A Lion Group Book

LAW SCHOOL
INSIDER

Law school should not be feared.
It should be understood beforehand
and appreciated for its duration.

ABOUT THE AUTHOR

Jeremy B. Horwitz is an attorney and writer whose work has appeared in print publications including *The New York Times*, *Basketball Digest*, *Soccer Digest*, *Edge* (U.K.), and *GamePro*, as well as several online publications. The magazine he created in 1994, *Intelligent Gamer*, was amongst the very first Internet-based publications prior to its 1996 acquisition and conversion into a print magazine by Ziff-Davis Publishing.

Raised in Buffalo, New York, Mr. Horwitz graduated *cum laude* from Cornell Law School in 2001, earning the degree of Juris Doctor with a concentration in Business Law and Regulation. While at Cornell, he earned a CALI Excellence for the Future® Award for his performance in Constitutional Law II: The First Amendment, and served as Internet Editor for the *Cornell Law Review*. He has worked for two international law firms headquartered in the United States, carries a Master's Degree in Business Administration from Canisius College, and earned a Bachelor of Arts degree in Political Science (with distinction) from the State University of New York at Buffalo. He now works and resides in Southern California.

Mr. Horwitz previously contributed chapters to two editions of Prima Publishing's INTERNET AFTER HOURS (A. Eddy, 1994, 1996).

LAW SCHOOL
INSIDER

The Comprehensive 21st Century Guide to Success in
Admissions, Classes, Law Review, Bar Exams and
Job Searches, for Prospective Students and their Loved Ones

by
Jeremy B. Horwitz, Esq.

A Lion Group Book

WWW.LAWSCHOOLINSIDER.COM

A Lion Group Publication
The Lion Group LLC
www.theliongroup.com
Amherst, New York, U.S.A.

First Published in the United States of America 2002

Publisher's Cataloging in Publication Data
Horwitz, Jeremy B., 1975-
Law school insider: the comprehensive 21st century guide to success in admissions, classes, law review, bar exams and job searches, for prospective students and their loved ones /by Jeremy B. Horwitz –1ª ed.
Includes index.
1.   Law students—United States—Handbooks, manuals, etc.
2.   Law schools – United States.
3.   Law—Study and Teaching—United States.
4.   Law students – New York – Ithaca – Biography.
Library of Congress Control Number: 2002094476
ISBN 0-9723766-0-7

Printed in the United States of America
Set in Optima
Designed by Lion Group
Cover and Interior Photography by Jeremy B. Horwitz

for

my parents, Larry & Tobi, who made this possible;

thanks to

S. Shujaat Ali, Erin K. Ardale, Christopher J. Frieda, Douglas S. Horowitz,
Steven L. Kent, Christian A. Munoz, Steven D. Park, and Eric M. Sprague,
for their suggestions, assistance, and friendship,

my sister, Elizabeth, for her insights and comments,

those educational institutions I have visited and attended, for informing
my perspective on the law school experience;

and special thanks to

Suchir Batra, for his tireless assistance, and
Heather M. Clark, for her special role in helping to make this book what it is.

Properly written, laws fade into the background of everyday life, gently regulating chaos to create the appearance of order. Occasional hiccups in the order demand new laws, but for the most part, a good legal system works because it governs most people invisibly while deterring or punishing those who would selfishly disrupt the peace.

To a newly-minted law school graduate, the streets of China circa 2001 bring the role of law squarely to the foreground of the mind. In Beijing, empty landmarks cast long, quiet shadows in the center of the public Tiananmen Square, replacing the students who once stood there to call for changes to Chinese law. Elsewhere in the same city, roads every day are a distracting, chaotic blend of bicycles, cars, trucks and pedestrians, frequently colliding without traffic signals to properly regulate their flow. In the *hutong*, historic Chinese pedestrian side streets filled with tiny shops and restaurants, food is served in conditions that would flabbergast first-world sanitary authorities, and merchants quietly trade in products banned by law.

Place yourself in my shoes for an hour, several days later. You emerge from a taxicab someplace in the middle of Shanghai, China, a futuristic metropolis today considered amongst the most modern of Chinese cities, and arrive at a hotel. As was the case in Beijing, the taxi ride to your Shanghai hotel was harrowing, full of near-misses with bicycles and pedestrians that would shock even New York or Las Vegas cab drivers. You enter the hotel tired from your day of travels and begin the walk from the entrance to your room, noticing armed Chinese police standing around the lobby of the building, glaring at you when you walk by. But you discover, to your relief, that they are merely looking for a local pickpocket, and you retire to your room for the same night's sleep as you would have had back in your bed at home.

Fast forward several more days. You arrive in a new country late one evening in September and check into your hotel. Considered among Asia's safest nations, Japan gives off a reassuring aura that leaves you with no concern whatsoever for your well-being. Compared with New York City, where the streets are kept quiet by a heavy, constant police presence, the streets of Tokyo are orderly without intervention. Then, as you settle into bed and turn your hotel television to CNN that first night, you witness the destruction of the World Trade Center on an international broadcast. By the next morning, armed police are on patrols and you're wondering how to get home. As an American in Japan with a pre-planned itinerary, travel to your next destination, Indonesia, no longer seems advisable. And when you arrive at a Japanese airport days later to return on the earliest flight back home, everything is different – your bags are searched repeatedly and air travelers are in a panic. Within several days, there are now new rules to follow in airports, and perhaps in daily life, for virtually every country across the world.

Every moment of your life right now wherever you are, and the alternate life I just described and lived through, is governed by law – though the extent to which you notice the law varies dramatically based on the places you go, the times you're there, and the things you do. In the United States, we stabilize our system of laws through redundancies, checks, and balances: when local and municipal regulations failed to insure traffic safety and order, state laws stepped in. If state laws were to prove inadequate to deal with common crimes, such as pick-pocketing, or regulate issues such as sanitation and the sale of banned goods, the federal government could step in and create a new layer of laws that govern every state in the country. And there are many layers of federal laws dealing with your rights and privileges as a traveler to foreign lands, and as an American returning home, which can be adjusted and made more uniform through international agreements.

But for the work of generations of citizens, you might never have been allowed, as a foreigner, to travel safely to China or Japan. Absent medical regulations and health codes, you might similarly never have survived long enough as a newborn to claim the benefits of American citizenship. And without the hurried work of today's lawmakers, you or I might never have had a safe way to return to the United States from Japan, lacking the hastily-drafted security regulations that placed soldiers in airports or the multiple checks on every person, piece of luggage, and aircraft entering or leaving an airport. Law defines all your rights and can restrict every freedom.

Those who would change, enforce, or create law must first understand it. Politicians or policeman may acquire some understanding on the job, but lawyers – those formally educated in the law as it was and is – possess a unique opportunity to stabilize or change society with the cumulative wisdom of centuries of scholarship. That said, I now turn to the task of disclosing the realities of undertaking a formal education in law.

J. Horwitz
Tokyo, Japan
Sep. 16, 2001

CONTENTS

CHAPTER

1

A. THE FIRST CYCLE

You are about to read a paragraph that will look entirely different when you read it again four years from now.

Nervous chatter fills a large room full of mostly young adults, many between 19 and 26 years of age. Then, like a thunderclap, the sound of a single voice coming from the front of the room instantly brings all other speech to an uncomfortable halt; those sitting as an audience ready their pens in preparation for one of the most important moments of their collective lives.

Prospective law students and their families will come to see that paragraph in distinct ways. A law student will personally live this experience at least four times in the course of his or her training, first at the administration of the Law School Admission Test (LSAT) before applying to law schools, when her eligibility to study law will be tested. The second time will be her first class on her first day of law school, when many seasoned professors will test her resolve to tough out long months of disciplined study and rapid-fire question-and-answer sessions. Third will be her first day of law school final exams, when she will be tested for the first and only time on materials she read three or four months earlier. And fourth will be on the first day of her bar examination, when she will be tested to see just how much material from three years of law school she can regurgitate in two or three straight days of questioning. Family members, by contrast, will never attend any of these events, but they will forever remember either the days themselves or the consequences that follow.

Though the settings will be similar, each experience will dwarf its predecessor in difficulty, preparation, and stress. The stakes will get higher and higher, yet so will the payoffs. Those who fail at any stage to thrive will retreat to lives in other professions; those who succeed will become living symbols of the learned profession of law.

These four experiences are collectively steps in one of the legal profession's many cycles, events spaced years apart yet bearing more than a passing resemblance to each other, increasing in both challenge and reward. Similarly, there are dozens of predictable and profound changes law students will go through – changes that will alter the way they look at common words such as "Erie" and "Chevron," and even language as a whole; changes that will alter their perceptions about the importance of judicial institutions such as the United States Supreme Court; changes that will almost certainly transform the ways they think, interact, and dream.

This book is intended to guide prospective lawyers and their families through many such cycles and changes – in fact the entire process from law school applications to final bar examinations, with pointers on how to succeed at every stage. The pointers are based in part on my own experiences, and in part on those best practices I have learned from others, whom I thank for guiding me towards a more successful life in the profession I respect so much.

B.   IMPORTANT NOTES ON MY METHOD

Authors consciously or unconsciously choose a tone when they write; I consciously made four choices when writing what you're about to read.

First, I chose a mostly conversational tone in the hope that this book will be easy to read, but neither condescending nor spoon-feeding. This is a difficult balance to achieve. On the one hand, there is considerable wisdom in the maxim that the study of law should be open to anyone who *makes an effort* to learn it; however, there's no point in reading a book about law school that intentionally strives to make that reading difficult. Moreover, this book isn't just for law students. It is designed to share the realities of the law school experience with prospective students, their families, and friends. My intent is to present the balance of insight and perspective appropriate to several different types of readers, in a manner equally accessible to each.

That leads to my second choice regarding structure. Though I've attempted to insure that this book contains just about everything that law students and their loved ones would want to know before it happens, I haven't crammed all of it into the narrative. For better or worse, law professors, lawyers, and judges hide really important stuff in their footnotes – you know, the little numbered paragraphs at the bottoms of pages that 98% of the population never reads.[1] I'm not going to tell you that I've hidden important information in my footnotes, but I will say that it will probably be to your benefit to read them if you're planning to go to law school – as is the case with the study and practice of law, you'll get more from this book if you sweat the details.[2]

Third was a choice regarding scope. It should also be clear from the beginning that this book is not limited to discussing any single law school or individual legal educational experience. There is a considerable amount of similarity between law students' experiences at the 180-plus American Bar Association-accredited law schools. Though I respect the authors of older law school books, I believe that every prospective student should go beyond Harvard-centric books such as ONE-L to get a sense of what the real world of legal education is like today.

Finally, there's my choice as to flow. There are many ways to present the law school experience, and chronological order with a largely narrative format makes the most sense to me. Steeped in years of tradition, the law school chronology is the same for most people, starting with the issue of whether to go to law school at all, continuing through three years of school and three

---

[1] Hey, you found one already. Congratulations!

[2] **If you're a parent, a friend, or someone who has already attended law school, skip the footnotes.** They won't help you much and may well impede your enjoyment of the book. But if you want to learn more about a topic discussed herein, the footnotes will often point you in the right direction. Citations to web sites are current as of August 2002.

summers of work, ending only after you take a bar exam and learn your results. To present the material in another way would, in my view, turn understandable trends and patterns into fractured, seemingly unrelated concepts. Still, if you decide to read the chapters out of order, the glossary may be a helpful tool towards understanding concepts that were explained earlier.

Taking these four choices together, you will hopefully find this book easy to read, but not insultingly so, and full of broadly applicable information, but not presented in a mind-boggling manner.

C.   SIDEBAR: WHERE I'M COMING FROM

After completing the LSAT, three years of law school and two solid months of studying for a bar examination, you would think that there wouldn't be much left that could intimidate me about the study of law. But at this moment, there's still one thing left.

As I write these words. I am on an airplane four days away from taking the California State Bar Examination, reputably the hardest of 50 separate state bar exams that will be administered across the United States starting on July 24, 2001. Every state's exam is different. Most last two days. California's will go for three days straight, from approximately 9am to 4pm; the second day of the "bar," as it is often abbreviated, just happens to be my birthday. I have studied for this exam literally every day since the end of May. Once it's over, three months will pass before I learn my result. If I pass, I will legally be able to call myself an attorney-at-law. If I fail, I will spend another two full months preparing to take the exam again, along with over 43% of the other people who take the California Bar Exam. Needless to say, I'd like to pass.

I've known for at least a year that I wanted to write this book. I just didn't think that I'd be starting it quite so soon; after all, the story of my life as a law student has not officially ended yet. My original plan was to start writing two weeks from now, during free moments on my upcoming post-bar exam vacation to Southeast Asia, and I would expect to finish the text over the course of a couple of months. If I had my way, I would instead be using every minute of this five-hour cross-country flight to study for the bar exam, but that's not going to happen because of the several crying, screaming babies who, as luck had it, were placed in the seats right behind me. But enough of that.

Conceived with a sense of the challenges that face modern students at American law schools, this book aspires to be something more useful than just a collection of my own experiences as a law student, yet more personal than the typical 'how-to' guide to admission and exam statistics written by a professor, or perhaps someone who never attended law school. I know such books are out there, but to my way of thinking, succeeding at law school results from preparation and perspective that enable you to avoid playing probabilities.

My aim is to offer useful and personal advice to others who might follow me into this profession, regardless of their pre-law backgrounds and the schools they attend. As of this writing, a perception persists in some quarters that lawyers generally come from wealthy or special backgrounds, or are the legacy-bearing children of the last generation's law school graduates. While this is no doubt true of some new lawyers, it is not true of all, or even most of them. Today, law is a profession open to all, admission to which is limited only by one's ability and interest in the subjects that constitute its formal study.

I won't claim to have possessed any special ability to learn law, or any other unique credentials in that regard. Neither of my parents were lawyers. In fact, to the best of my knowledge, there were no lawyers in my immediate family when I applied to law school. My grandparents were pharmacists, grocery store owners and housewives. My father was a computer engineer, and later a manager. My mother is a teacher. As you've probably noticed, nothing here suggests a genetic disposition to prosecute criminals, negotiate billion-dollar contracts, or host a program on Court TV.

But if genetics don't explain it, long-term personal interest in learning about the law definitely does. Like many of the lawyers I've met, my interest was piqued by a perhaps clichéd childhood experience – because I was an argumentative kid, my parents always joked that I would grow up to be a lawyer. As luck would have it, my grandfather had several close friends who were judges and politicians in Buffalo, New York, where I spent almost all of my life before law school. He introduced me to New York State Supreme Court Justice Theodore S. Kasler when I was 12 or 13 years old, a point when I was too young to understand just how important he was. I spent a fascinating summer "clerking" for Justice Kasler at that age, sitting in on conferences in chambers and watching felony criminal trials. Afterwards, I decided that I wanted to take every possible law-related class during high school and college, and from there, attending law school seemed inevitable. I've had other passions, but my interest in the law has remained a constant.

D. WHO ARE AMERICA'S LAW STUDENTS TODAY?

It is critical at this stage to note that no fact from my personal biography is a prerequisite to admission or success in law school. The stories of my classmates varied as much from person to person as could be expected in a country of over 280 million people; my graduating class proudly included a former sanitation worker, immigrants and the children of immigrants, and people from an impressive array of racial, religious and economic backgrounds. People come to law schools hoping to spread justice after suffering from domestic or parental abuse, and believing that the best way to right those wrongs is to work within the system. Others come fresh from backgrounds in science, math, and medicine, for reasons as diverse as those fields might suggest. And others, not surprisingly, come from traditionally 'legal' backgrounds, as well as backgrounds of relative privilege; some are the children of lawyers who were themselves the children of lawyers, others are the sons and daughters of people who earn livings trading in horses and real estate.

Surprisingly, *every person who comes to law school is challenged by it*, though the degree to which any person walks away changed by the experience is entirely personal and has little to do with background. Especially in the very beginning, the first year of law school is truly a great equalizer.

That said, there are many types of people who attend law schools across the country. It sometimes surprises people to learn that only a fraction of lawyers work in courtrooms.[3] Only some law students aspire to be litigators, the sort of lawyers portrayed on television shows and in movies, arguing before courts; others desire to practice what is known as corporate or transactional law, working on deals and contracts performed almost entirely outside of courtrooms. So it's fair to say that one needn't aspire to be like Johnnie Cochran or Marcia Clark in order to succeed as a law student.[4]

I personally had no such aspiration, and because of that, I was extremely concerned about one of the traditionally mandatory parts of first-year law instruction – a simulated trial against another student. I was especially nervous that I'd be humiliated by exceptional classmates. But like everything else in law school, I discovered two things when the day came to actually face my fear: most other people were just as nervous as I was, and the experience turned out to be a lot better than I ever could have imagined.[5]

Prospective students are often concerned about the people they'll encounter in law school, yet there's actually little reason to fear. Yes, it's true that some people have 'photographic memories' and are thus capable of quickly memorizing incredible amounts of information. And yes, there are people who do things now and again that would shock the conscience of any reasonable person. But let's get something straight: these sorts of people are few and far between in law school, and moreover, more people *think* they can succeed with old tricks than actually do. Memorization isn't enough to succeed in law school, and shocking behaviors lead to ostracism or expulsion, not success. At worst, your classmates will include some unusual people,[6] but few

---

[3] See Chapter 2, Section A, for a reasonably comprehensive list of the types.

[4] And, of course, one need not be a successful law student to be a successful lawyer, or even a judge. More on that in Chapter 5, Section C.

[5] See Chapter 4, Section C.

[6] Without miring ourselves in the statistics, the profession does have a reputation for attracting certain personality types. A recent California Bar Journal article illustrates the issue: "among all the occupational groups represented . . . attorneys had the highest prevalence of signs and symptoms of clinical depression. In fact, the rate of depression among the attorneys studied was 3.6 times the norm for all occupations." Richard Carlton, *The Stress and Impairment of Attorneys*, CALIFORNIA BAR JOURNAL, November 2000, available at http://www.calbar.org/2cbj/00nov/mclestdy.htm. (Note that the format of the

will be malicious or possess insurmountable intellectual advantages.

When I prepared for law school, and heard rumors about what I should expect, the personality type that concerned me the most was that of the backstabber – the person who tears pages out of library books or steals handouts so that others cannot prepare with them. Today, I believe that backstabbing has all but vanished – there was literally none in my classes – though there are infrequent stories about such behaviors at schools in major urban centers.[7] At any school, of course, there will be at least a small number of unpleasant people. My school had a small share of unhappy personality types, but it's best not to dwell for too long on the bad seeds.

It's more useful to focus instead upon the large number of different, yet equally successful types of law students that are out there today. Some find weekly study groups to be useful, while others study alone every night. There are many people with strong beliefs regarding sexual preference, religion, and race – in my own experience, largely positive, open-minded views on each, though there are of course rare exceptions. Moreover, there are just as many people who strongly prefer to hold no beliefs on these subjects and others, a lack of opinions that I never would have expected at a law school.

The diversity is often impressive. My class included members of at least two married couples who were simultaneously attending law school, several married people with families, and several people with domestic partners. Ages ranged from the bulk of students in their mid-20s to handfuls in their 40s and 50s. As previously suggested, students represented a wide variety of racial, ethnic, and national backgrounds, as well. Regardless of our personalities, skills, or backgrounds, we were all humbled by our years of law school. And we were enhanced by the experience, as well.

There are only a few common threads between all of the happy and successful law students I have known. First, all have had some level of **passion** for the law – intrinsic, extrinsic, or both. Those with an intrinsic passion find "the law" interesting as a concept. Those with extrinsic passions are motivated by interests in the specific ways the law is applied to people, or governs

---

preceding text, including the distinctive differences in font styles, follows what are known as "Bluebook" standards of citation – the orderly ways lawyers tell other lawyers how to find referenced source materials that back up the statements they've made in written documents. For more on the importance of Bluebooking to law students, see Chapters 3, Section M, and Chapter 5, Section A; the following footnotes will not use Bluebook standards.) For a student's perspective on anxiety and substance abuse in the profession, see Brooke M. Budde, *A Dismal Look Into the Realities of Substance Abuse in the Legal Arena* (2001), available at http://law.gonzaga.edu/ILST/CarnegieSeminar/budde.pdf.

[7] It is entirely possible to avoid such schools if you do your research before choosing a law school, but this is the sort of thing that you'll need to ask several current students about. Law school administrators are sometimes in denial that such practices continue, and only the students who have to live with it will know for sure.

situations – such as environmental law, international law, criminal law, and the like. It's my sincere belief that most if not all successful law students possess at least one of these two types of passion, and enough of it that they will remain motivated through some of the most difficult days they will ever experience in their educational careers. Those lacking passion are far less likely to enjoy or endure three full years of legal education.

Diligence – perhaps better described as a never-ending ability to labor – is the second thread. As a rule, first-year workloads are heavy and most students will at some points go for stretches of days with little sleep. The successful ones will slowly, but surely, improve their time management skills enough to make time for fun after conquering mountains of hard work. Others will instead opt to skip assignments and classes. In law school, diligent students do the best.

The third thread is **analytical reasoning ability**. Unlike other educational institutions, law school is not merely an exercise in memorizing information and regurgitating it on exams. And you have no prayer of success if you hope not to study and thus to fake your way through exam answers without understanding what's being tested.[8] Law school is entirely about analysis: you build up a base of knowledge about legal standards and learn how to compare and apply that knowledge to new situations. Sometimes you are asked to step through the reasoning of such comparisons and applications in front of your classmates. Every successful law student has learned at some point how to analyze questions in a 'lawyerly manner;' some students enjoy doing this in front of audiences, while others prefer to do it in less public surroundings.

Finally, I did not come to law school understanding the value of any of what I've just said. My perceptions of law school and the legal profession were shaped by popular culture and the media, infrequent interactions with lawyers, and third-hand stories from friends of friends who had attended law school. I knew that people worked hard, but I didn't think it would be considerably more work than other graduate programs, such as the M.B.A. I had just finished. I knew that there was something called a "law review" that most people hoped to

---

[8] On undergraduate exams, some professors offer decent grades to students who fail to demonstrate an understanding of the material but still write well. On a law school exam, you either display the skills that are being tested or do poorly. Typically, you are tested on how to step through a specific type of legal analysis and apply the right legal standards to the facts of a hypothetical situation. There is frequently room for creative writing, but only *after* you've hit the key points in an essay's analysis and have extra space to toss in some unique thoughts, hopefully for extra points. Unlike in undergraduate coursework, one's chance of successfully "winging it" through a whole law school exam is very small. Additionally, as your grade will generally be based entirely on a single exam per class per semester; there's too much riding on each exam to show up even once hoping to fake your way through it. These are the reasons why people tend to grossly over-prepare, rather than under-prepare, for law school exams.

be a part of.[9] I thought that the law somehow involved understanding Latin – at least, more Latin than was known by the average person. And I had watched legal movies and TV shows, which at that point I thought portrayed the profession quite accurately. In all candor, I was wrong on a few counts, and I was ignoring a number of things that were about to become significant. I was prepared just enough not to drown when I started law school, but I could have hit the ground running if I had known more.

To that end, I offer you the broad lessons I have learned before, during, and after law school, in the hopes that you might avoid my mistakes and improve on my successes. Some of what I will share comes from my own experiences at Cornell Law School, an Ivy League institution located in the northeastern United States, while additional insights were shared by students and graduates of other schools spread across the country. I thank Cornell for the superb education I received, and hope that any modest criticisms of my experiences there will be understood as intended: to prepare prospective law students and their families for what they might expect from law school. Even bad experiences are worth sharing precisely because they are not unique to any one school, and because disclosure may help others to avoid similar problems.

E.   THE BIG PICTURE

The formal study of law is an ongoing process with several easily identifiable stages. First you seek out and apply to law schools; then you probably attend one such school for three years, during which you might also intern with a practitioner; then you graduate from law school, take a bar exam, and ultimately, receive a license to practice law.

Many people are surprised even by the number of stages sketched out in this bare roadmap, but it's true that there's more to legal education than just going to law school. The law school part of the story alone defies common conceptions. It is most often intense beyond the wildest expectations of students who have attended even competitive undergraduate and graduate schools, yet offers unparalleled opportunities to truly understand ancient and mysterious concepts. Some people, of course, try to reduce the intensity level, and opt not to compete for places near the tops of their graduating classes. But others will compete, and thereby become eligible for even more incredible things; many will go on to enviable public or private sector jobs.[10]

---

[9] See Chapter 5, Section A.
[10] Hopefully, any post-law school job will be meaningful in some way to the person who secures it. Some of these jobs will have the extra benefit of prestige. A select group of highly competitive students will be offered assistant positions with the United States Supreme Court and its subsidiary courts almost immediately after law school. Such positions are coveted by thousands of law students, as law schools generally replace

But before they settle in to these jobs, they will need to be licensed. Most law school graduates receive the degree of Juris Doctor (J.D.), which does not itself include a license to actually practice law, in other words, to represent clients in legal matters. For this, one must obtain a license from a state "bar," the officially recognized association of licensed attorneys within a given state,[11] by passing a written bar examination and meeting certain state-specific requirements regarding one's morals and character.

And surprisingly, even after graduation and bar exams, legal education continues. Once admitted to a state's bar, practitioners are generally required to continue their legal educations for so long as they continue to practice, so that their experiences in law school do not constitute their only exposure to emerging legal trends and concepts. It is therefore a cycle of learning that never ends once started, unless you leave the profession.

Some might advise prospective students to plan early for all of these stages before starting law school, then follow the plans to successful careers and locations of their choosing. While this is possible, it's not always easy, and people are likely to encounter unexpected ups and downs that will change their plans. As you read, attempt to develop at least a general sense of whether you belong in law school and what you might hope to do with your degree thereafter. Then consider secondary and tertiary options for each stage, just in case things turn out to be different from what you initially expected.

As is the case when studying the workings of any individual law, the bigger picture of legal education will make more sense as each of its constituent parts is examined in turn. Following the chronology, we shall now begin with the earliest of the stages: finding good law schools and applying to them.

---

reverence for Presidents or legislatures with deep-seated commitments to the judiciary and its courts. These commitments are confirmed with formal oaths whenever attorneys complete their bar exams and are licensed to practice law.

[11] For sake of completeness, a "bar" is a given jurisdiction's organization of practicing lawyers, entrusted by that jurisdiction's highest court with the task of licensing new lawyers to practice law only within that jurisdiction's borders. Therefore, a license to practice law in Florida does not entitle you to practice law in California, or vice-versa. While there are many jobs available to those who earn law degrees but do not take or pass a bar exam, these jobs do not permit people to have legal clients of their own.

CHAPTER 2

(ABOVE) PEPPERDINE UNIVERSITY SCHOOL OF LAW, MALIBU, CA
(BELOW) YALE LAW SCHOOL, NEW HAVEN, CT

MODERN AND TRADITIONAL LAW SCHOOL CAMPUSES, 2002

For centuries, those who have desired careers in the law have come to the profession with abilities and experiences differing dramatically from person to person, and there is no single, exclusive path to success as a law student, or, for that matter, as a lawyer. Similarly, it goes without saying that there is no single correct way to seek out and apply to law schools.

But there are some things you can do to maximize your chances of getting in to a good school, then succeeding while you're there, and flourishing thereafter. The process begins when you try to understand yourself and your future goals, then continues as you take the LSAT, search for places that are likely to suit you and those goals, and submit applications to the schools you've identified. The process of understanding yourself is at least as important as any of the later stages in the process.

A. Before You Come to Law School: the Realities and Misconceptions

Though most lawyers enjoyed law school, few are willing to recommend it uncritically to others. Sure, this is partially because they don't want to see the already overcrowded legal market become even worse, but it's also because of a simple truth about law school: it's not right for everyone. Some people know this before applying. Others might not figure it out until they actually start classes. And still others will only realize it after final exams.

In my view, you shouldn't need to waste precious time and money to learn whether or not you're going to survive in law school; in fact, if you have three things, you'll know right now that you possess the minimum tools necessary to survive law school, and perhaps even succeed in it.[12]

The three things are **motivation, money,** and **maturity.**

1. Motivation

Motivation is perhaps the simplest concept of the three, but in reality, it's the most elusive. Law school is designed to be tough and overwhelming. To survive the first year, you have to want to be there – not blindly so, but at least enough that when you have your inevitable tough days, you will know that you really want to keep fighting through them because it's ultimately worthwhile. While it would take a whole book just to list every conceivable

---

[12] In the previous chapter, I identified "passion," "diligence" and "analytical reasoning ability" as keys to happiness and success in law school. This section deals only with the minimum requirements to *survive* law school, and not the additional factors that will make you happy or successful there.

proper motivation for coming to law school,[13] there are three universally improper motivations that will always lead to disappointment down the road.

- Are you considering a law degree largely because of family pressures?
- Do you believe that you have no other options besides law school?
- Do you misunderstand what law school is about, namely, do you think it's the no-brainer next step for any political science or government major?

Reading this book will help you avoid the last trap, but the first two points are something you'll have to deal with on your own – most likely by planning out a better alternative.[14] If your family is pushing you to become a lawyer and it's something you don't really want for yourself, be assured that with rare exceptions you can satisfy familial pressures by demonstrating a drive to do something focused and productive with your life.[15] You do have other options, and **law school should** – at least in my opinion – **never, ever be your fall-back choice**, or a place you wind up against your wishes. Law school is simply too stressful to be a comfortable alternative to other graduate work or real-world employment in political science, history, or the like.

---

[13] If you identified with the "passion" factor identified in the previous chapter, you probably have enough motivation to survive law school. But it's important not to confuse the feeling of "wanting to be there," which most people carry with them through law school, with wanting to be at the top of your class, a dream which at some point 75-90% of people must abandon while still carrying on with their lives. This is likely to be a point worth reconsidering during the tougher moments of law school, and perhaps thereafter.

[14] My parents never pressured me to come to law school, but my grandfather pushed my dad into law school with the belief that his undergraduate degree (electrical engineering) was worthless. Six months later, my dad left law school quite unhappy, went out into the world and got a job doing what he loved, and went on to become very successful in a fledgling field entirely unrelated to law – computer science. Countless people have had similar experiences. The lesson is clear: don't come to law school under any sort of pressure, either from your parents or from yourself. Only come if you want to be there.

[15] Make sure to distinguish unreasonable parents from reasonable ones. At first, many reasonable parents look unreasonable – they point to law school as the graduate school equivalent of military school for a wayward high school student, or as a necessary step to force a son or daughter into the family trade. At the core, some of these parents are actually only looking for a college-aged person to show self-motivation or any marketable skill. Consider these parents to be "supportive" of a future self-sufficiency, not unreasonable. By contrast, an unreasonable parent will try to force you into law school when you have already demonstrated a marketable competence and drive to do something else; this sort of parent will be far more difficult to convince.

If you find yourself in a position where you feel like you're considering law school against your will, it's time to enlist other family members to get a message across to your pushy relatives, and to start developing other realistic alternatives. On the other hand, if you feel as if your family is unhappy about your strong personal desire to pursue a law degree, now's the time to demonstrate your strong powers of persuasion and show them why such a law degree will be worthwhile.[16] This book will hopefully help in that process.

There are plenty of good motivations to want to attend law school – the best combination is when you desire a specific career related to the law and have a realistic sense of what law school will be like. Consider the variety of career choices law school graduates *might* choose from, and notice how differentiated the options have become.

TABLE 2-1	THE LARGE LIST OF MODERN LAW-RELATED CAREER OPTIONS
ATTORNEYS-AT-LAW As the most commonly recognized class of lawyers, Attorneys-at-Law represent the interests of their clients, ranging from individuals to companies and governments.	**Litigators**: Litigators are best known as the "courtroom" attorneys at the center of law-related television shows, but actually spend considerable hours outside of courtrooms, drafting documents, interviewing witnesses, and negotiating to avoid trials. Some of the specialized types of litigators include: • *Plaintiffs' Attorneys*: These litigators focus on civil (individual or company against individual or company) lawsuits instead of criminal (state or nation against individual) lawsuits. They represent people looking to initiate lawsuits (plaintiffs) against other people or companies (defendants), and can focus on anything from failures to perform contracts to injuries caused by accidents.

---

[16] This applies equally to parents and spouses. Some people are less than enthusiastic when their loved ones decide to join "a profession of sharks," and some think that the loved ones who enter law school good will come out bad. Such fears are unfounded; in truth, despite all that you learn, you will probably leave law school with pretty much the same personality as when you came in, but you'll be more disciplined and better informed. And even the most initially disdainful parents will eventually admit that it's always a good thing to have an attorney in the family, especially one you get along with. Spouses, however, will have stronger fears: most know the legends of long law school hours and extended law student anxiety; hopefully, they will take some comfort in the later discussion of first-year life with a law student spouse. See Chapter 3, Section O.

Though a significant number of attorneys today have narrow specializations (practices limited to discrete types of law), smaller law firms still offer lawyers opportunities to work on many different types of cases.

Personal Injury Attorneys may be the most recognized plaintiffs' attorneys because of aggressive advertising. These attorneys initiate individuals' lawsuits against entities alleged to have injured them physically, such as car accidents caused either by another driver, or by a vehicle defect traceable to the manufacturer. *Class Action Attorneys* are similar, but typically represent large groups of people against companies that are alleged to have injured them physically or monetarily, such as people injured by defective tires or medicines, or investors injured when a company misrepresented its stock. Other plaintiffs' attorneys, by comparison, may be *General Practitioners*, who initiate suits on a broader range of civil legal matters.

- *Private Defense Attorneys*: These are slightly less visible litigators who take on a high profile in certain civil and criminal trials; these litigators represent the individuals and companies that have been sued, such as the driver or manufacturer of a vehicle alleged to have caused an injury.
- *Public Defense Attorneys* (Public Defenders): These are less visible attorneys who represent indigent clients in criminal trials, such as homeless men or women accused of theft, rape, or murder.
- *Legal Aid Attorneys* (Public Civil Attorneys): These are perhaps the least visible litigators, namely ones who provide legal counsel to indigent individuals in civil (rather than criminal) trials where cash compensation is sought, such as if a homeless person sues or is sued by a person.
- *Appellate Attorneys*: These litigators are brought in at the second stage of a civil or criminal proceeding – typically when the client (plaintiff or defense) either has a lot of

money to spend or is indigent with a meritorious case. They generally try to reverse an earlier trial verdict by proving that mistakes of law were made. Private sector appellate attorneys often work on high-profile civil cases; public sector appellate attorneys work on death penalty appeals and other cases of allegedly wrongful sentencing.

- *Divorce Attorneys*: These litigators specialize in the dissolution or reconciliation of marriages, and represent only one side in divorce proceedings.

Transactional/Corporate Attorneys: These attorneys are generally much less visible than litigators, but handle a very considerable part of the legal work done for banks, corporations, and other businesses – they draft contracts and negotiate deals between various entities. Many large law firms specialize, at least in substantial part, in what's called "transactional" or "corporate" work. Within the profession, the transactional attorneys are said to be the ones who are called in to bring people together, and the litigators are the ones you call when things start to fall apart.

Counselors: These attorneys are similar to transactional attorneys, but have different sorts of clients – they either specialize in the affairs of a single client, or in a narrow class of clients (such as trusts and estates planning or family law). Some counselors never (or rarely) appear in court and instead take purely advisory roles; others make limited court appearances. Yet while this sort of practice sounds highly appealing to many people who come to law school, the actual number of people who practice these types of law fresh out of school is quite small, owing in equal parts to the likelihoods of special educational requirements, lower incomes, and scarcity of counselor positions within large firms.

- *In-House Counsels/General Counsels*: An in-house counsel is an attorney (sometimes one of many) solely employed by a single company; a general counsel is the highest-ranked attorney employed by that company. These attorneys handle much of a company's pre-trial and transactional work, and sometimes have some involvement in pre-litigation strategies as well. They may leave certain specialized or large deals to outside counsel (attorneys with law firms). In-House Counsel positions have a reputation for being cushier and more family-friendly than law firm jobs, in terms of the number of hours worked, but can be just as bad or worse in some cases. Many businesses will only hire mid-level (third or fourth-year) or senior (partner) attorneys from law firms to serve in these positions; new attorneys fresh out of school typically need not apply.
- *Family Law Attorneys/Trusts & Estates Attorneys*: These attorneys typically handle specific issues for families, including juvenile court proceedings, estate and financial matters, and occasionally counseling regarding marital issues. Such attorneys typically have lower incomes than litigators or transactional attorneys, and offer as much in the way of informal psychological counseling services as legal ones.

Government Attorneys: These attorneys are employed by federal, state or municipal governments to handle specialized matters limited to the mission of the government or specific agency in question.

- *Prosecutors/District Attorneys*: These attorneys exclusively handle various types of criminal prosecutions on behalf of federal or smaller governments. Federal positions are perennially highly sought-after, and with the exception of state murder charges, often involve the most serious penalties.

- *Agency Attorneys*: These attorneys handle regulatory enforcement and litigation matters on behalf of federal and state agencies, including such matters as antitrust, communications, and environmental law. They present the government's position on such issues, first attempting to negotiate compliance, and then forcing compliance if necessary through litigation.

Non-Profit Attorneys: These attorneys work for private organizations with political or social agendas, and can serve in roles as counselors and/or litigators. They run the gamut from advocacy group lawyers, including environmental lawyers, racial or religious group lawyers and consumer advocacy lawyers, to attorneys for political parties or candidates. Their work may or may not overlap with the work of public defenders and public sector appellate attorneys, depending on the specific organization's purpose; organizations include the venerable American Civil Liberties Union (ACLU), Lambda Legal Defense, and the Sanctuary for Families (Center for Battered Women's Legal Services). Lower salaries and uncertain tenures discourage many otherwise interested people from these practices.

Solo Practitioners, General Practitioners, and Contract Attorneys: These attorneys work for themselves and may perform all sorts of legal services; contract attorneys tend to focus on transactional work and negotiations, while both "solos" and "general practitioners" may have broad practices ranging from litigation to transactional to family law matters. General practitioners may work in small or large firms, however, they have decreased in number, especially at large firms, as specialization and salary trends have discouraged students and firms from general practice. Sadly, general practice has become a niche in many states, especially larger ones.

	Legal Consultants: These individuals perform services that fall just within the outermost edge of the legal profession, offering advice to small or medium-sized businesses on such legal matters as regulatory compliance and methods of negotiation. Though some legal consultants are not actually attorneys, these consultants seriously risk running afoul of state laws prohibiting the unauthorized practice of law.
JUDGES	Contrary to popular misconceptions, most judges are established and well-respected practicing attorneys whose pre-judicial careers involved some form of litigation practice. Thus, it is typically unlikely that a fresh law school graduate will become a judge without practicing law for at least some period of time – perhaps many years. There are numerous types of judges, ranging from several types of federal judges ("Article III" life-tenured, President-appointed judges to Administrative judges and others) to several sorts of state court judges (trial court judges, appellate court judges, probate court judges) and municipal judges such as town court judges. Some judges are elected, others are appointed. Judges who were not practicing lawyers are truly in the minority, and judges who did not attend law school are even fewer. Stories of non-lawyer U.S. Supreme Court Justices are exceptions.
NON-LAWYER LEGAL PROFESSIONALS Some of these individuals serve as assistants to practicing lawyers or work in quasi-legal capacities.	**Paralegals:** Paralegals are not lawyers and cannot sign court documents, practice before courts, or take active roles in negotiating settlements or counseling clients. These individuals perform low-level legal research and assistant tasks for practicing lawyers, doing a specific class of legal work that enables lawyers to focus on performing higher-level legal services for their clients. Practicing lawyers must supervise and take full responsibility for the work of their paralegals. Paralegals may or may not have attended law school, but in either case have not passed a state bar exam. **Arbitrators:** Arbitrators may or may not have attended law school, though they are often former lawyers or

Some people decide to leave the practice of law for one of these jobs, instead.

judges. These individuals act as hired quasi-judicial intermediaries, and seek to settle claims between adverse parties without a need to resort to litigation. Decisions made by arbitrators are typically binding and their procedures have fewer formalities than trials; few law schools focus in detail upon this subject and law students are not typically encouraged to pursue careers in arbitration.

Mediators: Like arbitrators, mediators are sometimes former lawyers, and they also act as quasi-judicial intermediaries to settle claims without litigation. However, their decisions are rarely binding upon the parties, and while attempts are made to encourage mediation as a means of dispute resolution, it is not looked upon as favorably by the American judiciary as arbitration. Law students are typically not encouraged to pursue careers in mediation.

Law Clerks: Law clerks work as assistants to judges either on a temporary or permanent basis, and have the prestigious responsibility of ghostwriting parts or wholes of judicial opinions. They are typically hand-picked by judges from the elite ranks of top American law schools, including schools based in cities near the courts and top schools around the country. A clerk is often required to sit for the bar exam of the state in which her judge presides, and will typically work for a judge for a term of one or two years. Though some people become professional, long-term law clerks, the population of such permanent clerks is small.

Politicians and **Political Advisors**: These individuals constantly evaluate existing legal systems while having the power to create, repeal, and modify laws; the less glamorous parts of these jobs include authoring of committee and subcommittee documents and draft proposals of laws. Politicians supervise advisors, who may take more hands-on roles in drafting laws and related documents. Law school graduates who enter politics or work as advisors to politicians possess a distinct advantage in understanding and creating laws, however, it is important to note that neither politicians nor most of their advisors need to have law degrees.

NON-LAWYER NON-LEGAL PROFESSIONALS

Members of these several professions need not have attended law school, but those who have may possess a distinct advantage within each profession.

Journalists and **Commentators**: These individuals write or talk about the law in newspapers, magazines, television broadcasts and web sites, lending their understanding of the legal process to bridge the gaps between non-lawyers and the legal world. The best legal journalists and commentators have often had some experience within the profession before leaving it, specifically as practicing attorneys.

Authors: These individuals write books about the law or legal topics, typically for mainstream consumption. They rarely write textbooks for use by law students; such is the business of law professors.

Lobbyists: These individuals contact politicians to propose changes to laws or the maintenance of existing laws, sometimes in person and sometimes in a written format. While law school graduates may be useful in lobbying efforts, especially in proposing seemingly subtle changes to the law, they become exponentially more useful as lobbyists when they have worked for politicians, served as politicians, or work for influential lobbying law firms in their capitol cities. In the latter instance, they may fall back into the "lawyer" category.

Analysts or **Fellows** of a Think Tank: These individuals may engage in academic and socio-political analysis of laws, and while one need not be a law school graduate to hold one of these positions, analysis is greatly aided by understanding the linguistic nuances and comparative methods taught in law school.

Expert Witnesses: These individuals testify at trials on behalf of plaintiffs, prosecutions, and defendants, serving as especially knowledgeable sources of information on very specific subjects. They are typically paid for their services, handsomely where they possess unique expertise or a proven track record of speaking clearly and unimpeachably to juries. Again, while a law degree is by no means required, study at a law school can dramatically educate a potential witness as to how to testify, and though this career path is atypical, it can be pursued by those with scientific or other specialized backgrounds.

EDUCATORS

These individuals teach others about the law, either as law professors, non-professor law instructors, or non-law school teachers. The vast majority of the first two categories of instructors possess law degrees; the latter category is far less likely to have attended or completed law school.

Law Professors: These individuals teach the law to students at law schools, and generally specialize in two to four specific subjects. They may author textbooks, as well. While law professors need not have passed a state bar exam, they typically have done so, practiced law at least briefly before teaching, and in many cases served as law clerks to judges – these are especially requirements at top law schools. It is unusual, but not unfathomable, for a professor at a law school not to have attended law school. Law professors at top schools are typically prolific writers, with numerous articles published specifically in law journals and other academic publications (rather than, or in addition to anything published in mainstream newspapers and magazines).

Non-Professor Law Instructors: These individuals teach law students about ancillary legal subjects, such as clinical work or legal writing, yet do not receive the status or tenure of law professors. They typically have practiced law for some period of time before teaching but do not often lecture on the substance of laws, only how to practice it.

Non-Law School Teachers: These individuals teach law in a generalized way for students at schools other than law schools. They could teach law-related classes at middle schools, high schools, and colleges, though their actual knowledge of the subject matter will most certainly increase dramatically (and qualify them for better employment) if they have attended law school. They need not have practiced law or served as law clerks, and most often have not.

This list is not exhaustive, but it does suggest the wide variety of options the modern law school graduate could choose from. It is also not intended to suggest that a prospective law student even needs to know with any degree of certainty at this point what sort of career he or she wants to pursue; you may well enter law school hoping for one type of job and wind up pursuing an entirely different one. You're doing just fine for motivation so long as something on the list appeals strongly to you.

But it's important to stress just how few of the jobs above actually require law degrees – with only rare exceptions, unless you want to be an attorney, judge, or law professor, law school isn't mandatory. Consequently, for those people who believe law school to be the next logical step after undergraduate studies in government or political science, there are actually many other options. Consider both the non-lawyer careers above and, of course, other graduate programs ranging from history to anthropology, and those tangentially related to the formal study of law, such as further studies in government and public policy. If one of these areas excites you more than the idea of having a law degree, you may well find yourself happier outside of law school.

2. Money

Money sounds like the hardest of the three items to obtain, but it's actually neither impossible nor terribly hard for most prospective law students to get. To put things in context, law school tuitions as of the time of this writing range from approximately $10,000 to $30,000 per year,[17] excluding costs of books, housing and necessities[18] during the three years of law school.[19] The lower end of the price spectrum represents a state resident's law school tuition for the state's public law school; it inches upwards for out-of-state residents and then

---

[17] Some public schools offer even lower tuitions for in-state residents – the University of Arizona ($5,240), University of Kentucky ($6,250) and University of Texas ($8,960) are among such schools.

[18] Necessities are generally limited to food and clothing, but one item that has increasingly become a necessity at law schools is a computer, preferably a laptop, to complete legal writing assignments and access the Internet. Note that a laptop computer wholly adequate for law school applications will contain a 350-500mhz processor, a dual-scan backlit LCD screen, and a CD-ROM drive – a specification far below the current standards for a $1000 laptop. Any modern computer will be overkill, from a 1.0GHz laptop with an active-matrix LCD screen and DVD drive, to a 2.0GHz desktop machine with a DVD burner. But higher end machines, of course, are more fun to own. Laptops are generally preferred to desktops because of portability concerns and the laptops' utility for taking class notes, an increasingly common practice.

[19] You can limit these costs somewhat by living with your parents, but you can't avoid buying textbooks or necessities. It's all but impossible to obtain the sort of access you need to a law school textbook without owning it, and this is not the right time to cut back on the nutrition and energy you'll need every day.

skyrockets for top private schools, which frequently hit the peak of the spectrum. Books are additionally estimated at between $700 and $1,300 per year, on-campus housing from $6,300 to $11,000 per year, and necessities between $2,000 and $4,000 per year. Some schools recommend that married couples, with one partner attending law school, budget an extra $10,000 for housing and necessities on top of these numbers. Tally up these numbers and you fall somewhere between $19,000 and $36,300 per year, assuming that the school doesn't raise tuition, and that books, housing and necessities stay the same price. But schools almost always raise tuition,[20] and the other numbers creep upwards – at least a little each year. And then there are application fees ($40-80 per school) and other expenses to consider. It's therefore safe to say that law school is a $60,000-110,000 commitment, and at this point, you probably think that raising such money is a daunting task.

In truth, few people come to law school with $110,000 in cash and walk out entirely debt-free. Those that do have either received family financial support or worked for some significant period of time before law school; the former is far more often the case. Most law students apply for and receive substantial student loans, which come due shortly after law school ends.

The consequence is that law school debts, which may take between five and fifteen years to pay off, cast considerable shadows upon their bearers and frequently create a tension to seek and accept higher-paying but higher-stress (and potentially less fulfilling) private sector legal careers over lower-paying public or private sector alternatives. Recent college graduates who enter law school hoping to work for the indigent often leave law school desperate to work for any big firm that will diminish their loans. It will be hard to appreciate the debt burden until you face it, so if you feel that public sector work is your calling, plan either to attend a public school or secure non-loan assistance.

Though numerous law school scholarships exist, both your chances of getting them and their pay-offs are smaller than those offered to undergraduates. Full-ride scholarships to top American law schools are reserved for exceptional cases, such as students with impressive extracurricular activities who are also described by recommending faculty as amongst the schools' top graduates. Less prestigious law schools sometimes offer full rides to students whose statistics clearly place them in contention for slots at significantly better schools.

Partial scholarships to any law school are offered to outstanding candidates who might otherwise choose other, better-known schools. How do you know if you fit into this category? If you've been accepted at a bunch of schools and the one you're about to accept is not as competitive in admissions as the one you're about to decline, you're probably in a position to seek a

---

[20] Cornell Law, as one example, raised tuition between 3-10% each year from 1997 to 2002, and its peer schools followed a similar pattern despite a non-inflatory economy.

partial scholarship. If the scholarship hasn't been offered to you already, you can go to your preferred law school's admissions office, let them know that you're on the cusp of a decision between them and the other school, and you're wondering whether there are any scholarship options that might weigh more heavily in their favor. But the usefulness of this tactic does vary dramatically by institution; scholarship fund endowments are often made subject to interesting conditions by graduates or the families of graduates. Candidates with different academic, athletic, gender, and racial backgrounds may find themselves at advantages or disadvantages, depending on the school. Those hoping to rely upon scholarships are advised to consult the financial aid offices of law schools prior to completing their applications for admission.

Even if you're lucky enough to have family assistance in funding your legal education, you might encounter certain constraints on your freedom to choose from any schools that might accept you. Some students have reported that if they were accepted at two schools that were very close in rank and specializations, yet the better-ranked school was considerably more expensive, parents asked them to choose the less expensive school or seek additional funding on their own. This isn't always the case, however; price sensitivity clearly varies tremendously based on the families and specific circumstances involved, and some families will take a far less hands-on approach to managing the law school decision than others. If family assistance or large loans aren't options for you, pre-law school employment as a paralegal might help to fund your education; some law students pay their way through law school on assets earned through earlier years' labor in professions entirely unrelated to the law.

A major reason that so many students are willing to take on loans is the ultimate value of a law degree, particularly a degree from the most expensive schools. Starting salaries for American private sector attorneys – those who work for law firms – range from slightly over $60,000 at small firms to as much as $135,000 a year plus bonuses, and the median starting salary is today upwards of $100,000.[21] A salary may increase each year by $5,000 to $12,000, depending on the firm and the attorney's performance. Yet as enticing as these numbers are, they may be an unreachable oasis for many law school graduates: few $100,000+ positions are available to students outside of the top graduates of top-tier law schools. Outside of the private sector, starting salaries are even lower. Government positions have starting salaries ranging from $25,000 to $65,000 per year, and public interest positions range from $30,000 to $40,000.

You can do the math and figure out the costs of attending a given school versus the earning potential of the type of job you aspire to have. On the bright

---

[21] While starting salaries may dip as low as $35,000 for private firms, these are truly outside the norm and, in fact, are so low as to almost moot the value of attending a graduate program such as law school.

side, once you've been admitted to a law school, securing funds will thankfully not be all that hard. But it goes without saying that unless you have a top-paying job and can contain your living expenses for several years, it will take quite some time before you will be able to pay off law school loans, let alone any that you have accrued before attending law school. Can you live with that? Or do you have plenty of personal cash already saved up, or family assistance in financing your legal education? These are personal questions you'll have to answer, and you'll have to live with the consequences of any financing decision you make.

3. Maturity

Maturity, the third and final prerequisite, is the most amorphous of the categories, but essentially boils down into two things – your mind needs to have a certain level of discipline,[22] and your on-paper credentials at least need to hint at this.

Unlike the admissions qualifications established for the study of medicine, admission to study law does not typically require formal undergraduate preparation in specific subjects. However, as American law schools are graduate institutions, they do require first-year law students to possess both a high school diploma and a four-year undergraduate degree of any sort.[23]

At least 50% of American law students come to their first years of law school some years after graduating from an undergraduate institution; this means that most law students have done something 'character-building' for at least a year after earning a bachelor's degree. This may include work in the 'real world' for a period of time, or graduation from business, medical or other graduate schools. Some students floated around, uncertain as to what to do next, or took a one-year hiatus in order to travel or relax before tackling the demanding experience of law school. Fewer than half come straight from undergraduate school to law school.

Do you really need a break of any sort before law school? No. Are there reasons to recommend one? Yes. As will become evident throughout this book, law school is both an intense and catalytic experience. It demands a certain level of emotional maturity which, believe it or not, correlates at least partially

---

[22] To some extent, the maturity factor encompasses the previous chapter's discussion of diligence and analytical reasoning skills, however, the minimal levels of diligence and reasoning skill required to survive law school are far lower than those required to truly succeed in it.

[23] As a point of interest, this is not necessarily true of foreign law schools. Therefore it is possible for foreign lawyers to arrive in the United States to pursue American law degrees at relatively young ages – 20, not 15 – and graduate with their second law degree at the time that Americans have just earned their first.

with age and perspective. A one- or several-year period after receiving a Bachelor's degree, coupled with the right sort of external experiences, can facilitate a calmer or more mature state of mind that's ready for the challenges of law school. Yet the same period of time, coupled with other experiences, can lead to a laziness or anti-educational attitude entirely incompatible with the requirements of the study of law.

My background prior to law school offers some suggestion of what's typical or unusual when admissions officers try to get a general sense of one's maturity and fitness for law school. Prior to law school, I had worked during college (typical) and earned a graduate degree (atypically mature), which meant that two years separated my undergraduate degree from the start of law school (typical). I didn't take a break to vacation, which while typical in the sense that most people had not spent an extended period traveling prior to law school, was atypical in that I had been in classes of some sort pretty much without any real down time since graduating from high school.[24] At a minimum, you probably achieve 'average' maturity for top schools by having one significant two-year activity, either real world or academic, outside of a bachelor's degree.

Academic maturity is another piece of the big picture. There probably is a threshold level of external academic awareness one needs in order to have a smooth initial law school experience.[25] I studied political science, which was the "pre-law" major offered at my undergraduate school.[26] Though I enjoyed the subject, I should not have relied solely, or even largely, on political science to form my understanding of what's important to know before studying the law.

---

[24] I strongly believe that you should do something – either real world or academic – after your bachelor's degree and before law school. Some of my classmates went to the Peace Corps or Americorps, others worked for companies, and still others pursued other graduate degrees. Though this is by no means a scientific conclusion, those who did something else before law school seemed more comfortable or confident during law school, as they were better prepared for the workload and schedule challenges that law school offers. This isn't to say that hard-working undergraduates can't flourish immediately thereafter in law school, but it's more difficult. Moreover, I would have taken at least a month at some point to travel and relax prior to my first year of law school – perhaps right before my first semester there. It helps to come to law school a bit worldly, yet willing to stay indoors.

[25] The nuts and bolts of this are described below, but it should be noted that part of the law school experience is, in fact, picking up whatever critical and commercial terminology and concepts you missed in your prior life. If you don't know a term you read in the textbook, you learn it – that means if it's not defined, you find another book and look it up. So it goes without saying that the more you know before law school, the easier you have it, but you learn the rest one way or another when you get there.

[26] My classmates included at least a handful of economics, mathematics, or hard sciences majors. The math and science majors had their own sets of challenges to face, but came well prepared for the logical reasoning components of law school classes.

Law school applicants should aim, if possible, to take four elective undergraduate or graduate-level classes that demonstrate breadth. Economics and business students had a leg up in understanding the fundamental language of contract law and other business law subjects, such as securities regulation. And as the mandatory first-year law school class called Contracts is among the only classes with terminology that you might pick up as an undergraduate, it's useful to prepare yourself beforehand.

Interestingly, some undergraduate work may handicap potential law students, but it's not what you might expect. You will hear that professors look for 'good legal writing,' which must be distinguished from 'good English writing,' the product of a zealous English or linguistics major. Legal writing is far more like authoring mathematical logic than any creative writing you'll ever produce in an undergraduate program. Good legal writing tends to be boring, tautological and formulaic, at least as it's taught in law school,[27] and math majors actually have slight advantages in certain parts of writing courses. By contrast, good English writers often find it hard to conform their previously honed skills to the requirements of legal writing programs, as the skills are almost opposite in nature. So while it benefits any potential law student to have an excellent grasp of the English language, you will not necessarily be rewarded for devoting your life before law school to studying it exclusively.

Like all things in the law, though, this is only a general rule and has its limitations. Contrast the learning process with the actual experiences of practicing lawyers, namely those who are courtroom litigators. A litigator's creative grasp of the English language is critical, especially when it will be used to communicate with a jury, a judge, clients, witnesses and other counsel. Here a knowledge of psychology, linguistics, or even theater arts and acting may carry special weight. Opportunities will be rare for students to use these talents,[28] but some practitioners will find such skills useful, if not integral.

Other types of people – namely those who have no desire to appear in a courtroom, and prefer instead to work behind the scenes on big contracts, deals, or the like – will find psychology and acting courses all but useless. For these people, business courses will be the best, with a sprinkling of economics and enough language and liberal arts coursework to have at least the fundamentals of a few subjects down by the time of admission.

The very last thing about maturity is a broad point which, while implicit in

---

[27] As suggested earlier, your opportunity to be creative in law school is constrained; you can exercise your creative mind after you've fulfilled the express purposes of an assignment, or by finding a new and better way to fulfill that end. But the latter is rare.

[28] Some law school classes – not many – offer the opportunity to go through simulated trials and practice other 'theatrical' skills. Almost every school has at least a class or two like this, generally called Trial Advocacy or Trial Practice; several law schools best known for their trial practice preparation are Northwestern, Temple and Georgetown.

the others, deserves separate recognition. If you're angling for acceptance to a top school, you need to be aware that elite schools tend to take the maturity requirement more seriously than other schools, and tend to view maturity as somewhat synonymous with well-roundedness. This means that, as much as it hurts to say it, if you're single-mindedly pursuing the study of law and have nothing else going on in your life, you need to take a step back and find some other hobbies. Law school admissions officers search for candidates who show commitment to several separate, demanding passions, some of them academic and at least one that's non-academic. You should come to the law school admissions process with at least a handful of interests having nothing to do with academia, preferably including at least modest aptitude in either a sport or a physically recreational hobby of some sort. While debate continues on the subject of whether consideration of such extracurricular activities is appropriate in assessing the capacity of a particular person to study law, there is little debate that such activities are considered in the admissions process, so take them seriously before applying.

B. A SPECIAL SET OF MISCONCEPTIONS – POP CULTURE AND THE LAW

When I prepared to apply to law schools, American popular culture offered plenty of opportunities to misunderstand the legal profession: from L.A. Law, Ally McBeal and The People's Court to Hollywood movies, legal thriller books and even C-SPAN, perceptions of lawyers created by the media are at the very least confusing and at the worst highly misleading.[29] Television emphasizes litigation and personalities, ignores transactional and business law, and skips over realistic but boring parts of the legal process. Books and movies tend to play up the snootiness of law schools and jaw-dropping surprises in courtrooms, when most law schools aren't snooty and few trials nowadays involve major surprises of any sort. And though I enjoyed C-SPAN's rare coverage of trials and trial-like proceedings, they begin and end at appellate courts and Congressional hearing rooms, when the vast majority of actual cases either wind up in very different lower trial courts or never get tried at all. And lower trial courts are very, very much unlike The People's Court, Judge Judy, Judge Mills Lane and Judge Joe Brown.

Though it's true that you can't get much of a real sense of the legal profession from the media, Court T.V. comes closer than most to representing reality, at least for the litigation side of the law. But much of the legal profession has little to do with courtrooms. Approximately ninety-eight percent of civil cases are settled before they ever go to trial, and many criminal cases are settled

---

[29] This isn't to say that all of them are entirely misleading, or even poor entertainment products. They're often fun to read or watch, and of course contain at least grains of truth.

via plea bargain rather than going before a judge and jury. Decisions every bit as important are made with the guidance of transactional attorneys and in-house counsels in corporate boardrooms. And the media rarely depicts the more commonplace, mundane activities of attorneys – researching legal issues, writing advisory opinions for clients and letters to opposing counsel, and so on. These are realities of the profession that you can only really learn about if you work for a law firm, business, or governmental agency.

Another misconception I harbored for many years was a belief that the law and politics were necessarily and fundamentally intertwined. I was a political junkie throughout high school and college, and thought that I'd be served well in law school by a constant diet of political television, newspapers and books. Yet as I'll explain shortly, knowing plenty of political trivia turned out to be all but useless for me,[30] and unless you're going to a law school in Washington, D.C., or planning to practice law there or in a state capital, my experience may well be similar to yours.

Despite all of what I've said above, a few pop culture references I missed initially would actually have been useful to prepare me for law school. The classic movie The Paper Chase, a story of several students' first-year experiences at Harvard Law School, turned out to be an at least informative, if not comprehensive account of the first-year law school experience as it was in the late 1970's. Contrast this with the 'blonde fashion plate goes to Harvard' movie Legally Blonde, which is neither especially informative nor accurate, and is probably not intended to be either. Jonathan Harr's book, A CIVIL ACTION, turned out to be a very useful guide to understanding how courts actually work – it discusses at length the critical parts of a civil trial[31] that take place before Court TV's cameras ever show up.[32] And other books dealing with the subject of law school and the legal profession, while sometimes either gimmicky or slanted, offer at least kernels of insight into the way things appeared to their authors to be at the time of their writing. If you're giving law school serious

---

[30] While a knowledge of domestic and international affairs may inform your general understanding of law school concepts and the basic operations of state, national and supranational governments, it does not play a day-to-day role in first-year legal education.

[31] There are two types of trials: criminal trials, where society (the general public as a whole) sues a person, and civil trials, where one person (or company) sues another person (or company). The criminal trial process typically begins with an investigator having reason to believe a person is guilty of a crime, arresting that person, and then presenting the accusation of the crime in a courtroom. The civil trial process requires no arrest or crime, but rather, that a person or company believe that it has been harmed by another person or company, notify that person or company that they are suing over the harm, and then present the claimed harm in a courtroom.

[32] Gerald M. Stern's THE BUFFALO CREEK DISASTER is often recommended by legal practitioners and professors as useful to building an understanding of the legal process.

consideration, at least peruse a few of these things to get a hint of what's out there, even if you won't want to take them all that seriously.

C. READING MATERIALS

One of the most common fallacies harbored by potential law students is the belief that they must enter law school with a comprehensive knowledge of law, politics, or history. Simply put, though it never hurts to know a little bit about these subjects, there is no need to know law, politics, or history before law school. As a general rule, law school has nothing to do with politics. It only tangentially involves history. And though it has everything to do with law, it's unfortunately true that you will probably not even read law in a useful way until you are actually at a law school and taking classes there.

As I prefer to be over-prepared, I'm definitely guilty of thinking that I could have an advantage by knowing about subjects that were clearly, in some way, related to the law. In the months leading up to law school, I picked up THE FEDERALIST PAPERS, books on Latin, and a bunch of used law books from a local store that was selling off discarded library books. I taught myself a bit of Latin with the thought that I would be exposed to plenty of ancient phrases that I would be able to quickly decipher. I read THE FEDERALIST PAPERS from cover to cover and highlighted parts that I thought would prove relevant to understanding the Constitution. I glanced over the law books I had purchased and re-examined notes from undergraduate classes related to the law and politics. In truth, none of these materials helped me even slightly in law school.

Relatively few basic Latin phrases actually pop up in classes, because the profession – in America at least – is thankfully attempting to reduce practitioners' use of confusing jargon. The two handfuls of Latin words that are worth knowing appear within the pages of a single book you need to buy for law school anyway; getting BLACK'S LAW DICTIONARY in advance might be worth your while.[33] The links between course materials and my prior reading of historical materials were few and far between; a general knowledge of American history is perhaps more useful than a specific one in law school because considering the specifics of history frequently distracts you from thinking about the specifics of law. And that's what law school is all about – the specifics of law. So wasn't it a good idea to buy some old law books recently discarded by a library? Not really.[34] They had been discarded because they

---

[33] BLACK'S LAW DICTIONARY (Brian A. Garner ed., 7th ed.) is considered to be the definitive legal dictionary, and is a recommended purchase at most law schools. You can test your first-year skills with the terms *quantum meruit*, tort-feasor, and *nolo contendre*.

[34] At most, gleaning concepts from their tables of contents would have sufficed. But getting modern, general "how-to" books on interesting areas of the law might have helped; Nolo Press for example publishes easy-to-read law volumes on many subjects.

were outdated, poorly written, or relatively useless. To have attempted to learn "the law" from them would just have confused me about the state of the law today, but in all honesty, I know now that I could never have really read those books back then in the way I would read them today.

Law school teaches you an entirely different sort of critical reasoning process that changes the way you look at books, and what you learn from them. Reading law books right before entering law school is, for the most part, a waste of time. You'll learn what you need to know when you get there, but if you have to get a head start, use modern materials.

D.   CHOOSING A GOOD LAW SCHOOL

As it turns out, I should really have been reading about law schools themselves, and the issues I should have considered are numerous. Admissions brochures from law schools are a good start, and there are some general pointers that might help in your initial canvassing of the field.

- When requesting brochures, think regionally and scholastically. Choose only regions where you will be able to survive for three years.
- For each region, aim academically above and slightly below the type of school you think you might be able to attend.
- Look for schools that cater to the kind of student you want to be, whether that's overachieving or somewhat lower-key. Though many top law schools deserve their reputations for stressing students out, other schools, particularly those outside of the country's top 20, offer less taxing alternatives.
- You may also consider whether the school does anything special to cater to your personal interests and specific demographic characteristics, which I'll call "Personal Preferences."

1.   *Personal Preferences*

Though many law schools brag that they have student organizations for women and racial, religious or sexual minorities, some are better known than others for reaching out to these communities. For example, law schools with fewer students are at a natural disadvantage when you consider the size of such student groups – the commonly named "Black Law Students Association" (African-American and other students of African descent) or "Lambda Law Students Association" (lesbian, gay, bisexual and transgender students) may only have four or five members in a given class of students. But through financial aid, hiring practices, or generous funding for these organizations, schools can do plenty to cater to specific groups of desirable students.

It's worth investigating a school regardless of its size if its other assets make it appealing.[35] Despite a small class size, a school may have a high percentage of female or minority students,[36] and moreover, may have an excellent reputation for handling issues of concerns to these populations.[37] Many schools – particularly those in the top 15 – offer admissions preferences and financial incentives to qualified minority applicants.[38] Conversely, other schools with significant minority populations may have poor track records on issues of importance to some students. If you're concerned, research specific schools in advance of accepting their offers of admission.

There are several issues of continuing concern to female law students in particular, including the number or percentage of women in their classes, the treatment of female students by professors, male-biased testing or grading, and any career-related limitations female graduates may face. The good news is that the legal profession is making tremendous strides in improving conditions for female law students and lawyers. Many law schools have male-to-female ratios of nearly 1:1, and some – including Cornell – have actually had classes where

---

[35] A recent U.S. News and World Report survey of law school diversity provides at least a general sense of the racial and ethnic composition of accredited schools, and may be viewed at http://www.usnews.com/usnews/edu/grad/rankings/law/brief/lawdiv.htm.

[36] As a reference point, the surveyed law school racial minority population as of 2000 was approximately 21% of the roughly 125,000 law students enrolled at ABA-accredited schools nationwide. Approximately 4% were "American Indian or Alaska Native," 32% were "Asian or Pacific Islander," 36% were "Black American," 9% were "Mexican American," 3% were "Puerto Rican," and 16% were "Other Hispanic." The statistics appear in the American Bar Association's *Minority Enrollment 1971-2001*, available at http://www.abanet.org/legaled/statistics/minstats.html; and the American Bar Association's *Legal Education and Bar Admission Statistics, 1963-2001*, available at http://www.abanet.org/legaled/statistics/le_bastats.html.

[37] You could contact representatives of a law school's student organizations to get a sense of how the school's administration has responded to issues in the past.

[38] Though the degree of advantage varies from school to school, minority candidates can be at significant advantages in admissions and scholarship funding. Duke Law School, for example, notes that it "is committed to increasing its percentage of minority students. Special care is taken in evaluating applications from members of minority groups who traditionally have not been well represented in the legal profession." See *Policies and Practices of the Admissions Office, Policy 1-1: Decisions*, available at http://www.law.duke.edu/general/info/s01.html. But for one example of the continuing debate over racial preferences in admissions, see Anna Clark & Jen Fish, *U. Michigan Law School Admissions Ruled Illegal*, MICHIGAN DAILY, Mar. 28, 2001, available at http://www.uwire.com/content/topnews032801002.html, and Mike Householder, *U-M Can Use Race in Law School Admissions*, THE DETROIT NEWS, May 14, 2002, available at http://detnews.com/2002/schools/0205/14/-489369.htm. Regardless of what may be happening in a particular state, however, minority applicants should not shy away from discussing their backgrounds in essays.

women were in the majority.[39] A survey conducted by the American Bar Association in 2000 showed that 49% of first-year law students are women, up from 42% in 1990, 36% in 1980, 10% in 1970 and 4% in 1950 and 1960.[40] Classes are now being offered at numerous law schools to appeal specifically to female law students, including courses in feminist jurisprudence and gender discrimination, and both female and male faculty members often work tirelessly to help female students seek clerkships and permanent employment following law school. It's not hard at this point to find many female-friendly law schools,[41] and your chances of finding an unfriendly one are quite small. In summary, though it's fair to say today that the law school experience is virtually identical for women and men, women can also look forward to classes at most schools that address their specific interests as women.

The bad news is that occasional gender-related issues do rear their ugly heads. A small percentage of professors are infrequently accused, sometimes correctly, of displaying favoritism or bias either for or against female students – behavior that might manifest itself as an over- or under-aggressive class discussion style with female students, but generally not in testing or grading (processes which are typically anonymous in law school). Even rarer are professors or job interviewers who sexually harass students, but, of course, these things happen, and students generally complain when they do. Having said this, it's worth repeating that these events are very few and far between, and much less likely amongst faculty than interviewers,[42] and even then, it's unlikely. As of December 2001, females accounted for almost 42% of the associates and staff or senior attorneys at major law firms, and nearly 16% of the partners at these firms[43] – numbers that are higher now than they were ten years ago. You should not be deterred from law school by the truly rare prospect of harassment. But if you are concerned by the prospect that these

---

[39] Other universities, including Stanford and two in Colorado, report similar gender parity. See Barbara Allen Babcock, *Women Poised for Real Revolution in the Legal Profession*, CNN Interactive, May 15, 2000, available at http://www.cnn.com/LAW/columns/babcock.05.15/; Jan Leitos, *Women in the Law*, KUSA Denver 9News.Com, Dec. 9, 2000, available at http://9news.com/issue/women.htm.

[40] The survey is available at http://www.abanet.org/legaled/statistics/femstats.html.

[41] Quite a few schools, including schools in the top 15, go so far as to hold special gatherings for female applicants who have not yet accepted the schools' offers.

[42] For experiences relating to job interviews, see Chapter 9, Section A.

[43] Though the partnership numbers are disappointingly low, representing only a 3.5% increase from eight years earlier, non-partner attorney numbers have gone up as a larger number of women have entered and successfully completed law school. See NALP, *Dearth of Women and Attorneys of Color Remains in Law Firms*, Dec. 3, 2001, available at http://www.nalp.org/press/minrwom01.htm. The statistics have not increased as impressively for attorneys of color, who represent only 3.55% of partners (a 1% increase from 1993) and 13.70% of staff/senior attorneys and associates.

sorts of things might happen to you, it's worth your time to contact the student associations at the law schools you are considering – they will likely be more open about such events, if they've occurred, than school administrators.

Married or committed students may have additional concerns, both for the stability of their relationships and their chances of finding appropriate employment or networking opportunities for their significant others. Though the stability issue will be discussed later,[44] it's fair to suggest now that relationship commitments where both people might relocate may well lead students to choose larger schools and/or schools in more metropolitan areas. The percentage of married and permanently committed law students is generally small relative to singles, thus for social reasons it may be easier to find other couples in schools and cities with more people. Similarly, spousal employment and other daily activities are easier to find outside of dedicated college towns.

In addition to your personal preferences, choosing the right law school will boil down to several considerations. The reputation and ranking of a school are generally critical factors. Many practicing lawyers would advise you to attend the best-ranked school you can get into, and to finance the expense if necessary through loans.[45] There is no doubt that the legal profession today places considerable weight on the national or regional reputation of the school you choose; it's no understatement to suggest that the school you attend may mean more to a potential employer than the grades you receive.

2. Statistical and Rankings Data

While personal preference is a useful starting point, it's not the best place to end your considerations. A properly thought-out law school choice should include a full canvassing of possible options, both through official sources and unofficial ones. This process might begin when you obtain brochures and course catalogs from law schools, check their web sites, or skim one of the annual statistical data books on all of the accredited law schools in the

---

[44] The first year of law school is generally the most challenging for couples; a student cannot alter his or her schedule and spouses or domestic partners are thus frequently left at least somewhat lonely. But this can, and most often does change after the first year. Significant others should make significant plans to keep themselves occupied during the first year of law school. For additional details on law school relationships, see Chapter 3, Section O.

[45] Some have even stated it in a manner I personally agree with: "you can't price the value of a degree from a top school." Your job prospects are enhanced tremendously, even if the quality of the instruction is the same from school to school – which it will probably not be. Better-ranked schools often have superior faculties, much better job prospects for their graduates, and higher bar passage rates, though the correlation is an imperfect one.

country.[46] Brochures and web sites only tell you so much, however, and books full of statistics can become mind-numbingly confusing.

That's why I'll suggest another, less official source. Several publications rank or otherwise offer guides to law schools; the one most respected by students (and despised and feared by the deans of law schools) is the annual graduate school guide published by *U.S. News and World Report*. *U.S. News* publishes an annual survey that ranks law schools by four "tiers" and also by "specialties," such as international law, intellectual property law and alternative dispute resolution. It lists the general combinations of GPAs and LSAT scores typically required for each of the country's over 180 **ABA-accredited law schools**,[47] and contains additional information to aid your decision, from location to school size. Some of the *U.S. News* metrics – such as reputation amongst academics and practitioners, or faculty-to-student ratio – are arguably outdated, less than accurate, or downright misleading,[48] but to get a general

---

[46] The Princeton Review publishes an annual COMPLETE BOOK OF LAW SCHOOLS, Penguin has a PENGUIN GUIDE TO AMERICAN LAW SCHOOLS, and Peterson's has an annual PETERSON'S LAW SCHOOLS series, as well. A course catalog should be read to see whether a given school offers classes that *generally* interest you – even though you may not be totally sure what sort of law you will ultimately practice after law school.

[47] There are four types of law schools – those accredited by the American Bar Association (ABA), those only accredited by a given state, those that lack ABA and state accreditation, and those that are not really law schools. **The *U.S. News* guide only includes ABA-accredited schools, which should probably be the only schools you consider attending** – a degree from any of these schools entitles you to seek admission to practice law in any state in the country, and typically includes a superior legal education than what's offered at non-ABA schools. This book deals solely with the legal education you're likely to receive from ABA-accredited schools. Graduation from any of the non-ABA schools not only tends to be less educationally beneficial, but in some cases will force you to pass special additional hurdles (such as certification and testing) before you're even allowed to take a given state's bar exam and practice law. Only consider a state-accredited school if you feel that you must study the law despite the fact that you cannot get in to an ABA-accredited school – and this is not likely to be the case. Be wary of schools lacking ABA or state accreditation, especially those that claim to be "seeking" ABA approval or in a "pre-accreditation" phase. For all practical purposes, your degree will be next to useless in helping you ultimately practice law. Finally, you may have seen advertisements for fringe organizations that purport to teach people the "law" necessary to "free them from government oppression and taxation," or something similar – sometimes they call themselves "law schools." They're not law schools, so be quite wary of any "school" that offers to teach you entirely by videotape or CD-ROM – you probably won't wind up with anything close to a law degree at the end.

[48] The numbers may be misleading because of behind-the-scenes trickery. Some schools maintain artificially large lists of faculty in order to suggest high faculty-to-student ratios. Realistically, no one should expect to be taught by a mostly retired professor emeritus or one who takes a multi-year or seemingly permanent sabbatical.

sense of what's out there, *U.S. News* is a great resource to suggest where you might or might not consider applying.[49]

3. Geographical Considerations

The previous advice regarding attending the best school that accepts you is applicable if the school in question is ranked in *U.S. News'* top 15. These schools typically have enough national prominence that you will be able to find a post-graduation job anywhere in the country regardless of where the school is located. This is not the case for the remaining 165-some schools. If your best acceptance comes from the top 25 and the school is local to the place where you'd like to be employed, your chances of securing a job are about as good as they get. Otherwise, you need to focus right now on the location where you hope to practice after law school, and target the best possible school(s) within that state.

First-year law students often want to choose a school in a region conducive to studying and not conducive to distraction; this is a good idea, but not mandatory, and not necessarily wise after the first year. Regardless of where you go, your first year will essentially be spent indoors and studying most of the time. While it never hurts to consider places that are geographically close to friends or family, at least by airplane, your real focus should be upon places where you could feel comfortable living and working after graduating from law school. Unless you're accepted into a top 15 law school, you will probably *need* to choose a school close to the state and city where you will ultimately want to work; many law firms only hire from a tight, local geographic area.[50]

There is only one exception to the general formula that you should pick a top 15 school if offered, and if not, a school as close as possible to where you want to practice. Schools in the third and fourth *U.S. News* tiers have disproportionately less success in placing students in jobs than schools in the

---

[49] *U.S. News* currently makes an abbreviated web version of their rankings available at http://www.usnews.com/usnews/edu/beyond/gradrank/law/gdlawt1.htm. Competing law school rankings have appeared and disappeared over the years. Princeton Review also offers law school rankings via its web site, though no one takes them seriously by comparison to *U.S. News*. Once in a while, columnists and other sources will attempt to create competitor rankings to *U.S. News'* product, sometimes seriously, sometimes in jest; *U.S. News* has continued to serve as the benchmark for most students and practitioners, and grudgingly, academics as well. See http://www.lawschool100.com for an alternative.

[50] This latter point is especially critical in tough economic times. Law firms are notoriously selective in hiring based on geography; local students tend to receive strong preference in hiring over non-local ones, unless the non-local students attended one of the top 5-15 schools in the country. Students from the top 15 schools can find work virtually anywhere, and those in the top 5 are in especially good shape in hiring.

first two tiers, so students with average undergraduate grades or LSAT scores sometimes opt to spend their first year at the best-ranked school they can attend, regardless of location, work like crazy to earn their way into the law school's top 10%, and then transfer to a top locally- or nationally-respected school immediately thereafter.

4. Course and Subject Matter Offerings

Of course, there are other considerations beyond geography, though location does have quite an impact on many students' law school choices. Another critical point, sometimes neglected, is to consider whether the schools you're applying to are capable of offering the types of classes that interest you.[51] As many students realize that the first year is almost the same at every school, rarely does a school's area of specialty matter to prospective students as much as it should, but for those hoping to eventually study international law, mediation, intellectual property law, or the like, it may be critically important to determine in advance the sort of classes a school offers, and rarely who the professors are. As suggested above, U.S. News is a helpful guide to the top schools for several specialties, but their specialty list is not comprehensive. The web sites of many schools will highlight their specific curricular advantages, and you might consider contacting students or relevant student organizations at each school to determine whether the schools are overstating their offerings.

To get some sense of the fields of specialization that are out there, Table 6-1 in Chapter 6 offers a collection of classes that often show up today in American law schools, linked to specific potential fields of study.

5. Financial Limitations

Especially for older students – those who have been out in the world doing something else for a number of years prior to law school – huge loans will be even less attractive than for younger students with fewer responsibilities and limited expenses.[52] Financing thus can be a fundamental concern, and while I

---

[51] Just to be clear about it, a law degree is a law degree, and once you pass a state's bar exam, you can theoretically practice any sort of law you desire with the exception of patent law. Therefore, you don't *need* to pick a school with classes specific to your interests; it only helps you learn more about what you like and avoid having to teach yourself later. So even if you attend a school hoping to practice international law only to become interested in intellectual property law, not a subject the school specializes in, you will still find a modest number of related courses at the school you picked. You'll teach yourself anything else you need to know afterwards. This is how the study of law works.

[52] Students older than 30 may also be concerned about their social lives at law school. This will depend a lot on the school's demographic characteristics, something that you

would advise prospective students to aim high in their applications and seek scholarships,[53] the choice may appear in the end to come down to dollars. The strategy I would advise as a general rule is to pick a better-ranked school unless the price differential is so profound and the ranking differential so slight that you can't justify picking a better-ranked school over a cheaper one. While geography, specialization areas, and finances are all important, it is unquestionably the case that one can invest three years in earning a law degree and leave law school unemployed. Picking a good law school is as much about what's inside the school as what will happen when you're finished. Err if at all on the side of practicality.

E.   AN ASIDE ON THE LONGSTANDING DEBATE OVER LAW SCHOOL RANKINGS

Rankings can be dangerous. To hear the story told by the Association of American Law Schools,[54] when it comes to ranking law schools, rankings are misleading, methodologically flawed, and perhaps even entirely inappropriate. Further, the Law School Admissions Council has published an open letter from law school deans to prospective students challenging the validity of rankings, particularly those published by *U.S. News and World Report.*[55] And the American Bar Association's Section of Legal Education and Admissions to the Bar has also come out strongly against rankings, stating that:

---

can research with a phone call or web site visit prior to or after application. Married students tend to spend most of their free time after the first year making up for lost first-year hours with their spouses and families, and unmarried students may find themselves hunting for people to spend time with. This is truly a subject that will require personal research on a school-by-school basis, and might skew one towards cities that are more metropolitan and thus not dependent on young student populations for a social existence.

[53] As of 1999, over $310-million per year in scholarships and grants were awarded by ABA-accredited law schools, a 12% increase over 1998 and a 199% increase from 1988. See American Bar Association, *Internal Grants and Scholarships: Total Dollar Volume Awarded All ABA Approved Law Schools,* available at http://www.abanet.org/legaled/statistics/grants.html. Many schools offer substantial scholarships to minority students, students who demonstrate considerable academic merit, or who will commit to careers in public service after graduation; programs outside of law schools sometimes offer additional support. See, e.g., University of Missouri-Columbia School of Law, *Prospective Students Financial Information,* available at http://www.law.missouri.edu/prospective/scholarships.htm; Florida Education Fund, *Minority Participation in Legal Education (MPLE) Program,* available at http://www.fl-educ-fd.org/mple.html.

[54] The AALS represents 164 member schools and 19 non-member, fee-paid schools, and commissioned a study contesting the validity of *U.S. News* rankings, which you can read at http://www.aals.org/validity.html.

[55] See http://www.lsac.org/LSAC.asp?url=lsac/deans-speak-out-rankings.asp.

Qualities that make one kind of school good for one student may not be as important to another. The American Bar Association and its Section of Legal Education and Admissions to the Bar have issued disclaimers of any law school rating system. Prospective law students should consider a variety of factors in making their choice among schools.[56]

So, with three formidable organizations on one hand, and a publisher of perennially popular undergraduate and graduate school rankings guides on the other, what is a prospective law student supposed to believe?

You'll hear plenty of different opinions, but my answer is: believe the rankings. At least, don't let law school deans and their various organizations dissuade you from considering them. Rankings may be dangerous, but they're far more problematic for law school faculties than their prospective students.

Depending on your general level of cynicism, for law schools to criticize law school rankings may fall someplace on a spectrum between hypocritical and knowingly intellectually dishonest. My own belief is that such criticism is merely hypocritical.[57] The simple logic goes like this: law schools rank students, law schools admit that their ranking systems are imperfect, yet continue to rank students, and therefore, law schools should not complain when people rank them and use imperfect systems to do so. But the issue is deeper than that.

Rankings made two statements: first, that "this is the way things are," and second, that "if you want to be higher-ranked, this is what you have to do." Law schools hate rankings for the same reason students do: unless you're at the top, rankings force you to work harder. It's easy to protest that you don't like the standards you're being judged by, and on occasion, it's even possible to change the standards.[58] But when law school deans protested the school ranking system and were pressed to suggest an alternative to the *U.S. News* format, they presented a mind-numbing list of 22 "most important" factors to students that were not being given adequate consideration, in addition to the 10 factors already used by *U.S. News*. Like students, law schools are trying their hardest to blur the ranking lines and add so many criteria that every school stands out as good in some way. And like law professors grading their students, *U.S. News* is

---

[56] See http://www.abanet.org/legaled/approvedlawschools/approved.html.

[57] Those who believe the criticism to be intellectually dishonest point to the facts that numerous law schools quietly take pride in their high rankings, many faculty members believe that the rankings have substantial merit, and that law schools cannot possibly believe that they are so unlike other academic institutions as to warrant a ban on ranking.

[58] At undergraduate schools, students show up to protest paper and exam grades all the time. At law schools, professors hardly even entertain protests, especially amazing when you take one test and get one grade for an entire semester of work. A grade is a grade, no changes, and in some cases, you might not even get an explanation of what makes your essay or exam different from that of someone who received a higher or lower grade.

sticking to a certain set of criteria and saying that even if every school is good – a doubtful hypothesis to begin with – some are measurably better than others. And while proposed LSAC criteria such as "law library strengths and services" might be important to some people, they are just not important enough to matter to the majority of law students.

The *U.S. News* rankings measure reputation, selectivity, student-to-faculty ratio, bar passage rates, and employability of graduates, factors which speak to some, but not all of the concerns students may have. In a nutshell, the rankings tell you what specialists think of the schools, how hard they are to get into, how large the classes are likely to be, how good a chance you have of getting a job with your new degree, and your likelihood of actually being admitted to practice law after graduation. Schools dislike these factors because they are essentialist.[59] But these issues are of considerable importance to students, often more than almost any of the deans' 22 proposed factors. If you don't realize the value of these factors already, you will when you're near or after graduation. And the four *U.S. News* tiers do a good, if imperfect job of letting students know where schools stand in a broad spectrum of choices.

True, these rankings do not speak specifically to the "breadth and support of alumni network" or the "quality of teaching," though these dean-proposed factors are reflected at least vaguely in the *U.S. News* employability and reputation factors. *U.S. News* does not speak at all to such other proposed factors as cost, location, breadth of curriculum, or international programming. But these and 10 other factors are ones that students can easily research on schools' web sites if they desire, and assign whatever weight they feel relevant in reaching their ultimate personal decision.

What students cannot meaningfully measure, either through official school web sites or rankings of any sort, are factors such as "collaborative research opportunities with faculty," "faculty accessibility," "quality of teaching," and one of my pet peeves, "commitment to innovative technology." Many schools claim to be excellent in all four of these areas, amongst others, and the only ways prospective students can learn the truth is either to read student

---

[59] Some schools have suggested that rankings compel the use of dirty score-raising tricks for factors such as "acceptance rate," including attracting unqualified students to apply and then turning them down. There are three answers to this. First, if you are satisfied with your place in the rankings and the students you are admitting, change nothing. Second, if you are dissatisfied with your rank but not your students, work to improve your reputation amongst lawyers, judges, and academics, your employment statistics, or your bar passage rates. Third, if you are dissatisfied with your students, raise your standards, admit fewer people, and/or convince better people to attend. Any school that would exaggerate its acceptance rate or student-to-faculty ratio to make itself look better in rankings, rather than working to improve its student satisfaction, areas of specialization, or breadth and depth of instruction, deserves the fate it will suffer as a consequence.

satisfaction surveys, speak with numerous students, or attend a school and observe first hand. *U.S. News'* omission of rankings for these important but hard-to-measure subjects should be viewed as an invitation to students to research specific places of interest in greater depth, a skill any hopeful lawyer should develop early on. Ultimately, gathering information from more than one source is always the best strategy at application time.

All of the above discussion ignores one other important point: in the real world, rankings matter. Virtually every faculty member considers the rankings in some way before accepting employment at a school. Many law firms use the rankings to determine the top national and local schools from which they should hire. Some even give hiring bonuses to students whose schools are in the "top 10." Like them or hate them, *U.S. News* rankings should not be the end of your research, but definitely factor them into your final decision.

F.   CHOOSING THE RIGHT DEGREE

One of the confusing, but relatively minor aspects of the study of law is the nature of the degree potential students are seeking. Generally, completion of the study of law in the United States results in the award of a degree of Juris Doctor, or Doctor of Law. This degree is abbreviated J.D., and replaces the degree that was formerly awarded to law school graduates of the 1960's and before – the Bachelor of Law (LL.B.) degree. While many practicing lawyers continue to possess LL.B. degrees, some law schools have recently awarded juris doctorates retroactively to their older graduates to reflect the profession's modern trend. LL.B. degrees are no longer offered in the United States.

The real confusion for most people starts with the degree of Master of Laws, or LL.M., which is a complement to (rather than substitute for) a J.D. or foreign law degree. The LL.M. degree is offered in one- and two-year programs, and tends to be in a specialized, specific area of the law such as tax, international law, or the like. Generally, no American law student would seek an LL.M. alone if she or he hoped to practice law in this country, but some students opt to graduate from American schools with both a J.D. and a LL.M. in some specific subject. Schools offering LL.M. programs will generally describe the breadth of their offerings in their admissions brochures. Cornell Law School, specifically, offers a LL.M. in international law which can be earned at the same time as a J.D., but requires considerable additional coursework during what could otherwise be a relatively low-key third year.

In my informal survey of law firm recruiting, the consensus was that the professional benefits of earning an LL.M. degree were minor, and in almost every case not worth the time and effort demanded during the already stressful law school experience.[60] Few lawyers have an LL.M., and thus few expect you to have one – unless you hope to practice international transactional law with a huge international firm, in which case an International Law LL.M. will help, or the tax department of a large American firm, in which case a Tax LL.M. may help. Even then, an LL.M. is generally an option, not a requisite, at most firms.

An unusual option, pursued in U.S. law schools primarily by citizens of foreign countries, is to complete a foreign law degree and then pursue an American LL.M. Typically foreign LL.M. candidates spend a year in the United States working on their degrees, and either return home thereafter or attempt to pursue certification from one or more of America's state bar associations. Sadly, some law schools offer vague glimmers of hope to foreign applicants who think that an LL.M. program will enable them to pass a U.S. bar exam. In my limited exposure to foreign LL.M. candidates who have attempted this, the bar exam failure rate is exceedingly high; an LL.M. is no substitute for the knowledge one receives from a J.D. degree when it comes time to take a state's bar exam.

Another joint-degree program is the J.D.-M.B.A., which arms graduates with both a J.D. and a Master's of Business Administration degree. This joint-degree program tends to take at least four years in total, and the result is generally a much more marketable credential. Typically, the student spends their first full year at either the law school or the business school, then the next full year at the other, and then mixes classes from both together in the third and fourth years to complete both degrees.

While there are great benefits to be derived from the J.D.-M.B.A., there are also some consequences. The first is simple; if you spend your first year at the law school rather than the business school, any friends you make in law school will have graduated by the time you start your last year of the program. A second is less intuitive; as investment banks and consulting firms traditionally paid better than law firms did, it should be noted that many law firms have been suspicious of candidates who possess both degrees. The thought is that these candidates are most likely to come to law firms for short periods of time, gain experience, and bail out for greener pastures. Thus pursue a J.D.-M.B.A. with great caution, bearing in mind that you'll have to really show a legal employer that you're purely interested in the law, as opposed to business.

There are several other joint degree programs to consider, as well, though they are far less commonly offered than LL.M. and M.B.A. programs. First is the Master of Public Policy degree, which may be the best joint-degree program for lawyers who aspire to legislative or executive branch employment in the future.

---

[60] In fact, I was accepted to the joint J.D./LL.M. program when I applied to law school, but after first-year discussions with a number of students and practitioners, I became one of a large number of people to drop the International Law LL.M. program based on its impracticality and time commitments. For a number of reasons, this later proved to be a wise personal choice.

Another is the Ph.D. in Economics degree, which helps those particularly interested in high-level commercial law for either the private or public sector. A Master of Dispute Resolution degree might be useful to those considering mediation or commercial law (rather than litigation) practices; many other Master-level programs, including Public Health and specific courses of non-legal international studies, are offered at various schools.

With the exception of the joint-degree J.D.-M.B.A. program, which has great utility to a specific class of people but little use for the majority of the population, I will describe myself as bearish on the practicality of joint-degree programs. Law school is not the sort of experience one should lightly compound with additional work. Your life could easily become overwhelming – as is does for most first-year law students – and then remain that way for three or four years – which it generally does not for students who pursue only a single degree. Enter these programs only if you find the second subjects both fascinating and worth the considerable amount of extra time and aggravation you will face in addition to your full-time life as a law student. In some cases, these programs will consume an extra year of your life and may limit your flexibility when seeking employment, so if you're going to work for another degree, be sure that it will be of some use to you when you finish it.

G. THE LSAT

Business schools have the GMAT. Medical schools have the MCAT. Other graduate schools have the GRE. Most ABA-accredited law schools use the Law School Admissions Test (LSAT), a harrowing half-day exam which is graded to a minimum of 120 and a maximum of 180 points.[61] Multiple-choice in nature, the LSAT tests skills widely believed to be useful if not necessary in law school: reading comprehension, logical reasoning (arguments), and analytical reasoning (games). The LSAT is administered by the Law School Admissions council, costs at least $103 (plus a potential $54 late fee) per exam,[62] and is offered in numerous test sites around the world four times annually – typically June, October, December, and February. Because of November and December admissions deadlines, most law schools will not consider applicants who submit their materials and then sit for the February exam; February is thus only an option for early birds or multiple test-takers.[63]

---

[61] See http://www.lsac.org for more details.

[62] Most law schools also require you to register with the LSDAS, a $95/year data accumulation service which produces form reports on your grades and letters of recommendation that may be examined by any law school you apply to. Each LSDAS report after the first "free" one costs either $9 or $11 depending on when you order it.

[63] For reasons to be developed, of the remaining dates, October is preferable. December is the latest exam you can take and still be considered for admission the subsequent fall.

Entire books have been written on the LSAT, so I will make no attempt to tell you how to ace the exam. But I will tell you that the LSAT is one of the two most critical components, for better or worse, that you will disclose on your application to law schools.[64] And there are therefore several important considerations any prospective law student should take into account before even considering the LSAT.

I confess that I made a mistake in the LSAT process: at a point in my life when I thought my date of application to law school would be more remote than it was, and without realizing the importance of the exam, I took the LSAT cold, without any preparation. In fact, I didn't even know what score I needed to receive in order to get into a law school, and I didn't really care because I wasn't planning to do it right away, any way. This was not the world's most brilliant idea. My score was good enough for a top 50 school, but not good enough for the top 15 or top 10 schools I would ultimately hope to attend.

As it turns out, LSAT scores are kept on file for nine years, and you generally can't take the LSAT more than three times in a two-year period. Law schools have different policies on whether to accept your most recent score as your "actual" score, or average your score based on however many scores you've received. Most schools do the latter. In essence, this means that if you do what I did, you seriously risk diminishing the impact of whatever score you ultimately hope to achieve on the exam, and to state that point more clearly, you should not take the exam until you have relative confidence that you can get the score you need for the school you want to get into.

This opens up a big can of worms. How important are the scores to law schools? How do you know what scores a law school will be expecting of their successful applicants? How can one have any confidence in the score one will receive, before taking the exam?

First, top 50 law schools take the LSAT quite seriously – perhaps too seriously. There are plenty of ways to evaluate potential law students, and as virtually everyone agrees at this point, multiple choice exams are not a perfect way to determine who should and should not attend the top schools in the country. However, as has often been said of democracy, the LSAT may not be the perfect solution, but it's the best one developed so far. It does test relevant skills. It omits graded essay writing and other practical skills, but individual law schools may examine these in your separate applications. Most accredited schools, and therefore all graduate school rankings guides, use LSAT score cutoffs to determine what supposed caliber of students are being admitted. Whether or not each school feels comfortable about the LSAT, most law schools give your LSAT score considerable weight.

U.S. News and World Report publishes a list of the approximate 25%/75%

---

[64] The other is your undergraduate GPA.

LSAT spreads used by each law school in accepting candidates. For example, a school's 25% mark might be 152, and 75% mark 158. As 75% of students applying to that school have scores of 158 or lower, students submitting applications with LSAT scores at or higher than 158 have a pretty good chance of getting accepted. As only 25% of the applicants have a score of 152 or lower, students submitting LSAT scores at that level are less likely to be admitted. What is unpublished, but widely rumored, is that those accepted at or below the 25% level typically either have excellent undergraduate or graduate GPAs, previous ties to the school, or express unique personal characteristics in an essay, such as diversity/affirmative action characteristics of some sort. In other words, if you have a score at or below the school's 25th percentile, and fall into one of these categories, you're not as much of a long shot for acceptance as someone who is not.

The 2002 *U.S. News* survey showed that 150 was the lowest 25% mark for a school in the first tier (top 50 schools); 174 was the highest 75% mark. Second tier schools hit a 25% low-mark of 149, and a 75% high-mark of 163. Third-tier schools hit the 25% low-mark of 143 and 75% high-mark of 160. Fourth-tier schools hit the 25% low mark of 139 and 75% high-mark of 157. These ranges of numbers might suggest general targeting guidelines for both your preparations and your later applications.

The final, and most important issue, is how to anticipate your possible grade on the LSAT. Frankly, though this will no doubt freak out plenty of potential law students, the answer is to prepare heavily in advance – if you are really concerned about your score. Average (50th percentile) scores tend to fall between 145 and 150; typical law schools offer easier acceptance to those in the mid- to high-150s, and the most selective ones have averages in the upper 160s. Few people come close to the perfect score of 180, and few people should; again, the LSAT is not going to be the sole reason any candidate gets into a law school. Don't think that Legally Blonde's portrayal of a 179 score recipient is either likely or even believable. Most practicing lawyers came nowhere near that number.

But then, most practicing lawyers did not go to the country's elite schools. If you have a need to aim especially high, Kaplan and The Princeton Review are among the companies offering full classroom-style LSAT preparation courses for prices around $1000.[65] That's a lot of money, but frankly, for those who need encouragement to study hard, it could be a worthwhile investment if

---

[65] As of the time of writing, Kaplan's two-month classroom course, consisting of 11 three-hour sessions, cost $1100, and the Princeton Review one-month course, consisting of 12 three- or four-hour sessions, cost $1000. Students taking Kaplan are guaranteed that their scores will improve over a certain threshold point-level of performance or they can receive their money back.

you're serious about getting into a good law school.[66] Unless you're exceedingly self-motivated, studying on your own with a LSAT preparation book is not as likely to produce a beneficial result as Kaplan; this is mostly due to the fact that taking a course imposes the discipline upon your studies that you might otherwise personally lack.

Each course meets for weeks prior to an exam, offering practice exams, classes and self-administered drills in preparation. You start at a base, unaided level of performance based on whatever skills you've developed without any practice. From there, six or seven point increases in score are typical; my unaided base level of 159 shot up to a 166 after taking Kaplan. A few pointers:

- You'll maximize your score if you take every drill seriously and know exactly where you stand on practice exams before doing the LSAT.
- If you want to be especially serious, do some studying on your own before taking a class, just to familiarize yourself with the style and nature of the questions.
- Definitely work hardest on those things you have the most trouble with; you will be surprised at your enhanced level of performance thereafter. After mastering each part, target your next worst section.
- If you plan to attend a good school, you really have to make it your personal responsibility to practice until you feel confident with even the hardest material the course offers.

This is not to say that Kaplan or other courses are perfect. In truth, with the exception of their practice exams, which are pretty much on target in estimating your actual exam-day performance,[67] prep courses tend to be amateurish. This owes to the fact that their lesson plans essentially consist of practice exams and structured self-teaching sessions; they motivate you to do what you could be doing on your own.

If you are widely known by friends and family alike to be self-disciplined, consistent practice with professional course materials, in my view, will be entirely adequate to earn you a stellar score on the LSAT. There have been reports that disciplined self-preparation produces LSAT scores on average only

---

[66] More dubious is the value of Kaplan's private one-on-one tutoring, an option I've known no one to take, which runs from $2000-4000 depending on the number of hours (15-35) of tutoring one takes. Take this as you will, but I can't imagine the circumstances or the materials which would merit spending nearly half of a full year of law school tuition just to prepare for the admissions exam; my view is not necessarily shared by those who, in hindsight, received lower scores than necessary to attend certain schools and believe that tutoring might somehow have made a difference.

[67] Barring unusual testing conditions, the estimates are largely accurate.

one tenth of a point lower than Kaplan class preparation.[68] Whether you would benefit from externally imposed discipline is a question only you – and people who know you well – should answer.

Viewed from a distance, the LSAT is not the world's most difficult graduate school exam; by comparison with the MCAT, it's probably a lot easier.[69] But there are no guarantees of fairness in conditions of administration. The climate and the testing rooms tend to be relatively important factors in taking the LSAT, as tests are offered across the country (and beyond) at sites selected not so much for hospitable conditions as their inexpensive availability and space. Some LSAT sites are downright inappropriate for a test of this gravity.

As you may well take the LSAT in either in June or December, it might help to take the exam someplace that is spared the extreme conditions of climate; I took the LSAT in Buffalo, New York, once during the summer, where the room was blazing hot and a loud soccer game was in progress outside when they opened the windows, and once in the dead frigidity of a Buffalo winter storm, when either the LSAT proctors or school had literally forgotten to turn on the heat in the building, and students were forced to take the exam wearing gloves and jackets. Though not as important, sites also vary in the types of desks used, and obviously, the people administering the exam. Stories abound of staff that failed to follow directions or give proper "minutes remaining" notices, desks uncomfortable for taller-than-average people, and other miscellaneous problems. Needless to say, it helps to be somewhat resilient when taking the LSAT. And American test-takers might best be advised to take the October exam rather than the February, June or December ones, as climate will probably be least a factor then.

In short, doing well on the LSAT is important. Some of your performance is controllable. Some is left up to last-minute chance, and factors beyond your control. If you're aiming to get into just any law school, hard-core preparation is probably unnecessary, but preparation of some sort will be to your benefit. If you're aiming for a top-tier law school, serious preparation is in your future, so take whatever steps you believe to be necessary to maximize your score.

H. APPLICATION SEASON

Application season begins for most prospective law students at one of

---

[68] See Sarah M. Lee, *LSAT Awaits Law School Students*, THE DAILY ILLINI ONLINE, April 3, 2001, available at http://www.dailyillini.com/apr01/apr03/news/stories/news08.shtml.

[69] The legal sphere makes up for this by administering a far more punishing exam (the bar) when it comes time to begin practicing law than doctors must take (medical boards) before practicing medicine. A few law schools admit students on the premise that some students won't pass the bar exams, and therefore will never practice law. Medical schools generally admit only students who will ultimately be permitted to practice medicine.

several points in their lives – near the end of one's junior year of college, in the middle of one's last year of another graduate school, or roughly a year before a non-student plans to leave a job. Yet all three of these times have one thing in common; as most schools do not offer year-round "rolling" admissions, applicants will be submitting documents at a certain point in the standard application cycle of a given law school, often from late summer until early winter. My strong advice, especially if you are a candidate on the margins of a school's numerical admissions numbers, is to have your completed application ready to send out at or near the very beginning of the application cycle. This means taking the LSAT early. It means guessing that this year's essays will be pretty similar to last year's when schools publish their annual application forms. This may, but not need, be accomplished during a "year off" after college.

The benefits of this strategy are threefold. First, submitting any application early – so long as it is appropriately prepared – is a sign of diligence and interest that will serve you well in any profession. Second, an early application reaches the eyes of a less weary admissions council at the school you target, rather than showing up when they have already sifted through piles of applications that are no doubt very, very similar. Third and most importantly, you have some advantage in the numbers game, in which schools unquestionably hesitate at some point to admit candidates with scores that are just "too low" because it would drag down their numeric averages by comparison to other schools. Don't fool yourself; this actually is a consideration for law school admissions offices. While an early application can't completely escape the LSAT and GPA numbers game, there is a much greater opportunity for an admissions panel to let you in at the margins – or at least place you high up on a wait list – where your numbers are perceived as ones that the rest of the pool will eventually correct for, rather than ones that are perceived to have shown up late only to weigh down the pool.

Now let's be realistic, if not a bit cynical. One of the most common comments made about the law school admissions process, and about many other cattle calls in the legal profession, is that it's all really a crapshoot in the end. Unless you really aimed too high, you'll surprise yourself by getting into some schools where you thought you didn't have a chance. And you'll be denied admission to schools where you otherwise seemed a likely candidate for admission. And in many cases there will be no special rhyme or reason for the decisions, at least as it's apparent to you. Rarely should one take personally the decisions of schools' admissions boards; they may have agendas that transcend whatever numbers, life experiences, or special skills you want to offer them.

At the same time, however, don't forget that you do have some control over the process. If you submit an application that is clearly consistent with or superior to a school's average LSAT *and* GPA, you probably come in with a presumption in your favor; the question is then what you can do at such a point that ultimately denies you admission. Timing, clearly, is one such thing; submit average scores when the application season is almost over and your chances are reduced. Saying something especially stupid on an essay – and by stupid I mean offensive, not naive – probably diminishes your chances. Ignoring or misreading the heart of an application question, namely exactly what it is asking for, would also likely be problematic. Finally, declining a school's invitation to come visit, if extended before you're accepted, is probably another bad move. This boils down to several simple recommendations: apply early, make sure each application meets all of the requests made by that specific school, don't say anything ridiculous or offensive in your application, and show up if they invite you before you are accepted.[70]

There are some schools that, at least theoretically, would offer you a place in their incoming classes even if you did make all of these mistakes – so long as your numbers were right. The dean of one law school told me that, based on the weighted average of my GPA and LSAT scores, I was an "automatic admit" to his school, regardless of whatever I said in my essays. At some threshold, in some places, your numbers alone are enough to get you in. But don't hold your breath for this sort of practice at the first tier of ranked law schools. They tend to be more selective because they can afford to be; Yale, for example, admits roughly 180 students each year from an applicant pool of over 3000 people, and while numbers are important, they are clearly not dispositive. Many people with outrageously high LSAT or GPA numbers are rejected from top schools for other reasons.[71]

I.   VISITING SCHOOLS

If you're like most people, it will not be especially convenient for you to travel to each of the schools that will ultimately appeal to you. There are, however, clear advantages in visiting places before you commit to attending

---

[70] Law schools rarely invite unaccepted candidates to visit the school, but when they do, it probably means that you're in an intermediate acceptance pool – show up, come across as bright and honest, don't act weird, unfriendly or immature, and they will probably accept you. Though interviews are atypical for law schools, the trend is to increase their use, but not for *clearly* qualified and otherwise 'normal' candidates. If there's something the school really needs to observe or speak about firsthand, they'll invite you to visit.

[71] In the broader graduate school world, where programs admit only 18 students per year, virtually all acceptable candidates are asked to show up at the school in person, at the school's expense, to talk about their interest in the specific school in question. The schools typically pick and choose the best students from those who show up. In the law school world, even if you're invited, you pay your own way, and if you don't show up, you will probably remain in the 'maybe' pile, depending on why you were invited and who else applies for the open slots in their class.

them, and there are at least three points when you'll be able to do this. The first will be prior to submitting an application; doing a full tour at this point might be appropriate if the school is in a place with which you are largely unfamiliar, but is probably overkill if you have some level of comfort with the area or the school. Those from the West Coast who have never been to the East Coast should probably make a visit to a school or two during winter, just to see what they might be committing to living with for three years. The second is if the school asks you to come; if so, you should visit if you want to get in, even if you're afraid of the impression you'll make. Dress in business casual attire[72] and be on time. A third opportunity will generally present itself if and when you are accepted to a school, on the school's "accepted students day(s)," where groups of potential students are invited to tour around together and meet with selected faculty and administration members.

I would strongly suggest you visit any schools you are seriously considering. Some people have experienced profound culture shock upon arriving for the first time at their new school without realizing how isolated, busy, or unusual it is. This is particularly the case with transitions from the Southern United States to the Northern ones and vice-versa, East Coast to West Coast and vice-versa, and city to rural and vice-versa. While many adapt, some do not, and regardless, you probably want to avoid this sort of unnecessary dismay as far in advance as possible.

But tours aren't just tools to eliminate schools from an overcrowded list: they can also be fantastic opportunities to find a place with near-perfect fit for your needs. And even if you're familiar with a university's campus already, it may be worth taking a specific tour of the law school. I decided to tour Cornell's law school in 1997, even though I had attended a Cornell summer program in other undergraduate buildings years earlier and was somewhat familiar with the rest of the campus. I had loved the classes but felt a bit uneasy with the location, which was an hour away from a major city.

Visiting the law school turned out to be providential; I felt instantly comfortable there and learned that, unlike the rest of the sprawling campus, the law school was relatively close to a nice collection of stores, restaurants, and parking – things absent in parts of the campus I had visited before. And I was also exposed to some of the charming little details that would endear me to the school – including a beautiful, carved-wood cathedral of law books called the Reading Room, similarly magnificent classrooms, and the massive bronze seal of the school set in the ground in the school's stately courtyard.[73] I also met a

---

[72] Pick business casual as that term is locally understood at the school, unless you're interviewing at an Ivy League school, in which case you might ask an admissions officer or secretary in advance what to wear – perhaps something more formal. Dress for success.
[73] Students avoided walking on the seal based on a legend – or superstition – that a person who touched the seal would be called on in class that day.

few students, and felt both impressed by and comfortable with them as people; one continued via E-mail to offer insights into the school that further reinforced my interest in attending. It was as if I had an all-new slant on the school I had visited years before, and I wouldn't have known it without visiting again.

You can typically contact a school's admissions office to arrange a tour. Do not assume, or even believe, that taking a tour makes you a stronger candidate for acceptance, unless the law school is among the few that actively interview candidates in person prior to acceptance. If you're seriously interested, call far in advance and determine possible dates of availability. Other people may or may not tour on the same day as you do, and if they are, that's probably a good thing, because you'll benefit from hearing other people ask questions you might not yourself have raised. Parents tend to be welcome on the tours; ask the admissions office beforehand about parent-student tours if a family member's presence would comfort you.

J. WRITING THE APPLICATION

Until you actually attend law school, there are few things in life as taxing as completing law school admissions applications. The process can take weeks, sometimes more, not including the time you'll spend chasing down recommenders and their completed letters of recommendation. And most of your time will be spent filling out lengthy questionnaires and editing down different essay answers to fit the schools' required page lengths.[74]

If you were considering medical schools, you would find that you were asked to complete only a single form, which though lengthy could be submitted to almost any medical school you were interested in attending. Fortunately or unfortunately, law schools do not follow the same applications methodology. This is unfortunate in that you must separately complete many applications, each of which is likely to be quite long and demanding; it's fortunate in that you may have a greater chance of standing out at a given school because of the unique questions each asks and the special responses you give. Also, though there will certainly be differences between various schools' applications, you will notice that there is a great commonality of concepts between the applications we discuss.

---

[74] At the time of writing, the Law School Admissions Council offers an easy-to-use but expensive, annually updated CD-ROM- or Web-based compendium of official law school applications. For $59 (CD) or $54 (Web), you get electronic access to over 180 schools' applications, which then may be completed on and printed from your computer. Your other option, personally calling or E-mailing each of your target schools' admissions departments, is considerably cheaper but also more time-consuming.

We will look here at the applications of several schools, and discuss some of the more important or interesting parts of each of them in turn.

- **Columbia Law School**, based in New York City, New York, breaks its application down into six key parts. First, there is a basic, fill-in-the-blanks "Biographical Information" section. Second is a "Personal Profile" sheet, which also offers a fill-in-the-blanks format and requires you to submit a single essay. Third is a "Dean's Appraisal/Certification" form. Fourth is a set of two identical "Faculty Appraisal" forms. Fifth is a "Request for Early Decision" form. Sixth and finally is a set of "Cards and Stickers."

- **Stanford Law School**, based in Stanford, California, has a four-part application. The first is an "Application for Admission," which consists exclusively of fill-in-the-blanks biographical information. Second is a "Statement of Current Undergraduate Dean of Students or Comparable Administrative Official." Third is a generic request for a personal statement of "about two pages." Fourth are two letters of recommendation called "Statements of Instructors," which you may, at your election, replace with letters submitted to the LSDAS letter service, except for the caveat that the LSDAS service "will not accommodate any letters written on your behalf in which your recommender describes your qualifications specifically for Stanford Law School. . . . While it is your decision whether to utilize [LSDAS], please be aware of the high value Stanford places on school-specific letters of recommendation[.]"[75]

- **Pepperdine University School of Law**, based in Malibu, California, has a five-part application. First is a fill-in-the-blanks "Application for Admission," which includes instructions on preparing three other pieces: a full "Resume . . . including record of employment, scholastic honors, extra curricular activities, and community involvement," an essay titled "Response to Mission" answering how the candidate expects to contribute to the Christian mission of the school, and a 'brief' "Personal Statement . . . indicating fully your reasons for wanting to study law, why you chose to apply to Pepperdine . . . significant extracurricular and/or civic activities, and any further information which you feel should be considered[.]" The Statement may include diversity factors, as well. The fifth and final component is

---

[75] What should you do in a situation such as this one? Unless you know the entire admissions panel personally and they love you, go out and get a specific letter. And find a professor or two, if possible, who attended Stanford or a comparable school – better as a law student than as an undergraduate, but either will suffice.

submission of two "Letters of Recommendation," which Pepperdine mandates come through the LSDAS service.

- **The State University of New York at Buffalo Law School**, based in Buffalo, New York, has a five-part application. First is a "Data Sheet" detailing basic personal mailing address and application information, followed by the second piece, a "Biographical Data" sheet with information on your parents, "character," and possible diversity factors. The Biographical Data sheet also allows you to attach two or three sheets detailing diversity and character factors. The third part is an "Education and Employment Data" sheet, to which you may attach a resume, and the fourth part is a "Personal Statements" sheet requiring you to complete two separate essays. The fifth part is mandatory submission via the LSDAS of two "Letters of Recommendation."

- **The Thomas M. Cooley Law School**, based in Lansing, MI, has one of the shortest applications out there: because the school explicitly uses an almost strictly mathematical admissions process based on GPA and an LSAT score, Cooley's entire application is but four pages long. Letters of Recommendation are "not used in the admissions process," and submission of a personal statement is entirely optional. You fill in the blanks on the forms to indicate essentially the same biographical material requested by other schools. As such, there is nothing especially distinctive about the application, save its simplicity.

We'll use Columbia Law School's application as an exemplar for comparison because of its relative comprehensiveness. Material differences between the applications will be pointed out where appropriate.

1.   Biographical Information

Columbia's biographical information questionnaire is fairly typical. At first, it requests such information as your name, social security number or LSAT LSDAS number, country of citizenship, mailing address(es), and gender.

Then, Columbia requests information on all of the high schools, undergraduate and graduate institutions from which you have graduated, and their locations, dates of attendance, the degree(s) you received, and your major fields of study. That Columbia requests this is entirely commonplace; however, it should be clear that schools in the first- and second-tiers tend to be more selective than others regarding their applicants' prior educational backgrounds. While an applicant must be completely honest and truthful in disclosing his or her prior educational history, and top law schools accept candidates from many disparate economic, educational and cultural backgrounds, admissions committee members unquestionably make distinctions between applicants coming from community colleges and those coming from top-tier undergraduate schools. Top law schools look for demanding courses of study – frequently established liberal arts or hard science backgrounds. Though no reputable law school would unblinkingly admit an incoming class stocked only with Harvard undergraduates, it never hurts in the admissions process to have recognizable credentials. Some tips to bolster your resume include:

- Participating in summer courses offered at top schools.
- Working with professors who attended the schools you're targeting, at least as undergraduates, hopefully as law students.
- Making choices regarding undergraduate school transferring or pre-law school graduate program selection with your future law school goals in mind.

The Columbia application also includes a variety of questions regarding previous experiences that might help or hurt your candidacy: past military service tends to be a plus, while having been subjected to disciplinary action by prior schools or criminal courts tends to be a minus. While former soldiers need not explain their service, those previously accused or convicted of inappropriate behavior are asked to explain in a "full descriptive statement" what had happened.

It goes without saying that a reasonable explanation mitigates what otherwise could be a major problem for a potential applicant. But don't even think of trying to deceive a school's admissions panel. Not only are law students subject to honor codes, as will be discussed in greater detail later, but they are also required at several separate stages to submit to ethical examinations – first during law school through a course in professional responsibility, second for the MPRE – a Multistate Professional Responsibility Exam which certifies you as ethically competent enough to practice law – and finally during any state's bar admissions process, where one's 'moral character' will likely be examined yet again. Incidents displaying gross deviation from reasonable standards of behavior may cast doubts upon one's ability to practice law. Law schools screen candidates even at this early stage to avoid later disappointments at the time of bar application. If you lie here and it's discovered later, you'll be living every law student's nightmare – spending years of your life slaving away in law school with no ability to practice the law.

This section of the application comes near its close with simple questions regarding the dates that you have registered to take the LSAT and placed yourself on file with the LSDAS. Several separate lines are provided for LSAT dates, should you choose to re-take the exam multiple times.

Finally, the form asks the candidate to certify that the "above information is true, correct, and complete to the best of [his or her] knowledge," and requires the candidate to "promptly amend the foregoing application should there be a change in any of the facts therein." While a signature line is typically not something that attracts a great deal of attention, these particular application signature lines are important. By signing, you accept an affirmative responsibility to continue to provide the school with new information about yourself relevant to the application. If, in the intervening period of time between your application and hearing back from the school, you should be charged in a criminal case, or have a grade changed on your previous transcript, you must disclose that fact to the school immediately. In other words, be on your best behavior – both before and after applying to a law school for admittance.

2.   Personal Profile Sheet

The second component of Columbia's application is a Personal Profile Sheet, which though similarly named to the Biographical Information portion, has a somewhat different bent. This form requests that you describe the scholastic, civic or professional awards you have received "after graduation from high school, including scholarships, fellowships, prizes and memberships to honor societies." Only three lines are given. What's the best approach to take with this sort of space, both for those whose resumes overflow with awards and those without such long lists? Both types of people should make their best attempts to use the space in a balanced way. First, the space limitation is somewhat artificial. Cramming every line full of tiny words and semi-colons will look impressive but cluttered; a separate sheet of paper with a clearly typed or written list may be more appropriate. However, this does not mean that full descriptions of every award are necessary – in fact, do not waste the reader's time with extended verbiage. Explain only those details which are not obvious on their face, such as an honor given by the Okomatu Society which might usefully be parenthetically explained with a description of what that society is, and where it is located.

Those without significant honors or awards should not be intimidated by the three lines, either. Though top law schools look for applicants with previously recognized or rewarded talents or behaviors, they do not look exclusively to this category when admitting students. Simply state that which you have earned, being appropriately descriptive, and do not dwell on this. Of course, don't even think about making up awards. It's a seriously bad idea.

The next part of the Personal Profile inquires about "the major extracurricular, community, and professional activities that have been most important to you." If nothing else may be generalized about in the law school admissions process, it can be said with confidence that the vast majority of schools love to see something more to a person than just high LSAT and GPA numbers. A candidacy on the edge is routinely helped by a plausible, honest list of one's interesting activities outside of the classroom, and it is nearly mandatory for an applicant to possess at least some sorts of outside interests besides just 'law.' Imagine the variety of applications that include 'politics,' 'law,' and 'history' somewhere in a list such as this one. Think of the other things that make you a human being. Consider those things that give you commonality with those who will be reading your application – running, cooking, soccer, writing poetry, or swimming, as examples – and include them where appropriate.

The Profile then asks about your undergraduate employment history or assumption of "significant family responsibilities" during that time. The reason for this is obvious; schools will give you an extra boost or mitigation if you held a steady job or were in some special way providing care for a family member during the time you were an undergraduate. This is not the place to mention that you were a good son or daughter if that's all that you've done; it's a place to mention the elderly grandparent or newborn child you cared for, or the infirmed relative you helped through a sickness during a time when undergraduate studies otherwise would have been your primary focus. If you started your own business or worked for someone else, it's worth mentioning here, especially if it in some way impacted your studies – either positively or negatively. Columbia also requests, separately, a full list of your prior employers, and permits you to submit a resume if you choose. Be prepared to make a full disclosure, and if you submit a resume, make sure it's good enough to impress someone with an already imposing stack of applications waiting.

Family background is another interesting component of the application. The names, ages, current employment and prior educational histories of your parents are requested, which might lead one to ask what role, if any, such details play in your application. More likely than not, such details will not hurt you; they might help you if one of your parents is a legacy (prior graduate) of the school to which you are applying, but there's nothing wrong whatsoever with mentioning that your parents never attended colleges or graduate schools. Many lawyers are first-generation college graduates for their families, and this information is generally not requested for purposes of discriminating against any candidate based on the successes or failures of their parents.

A final important part of this section is Columbia's requirement that candidates submit "a personal essay or statement," which "may provide the Admissions Committee with information regarding such matters as: personal, family, or educational background; experiences and talents of special interest; one's reasons for applying to law school as they may relate to personal goals and professional expectations; or any other factors that you think should inform the Committee's evaluation." Columbia limits this statement to one or two printed sheets. If you are uncertain if that includes both sides of a page, contact the specific law school(s) in question.

This personal statement can be among the most interesting and important parts of an application to law school, assuming that all other portions of the application are relatively unimpressive or average. Most schools emphasize in their application instructions that the personal statement receives a disproportionately large amount of attention – **take this seriously**! Clearly, the statement is an opportunity to present oneself to the reader in a manner which intrigues and captures the reader's interest; moreover, it is a critical opportunity to reveal a story of your personal triumph over long odds, a previous success that explains something about your character, or something that relates your present life clearly to what you hope to be as a graduate of a law school. And it needs to be relatively compact – follow the school's explicit guidelines or assume a two-page limit if they don't give you one. No matter what you want to express about yourself, make it succinct, logical, and punchy. This is not a place for rambling, non-sequiturs, or jokes.

To be frank, this is a component of the application that is important *because* it is so personal. There are plenty of numbers elsewhere on the application for the reader to consider. This is the place where you make the reader understand who you are outside of classes, and who you want to be once you leave law school. It might be the best possible place to discuss your spouse or committed partner if you have one, and might help to explain why a specific city, state, or school is particularly important to you. But don't assume that a personal statement will mean the difference between acceptance and rejection if your grades and LSAT scores are abysmally low; rather, assume that a good personal statement will be the factor that helps you impress a school where your numbers are statistically average or slightly below average.

When I applied to law schools, I sought the advice of several professors and professionals as to how I should approach this essay. One common recommendation was to avoid waving the patriotic flag or talking about your pure and undivided love for law, especially through attempts to use legal language or the like. No matter how much you may love America, or how steeped in history or law you may consider yourself to be, it is rare that these sorts of sentiments will, at least in their most commonly expressed form, win over admissions committees. Succeeding in law school is not about loving your country or about having read Jefferson and Madison; it's about understanding that your education will one day be used, hopefully, to achieve results of some sort for people who need your services because they cannot achieve the same results on their own – not just the indigent, but any sort of person who might benefit from the services of a lawyer. If you're thinking of becoming a law professor or judge and wish to disclose it, do so, but make sure to convey an understanding of either profession that will convince a skeptical reader.

The best personal essays tend to connect one's personal past with the results one hopes to achieve in the future with a law degree. They also emphasize things that other parts of the application might not adequately explain. That said, there is no perfect formula to writing such an essay. Let yourself shine in the manner you believe is best, but just make sure you demonstrate an interest in both the degree and the school.

3.   Dean's Appraisal/Certification and Faculty Appraisals

One of the unusual common components of law school applications is the request for outside appraisals of your candidacy by people who either know you or should have known you, in the law schools' opinions. Though this is unusual when contrasted with other academic applications you may have filled out, it is somewhat universal in the legal realm – your identity is essentially a reflection of what verifiable others know of you. Therefore, if you're a virtuoso pianist who plays only for an audience of herself, you might just as well consider your performances irrelevant for purposes of this component of the application. Your goal is to first seek out two faculty members who have seen you at your best, and are responsible enough to submit appraisals of your work without badgering, then to secure a somewhat more cursory recommendation from the dean of your most recent educational institution.

The Columbia application is somewhat more probing than others in the questions it asks of your dean "or other administrator who has access to your complete school records." If he or she wishes, the dean may mark with checks a series of boxes indicating just how special you are in terms of "overall intelligence," "analytical skills," "independence of thought, originality," "problem solving skills," effectiveness of oral and written communications, "academic motivation," "self-confidence," "concern for others," "energy," "emotional maturity," "personal initiative," "judgment," "leadership ability," and "organizational skills." It goes without saying that, although there is a box that can be checked for each category marked "no basis for judgment," one would prefer to know a dean or administrator who could render judgments on at least most of these characteristics. However, note that most schools are not so probative on this issue, and even Columbia phrases this inquiry in such a way as to suggest its optional nature. Do not fret if you have failed to demonstrate your "energy" to a dean. Few people have. Columbia continues on this path by later requesting the recommender complete a "summary report" on you which might include discussions of your academic, extracurricular and personal activities, plus any special factors that might merit consideration.

Where the Columbia application is most similar to others is in its request that the Dean describe anything that leads him or her to believe that your character is lacking, and to note your prior history of academic misdeeds, if any. Most schools treat the Dean's report as a means to disqualify candidates who have behaved so poorly before law school as to merit exclusion from the profession for reasons of character.

As suggested in the breakdown of different schools' applications above, some schools have dispensed with the need for a Dean's certification altogether, relying instead upon simple certified copies of your transcript and your other letters of recommendation to get a sense of your academic background. And schools are gradually moving away from customized letters of recommendation towards the LSDAS' standardized recommendations system, though highly selective schools such as Stanford and Columbia do more than hint that they prefer to receive personalized letters. It's fair to assume at this point in time that candidates who can convince their recommenders to deliver such personalized letters will benefit at least marginally from doing so, though whether it's worth the effort depends entirely on your personal preferences and the selectivity of the schools you're hoping to attend.

4.   Request for Early Decision Form

Columbia is among a number of schools offering an "Early Decision option," under which candidates who have a strong preference for one school over another submit their materials by December 1 of a given year and "commit themselves to matriculate . . . if admitted on this special basis." You must agree to "withdraw all [of your] applications to other schools and to initiate no new ones if and when accepted to Columbia as an Early Decision candidate." Furthermore, you must agree not "to enter an Early Decision agreement with any other law school."

The Columbia Request for Early Decision Form contains that much language and little else; you needn't explain why you are requesting an early decision, but if you're filling out this form, you should probably make an answer to that question a sub-theme in your personal statement. What sort of reasons might you have?

- A family member, mentor, or close friend attended and loved the law school in question. Be careful if this person only attended the school as an undergraduate and not the law school; unless it's a parent, rarely would this be of any value.

- A special professor, course, or area of specialization appears near-exclusively at this school. Putting all your chips on one person or course probably isn't wise,[76] but if you're looking to

---

[76] That person might have left the school or be despised by a member of the admissions panel, or the course might have been cancelled, amongst other things. Be careful with such an explanation.

come to a school because it has a highly-regarded international studies, alternative dispute resolution, or other specialization program, then mentioning it here is a great idea.

- You have a previous personal tie with the school, such as having attended it as an undergraduate or graduate student. This can work for you or against you; be sure that your grades were either at or above the school's curve and that you choose decent academic recommenders.

- Your spouse or fiancé attends the same school as an undergraduate or graduate student, or works there professionally. This almost always tends to work in your favor.

For numerous reasons, you shouldn't put a lot of faith in the Early Decision option as a means to secure yourself a spot at a school where you'd otherwise appear unqualified, but if you're on the edge of acceptability and show a strong preference, you might stand a chance. Consider this a chance to demonstrate a strong legitimate interest in your top-choice school, and be conscious of the responsibility you'll have to accept their offer if they make it to you.

5. Other Essays

Columbia Law's essay portion, like that of many schools, is relatively short and straightforward: provide a statement of one or two pages discussing "such matters as: personal, family or educational background; experiences and talents of special interest; one's reasons for applying to law school as they may relate to personal goals and professional expectations; or any other factors that you think should inform the Committee's evaluation of your candidacy for admission."[77] Compare this language to what's requested by the State University of New York at Buffalo: "explain what makes you particularly well suited to the study of law . . . You may, but need not, describe your career goals after law school. [Y]our background and experience . . . as well as other topics, such as employment and community activities, educational and intellectual activities, obstacles you have overcome, and change and development in oneself, can be extremely helpful to the committee." And Pepperdine University School of Law requests, in one of its two essays, "a brief personal statement indicating fully your reasons for wanting to study law, why you chose to apply to Pepperdine[,] significant extracurricular and/or civic activities, and any further information

---

[77] Be judicious in listing experiences and talents. It's cute to mention your singing voice, piano playing, or mountain climbing; these might resonate with someone on the admissions panel. It's not so cute to talk about your odd habits unless they've been validated as interesting by the people you've asked to proofread your essays for you.

which you feel should be considered by the Admissions Committee. If you desire, please discuss any applicable factors which would bring diversity to the class including racial or ethnic origin, age, work experience, geographical origin, and socio-economic background."

Consistently these essays ask you to think about why you want to be at law school, and whether or not they make it explicit, they'll probably give at least modest preference to students with minority or socio-economically disadvantaged backgrounds. The key to success on any admissions essay is a focused, narrowly-chosen essay topic rather than a scattershot collection of thoughts vaguely relating to the essay question asked, plus a more than cursory statement someplace within the essay explaining why this particular school is special in your mind. A secondary pointer is to have thoroughly grammar- and spell-checked your work before mailing it off. You'd be surprised at how many people fail to do this, and how much your application will actually stand out if it's properly written.

You might also poll friends and family members to get their perspectives on what makes you specially suited to study law. It will at least inform your perspective, if not offer useful tips on what you can write about. Then you should consider the materials in the later chapters of this book, as they will give you insights into what you'll actually be studying and how best to focus on legal areas that you're actually suited for and excited about.

As you'll recall from the list of various schools' applications, though most schools include a personal statement essay of this sort, many schools also require the submission of a second essay on another, totally random topic. SUNY at Buffalo asks you to write about two books you've recently read, Pepperdine asks for your response to an inquiry about its mission as a Christian school, and other schools, including Yale as another example, let you choose a topic yourself and write about it.

There is no single way to prepare for all of these types of essays, but each essay needs to be given special attention – if you're seriously interested in attending the school in question. If you're asked to speak to your personal feelings on a subject specified by the school, spend some time thinking about why the school chose that subject, and what 'good' or 'bad' answers would look like in the abstract. Then answer the question honestly in a way that comes closest to the good answer you've pictured.

If you're asked to choose a topic of your own, your goal should be to demonstrate your strength as a writer, regardless of the topic you select. You should probably avoid attempts to emulate legal writing, even if you've had some exposure to it, and stick with style and substance that are personal to and comfortable for you. Select a subject that will capture the interest of your reader amidst a pile of entries, and if there is a space limitation – Yale gives you 250 words – inspire yourself by reading some short poems before trying to write.

Cultivate a personal sense of how to express interesting ideas in small quantities of compelling words.

Be careful in advance to allot an appropriate amount of time to each application you consider important. Managing the stack of essays – particularly editing them to fit in the space provided – takes a lot of time and discipline. Give yourself at least a few weeks to get your essays together. My biggest problem with every essay was finding a way to fit my thoughts into the space provided, which should have signaled to me that I was being overly broad in my approach. Like the personal statements, being succinct and punchy helps to make these essays stand out for their readers.

K. CHOOSING YOUR RECOMMENDERS

One of the interesting and odd things about the legal profession is its relative dependence on self-reporting as a means of information gathering at the times of admissions to law school, and to various state bar associations, as well. In essence, both law schools and state bars give you a relatively simple task: find a handful of human beings who know you pretty well and like you enough to tell other people that you're qualified to enter the legal profession. This task is complicated, for better or worse, by several factors.

First, in the case of law schools, you'll need to get recommendations from two or three college professors and one "dean or administrative official," with some modest exceptions where the applicant no longer attends school and allows you to use an employer or employers instead. Refer to the specific applications you've solicited to confirm their distinctions, but be aware that even if most schools only require two recommendations, there may well be a school amongst your choices that requires three. And thus you'll need to find a third recommender for that school alone.

With the exception of that rare third recommender, you might be handing a big stack of questionnaires and envelopes to the people you choose. The people you select will be responsible for either filling out each questionnaire and returning it to you, sealed in a signed envelope, or mailing it off to the law schools you hope to enter. You generally are responsible for paying for all of the postage and making certain that your recommenders receive and submit the questionnaires on time.[78]

---

[78] This process has eased somewhat in recent years because of the Law School Admissions Council's recent addition of a recommendation letter collection service to the list of LSDAS services. In concept, you could have your recommenders author only one letter each and see those letters copied and mailed on time by the LSDAS. But as mentioned earlier, some schools have seemingly unique requirements for their letters of recommendation, confounding what would otherwise be a standardized submission of

When it comes to professorial recommenders, there is obviously a major threshold challenge in finding people who know you well enough to fill out a rather specific questionnaire about you. This requires, obviously, that you've made some sort of personal connection with your professors outside of just grading your papers, and in the case of law schools, that you've demonstrated to those people at least some propensity for the vast majority of characteristics schools ask about – logical reasoning skills, decent oral and written communication skills, and the like. This component of an essay clearly disadvantages students who attend large, anonymous schools and do not in some way stand out from their peers. It advantages those who have either been naturally gifted with stand-out radiance or have prepared well enough in advance to feel comfortable talking with professors outside the setting of a classroom. It also advantages those with professors who understand the value of recommendations.

In my personal case, coming from a large school with mostly huge classes full of people, I sought recommenders who taught smaller classes in subjects I had particularly enjoyed. To my great dismay, I found that with a one-year break between my graduation and application, two of my favorite professors had left the school entirely – the two I had originally hoped to rely upon. When I was left to request recommendations from professors who did not know me quite as well, I opted to arrive at their offices prepared to leave them with short, less-than-one page typed bullet point lists of my reasons for interest in law schools and law, my grade(s) and performance in their classes, and any other highly important topics that were mentioned explicitly in the recommendation forms. My goal was to be sure they had as much information as they needed without having to sift through a big stack of stuff to find it, and to do it in a polite, rather than aggressive way. It apparently worked pretty well.

A second challenge comes in finding a professor who is dependable enough that you can rely upon him or her to send out the letters early – or even on time. One of the biggest stresses in the applications process is depending on others to send in your forms, and the number of people who have encountered admissions problems because of this can hardly be overestimated. More often than not, your favorite undergraduate professor will be someone who you can come in and talk with at any time, someone who is fantastic with a class full of people and obviously gifted in their subjects of expertise; you may well discover that he or she will also for some reason or another be incapable of getting anything done on time. And in the case of the law school admissions process, the last thing in the world that you want to do is choose someone who will either fail to perform entirely, or will require repeated nagging phone calls

---

forms. Consult with the admissions office of a law school before relying on LSDAS to provide it with letters of recommendation.

to force performance. Neither of these things leads to a pleasantly completed applications process.

A third challenge is finding a person who will portray you in an appropriate light. Believe it or not, this can actually in some cases be a challenge, even when you have a professor who appears generally enthusiastic and interested in your candidacy. Rare stories have circulated of applicants who relied upon seemingly benevolent professors and later discovered that their "recommendation letters" were scathingly negative. While in some cases this is entirely the fault of the candidate – either for behaving in a manner that earned the professor's scorn (before or during the recommendations process), or for not screening recommenders carefully – in other cases there are weird things going on behind the scenes with the professor that cannot be anticipated. Some professors hate lawyers and will try to scuttle your chances of becoming one, even if you are entirely qualified. Some have other personal issues.

As a general rule, then, it's a good idea to know your recommenders well enough that this sort of problem is minimized. How could you actively avoid this? You could be daring and request to see the recommendation before it's sent out. Few people do this, as it's clearly a bit presumptuous, and has more than a tinge of seeming impropriety. On the other hand, some have taken the position that they have the right to know what others are saying about them, particularly under circumstances where they had been assured favorable recommendations, and given the potential for dramatic consequences if the letters are in fact negative. There are, of course, stories of people who have asked and been denied an advance look at recommendations, for many reasons, not the least of them practical.

One major obstacle that you may or may not be able to hurtle is finding recommenders – especially in the ranks of hard-core academics, or employers if you're outside of school – who can clearly and effectively communicate in writing. It will especially help if the recommender is familiar with, and can write favorably about your personal writing skills. A friend noted that although "many a professor is no doubt a genius and has written volumes on his subject of expertise, it is often overlooked that his latest book was the subject of many hours of hardcore editing so as to produce something in intelligible English." Similarly, people who could enthusiastically recommend you might also have no writing skill whatsoever; I personally avoided one highly favorable recommendation from a very relevant authority – one of two judges I knew – on the basis that he was known not to be an effective writer. Though you may not be able to control this in advance, you may find that your best writer-recommender is someone who teaches and evaluates writing professionally.

Again, early preparation and strategic undergraduate class scheduling may be your best bets, and a bit of resourcefulness might also play a part. One might procure applications one year in advance and get the forms into the hands of recommenders very early, requesting completion by a given certain date. The recommendation forms do not appear to change much, if at all, from year to year, but there is obviously a risk of change to consider. Additionally, especially suspicious students in the past have tried to protect themselves by including one dummy recommendation form – part of an application they ultimately will not submit – and inspected the recommendation written for that school. I can't recommend this strategy, but at the same time, I feel somewhat disturbed by the thought that recommenders might offer their services under false pretenses and deny qualified applicants an opportunity to attend good law schools.

A final note on recommendations relates to the Dean's Recommendation, which on some levels is the trickiest of all of the recommendations you'll be asked to supply. There are two philosophies about these recommendations: the modern one is namely that colleges are huge schools where deans are highly unlikely to know candidates personally, and the traditional one is that a good law school applicant would be close enough to a person in this sort of position that they can call upon them for a personal reference.

The modern approach, adopted by the vast majority of schools, understands that you may not know your dean well enough for him or her to offer any personal opinions on you, and thus the questionnaire is limited to general issues of your academic record and history, if any, of disciplinary or moral offenses. These applications typically leave a space for the dean to make comments from his or her personal knowledge, if any, and thus it would still likely be highly useful for you to know your dean well enough to elicit this sort of personal statement.

The traditional approach almost assumes that you do know the dean, or at least, one dean or administrative official, well enough to secure some sort of personal evaluation. While you should pay close attention to the specifics of a given application, you may be able to use the dean of your specific undergraduate major as a reference, so long as he or she has access to your academic records, and this may offer you an advantage in the applications process. Consider yourself the recipient of considerable style points – for sheer sake of rarity – if you can secure a positive, personalized letter from a dean who has attended the specific school you hope to attend. Speaking for myself, as a graduate of a very large and anonymous college, I found this particular recommendation to be the most problematic. If I could do it over again, I would speak with the dean of my undergraduate major. It would have looked better than securing the generic registrar form I ultimately obtained.

L.   WAITING AND MAKING CHOICES

One of the oft-repeated cycles in the legal profession is the waiting game;

it seems that for each of the four critical points in one's legal education,[79] there is a commensurate waiting period that makes the stressful exam or application seem comparatively easy. Just as LSAT scores take time to arrive,[80] the application period typically takes even longer to resolve itself – months. And some very interesting things happen in the meanwhile.

If you have friends who are also applying to schools, this will no doubt be a time of much discussion over who has received what postcard or letter from which school, which places everyone hopes to get into, and what sort of disappointments people have unexpectedly or expectedly faced along the way. For some people, the experience will be humbling and unsettling, while for others, it will be surprisingly pleasant. Many people will find a mix of each type of experience awaits them.

The first letter I received, for example, was an acceptance to a school I was excited about. It arrived quickly - within a month, because the school had a rolling admissions policy - and thereby preceded other responses by three or four weeks. When I first received the letter, I was thrilled, but also excited that perhaps more quick acceptances were to come. The next several letters I received were flat rejections. My spirits started to slump, though I knew that under the worst circumstances, I still had a great school to attend. Then I was wait-listed at an even higher-ranked school, but one with somewhat of a mixed reputation. Another wait list letter arrived soon thereafter. Another acceptance. And a couple more rejections. The entire process took several months, but the wait lists kept me waiting until the very last minute. I dropped off of one wait list and remained on another one, which conceivably could have invited me to attend at any time before their classes started. I accepted the offer of the school I was most excited about, and attended it – Cornell Law School.

I would learn later that several of my classmates had also been waiting on the same wait list I was sitting on – the University of Chicago Law School. By reputation, Chicago apparently had a tendency to waitlist people and thereafter remain surprisingly non-communicative, which had been my experience and that of some new friends. Another classmate, interestingly, continued through the first week of classes to remain on the wait list at Yale, where he was a legacy. When I asked him if he would uproot himself from Cornell if Yale called, he replied as if there was no question in his mind: "I'd be gone so fast you wouldn't even know I was here." But Yale never called. His experience was only unusual in how long he waited for the news that he wouldn't attend. Other people have gone so far as to acquire housing at given schools only to receive and accept better offers.

There are frequently unexpected benefits of the admissions process, which

---

[79] As mentioned in Chapter 1, Section A.
[80] LSAT wait times have decreased to a two week minimum, five week maximum.

cannot necessarily be understood at the start of one's formal legal education. Rejection from a big-named school can be a good thing, in as much as other schools may offer more accommodating social or cultural experiences, better geographical locations, and in some cases even more practical legal educations. Some would say that the benefit of not going to Yale is that you don't have to deal with the attitudes and problems that Yale is known for; in the cases of other law schools, there may be other factors, such as some top schools' penchants for theoretical rather than practical instruction, that may weigh in favor of attending a lower-ranked institution.[81] In summary, you shouldn't view rejection from your first choice school as the end of the world. It may well be the beginning of a much better one.

But if you're convinced that you deserve to be some place other than where you were accepted, you have two choices: decline admission and apply again next year, or accept admission to another school and take your chances as a transfer applicant after completing your first year. To be honest, your chances aren't great under either of these scenarios.

Declining admission on the premise that you might re-apply again and be accepted is a risky venture. You're essentially betting that one of two things happens: either you hope to submit a document that is superior in some way to what came before, or the committee reading your application could find it more appealing on the second run-through. One factor undermining both of these premises is that many schools retain previous records of previous decisions on applications, and some application forms even request that you indicate whether you've previously applied. Something short of a miracle would be needed to change minds previously made up on your application; what exactly this is, I will leave open to your speculation. If you sat on a wait list hoping for a space to open up, you probably have a much better chance of getting in on the second attempt than someone who was denied outright; it might help to indicate in your personal statement that you wanted to attend this

---

[81] A number of highly-ranked schools, including the University of Chicago, reputably place a considerable emphasis on abstract teaching of legal concepts (theoretical instruction) in order to prepare young intellectuals for later careers as professors and judges. Theoretical instruction focuses on trends or concepts in judicial and academic thinking, such as theories, types of logical reasoning (such as syllogisms), and interactions between the law and other spheres (such as economics or politics). By comparison, practical instruction focuses more heavily on specific judicial opinions, their actual impact on practicing professionals, and techniques such as professionals actually use. When it comes to finding employment over law schools, practical schools are sometimes said to prepare their graduates better for real world practice, although there is little question that many large law firms recruit disproportionately from higher-ranked schools, no matter whether their instruction is slanted towards the theoretical or practical.

school so badly that you waited for them rather than attend another school. Even then, this doesn't seem like the sort of thing you want to spend a year praying for, unless you were waitlisted at a truly outstanding school.

As for transferring, though anyone can try to transfer, candidates in the upper ten percent of a class are generally considered capable of transferring out of a school to someplace 'better;' however, half of those will typically remain, meaning that there will only be openings to fill for less than 5% of a given class of students. To simplify, in a class of 200, the top 20 people could conceivably leave for a "better" place, but only approximately 10 will, and perhaps 10 slots will therefore open up for transfer students. Competition for those slots will be tight, so betting on admission is rarely a winning gamble. But it does happen.[82]

M. MENTAL STATES: WHAT DOES ACCEPTANCE MEAN, AND WHAT SHOULD I BE THINKING RIGHT NOW?

Though some people enter law school without any doubts as to the career they want to pursue three years later, few people make it through law school without reconsidering that issue, and some people even start law school far from certain on the subject. Thus we'll begin from the premise, which may or may not be applicable to you, that you're wondering at this point just what this whole career concept is supposed to be about, and what sort of lawyer you're hoping to become.

As someone who takes planning and decision-making pretty seriously, it's hard for me to say this, but you really don't need to have answered this question yet. In fact, any answer you formulate at this point has a good chance of being only tentative, because if you're like many people – myself included – you had at least some interest in law even before you knew what people within the profession actually do. Now that you know at least a bit about the options that are available, let's revisit the most common misconceptions.

- Not all lawyers work in courtrooms, and you've probably never seen the inside of law firms or other offices where you could work with a law degree. Is it worth exploring the lifestyle of a litigator in greater depth? The lifestyle of a transactional attorney? Other jobs?
- You won't become a judge as soon as you graduate. If that was your ambition, what sort of law will you practice as an attorney before you are eligible to become a judge?[83]

---

[82] Personal motivation seems to count for a lot. Intelligent people who were average undergraduates frequently fail to get in to first-tier law schools, but if motivated to succeed, kick their studies into high gear, become top-ranked at second-tier schools, and transfer into higher-ranked law schools for their second and third years.

[83] The specialization list at Chapter 6, Table 6-1 could provide a useful starting point.

- And it's hard to pick a specialty area, such as Internet law, and come out three years later actually practicing it, because the market may not be there, so is there a fallback area of law you would find interesting?

To some extent, prospective law students (and those already in law school) need to have some flexibility about what they might want to do, as both experience and classes help people to better understand their true interests and abilities. You may well discover that you are capable of more than you imagined. You may also find that you seriously dislike something in the law which seemed completely fascinating at one point.[84] Reality is frequently much different from one's expectations, especially where the law is concerned. It therefore helps to keep an open mind about what you are about to start learning; it makes the days go by faster, and enables you to see where you 'naturally' thrive, and what you need to work on.

Thus at this stage, you need not know precisely what sort of lawyer you hope to be, or what type of law specifically you want to practice. But, of course, it helps to have at least something that interests you, and to this end, it's worth taking a look through the course catalog of the law school you're going to attend to determine what sorts of classes you will ultimately hope to take there. It might also be worthwhile to think about this topic on your own for a little while, just to center yourself as to why it was, really, that you decided you wanted to apply to law schools in the first place. The answer may well prove useful to you on those long days ahead when you feel like you might just be in too deep for your own good.

---

[84] A legislative maxim has it that writing law is like making sausage, because regardless of the quality of the final product, the process is so disgusting that no one wants to see what really takes place when it's being made. The study and practice of law are similar. You might love an area of the law or a legal concept, yet find that the reality of studying or practicing it is awful. This is entirely normal, and perhaps surprisingly common.

CHAPTER 3

LAW LIBRARY READING ROOM, CORNELL LAW SCHOOL

LAW CLASSROOM, UNIVERSITÉ PARIS I PANTHÉON-SORBONNE
FACULTÉ DE DROIT (PARIS I UNIVERSITY FACULTY OF LAW

A. ITHACA: A TYPICAL COLLEGE TOWN

With the exception of those who attend the law schools offered by their undergraduate institutions, every first-year law student starts fresh in unfamiliar surroundings. In some, if not many cases, America's law schools are situated in cities with little cosmopolitan vigor, such as state capitol cities. Some of these cities are thriving college towns. Others are quiet and boring.

Ithaca, New York is neither the state's capitol, nor a major city.[85] It is known almost exclusively for Cornell University, and more than quadruples its population when school is in session. Even at the height of its activity, it is by no means an exciting place to be; first-time visitors are often heard to remark that "there's nothing to do in Ithaca." Yet it is full of natural beauty, has ties to the women's suffrage movement, and hosts one of the country's most famous vegetarian eateries, Moosewood. Some people think of it as Berkeley minus the California school's nearby high-tech sector. I knew what I would be getting into when I came to Ithaca, and was able to rationalize it because I had resigned myself to go to an excellent school anywhere outside of New York City, no matter where it was.

In some ways, Ithaca is a perfect place to spend your first year of law school. The first year at any law school is typically spent studying at a level hitherto unimaginable by most students, and as a result, there are benefits to being in a place without distractions. Owing to its distance from other major cities in the state,[86] it's unlikely that you will be especially close to families, friends, or most of civilization in Ithaca, unless you bring them with you.

And this is the flip side of the situation. Choose a city such as Ithaca and you won't be able to do any serious shopping unless you drive an hour or more to a major city. You'll see movies, so long as they're playing at the city's single large movie theater or one of the scattered art house theaters. If you, a friend, or a family member needs to catch a plane, you can do it to and from Ithaca, so long as U.S. Airways operates it and it's not full. And oh, yeah – if your favorite flavor of ice cream is Ben & Jerry's Coffee Heath Bar Crunch, as mine happens to be, there's a good chance that you won't find it at any stores here, though there is a Ben & Jerry's shop downtown. Health food stores are more prominent. Isolation, which has its benefits for the student as a student, also has its costs for the student as a human being.

Though none of the sprawling campus would be a lengthy walk to such

---

[85] Outsiders frequently confuse Ithaca with Attica, New York, which is best known for its correctional facility and famed 1971 prisoner uprising. Though Ithaca may be similarly confining, any further connection is entirely coincidental.

[86] Any city you're likely to know in New York State is at least an hour away, with New York City and Buffalo out three hours or more.

amenities as groceries, barber shops, and restaurants, Cornell's law school is within a very short walk of Collegetown, an almost stereotypical amalgam of small convenience stores, bars and restaurants that a university's population demands. Surrounding and within Collegetown are apartments, rental homes, and parking lots – all means of access to the law school and the larger university. And, of course, there are roads leading elsewhere into the city's modest downtown, towards its shopping mall, and out of the city entirely. Ithaca is like many other college-dependent cities; small and unimpressive, yet easy to navigate and understand.

While this book will not attempt to survey housing conditions in all of the various cities of the over 180 accredited law schools, a few personal experiences are worth sharing at this point. They're broken down into two topics: my housing considerations, and my mistakes.

1. Housing: How I Planned

In truth, I didn't give a lot of thought to housing in Ithaca; in the weeks that had passed since I had accepted Cornell's invitation and submitted my cash deposit to secure a place in their class of 2001, the school had mailed me collections of materials to fill out and read through, detailing the dormitory, the basics of orientation, and some of the vague details of classes that were to come. There was a lot to read and I was still in the midst of finishing up business school, so I made the assumption that living in the dorm would be preferable to other housing options. But there were still some lingering thoughts in the back of my mind – I had an apartment in Buffalo to vacate and I hadn't been eliminated from the University of Chicago's wait list yet. There was always the chance, no matter how small, that Chicago might call and I might still be interested. But for now, I was going to Ithaca.

When it came time to commit to a Cornell housing option, my decision was fueled by two hard facts. First, I knew that I would be doing a lot of studying. Law school is like Japanese Geisha training; you leave home to live at school and are absorbed, morning, noon, and night with your studies. By the time you leave, you have been transformed. If I was going to take my studies seriously enough to transform, I needed to live close to the law school.

This was because of the second hard fact; it was going to be a challenge to do the whole law thing morning, noon, and night because I have never been a "morning person." If I had to be awake at 8:00 for a class, I wanted to be as close to the school as possible. I was also aware that Cornell, like many schools, had a long-standing parking problem which had never quite been resolved. I didn't want to start my day with a 45-minute hunt for parking as I had as an undergraduate. Cornell's parking situation offered potential for even longer hunting experiences, as some of its lots were miles from the law school.

So I was glad to learn that Cornell offered a dormitory located not only literally next to the single-building law school, but physically connected to the law school via a walkway. I had never dormed as an undergraduate, and although I had no great need to do it, I felt that for convenience's sake and as a positive learning experience, I would give dorm life a try. The little research I did on the rooms suggested that they ranged in size, were grouped in two-to-five room suites, and were randomly assigned to students. I was assigned a four-person suite with a modest one-person bedroom – number 502 in the Hughes Hall dormitory, named for former U.S. Supreme Court Chief Justice (and former Cornell Law professor) Charles Evans Hughes. I would share the two-shower bathroom with three other men; the six floors of the building alternated between the sexes. The 80-person dorm shared one communal kitchen.

I hastily cleaned out my apartment in Buffalo and reduced its contents to items that would safely fit in my car. The balance went into my parents' basement, at least temporarily. There was something truly unsettling about the idea that almost everything I owned in the world could fit into a SUV. It was the first time that I'd come to that realization.

2. *Housing Mistakes & Lessons*

The only mistakes in my reasoning process turned out to be ones of degree, rather than fundamentals. There were, in fact, similarly-sized apartments right next door in Collegetown, and I might have learned more about them if I had researched with the Internet – a Google search for "Ithaca" and "Apartments" would have produced many options. Of course, they would have cost a lot more, but I would have had my own bathroom and kitchen.

There's something considerable to be said for having either a kitchen or the variety of restaurants that would have been at my immediate disposal in Collegetown; the law school dorm housed only one kitchen and one part-time restaurant, and neither were any good. Lest the kitchen issue be glossed over, it's safe to tell you at this point that mealtime often takes on new relevance for law students, as it may be one of the only times you'll have for social activity during the day, unless you can get in and out of a kitchen pretty quickly.[87]

Finally, the dormitory's parking situation turned out to be less than ideal; notoriously hilly Ithaca compelled the law school to place its parking lots on

---

[87] You can't really talk with other people while you're reading for classes, and that activity will consume almost every waking hour in the early days of law school. If you enjoy cooking, as I do, you'll discover that you don't have a lot of time for it unless it's your only major leisure activity in a given day. Not having a kitchen next to my room and sharing a fridge with so many other people reduced my desire to cook, so I became very dependent on finding nearby, cheap places to eat.

hills, and while the faculty lots were right next to the school, the student lot was at the very bottom of a huge slope. In Collegetown, parking lots were right next to the apartments. Admittedly, I could not have rolled out of bed and walked two minutes to a classroom, but a five-minute morning walk wouldn't have been that bad. In summary, if I was willing to pay more, I could have lived almost as close to the school and had a few more conveniences at my disposal.

Living accommodations are similar at other law schools, and the most frequent complaints of law students around the country relate to housing and parking. Half an hour of driving and parking spot-hunting time before school can, in and of itself, become a major problem for a first-year law student, so you will truly thank yourself later if you plan to live within walking distance of the building where you're taking classes. And start planning early, so that you can find the best places before other people take them. Unlike undergraduate life, law school offers plenty of housing options. Plan your ideal, or less-than-ideal-but-adequate living situation accordingly.

B.   THE FIRST SEMESTER BEGINS

I planned my arrival in Ithaca so that I would get to the campus in time for the earliest optional orientation events – one was a computer training course that needed to be done either early or at some point closer to the start of classes. I wanted to get it out of the way, and I wanted the maximum opportunity to meet other people quickly.

With car packed, music and school paperwork ready for the trip, and my old apartment vacated, I had only one thing left to take care of: my family. And this proved to be the most difficult part. Both of my parents were crying as I left for Cornell, the first time I had left my home town to attend a school 'far away.' Their tears were, I later came to understand, a mix of pride at my law school acceptance and 'empty nest syndrome.' That my law school was only a three-hour drive from home was not especially significant to anyone at this point, and I was more than a little choked up myself. Over the course of my three years at law school, the three of us would always have uncomfortably sad moments at the end of a visit home when I had to return to school.

But soon enough I was on the road, and within three hours, I was at the law school – just in time for the computer orientation. And honestly, I was really very excited just to be in Ithaca. Despite the teary moments with my parents, I had really been looking forward to law school for a very long time, and I came possessed of a pervasively positive attitude towards whatever I was about to study: since I knew I learned best when I was engaged by the material, I was determined to find something interesting about every single subject. I was going to attend every possible optional event I could attend, meet people, and learn as much as I could.

So it was almost with a jump out of the door of my car that I left my computer, bedding, clothes, music and gadgets sitting in the parking lot of the law school. Fresh from sitting in the car for three hours, I sat through the one-hour computer class, in my excitement vaguely oblivious to the fact that it was a complete waste of my time ("here's how to use the Internet in 60 minutes") and that attendance would probably not even be checked. When the class was over, I returned to fetch my room key from the dormitory building and start hauling stuff out of my car.

At the dormitory, I found, not surprisingly, that many people were going through the same move-in procedures as I was; the difference was that many of them had brought family or friends along. I was moving in alone. Some people had parents there; many people had siblings or significant others with them.

I also started to notice some real differences from my undergraduate experience: surprisingly, there were many more attractive people, both as students and as family members. More social classes were represented, unlike my undergraduate school, which was largely middle- and lower-middle-class. And there was a much broader ethnic and cultural mix; my undergraduate school had been a very black-and-white institution, whereas Cornell was already looking like a Benetton advertisement – all colors of the rainbow.[88] And I liked what I saw. As a person with ambitions of world travel and a long-standing interest in Asian cultures, I now felt as if I had a good chance of meeting some worldly people at Cornell. And perhaps a girlfriend, too.

When I arrived at my suite, there was another pleasant surprise: two of my suitemates had already arrived and were offering to help me bring stuff in. We acquainted ourselves briefly, and I learned that both were Korean-American, a fact that especially excited me at that point because I had coincidentally

---

[88] As it turned out, the law school had at this point already hosted its annual special introductory program for newly admitted minority students, a several-day long orientation which gave the school's one-quarter population an early heads up on what the law school experience would be like. Some of the friendships forged during these early orientations became pivotal in students' lives, although minority students quickly went beyond racial lines in making friends and connections within the law school.

recently learned to read the Korean alphabet and cook Korean meals.[89] It was a great and unexpected point of commonality. Our other suitemate arrived later; he turned out to be a former East Asian studies major. It seemed for the moment as if I was in the perfect suite. I wondered how much of this had been planned by Cornell housing, and how much was just random luck.[90]

At some point after I had moved in, we all discussed the orientation schedule and learned a classifying detail that proved to be critically important in the next several months: our "section" letters. One of my suitemates and I shared the same section: section F. The other two suitemates shared section B. As we were about to discover, our section letters would determine just about everything in our lives for the next year: the teachers we would be assigned, the hours we would wake up for class and go to sleep each night, and the people who would be our classmates, potentially 'competitors.'[91]

C.   MANDATORY COURSES

Something missing from the law school's previously mailed materials was a class sign-up sheet or list of teachers one could select from. This was for good reason: in law school, all first-year students at a given school take the same classes, and moreover, the classes are virtually identical from school to school. Each fundamental subject is taught by two, three, or four different professors,[92] one of whom will be selected for each section, and students generally have no right to request sections or professors. You get what and whom they give you. And this is generally a good thing.

All six sections, A through F, would take the same subjects and would have classes at roughly the same times of day, though some sections would have earlier classes on different days of the week. Where appropriate, two or

---

[89] Though I didn't have much time for it during my first year, cooking authentic Asian meals is one of my favorite hobbies, and was excited to learn that the university offered an excellent gourmet cooking class that upper-class law students could attend.

[90] I learned later that the housing was more or less randomly selected; I was just lucky.

[91] At Cornell, the 180-person first-year class was broken up into six 30-person sections, an intimate size that quickly built close relationships between section members. Compare this with Harvard Law, which after years of using 140-person sections for each entering class of 560 students – an astonishingly large section size that gave students little in-class interaction with faculty – has just switched to an 80-person section size. With rare exceptions, members of Cornell's small sections did not treat one another as competitors, though there was a vague awareness that awards of some sort would be given out at the end of both semesters to the top-scoring person in each section for each class. Many believe that the lack of vicious competitiveness is a result of the small section sizes and friendships that developed.

[92] The number of professors will, of course, vary from school to school based on a number of factors, including the size of the entering class and the number of sections.

more sections would be instructed simultaneously by the same professor, and every section had at least two intimate "small section" classes with only one teacher. Every student's first semester would consist of 16 credit-hours worth of time divided into five classes – Contracts, Constitutional Law, Torts, Civil Procedure, and Legal Methods. Section F's small sections were Constitutional Law and Legal Methods.

With the exception of Legal Methods, all four of our other classes were 'traditional' first-year law school courses taught in a manner nearly universal from school to school. Every day, students arrive in class after reading 'cases,' published resolutions of legal controversies decided by judges, and professors call on students at random to discuss the cases. In the United States, judicial decisions serve as 'precedent,' or binding interpretations of law used by later courts. A professor attempts to have one student explain the important legal principles set forth in a given case, and thereby help the class understand how legal controversies are resolved. Students need the explanations because their textbooks intentionally only contain cases, not explanations, and because the process of discussing possible case meanings in a classroom prepares lawyers to understand brand new cases once they've left law school. Each of the four typical classes focused on understanding one particularly important area of law – the ones so important that every lawyer must learn them before practicing.

Contracts is perhaps the most practical of the first-year classes, because it deals with topics everyone knows from daily interactions – agreements to buy, sell, give away, and freely obtain goods and services. Over the course of a semester or two, Contracts exposes students to hundreds of court decisions on real-life business deals gone awry. Based on famous or semi-famous judicial opinions on the meanings and principles of certain contract concepts, students learn how courts interpret oral and written agreements between individuals and businesses, and then what financial penalties might result if the agreements are breached.[93] Students also learn why contract breaches are generally compensated with money, rather than more severe punishments such as arrests.

Contracts becomes complex when students realize that they're not just learning how everyday dealings work between average people, but also how highly complex deals work between very sophisticated businesses – good contracts plan around possible failures of one side or the other to perform. In many Contracts classes, students are exposed both to contracts principles that have evolved over centuries, and also the Uniform Commercial Code (UCC), a respected collection of history's best practices of contract interpretation that legislatures have adopted as binding law across the United States. For those

---

[93] In the broader scheme of things, Contracts is a class all about private law – the laws people make between themselves via agreements, and the way courts (as agents of the public) will enforce or refuse to enforce those agreements.

inexperienced in business, or those who know little about commerce, undergraduate classes in business might make Contracts less abstract.

Constitutional Law is the bread and butter class that many pre-law students believe will be representative of the law school experience – more than any other class, it blends small bits of history and politics with a lot of interesting, fundamental American law. To grossly oversimplify, this is a class about the Supreme Court's ongoing attempts to define the powers and limitations of the Congress, the President, and the courts, when each has attempted to act in ways that might overstep Constitutional boundaries. At times, it also discusses the relationship between the federal government and the 50 state governments, particularly when one such state may have stepped out of line.

But it's not representative of the law school experience as a whole. Unlike most other subjects taught in law school, Con Law is largely impractical for most attorneys, considering how few people actually deal with cases directly implicating the federal constitution. When contrasted with Contracts, which speaks to the common, everyday events in one's commercial life, Con Law's concepts are far more abstract, laying the ground rules for other forms of law.[94]

Torts is a fascinating subject, and probably the second most practical of the first year, first semester subjects. Whereas Contracts teaches you how to handle everyday buying and selling business dealings, Torts explains your rights when someone physically, mentally, or financially injures you, no matter how the injury was caused. Simply put, "torts" means "wrongs," and this class tells you how you will be compensated if you or your property is damaged intentionally or through someone else's negligence. It does not deal with criminal punishment for your injuries – that's another class (Criminal Law).

Torts teaches you the key laws applicable to any sort of harm one person can cause another, either intentionally or accidentally, from assault and trespass to the negligent infliction of emotional distress. In its least savory public form, tort law is the basis for the increasingly obnoxious personal injury law commercials on television – a tort includes physical assaults that cause injury and a car accident that's someone else's fault. In its best form, tort law is the means by which large corporations are held accountable for injuring unsuspecting users or victims of their products, and where America is made safer in the process; oil spills and air pollution are considered toxic torts, for example. At its core, tort law defines the appropriate boundaries of your 'personal space' and assigns liability to those who violate it.[95]

---

[94] In the larger scheme, Constitutional Law is a class all about the highest level of public law – the sweeping principles that guide and limit the development of all public and private law in the country.

[95] In its broadest sense, Torts is a class that deals with relatively low-level public law – non-criminal laws drafted by legislatures to preserve the public order and compensate people with money for their injuries.

Civil Procedure, or "Civ Pro," is the subject that humbles even the most enthusiastic first-year students. It teaches budding lawyers the most typical procedures used in courtrooms – the right ways to file a lawsuit, take it through trial, and conclude it. A civil lawsuit, as brought by one person or entity against another, starts out with the filing of documents called a complaint and an answer, continues with a process called discovery to expose as many facts as possible, and only after many motions have been filed will reach an actual trial, where a jury may be empanelled and parties will present their sides of the case.

Civ Pro is not a course in how to actually argue the substance of a case; rather, it is entirely about the procedures lawyers and judges must follow to make a case go smoothly or stop it dead in its tracks. The innumerable tricks of civil procedure continue to mystify even practicing lawyers, as many of the rules are optional and are evoked only under specific circumstances. And that's part of the reason that some lawyers are considered great without even having to put a witness on the stand: if a defendant's lawyer can end a case without paying a settlement or even speaking to a jury, the lawyer is probably well-versed in civil procedure. If you've ever wondered how a lawyer knows about everything from the dates for filing documents to the typical judicial mistakes that can be appealed in a bad trial, this is the class that teaches such things.[96]

Finally, Legal Methods is one name for a legal writing program, a relatively recent addition to Cornell's schedule, paralleling the addition of such programs at other institutions. Based on complaints from practicing lawyers that law students were not being required to learn how to properly write legal memoranda – the documents lawyers write to dissect and discuss specific laws – several schools opted to develop writing classes to improve the marketability of their students. The first-year schedule, however, was already pretty packed. So law schools were forced to either jettison another subject or make the difficult first year even more onerous. Cornell opted, after many years of consideration and debate, to remove from the first year schedule a course in legal jurisprudence – a philosophical course that has similarly become optional elsewhere. Now first-year students spend a year learning how to write legal documents, and as legal writing is technical and dry, it is this subject which often frustrates the best English students the most.

At its core, the legal writing class is the one that teaches you what is and is not fair game when drafting documents that will be submitted to judges and other attorneys; how far you can go, what you may and may not say, and so on. It is intensely practical, and will be your first official exposure to the much-dreaded BLUEBOOK – a tool used to universalize the manner in which legal

---

[96] In the broader scheme of things, Civ Pro is a class that deals with highly technical public law: the precise rules that must be followed when dealing with courts, as agents of the federal and state governments, and the consequences for failing to follow those rules.

practitioners and academics reference or cite the sources of information they consulted in preparing documents.

D. PEOPLE AND PERSONALITIES

As my first day wound down at the law school, only a few people grasped more than 20% of the aforementioned details. Most had come to the law school with little concrete sense of what, exactly, they would be studying.[97] After all, they were here to learn the law, and the school was going to tell them what the law was or is. For now, a less than intuitive part of the law school experience was taking place in the background: the earliest form of networking. Cornell took the time before classes to make formal attempts to introduce people to one another, and those of us in the dorms were aggressively starting to develop our circles of friends. It's safe to say that few things are as important in the legal profession as a good name, reputation, and contacts. The first days of orientation were all about making early legal contacts. With time to prove oneself inside and outside of classes to your peers, the name and reputation parts would surely follow, to each according to his or her contribution.

Most people were in a similar state of mind at this point: putting on friendly faces, shaking lots of hands, trying to remember names, and so forth. And Cornell had set up several official, more or less mandatory events through which students could meet each other and some professors. The first such event for most students was a celebratory luncheon at the Ithaca Yacht Club, which offered a paradigmatic taste for the new students of what they could expect in their new lives – at least at the law school, if not professionally thereafter. The event was interesting on several levels. For some people, including me, this was the closest we'd ever been to a yacht club. It was also the first time some of us had ever been patted on the back just for getting admitted to an organization; we were made to feel as if we were a select group within the population. And finally, we were given a sense of the burdens we would bear in exchange for the status we were to obtain as lawyers.[98]

---

[97] As it turns out, there are ways that incoming first-year students can arrive with a heightened level of sophistication about these classes. Along with this book, people can and should consult BAR/BRI, a company that offers law school and post-law school preparatory outlines and instructional videos. Their central web site at http://www.barbri.com is a little confusing, routing first-year students to the Gilbert series of course outlines; choose a state, such as New York, and look for information on BAR/BRI's First-Year Review Volume. Get the review materials, if possible, far in advance of final exams – even consider sitting in on classes or watching video tapes before law school. Is this really worthwhile? Successful friends have sworn by it.

[98] Though the initial orientation events differ from school to school, and few are as mandatory as Cornell's, it's fair to say at this point that even if it's not made expressly clear

The law school had organized a slate of speakers – a couple of students, some graduates of the school with careers in public and private service, and professors who shared interesting thoughts on their own first years of law school. Around this point is when it became clear to me just what sort of experience the first year was going to be: people spoke of it as a rite of passage littered with obstacles to hurdle or stumble over. It was understood that the work load was going to be heavy and that there was at least an informal competition, of sorts, to see who would be at the top of the class. But by the same token, there was a certain attitude all of the speakers had about the study of law that was somewhat amazing: the panelists strongly suggested that everyone from our school was going to graduate and either have a job immediately or find one very quickly, no matter where one fell in the 'class rankings.[99] Success at Cornell made it easier, rather than conceivable, to find a job. Therefore, the atmosphere could be competitive, but not cutthroat. No one needed to fail for you to succeed.[100]

This is an important part of my law school experience, and one that may differ dramatically not only from students at other schools – whether higher- or lower-ranked – but also in different economic times. Of the 180-some students who became the Class of 2001 at Cornell, virtually everyone initially worked hard to do well, but virtually no one did so at someone else's expense. Camaraderie stamped out over-aggressive competitiveness. But this is not necessarily the case at other schools across the country, at least, right now. In positive economic times, students from schools ranked in the top 15 or 20 nationally tend to have positive experiences when it comes to getting jobs,[101] but there are over 180 ABA-accredited law schools. Though some schools deny it, as the job market tightens, some students resort to cutthroat behaviors, pressures generated in part by the consequences of 'average' grade

---

by one's school, the beginning of a law student's life is special: it's an entry into a prestigious profession with the potential to do so much, yet loaded with obligations that could cripple one's use of that potential. This is true no matter what school you attend.

[99] Different schools have their own policies on class rank. Cornell does not publish ranks of its students, but generally makes them aware (personally, not publicly) that they fall into the top 10, 30, or 50% of the class. Other schools publish class rankings for public consumption. Most schools carry out individual GPAs to four decimal places because of the ferocity of competition; a 3.9876 would place you high up near the top… unless your school issues A+ grades, in which case a 4.3000 is the theoretical maximum GPA.

[100] It's important to distinguish this sentiment from a simple law school reality that comes whenever you have a forced grading curve, as described in Section Q of this chapter: because a curve requires an "average" with people higher and lower than that number, not everyone can or will "succeed" in classes relative to their classmates, yet even lower-ranked people in a class can still find jobs and thus succeed in legal careers.

[101] And that's what law school means to most people: what they'll be doing afterwards.

performance: major law firms frequently hire only from the upper 10-25% of the classes of schools below the national top 20. People fight to get into that top quarter or tenth of their class, and the fighting sometimes gets distasteful.

With only rare exceptions, my classmates didn't show a hint of this sort of cutthroat behavior. Owing perhaps to the fact that virtually everyone had something unique in his or her background, Cornell was a place where one's successes stood on their own and did not need to be compared against those of others. Especially early on, most people gave off an air of confidence that was later shown to be at least somewhat a front, but definitely made everyone feel as if they were in generally very successful and intelligent company.[102]

There were exceptions, of course. A few people stood out from the beginning as arrogant asses, and as a general rule were either later shut up by poor grades, emboldened by good grades to transfer out, or in a rare case or two continued obnoxious behavior and suffered as a result. Some of the traits that quickly lost potential friends for a person were: repeatedly making reference to all of the judges or lawyers in one's family, repeatedly referring to one's pre-law school abilities or experiences as predictive of future success, or repeatedly interrupting other people in the middle of their sentences to counter with different beliefs. But the point must be stressed: these people were exceptions to the rule of great civility.

The irony of early snootiness was that law school, at its core, is a great equalizer. One student who spoke most loudly of his disposition to become a judge was thereby among the most publicly humbled when he made mistakes in first-year classes. Rare is the soul who enters the study of the law and leaves unchanged for the experience; no matter how many judges or lawyers one could claim to be related to, or what sort of career one had before law school, such factors appeared to play little if any role in who succeeded or failed in classes. The majority of the subject matter was new on most cognitive levels to any student who came to it, and those who thought they knew the most coming in often found it the hardest to change when they belatedly discovered how little value their previous knowledge could be. Some of the most pompous souls embarrassed themselves in classes by presuming incorrectly that they knew it all; professors would roundly but gently humiliate them.

If there were any initially intimidating people, they were the few individuals with incredible gifts for memorization, and at first, that caused plenty of undue concern. How could I, with my so-so memory, even hope to compete against people who could memorize entire books just by looking once through them? As it turned out, many of those with photographic memories

---

[102] The same scenario plays out year after year at Cornell; even in economically rough times, the school's career office helps to secure a job for virtually every person who needs help. It's perhaps easier to avoid cutthroat tactics when they're perceived as unnecessary.

rested on that ability and never developed their reasoning skills; as a result, they rarely stood out in classes or achieved outstanding grades.

Your law school class will most likely have a mix of interesting personalities, the majority of whom you may never get to know if you attend a school with large class and section sizes. Anonymity often prevails at such schools, say nothing of common feelings that people are just numbers in machines far bigger than themselves. Some people may believe before law school that they would do better at large, anonymous places; as someone who did not think of himself as a 'people person,' I found that choosing a school where I got to *know* people was an excellent choice, especially when I later heard people from other schools complain about their huge class sizes.

E.   A "HAPPY" HOUR: THE RUMOR MILL BEGINS

One of the other traditional law school events, and one I did not at first plan to attend,[103] was a pre-semester happy hour – a chance to mingle with second- and third-year students at a local bar and discuss what is to come. With the incentive of free alcohol, turn-out was relatively heavy amongst upper-classmen and the stories quickly became astonishing. As school had not yet officially started, the happy hour was the start of a discussion within the law school's social universe that continued unabated for three full years, and perhaps thereafter with successive generations – the time when we first heard about our professors' skills, attitudes, and unusual character traits, some of our more notorious upper-classmen, and how happy all upper-classmen felt to be finished doing what you're about to go through.

The annual first happy hour is as much a hazing experience as the upper-class' legitimate effort to get to know you and share their experiences. Depending on the participants and the topics that come up, it can ruffle already sensitive feathers. Ours mixed chatter about professors and the challenges of the first weeks of classes. In essence, we had the shit scared out of us.

We learned for the first time about our place in the hierarchy: we were 1Ls – traditional shorthand for first-years – and above us were the 2Ls, who at this point were fresh out of their 1L years and thrilled to be done, and the 3Ls, who were closest to graduation and largely ready to move on to jobs awaiting them in the real world. The event was, for some reason, attended primarily by 2Ls

---

[103] On a personal note, events such as this one were events that I might not have attended as an undergraduate – unlike a large part of the population, I wasn't a big fan of alcohol and I hated bars. But I went anyway, and it was a highly useful experience; a good chance to meet people and learn the legends of the school. Even if it was intimidating to hear about classes that were about to beat us up, the ability to socialize and bond with people from other classes made it worthwhile.

and not 3Ls. We would not share classes with either; we would, for the entire first year, be split off in our sections and attend classes only with those other 1L sections who were assigned the same professors. Our interactions with 2Ls and 3Ls would be entirely social, and frankly, many of them wanted as little to do with 1L life as possible. They told us to expect that certain professors would be tough, other ones moderate, and a few even gentle. No one had a slate of entirely gentle professors. Everyone had at least one, if not two tough ones.

But we also heard some juicy gossip about professors, which was something to talk about and share with others as we attempted to make new friends and acquaintances. This was the true start of the rumor mill – a gossipy look into the lives of all of the law school's personalities, faculty and students alike, accentuated by the small class size and confined surroundings. Certain stories stood out from the rest, namely rumors that a few professors had once been intimately involved with students – supposedly outside of the classroom setting – a phenomenon that was widely thought to be the case at many law schools. While no one believed that professors would get involved with their current students, stories circulated that one unmarried professor had been involved with a former student, a student organization advisor was involved with the head of that organization, and another had married a student then acrimoniously divorced in a notable, published law suit years later.[104]

The rumor mill is one of those social phenomena that you can't avoid in a small law school unless you either drop completely out of sight or remain entirely below classmates' radar screens. Many rumors turned out to be just the grade school "telephone game" at work – one person hears a story, passes it on, and as it passes from person to person six or ten times, the story is distorted beyond recognition. In other cases, rumors were entirely true. In either case, they filled dead air when people wanted not to discuss law.

F.   THE GLASS CASE

At some point in the orientation we became aware that our initial assignments had been posted in a glass case in a central hallway in the school. As I walked down the long hallway towards the case, I saw scattered   groups   of   students

---

[104] Someone took the time to research the latter story by locating, printing, and sharing the case with anyone who was interested.

85

approaching the case, jotting down page numbers, and leaving to buy their books. And what followed when I personally went through this simple set of events was one of the most surprising experiences of my law school career.

I remember feeling relieved when I saw the first class assignments. Most classes asked initially for 12-16 pages of reading a piece, with a rare exception coming in at 25-30. Twelve or 16 pages was nothing to me. As an undergraduate, and even as a business graduate student, I could polish off 16 pages in less than half an hour while waiting for a class to start. This law school thing was going to be a lot easier than I'd imagined. Especially considering that some of my textbooks, though 1000 pages thick, had compact sizes with relatively fewer words per page than they might have had.

Then I actually tried to read the books.

On the first book, the first assignment's pages were so packed with text that I flipped through to see if the text ever became easier. It didn't.

There were, of course, no pictures on any of the pages, except for a grim cartoon or rare photograph on one or two pages of one of the books, put there as gallows humor, someplace near the end.

There was little to no narrative in the books, either. They were structured not as point-by-point stories, but as strings of transcripts of judicial opinions, tossed together with a random explanatory sentence once in a long while. What was I supposed to be getting from one of these cases when I read it?

Some of the cases seemed to be written in Old English. Every one of them was dense in a manner that I had never been able to imagine before. It was as if every sentence appeared to have special meaning in its own right. And in fact, the vast majority of them did. How was one to take notes on this? And why was it suddenly taking me 3 hours to read 30 pages and make simple notes for myself? I used to read so quickly that people nicknamed me "Flash." Now it seemed as if I was completely and totally screwed.

Oh, and those law books were heavy,[105] too, especially when they were all together in one bag because we had four classes in a row. This whole law school idea was not looking even slightly possible, by my previous graduate or undergraduate standards. At the rate that I was going, I would spend every moment when I was not in a classroom just reading and preparing for classes.

And there was no way that I could read a case or three right before class started and hope to be able to understand it.

And the classes sometimes came three or four in a row, without breaks.

And each class met at least three times a week.

And there were other things in the glass case that needed attention.[106]

---

[105] And expensive. The costs are discussed in Chapter 2, Section A.
[106] One of the unusual means by which a few states limit their numbers of bar applicants is the "far in advance registration process," by which first-year law students must register

This was not looking good.

This was me, in panic mode, my first year. Especially my first semester. It is the experience virtually every law student goes through, at least for several days, more often for weeks or months.

Every person responds in some predictable way. Some decide not to read the material too carefully. Others burn out trying to memorize it all to a superhuman level of detail. Predictably, most people fall in between.

At this point, I just needed to keep up with the reading *and* attend classes.

G.   OUR PROFESSORS

Along with the assignments, we had learned the names of our professors,[107] and some people had already researched the professors' backgrounds. My section had been assigned John Wakeman for Contracts, Alexandra ("Alex") Spitzer for Constitutional Law, Robert Alighieri for Torts, Laura Edwards for Civil Procedure, and Janice Crosby for Legal Methods. Three other sections had received Thomas Winter for Contracts and Charles Savard for Civil Procedure. None of these names meant much to me at this stage. I certainly wasn't aware that any of them were especially famous.

Through the grapevine, I quickly learned what our section's schedule meant. We had apparently been given an excellent assortment of professors, though not necessarily all of the best-known names. Professor Winter, for example, was considered almost a living deity of contract law. By reputation, he had authored parts of the aforementioned UCC, a document so well-regarded that it had been adopted by nearly every American state to regulate commercial transactions. But he was also notoriously prickly with his students and inspired performance through fear. My section had avoided him, which inspired mixed feelings; on the one hand, fear inhibited my learning. On the other hand, there are advantages in taking a class with a well-known professor.

Professor Savard had a similarly excellent reputation. He co-authored the Civil Procedure textbook and also a widely used commercial outline for the subject – a treatise-sized outline to help students understand the textbook.[108]

---

with the states as many as three years before actually taking the states' bar exams. If you're considering practice in a state with requirements like this, be sure to register early, no matter how much first-year work you have on your plate, else you'll be in for a real disappointment when you graduate. Filing times are always critical in the legal profession.

[107] Names and some biographical details, such as school names, may be changed herein.

[108] "Commercial outlines" are professionally-written explanations of the current state of the law in specific subject areas. These outlines range from ultra-compact (laminated one-sheet outlines, front and back) to unabridged formats. Bigger outlines, including Savard's 300-page outline of civil procedure, look more like treatises – comprehensive, logically-arranged explanations of specific law subjects that (unlike outlines) are never short.

But the professors we were assigned turned out to be impressive in their own ways. Professor Spitzer was a noted scholar of feminist jurisprudence whose widely-read articles had actually inspired many people to apply to the school. Though students naturally deferred to her, and all other professors, by calling them "professor," she was our primary small section teacher and encouraged students to call her Alex, her nickname. Professor Alighieri was a relatively young, entertaining lecturer on Torts. He had a gaunt but vaguely Kennedy-esque look that endeared him especially to female students, and had clerked for a Supreme Court justice after graduating from law school.

And Professor Edwards was to be our drill sergeant. I think that most law schools make sure that students are exposed to at least one such person during first year, if not more: she was the one who made up for the fact that we didn't have Professor Winter, and would be the person we feared. No matter what people thought of Civil Procedure, they would know it by the end of the course, because she would, by reputation, beat it into them. But by the end of the first semester, many people loved her, or at least respected her.

Our Contracts and Legal Methods instructors were not quite so well-known. Unlike our other professors, both were Cornell Law graduates who now taught at their alma mater. At many schools, including Cornell, legal writing instructors are deemed lecturers, not full professors, and though Janice Crosby was by reputation the best and most friendly, there wasn't a lot we could know about her in advance. Our Contracts professor was similarly anonymous; he essentially lived in the shadow of Professor Winter, who was the school's prominent expert on the subject. Advance opinions on his classes ranged from "boring" to "mildly amusing," depending on the person you were talking with.

H.   THE FIRST DAY OF CLASSES AND THE SOCRATIC METHOD

**"I'm from New Jersey, and in my free time,
I like to play blackjack."
Tim, a first-year law student, introducing himself
to his small section class at the professor's request**

**"Oh, that's very interesting, Tim.
What is this 'black jack?' "
Narrowly brilliant professor, graduate of Yale Law School,
inquiring seriously to the astonishment of the class**

Some of the moments in one's legal education are preceded by terror, or at least, a great irrational temptation to fear what's to come. The first day of classes, despite its importance, is not necessarily among them. I awoke from a sleep only mildly influenced by the uncertainty of the first day of classes at a new school. I was probably more excited than nervous.

In all candor, my own first day of classes was only modestly intimidating. The readings had taken a long time, but were short enough that I thought that I generally understood where they were going. Most of my professors initially came across as nice enough people,[109] and the first class discussions about the readings were relatively gentle, conducted with the understanding that students were new to the concepts of reading cases and discussing them in front of large lecture halls full of other students. The professors would later ratchet up the difficulty as the days passed. Other students with less benevolent professors had more of a shock on the first day, as the professors instead started classes aggressively or inquisitively, only to relax somewhat as the semester progressed. It's hard to know before receiving your class schedule just what sort of initial experience you're going to have.

Regardless of your slate of professors, however, you cannot entirely avoid the most commonly feared part of the law school experience, which despite frequent complaints continues to persist even today.[110] This absolutely classic component of every law student's educational career is the Socratic Method, a style of law school teaching that most law professors use in some form or another; at best, it will initially be used in a gentle form only to become more intense and less forgiving later on.

Without trying to sound too much like Bill and Ted's Excellent Adventure, it's fair to say that the teaching methodology pioneered by the Greek scholar Socrates has maintained a surprisingly consistent reputation in the world of law.[111] In theory, the use of the Socratic Method is a teaching tool by which a professor foregoes the standard 'I speak and you learn' lecture format and instead chooses students for one-on-one question and answer sessions, leading them through case-specific factual and legal analyses in front of their classmates. Each Socratic dialogue is designed to teach students how lawyers

---

[109] In retrospect, those who lived in fear of professors missed obvious signs that the professors were only human. Even the brightest professors had soft spots, including a classic intellectual's Achilles' heel: lacking 'street smarts' or common sense. On the very first day of one of our classes, a particularly academic professor asked each student to say his or her name, hometown and hobbies. One student from New Jersey said that he played blackjack in his free time. The professor seemed perplexed, and to the astonishment of the class, asked what "black jack" was, and upon explanation responded, "you will have to teach us how to play it, some time." The moment was too surprising to be fully appreciated at that point, but suggested that our professors were not as universally brilliant as they were about the law.

[110] The Socratic Method owes its longevity to tradition, perceived legitimate value in building skills necessary to at least some members of the profession, and lastly the amusement of the instructors who use it.

[111] The late Harvard Law Dean Christopher Langdell is often credited, spitefully, with pioneering the application of the Socratic Method in American law schools.

think and explain themselves rationally while attempting to reach conclusions.

In practice, this can and will be a terrifying first experience for most law students, but it's hard to be sure on your first day just what it will be like with your personal set of teachers. Under the strictest form of the Socratic Method, your name will be bellowed by the professor amidst a silent classroom full of your fellow students, and you will be asked a series of never-ending questions. The questions will keep on coming regardless of how right or wrong your answers may be, but if you can think straight enough, you may come to understand when you're on the right or wrong track. A strict Socratic practitioner, of whom there are few remaining, will continue to prod you even when you are wrong over and over again, and have given up all hope. And it is believed by such a practitioner that from your state of despondence you will eventually emerge, bearing an answer that gets you back on the right track, and then to a successful conclusion. In the meanwhile, the class listens and hopefully learns – occasionally more from mistakes than from right answers.

The advantage of a purely Socratic-style class is also its disadvantage: you read the material at your own pace and draw your own conclusions, aided only by what you can glean from the professor's approval or disapproval of the student's comments in class, and the rare summary comment the professor makes thereafter. In an ideal environment, the professor asks questions, sums up concepts, and then moves on. Some Socratic professors are not good, however, at leading logical discussions, and may confuse more than they instruct. A few professors become so absorbed with hypothetical questions that their interrogatory purpose never becomes clear to students. The following example of Socratic dialogue in the context of a Torts case will illustrate the difference between good and bad use of the Socratic Method.

Professor: Ms. Smith, what happened in this case?

Ms. Smith: A young man kissed a young woman on the face, and she sued him for battery.

Professor: Battery, you say. *(to the class)* We know she's not talking about a portable source of power. *(to Ms. Smith)* So, what is battery?

Ms. Smith: As the court says it, battery is...

Professor: Ignore the court for a moment. What do you think battery is?

Ms. Smith: It could be many things. I think it's a violent attack on one person by another. But it could be more.

Professor: What do you mean by violent?

Ms. Smith: Well, anything aggressive, forced, surprising.

Professor: And when you say attack, what do you mean?

Ms. Smith: Something physical, a connection made by one person against the other.

Professor: Very interesting. So what does the court say a battery is?

Ms. Smith: "An intentional and wrongful physical contact with a person without his or her consent that entails some injury or offensive touching."

Professor: That's good. Can you tell me, Ms. Smith, how your definition differs from that offered by the Court?

Ms. Smith: (brief silence) I'm not sure.

Professor: Give it a moment. Can you think of a difference?

Ms. Smith: (extended silence) They're very much the same.

Professor: (pause) That's true, but the differences are what we're after, here. Can somebody else see one? (hands are raised) Mister ... Jackson, is it?

Mr. Jackson: Yes; her definition includes violence, and theirs does not.

Professor: Correct. Going back to you, Ms. Smith, do you think that when a man kisses a woman's face, she should be able to sue him for battery?

Ms. Smith: Not necessarily.

Professor: But the Court here says that she wins, does it not?

Ms. Smith: Yes.

Professor: So why the discrepancy?

Ms. Smith: Because the Court explains that she did not consent.

Professor: Is that really the reason? Ms. Smith, do you think that a person need always consent before being kissed? *(to the class)* Should the young man bring a consent form, or perhaps a waiver, every time he wants a kiss?

Ms. Smith: No. But the Court explains that the young man's act was also wrongful.

Professor: Very good. And why?

Ms. Smith: Because she had told him before that she did not want to be kissed, had pulled away when he tried to kiss her, and immediately ran away after he did it.

Professor: So who says what is wrongful? What if she said "kiss me" and then said "don't kiss me," and then quickly pulled away?

Ms. Smith: That's a question of consent. The court says that what's wrongful can be inferred by the jury from the circumstances and societal standards.

Professor: So if society says "it's okay to kiss a woman even if she pulls away," then no punishment. Does that sound right to you, Ms. Smith?

Ms. Smith: No. Well...

Professor: But didn't you tell me earlier that you didn't think a woman shouldn't be able to sue a man for battery just for kissing her on the face?

Ms. Smith: I guess I did.

Professor: Can you explain what's changed in your mind?

Ms. Smith: Well, I don't necessarily agree that a person should be allowed to engage in poor behavior because society says that the behavior is okay.

Professor: *(to the class)* This has been an exercise in understanding the tort of battery – we discuss how the law determines "wrongful" conduct. Ms. Smith has presented a classic dichotomy; the objective standard, or what society says as a whole, versus the subjective standard, or what one person feels and believes. In this case, we see the court explaining that we will know if the kiss was wrongful by looking to what society thinks of the behavior as a whole. That's a question for the jury to answer – what do you, as representatives of society, believe? Then we will look to the circumstances of this case to see whether there was, or was not consent. And finally, to figure out whether there is an injury or offensive contact, we will consider both the victim's personal, subjective feeling of offense, and then society's. In essence, if the jury agrees that the behavior in question was wrongful, and the evidence shows that the victim was injured or offensively contacted, she will be compensated. You can't win in court just by saying someone made you feel bad. Your feeling must be justified.

You may well have been confused by the direction of the dialogue, at least until the end; many first-year students initially are. There are several differences between a useful Socratic dialogue and a confusing one. First, some professors end the dialogue or class before presenting any final summary thought, and you might or might not understand where the sample professor was going with his questions. Note that the professor above didn't explain anything until the end. That's often the way it really goes in a class, and your notes might look like questions without answers. Second, this professor was trying to test and explore each of the variables in the court's statement of the law of battery, see whether the student could explain what they really meant, and contrast them with the student's existing conceptions.

In real Socratic dialogues, professors ask lots of other questions, some of which are useful, and some of which will cloud the discussion even more. Professors who endlessly ask "what if?" questions tend to infuriate students, and only a handful of people come to understand what they're getting at. In the end, what you're really supposed to be learning is the standard for battery as stated by the court, the way that the court interprets each word of the standard, and the process of distinguishing between your personal feelings and those that courts and juries may hold.

Third, though many professors will ask a personal question or two just to loosen you up or elucidate a point, other professors will stick purely to the words in the case, sometimes to a point where you focus on all sorts of lessons not directly related to your exam, but rather more generally to the lawyering process. You might not realize what points are specifically important for your test, and which are just general lessons about the way that lawyers do things.

If you are 'on the spot,' 'in the chair,' or 'cold-called,' as the terms exist to describe those unlucky souls who are being subjected to Socratic inquiry, you will barely take notes. You will likely need to depend on a classmate to tell you what you've said, and whether the Professor agreed or disagreed. You might, if lucky, be able to gather yourself enough to jot down the summary paragraph, if your professor enunciates one. But you won't realize what you missed.

For reasons that may be apparent, the Socratic Method has some detractors. Contemporary professors tend to either use a light version of the Socratic Method, calling on several students at once or giving students advance notice, or leaving a student alone when he or she clearly has no idea what the 'correct' or helpful answer could be. Some, but not many, engage in pure lectures, clarifying otherwise difficult course materials in a straightforward 'black letter' format that can later be reviewed and understood.

My professors, I learned at the happy hour before classes started, were all Socratic lecturers – at least light Socratic, if not more severe.[112] And it is quite common on the first day of classes for the first words out of your new professor's mouth to be the name of a student, chosen apparently at random, who then sits figuratively in the hot seat answering questions for between five and twenty minutes straight. In reality, the student generally remains seated in her chair wherever she happens to sit in the class, and quivers uncontrollably while answering unless possessed of a false sense of confidence.

Such was the scene that played out on our first day of Civil Procedure. Professor Edwards, an imposing African-American woman, entered the room with the poise, charisma and confidence of an imperial general. When she started to speak, the room instantly went completely silent. Her reputation had preceded her. Several brief sentences about the course shot out of her mouth. And then she called someone's name. It was as if a lightning bolt had hit the room and one person in particular. Oh, what awful luck it must be to have your name called on that very first day, that very first question. It happened to me on the first day of the second semester. But at least I knew by then what to expect.

Our first day of Civil Procedure was almost exactly the same as every day that followed. Professor Edwards taught from the book written by Professor Savard, and did not teach the subject for clarity as Savard did. Rather, she employed the second-to-most hard-core version of the Socratic Method, focusing her attentions entirely upon one student at first, then moving to his neighbors in straight lines, vertical, horizontal, and diagonal, to as many as three neighboring souls whenever the first student would make a mistake. The class was thus an endless series of interrogatories, many of them based on incredibly difficult questions posed at the end of readings in the textbook. Rarely did she end a sentence with a period or exclamation mark; mostly she ended with a question mark or an ellipse, trailing off or standing silent as a

---

[112] This experience is typical. Most law schools intentionally cultivate a mix of personalities within their pool of first-year professors, a fair blend of tough ones and nice ones that today skews more towards the "nice" than before. Schools generally try to insure that each section gets a mix of each type of professor. Our section's compassionate, softer professors were Alex Spitzer and Janice Crosby, and our tough professor was Laura Edwards – together, these three represented a very wide spectrum of female instructors: all three highly intelligent and motivated, but one who was especially intellectual and academic (Spitzer), one who was practical and approachable (Crosby), and one who was tough as nails and fear-inspiring. The male instructors were simply less interesting by comparison. John Wakeman was a dry, nearly monotone Contracts lecturer, and Robert Alighieri was a friendly man who became surprisingly distant outside the classroom. Other sections had the withering Winters for Contracts or a somewhat hard-edged instructor for Con Law, Torts or Legal Methods, but made up for them with the brilliant but approachable Savard for Civ Pro, or one of two other friendly Con Law professors.

student pondered in 15 seconds or less how best not to embarrass himself when his mouth started and stopped moving. This paled only by comparison to the one-student-per-class version of Socratic employed by Professor Winter and many of his old-school contemporaries.

The experiences can be terrifying. But there are some surprising good points to the Socratic Method, too, besides the oft-stated reason that it 'helps you learn to think on your feet.' First, it builds a sense of camaraderie amongst students, who can associate with the fears and misconceptions of their classmates, and learn from their mistakes. People shared their notes freely with those who had been called on each day. Even when people had tough days under the grilling of the Socratic Method, other people would randomly stop by to congratulate them on surviving the ordeal, regardless of how it had gone. Everyone goes through it.

The second point may be of small comfort to those especially fearful, but if you manage somehow to do really well, you earn the respect of your classmates in addition to their empathy. In my classes, only one student in the entire Civil Procedure course managed to hold the floor uninterrupted for an entire class session. It was viewed, appropriately, as somewhat of a miracle. When you're being asked a new question every one or two minutes for 50 or 55 minutes and you never make a mistake, both the class and the professor tend to be surprised. I was frankly amazed when it happened. And at some point in that process, the mythical inevitability of failure is dispelled and it becomes evident that there may be, in fact, a way to master the material.

But for 99% of law students, being able to hold the floor uninterrupted will be either an elusive goal or something dreaded, rather than desired. The Socratic Method thus forms cloud clusters over first-year students' heads which only lift, cloud by cloud, in a given class for a given student on the day after she has been called on – the point at which she knows she is not likely to be called upon again, out of the blue, perhaps for the rest of the semester. But in small classes especially, those who are called early in the semester tend to fear getting called a second or third time; in my experience, it happens, but rarely more than twice unless a professor really likes your answers, you volunteer, or they have an unusual need to communicate with many people every day.

It's hard to overstate the psychological impact the Socratic Method has upon students. Its use influences the way people take notes – if you think you might be the next person to be called on, you write hurriedly and imprecisely, and if you're being called on, you're best off to ask a friend for his or her notes that day – you won't make any sense on your own paper if you're devoting yourself to making sense orally. This forced tradeoff – one student's day of performing while other students are learning, but in fear – is at the core of the debate over whether to preserve the Socratic Method when otherwise every student might be learning without fear.[113] Yet the Socratic Method has its benefits; it focuses students upon specifics, rather than encouraging them to take leisurely, generalized notes and broad glances at the material. It teaches *thinking* skills, not just *memorizing* skills. And it significantly decreases the amount of background chatter in classrooms – people frequently stay quiet to avoid drawing attention to themselves in classes where a professor is looking for someone to call upon. For many reasons, it's safe to conclude that the Socratic Method is here to stay.

I.   BEATING THE SOCRATIC METHOD: AN IMPOSSIBLE MISSION?

In most cases, those students who "beat" the Socratic Method accomplish it with apparent trickery: through paced over-preparedness. Those who consistently came closest to perfect Socratic performances were those who read materials beyond the scope of the textbooks almost every day and had gained some perspective on the material transcending just the days' lessons.

But let's be realistic. The first year schedule, even when you're simply completing the daily assigned readings and nothing more, is intentionally designed to be overwhelming. Professors almost never go a night without a new reading assignment, and there are Legal Methods papers and other activities to occupy whatever free time you might have left. Moreover, law schools repeatedly have resisted pressures to decrease the first year workload by even a single credit hour, and the American Bar Association has kept the pressure on to maintain the same number of hours of instruction every year.

Despite all of this, the best students take the time to supplement their mandatory readings with treatises or commercial outlines that provide structure and context for lectures and assigned cases. The Civil Procedure superstars relied upon Professor Savard's commercial outline, published in a format which certainly presented the subject more succinctly than his jam-packed 1,400-page textbook. And then they tried to actually understand each case and lecture, and how they fit into the bigger picture, and succeeded. I call it paced over-preparedness: spending a little time each night trying to understand the bigger picture for the next day's materials instead of rushing to build big-picture understanding right before exams. It takes time, but pays dividends.

The trick therefore is not so much a trick as a reality of the first-year study of law: few students take the time or have the necessary perspective to go

---

[113] Some schools reputably achieve some compromise on this issue by giving students warning, far in advance, of the specific date when they will be called upon. Though this has the advantages of mandating class participation and using individual students as teaching tools for classes, it does not encourage the vigorous study of materials required by pure Socratic disciples.

beyond the textbooks,[114] or even truly understand what's in the textbooks. They try to understand the individual class lectures on an undergraduate level – writing down key words and phrases every day in the hopes that it will all make sense at the end. Only the rare first-year professor will communicate that undergraduate learning techniques don't work in law school, and only the rare student will both believe that, and know how to change their habits.

As a result, students who know to start out using treatises or commercial outlines are at a seemingly unfair advantage. They show up for classes and, in many cases, know answers to questions before they're even asked. Their Socratic responses impress professors and stagger fellow students. True, they're not thinking on their feet. But then, should they have to, if they spent an hour more than the average student thinking about it all the night before?

Some professors, however, actively discourage the use of treatises and outlines. Why would professors not want you to use something simple and effective to organize your thinking? Moreover, why don't they just use treatises and outlines to teach classes in the first place?

Part of their answer is that law school is supposed to teach you how to reason, not just memorize.[115] The other part is that law school isn't supposed to be easy. If it was, the world would have far too many lawyers instead of just too many lawyers, as is the case now. So law professors try to make the process difficult by "hiding the ball," or taking clear points and making you work to figure them out. They tease answers out of people in public settings in order to expose flaws in reasoning and suggest alternate ways of looking at concepts.

If professors were all equally excellent with the Socratic Method, law school would be fantastic: properly applied, the Socratic Method builds reasoning skills while conveying information, an efficient way of building better lawyers. But improperly applied, the Socratic Method never teaches reasoning skills; instead, students become confused and have to teach themselves both the information and how to reason. As people have problems learning from the

---

[114] It must be stated, however, that there is such a thing as going overboard in one's absorption of outside materials. In addition to purchasing commercially-prepared case briefs, guidebooks and treatises – the latter of which should be adequate to assist you – students sometimes get wrapped up in reading every piece of ancillary material mentioned in footnotes or in asides by professors. More than anything else, fear drives this compulsion to consume, and though it is conceivably possible to read so much that everything starts to click, it is far more likely that you will overload and burn yourself out. Glance over the outside materials, pick one form of supplementary material that works for you, and stick with it. Don't be intimidated by classmates who load up on every book out there; no matter how confident they seem, they may well be more confused in the end than those who stick with one source and really understand it.

[115] The ability to reason in a recognized 'lawyer's' manner is, in large part, what separates lawyers from historians and other professionals.

Socratic Method, or because professors have problems using it, self-teaching – through treatises – becomes a viable way to succeed in your classes.[116]

The other part of weathering a Socratic dialogue is self-confidence or self-esteem. Though preparedness is necessary, it's not sufficient to survive the twisting and turning of one issue in five or ten different directions. Successful students maintain a level of comfort with the questioner, understanding that the point of the dialogue is not to trip up students, but rather, to try and produce one direct answer to each question. Fear of questions or embarrassment only leads to greater fear and embarrassment; realizing in advance that everyone goes through the same experience, and that the goal is not to cower but to participate, will lead to at least some confidence when you're preparing.[117]

It bears mention that older students, particularly considerably older ones, often do better with Socratic dialogues than younger ones. One student had graduated from medical school and was not about to be intimidated by even the most cowing professors. The reasons for older students' success were apparent: they are closer in age to the professors, don't fear them quite as much, and don't think of one bad Socratic discussion as the end of the world. But if you look at successful younger students, they possess the same latter two characteristics: less fear and some perspective on the value of the experience. They're just lucky enough to have developed such understanding earlier in life.

J. PRESSURES OF LEARNING AND THE DAY OF EPIPHANY

From the aforementioned premise that only the best students really take the time to understand the material in its broadest sense, it follows that everybody else doesn't truly understand what they're learning. And this may, in fact, be true. Many people spend their first year, especially their first semester, trying to figure out what they're doing. They show up for lectures, do most of

---

[116] As a cautionary note, rely on treatises or commercially-prepared outlines when trying to build initial understanding, not outlines prepared by fellow students. Student outlines may be poorly organized or wrong, and though this is also possible with treatises and commercial outlines, it's far less likely.

[117] Though most people initially have trouble learning through the Socratic Method, a small number of people find themselves unable to adapt to it at all for a semester or two. If you feel that you're really having problems with a class and you're just not understanding the subject at all, act quickly. Consider purchasing commercial outlines or treatises, or use one in the law library to see if it helps. If that doesn't work, talk with an administrator such as a dean about the problem, have an additional discussion with the professor, or get a tutor on the side. Any of these would be positive proactive ways to avoid "sinking into the depths of misunderstanding that may come with the Socratic Method," as one friend put it. While the struggle to understand legal reasoning on your own may be a valuable learning experience, it may also lead you down a road to poor grades, so protect yourself.

their readings, and don't try to make sense of it all until the end of the semester. And this is the reason that first-year law school grades frequently come as such a shock to so many students.

It's often said that after the first semester of law school, 90% of people are disappointed with their grades. While this is derived from the law school maxim that everyone wants to be in the top 10% of their class,[118] there is more truth in the statement than most would admit – no matter what school you're attending. A good part of the disappointment results from a testing practice nearly unique to law schools – the single-semester test.

At most law schools, students never get a second chance to redeem themselves after poor mid-term showings. There are no mid-terms. With the exception of your legal writing class, where you submit papers, you get a total of one exam per class, and all of the exams will be given over a two-week span with only days separating them. The pressures to perform well on these exams are immense. And during the first semester, almost no one knows exactly what they're supposed to be doing to prepare for the exams. There's so much material that it initially seems impossible to read it all, let alone organize it in your mind in time for an exam.

The trick to success, again, is paced over-preparedness. Keeping up with daily class assignments is one part of the process. Some students find that reading several days ahead of the material gives them the perspective they need in order to understand the broader concepts of specific class assignments. Others focus entirely on one day's reading and attempt to connect that reading, logically and somehow on paper, with what came before. A few others are willing to actually read more – namely treatises or commercial outlines – to get an outside perspective on how to organize the information as experts have been doing it for decades or centuries. At some point in the semester, you'll even be ready to develop your own outlines based on the course materials.[119]

Another part of the process is the review of past exam questions. Many law schools make publicly available most if not all of the past essay exam questions written by past and current professors. But they don't give you the answers; professors occasionally, but not frequently, offer one or two sample answers to

---

[118] A friend helpfully suggests that incoming law students should set their goals early in the process: decide up front that you're aiming to be a top performer or let yourself realize early on that your grades don't matter. The sting of failing to make the top ten percent, she says, is much more bearable when you decide going in that it's not meant to be. It's easier, she says, to perform well when you make the conscious decision to do whatever it takes to do well. My own opinion is that, even given the choice, many people would choose top performer status and wind up disappointed anyway – perhaps even more so because they gave the choice serious consideration and then met with an unexpected result, rather than not thinking about it and letting the chips fall where they may.

[119] See Section Q, and for examples, Appendix D.

selected classes, but rarely if ever publish then. Essay question books for twenty or more years were on file at Cornell when I graduated.[120] Multiple-choice and short-answer questions typically were never published.

At a minimum, the essay questions give you an opportunity to understand the scope of what you must be able to speak to on the exam. At a maximum, a professor may harken back to the same or a highly similar theme in a question on your exam. It's generally true that only so many different types of questions can be asked about subject matter that stays pretty much the same from year to year, so studying one year's questions might well prepare you for the next year's exam. It bears mention that your first look at the questions may well intimidate you. They're often designed to do that. Better to be intimidated weeks before your final exam than during it.

As you probably see by this point, for students who hope to succeed early in law school, there is a lot of studying going on: class books, supplementary texts, and old tests. Groups form to discuss class materials, with varying degrees of success based on their membership and their structures; readers who prefer solitude should note that there was no correlation between success and participation in study groups. Groups proved helpful for some people, but just as many people studied alone, or dropped out of them and then studied alone.

At some point during the first year, the average struggling, tired and stressed-out law student has an epiphany of sorts. It's mostly a point of confidence with the materials that stems from knowing that the workload isn't getting worse, your schedule has finally become manageable, you are seeing at least a little in advance where class discussions are heading, and you are no longer especially fearful of being called upon. If confidence does not fully capture the concept, the other part is intellectual sobriety, essentially the ability to admit to yourself what you truly know and what you don't, and to be able to review materials in a manner which truly creates new understanding.

Obviously, the earlier the epiphany happens, the better it is for one's grades, and for some people, the epiphany doesn't happen for a while or happen at all. Not every student can earn A's in all of their classes, and in fact, very few do. Many people hear that they will have an epiphany and keep on waiting for it to happen by watching for it to just appear one day. Trust me when I tell you that it will happen, but like water coming to a boil, it won't start when you are watching it. Follow the instructions and it will just happen.

---

[120] For a more or less typical sample of law school exams, you can see examples of previous Duke Law School essays on the Duke web site at http://www.law.duke.edu/curriculum/e_reserveExamsFrame.html.

K.   THE FUN OF IT

I've spent a lot of time talking about the harder moments of the first year, but there is some very good news to share: even with all of law school's tough days and hard work, there is plenty to enjoy about the classes, too.

First, you're bound to meet some great people. Though it will depend somewhat on the school you attend, many of your classmates can and will be fascinating, charming, and amusing – if you get to know them. Once in a while, a student will find a non-obnoxious way to make an entire classroom full of people – including the professor – laugh very hard. This happened early in our Contracts class when the professor cold-called a student on a trivial $5,000 dispute between parties: "Mr. Berkowski, what sort of damages would *you* seek if *you* were the lawyer in this case?" Without missing a beat, our classmate over-aggressively responded, "three million dollars." The words "why not?" were unnecessary; the answer had the class roaring as the professor, staggered and laughing, attempted to force a straight face and ask why.

There are also impressive moments where you get to see your classmates' minds working, and working well. People respect and enjoy hearing others who manage, without being obnoxious, to clearly answer questions. This tends not to apply as much to those who persistently raise their hands to volunteer, or wait for others to apparently make mistakes before raising their hands to derisively "correct" their peers. The obnoxious intellectuals quickly become known as "gunners," a term used by students at many law schools to separate the bright and quiet people from the bright people who persistently gun for a professor's attention.[121] In my experience, the positive classroom experiences with people far outweighed the few negative ones caused by overly aggressive gunners, and though it is probably true that every school will have its jackasses, it's really a matter of how much you let them ruin your experience.

And most first-year students truly enjoy at least one of their first semester classes: torts, and for odd reasons. Professor Alighieri, like many Torts professors, found snide humor in cases that hadn't initially seemed quite as funny. You learn about people intentionally and negligently doing nasty things to each other. You hear about some of the most improbable circumstances in history that have led to injuries, and may well begin to find them funny, in a perverse way. And you get to see what some of America's greatest judicial

---

[121] There is a great deal of temptation in larger, more anonymous classes to relax, fall behind in readings, and enjoy the social dimensions of law school. In-class games such as "gunner bingo" are outgrowths of this temptation: groups of laid-back students draw up bingo boards ahead of class with the names of known gunners in the place of numbers, and the winner is the one who completes a bingo-style line of five names and immediately either asks or answers a question in class by including the word "bingo." But such games say as much about their players as the gunners.

minds did when confronted with these problems.

Some of the classic torts cases are known to virtually every American law student: the one about the Coke bottle that spontaneously exploded, injuring someone.[122] The one about the naughty little boy who pulled the chair out from under a woman, injuring her.[123] The one about the two turkey hunters who somehow managed to fire buckshot rounds at a man who turned out not to be a six-foot tall turkey, injuring him.[124] And the person who had a package of fireworks knocked out of his hands as he got on the subway, dropping the fireworks through the elevated tracks, exploding the fireworks, and thereby knocking over some construction materials and injuring someone a great distance away.[125] These cases, and others like them, form the foundations of American personal injury law.

There are occasions when you have the opportunity to truly savor beautifully written judicial prose – rare occasions, but occasions nevertheless. In *Palsgraf*, the fireworks case from above, Justice Benjamin Cardozo, widely regarded as among history's finest jurists, created a legal test today applied in most if not all personal injury cases: the so-called foreseeability test, a point at which someone cannot be held legally responsible for injuries caused only indirectly by their acts or omissions. In 1928, if a person could not have foreseen that by carrying fireworks in a wrapped package that the fireworks might fall, ignite, hit something, and make that something topple and injure another person, the American legal system would find it unfair to punish that person for dropping the fireworks. Cardozo wrote this 75 years ago, and as a result, the legal system was changed and improved – a powerful thought.

There are similar moments of inspiration for many people in Constitutional Law. While Con Law classes vary in content from school to school, and even from professor to professor, much of the subject matter is technical and less inspiring than one might initially expect. You learn about the power of judges to decide what legislatures' laws are supposed to mean, the conflicts between branches, and Congressional power to regulate virtually everything in the country through crafty use of the Constitution's Commerce Clause. But there are also some beautiful and intellectually stimulating decisions in Con Law speaking to the redress of racial and gender grievances, religious rights and freedoms of speech and privacy.

And when you first come across judicial opinions that are interesting to read, and recognize just how important they later became, you begin to appreciate the human dimension of the law. Laws are words initially written by

---

[122] Escola v. Coca Cola Bottling Co., 150 P.2d 436 (1944).
[123] Garrett v. Dailey, 279 P.2d 1091 (1955).
[124] Summers v. Tice, 199 P.2d 1 (1948).
[125] Palsgraf v. Long Island R.R., 162 N.E. 99 (1928).

legislatures – human beings who sometimes don't fully think about what they say or how they said it. With the aid of lawyers, judges interpret the words of laws and give them deeper meaning, reconciling new laws with values from our common American heritage and notions of justice. Average citizens – including elected legislators and those who work for legal change – can play an important part in making good laws. Lawyers have even more potential to do so. And the realization that modern law is a human creation, made better when participants agree on the meaning of words, is something that makes the first year's struggles to learn the language of law so much more bearable.[126]

L. AN APOLITICAL ENVIRONMENT

Despite their common roots, the differences between law-making and politics were the real foci of my first semester. When I arrived at law school, I fully expected that I would continue the sorts of politically-charged discussions I'd had with undergraduate friends. Though I'm sure this differs dramatically from school to school, and from year to year, I was startled that my classmates were as seemingly apolitical as they come. Only a few people ventured opinions regarding the then-current Lewinsky affair or the impeachment of President Clinton. Most expressed little interest, including professors: clearly, law school is not just a place for political science and government majors. A fair summary of the attitude was that, regardless of one's personal beliefs about the behavior of individuals, the laws remain the same and continue to be enforced. Classes in Constitutional Law and the like weren't about to change, or even stop for more than a brief joke, just because of the news.

This came as a surprise to me on two levels. Much of my pre-law training suggested a strong interconnectedness between law and politics, though as I came to learn, the tie is not as direct as one might think.[127] Also, the events of the Clinton saga, especially the impeachment, seemed so ripe for legal discussion inside or outside of the classroom that I couldn't believe that they'd be entirely ignored. But with the rarest exceptions, most students and professors remained relatively quiet about their political beliefs or agendas throughout the first year. To reiterate a point made earlier, politics had almost nothing to do with my initial law school experience.

You may well have a different experience, and this is not to say that it's impossible even in a relatively apolitical environment to find people who care

---

[126] Some will even enjoy learning new legal terms regardless of the circumstances; first-year students are routinely exposed to odd terms such as stevedore, boilerplate, Blackacre, springgun, *actus reus*, and *mens rea*, sometimes just for a professor's kicks, and other times as initial exposure to critical legal concepts.

[127] Only 24 of America's 43 Presidents were lawyers, for example. The statistics become even more interesting for Congress and state governments.

about politics – it's just not what the formal law school experience is all about. In law school, people often become focused upon specific hot-button issues rather than party politics: the death penalty, civil rights and racial issues, women's rights, domestic abuse and child abuse are modern, perennial law school topics that generate enough interest to create student organizations.[128] While these subjects are tackled largely in extracurricular settings, students may have opportunities to tackle one or two such issues in their legal writing courses – not at their election, but at the instructor's.

M. LEGAL METHODS

Unless one of your first-year professors is willing to raise political issues in class – and that class, if any, would probably be Constitutional Law – your only chance to tackle pressing social issues during first-semester class time will be in the context of your legal writing program. Janice Crosby, our legal writing instructor, had a special interest in juvenile justice, and chose the issue of battered child syndrome as a launching point to teach us how to properly write court documents, in this case dealing with an accused teenage murderer.

The corollary to my earlier point about the writing of Benjamin Cardozo is how few judges or lawyers, past or present, could write with the elegance he employed. Legal writing has often been condemned as abysmal, and rightfully so. Documents prepared for and by courts are often unnecessarily difficult to read, and poorly edited. In the past, lawyers were never required to learn how to write well, and many substituted flourish for substance.

Legal writing programs are the present solution to this problem. They consist of instruction in several key areas: tightening of writing style, elimination of jargon in favor of Plain English, and universalization of document creation formats. These premises sound technical, but they're easy to understand.

A good legal writing program attempts to take all comers and churn out future lawyers universally capable of being understood easily by their superiors. Law students come from all sorts of undergraduate majors and schools, some of which have cultivated or tolerated flowery, superfluously long writing styles, and others that have barely taught their students how to write at all. This is not to say that law schools accept illiterates, but that some undergraduate schools and majors place less emphasis than others on creating effective written communicators. It's equally clear that undergraduate Math majors and English majors will, most likely, approach the same writing task from very different

---

[128] One exception to this general trend is the Federalist Society, an organization that exists at numerous law schools and self-identifies as conservative and libertarian across a wide variety of political issues. Another is the presence of ethnic and religious student organizations, which exist not so much for political reasons as social networking ones.

angles, and achieve very different results.[129]

A legal writing program tries to take those who waste space with cluttered or repetitive ideas and force them to edit the same thoughts down to a reasonable page limit and clear organizational structure. No attorney wants to sift through a junior lawyer's 100-page brief for the answer to a simple legal issue, and even though some judges like to write a lot, very few like to read a lot. At the same time, the class also tries to teach conclusory, overly abbreviated writers to avoid presenting instant final answers without explaining reasoning.

Elimination of legal jargon is another typical aim of a legal writing program. For centuries, American legal documents have been filled with "boilerplate," worn-out phrases and odd Latin and Law French words that judges – and perhaps more importantly, clients – had problems interpreting. Legislatures and courts have been promoting and in some cases mandating Plain or Clear English writing, essentially turning away submitted documents that were not clear by their own terms. Legal writing courses attempt to drive out the law student's tendency to include an *ipso facto* where a clearer English phrase would be more readily understandable.

Finally, the typical legal writing program tries to teach students what sorts of document formats are commonly in use in law firms, and state and federal courts, and how generally to prepare them. In learning how to write a 'statement of facts,' for example, you learn which *facts* adverse to your client a lawyer must, as an officer of the court, disclose anyway. You also learn what *laws* adverse to your client you must disclose anyway when rendering a legal analysis. And you learn how and when to write persuasively or objectively, as situations demand specific styles: when you argue for your client, you are typically persuasive, but when you speak to your client, you are objective.

Another major part of document format universalization is the teaching of proper citation, briefly discussed earlier. Citation is the method by which a lawyer backs up her words – by pointing to other published sources that have said the same things she's saying now. You 'cite' to a source by stating a proposition espoused by that source and then placing a tag on the statement

---

[129] Ironically, the math major tends to be at an advantage in legal writing, because legal writing is often formulaic. While it is not necessary to master the syllogisms favored by Supreme Court Justice Antonin Scalia, legal writing is all about creating structured, persuasive, logical arguments. Understanding the power of syllogisms as logical tools helps one to succeed in legal writing. Many English majors do have one advantage that manifests itself when they are asked to work with the facts of a case. Math majors see the facts as black and white. English majors often find it easier to see the shades of gray. Legal writing is both an exercise in discussing the law, and then applying that law to the facts of a real or imaginary situation. You win if you can make your facts fit the law, and English majors with creative writing experience tend to be better at finding tricky ways to make the ambiguities in the facts work out in their favor.

that tells other lawyers where to find the source and verify it. Unless you've gotten an early start on the process, a legal writing class will likely be your first official exposure to the so-called BLUEBOOK that explains all the 'right' ways to cite different materials, and thus becomes a reasonably important part of any lawyer's life. The BLUEBOOK is so named because it uses blue-colored paper stock as a cover. It is not by any means the most exciting tool in a lawyer's arsenal; as mentioned earlier, it attempts to harmonize what otherwise would be various methods of document citation used by lawyers and law students in court documents and journal articles.[130] Legal writing courses typically introduce you to the BLUEBOOK, explain its importance, and leave real mastery for others, including law journals, to teach you.[131] It bears mention that those who begin to really follow the BLUEBOOK's standards early in their legal educations are at a distinct advantage in ways to be explained later.

I go into detail about the legal writing program for several reasons. First, it's the only first-year class where you have any meaningful control over your grade. You typically get to draft and re-draft documents based on objective evaluations of your writing performed by your instructor. You can practice Bluebooking. You can talk with your instructor and learn how to improve your work. And you can ask for pointers when you continue to make mistakes.

Secondly, it's an increasingly important part of legal education. Lessons you pick up in Legal Methods are the ones lawyers rely upon most every day, as many practitioners attest. Legal writing programs expose you to online legal research tools such as Lexis and Westlaw, and help you learn how to walk into any massive law library and quickly locate what you're looking for.

Third and finally, despite all of a legal writing program's assets, it can be a major, major pain in the ass. Especially with a legal writing program in transition, as ours was when I started law school, the deadlines for paper submissions can conflict dramatically with your other class assignments. A big paper deadline may prevent you from participating in an optional, important extracurricular activity such as Moot Court, or stress you until the wee hours of an otherwise unremarkable night. A lot will depend on the quality of your instructor, the support your school gives to its legal writing program, and the quantity of work you are given.

It is because of the legal writing program alone that I have a personally untested pre-law school recommendation that may be of some benefit to others – it's something I've heard about but did not do myself, because I didn't know about it early enough. People who came to law school after working as

---

[130] Notably, the Association of Legal Writing Directors (ALWD) has a competing and similar citation standard, which you can view at http://www.alwd.org, and every state's court system has its own unique rules for citation, which rules you will likely learn (if necessary) while working at a law firm in a given state.

[131] See Chapter 5, Sections A and K.

paralegals tended to do better in legal writing classes, and sometimes law school overall, perhaps because their paralegal work exposed them to concepts and responsibilities strongly similar to those involved in these courses. Paralegals see firsthand how lawyers reason, research, and write. If you're looking for the maximum chance to excel in law school, especially writing courses, paralegal work at a decent firm can be key to later benefits.

Having said that, I don't think paralegal work is for everyone. You should explore it thoroughly before considering it as a pre-law school preparatory option, and recognize that it's truly a 'low man on the totem pole' field of employment with plenty of potential for discouraging experiences. Stories of abused paralegals are numerous across many law firms, and in truth, few law students were paralegals first. But if you still love the law after being a paralegal, and still apply to and attend a law school, you may well wind up in a better position, grade-wise, for having done it. Few things are better preparation for your legal writing course.

N. THE DAILY ROUTINE – A JEALOUS MISTRESS

Even with the uncertainties of legal writing paper deadlines, a law student eventually develops a daily routine to cope with the workload, and a weekly calendar of sorts which has a predictable hump at some point to get over. My first and second semester humps were on Wednesday and Tuesday, respectively, days when I had four or five classes in a row and thus had to spend an abnormally huge amount of time preparing the day in advance. A Wednesday hump therefore was a two-day stretch – a normal day of classes with one especially heavy night of reading, followed by an especially long day of classes with a normal night of reading.

As a first-year student, I gave up at least a good part of one day each weekend. At some point, I found it necessary and useful to declare either Saturday or Sunday a work-free day, and therefore to spend the other day finishing reading for Monday. Generally, Saturday was a better rest day than Sunday, but if I waited until Sunday, I thought about work all day Saturday.

This was my reality in the first year of law school, and I think it's a very common one.[132] Law students have many, many sleepless nights – or at least nights with four or five hours of sleep. There were infrequent, but memorable nights when my dreams were consumed by the readings I had finished. It was very uncomfortably close to a complete consumption of my being. Many people I knew had similar experiences, both in terms of the sleeplessness and

---

[132] Everybody imagines before law school that they might find a way around this lifestyle, but very few people succeed – those who do typically have written off part of the law school experience.

the dreams. It may well not be universal, and I'm sure it's not as much of a problem for those who have little concern for their grades, but in the early stages of law school, virtually everyone has such concern.[133]

The stresses of the first year are all but impossible for outsiders – including family and friends – to truly understand. My experience was made somewhat easier because I was blessed with understanding parents and friends who understood that I was serious when I told them that I'd heard that I might not be able to communicate with them much, if at all, for the better part of a year. They understood when I felt that I had to miss driving home (six precious hours there and back) during our short Thanksgiving break because I had to work on class outlines, something that later turned out to be a wise choice.[134] Though time crunches become less of a reality once you master your schedule, true mastery may well not come for eight months. I feel as if I only achieved a true comfort level after around that much time.

My lunch and dinner breaks, roughly an hour a piece, sometimes a little more, were just about the only time I spent during the work week away from law books. Some people set aside an hour per two days for limited exercise or other small activities. Inevitably, my daily breaks were spent with law student friends, and conversation would often focus on law or class experiences, occasionally departing from those themes entirely. For us, the law had taken over much of our lives. It gave meaning to yet another famed legal maxim: law is a jealous mistress. Especially at the first year, but continuing on, by the traditions of the profession at least, through your career, legal research takes you from your family and incites pangs of guilt when you're not fully prepared. Over time, it transforms the way you talk, dominates your conversations with friends, and distances you temporarily from those you loved before.

I acknowledge up front that there are a minority of people who might disagree with my characterization of the first-year experience as this engrossing. Some went to less demanding schools. Certainly there is another fraction of the population that can expend considerably less effort than the rest of the

---

[133] This gets back to the earlier recommendation about trying to choose in advance what sort of law student you want to be – a top-10% student or just a graduate. It's hard to really decide until you see the workload first-hand. And rumors of workloads at certain law schools may well influence your choice of where to go, as well.

[134] The prospect of getting sick later in the semester is but one reason to be highly prepared for final exams by the end of Thanksgiving break. Because this holiday comes at just the right time in the semester, enough first-years will be working straight through it that schools typically hold their own Thanksgiving dinners for those stuck in town. If your first semester ends right before Christmas, a good goal is to have two of your four outlines complete – up to the most recent class – by the end of the break.

population and achieve comparable, and in some cases superior results.[135] And finally, there is a fraction that had little concern for the quality of their results, and therefore would never expend so much effort in any educational setting, let alone when studying the law.

Take this as you will, but for better or worse, they're not writing this book, and if they were, and had offered you the advice to spend your first year of law school relaxing rather than working hard and often, I could virtually guarantee you that you would utterly waste your first year. Moreover, for every tale you may hear of a law student who screwed around, there are far more people who quietly toiled and developed into excellent professionals. From my perspective, if you're looking to get a job as an attorney, you want to be a toiler in your first year, not a statistic, but that's ultimately your choice to make.

O.   WHAT OF LOVE AND FAMILIES?

This is not to say that devoting yourself to legal studies is a choice without consequences. It has the strong potential to seriously impact relationships, especially those being conducted across long distances. And this issue – the relationship question – is amongst the items that aroused the most interest amongst law students I consulted regarding this book.

It's probably impossible to estimate how many people come to law school in the throes of a relationship of some sort or another. It tends to be more likely than when you arrived as a first-year undergraduate, just because law school comes later in your life. But it's not likely to be really late in one's life. Comparatively few people are married, and though I will devote some words to that subject, their situations vary dramatically from those who are either engaged or in other stages of what I'll call not-legally-recognized relationships.

One of the earliest things that happened during my first year was something that unexpectedly wrinkled many first-year men's brows. Understanding that "fresh meat" had entered the marketplace, second and third year students organized early semester parties which were, not surprisingly, opportunities to check out the new women who had come to the law school. All of my male classmates had quickly noticed the fact that we had a significant number of attractive women in our first-year class. Some had made aggressive moves to get involved with the 'available' girls. Within several days of the end of the orientation week, the second- and third-year guys were already sizing up their new opportunities. And so, to a much lesser and less conspicuous extent, were many of the second- and third-year women, who were tired of the guys they'd known for at least the previous year.

---

[135] In my experience, most of these people still spent a lot of time in the library studying, but they just denied it later.

First-year women came to these events with different perspectives. In a past era, the half-serious joke was that women would attend graduate schools to earn their "M.R.S." degrees, namely not for the academia but for the prospect of meeting eligible bachelors. Regardless of whether this could be true in other graduate schools, this is not the case in today's law schools, and the mere suggestion rightfully offends many women. As a sweeping but accurate generalization, female law students arrive interested in studying and eventually practicing law, and many are more focused than their male colleagues. Some arrive so driven to succeed that even dating during the first year seems out of the question, and beyond just personal drive and raw intellectual ability to succeed, many women have commented that men in law school make for slim pickings – there aren't enough guys worth the trouble of getting involved.

But every person is different and many people do, in fact, date during their first year of law school. It can fairly be said that the seeds of numerous long-distance relationship breakups were sown in the very first few weeks of each new year of law school.[136] It was a cycle I would see repeated again and again, though from different vantage points in my first and second years. Some of this was a result of the inherent instability of the relationships prior to those points, and some were a result of combinations of alcohol, stress, and very aggressive maneuvering between effortlessly charming and charmed people.

A refrain heard with great frequency in the first few weeks was that the most attractive and interesting women in our class already had boyfriends when they arrived. Few had fiancées. With only the rarest exception, each of these relationships was in some way dramatically interfered with during the first year of law school, owing at least in part to its long-distance nature. Most of these women wound up either breaking up with their long-distance boyfriends or indiscreetly cheating on them from a distance. Some became involved with other first-year students – in the case of breakups, this was largely confined to the dormers, those who most wanted to meet other people. Others became involved with second- and third-year students. Rarely, if ever, would someone break up with a long-distance lover for another random graduate student.

A good part of this was just the proximity. A law student is surrounded constantly by other law students. Part of it was the functionalist issue – some people just arrived at law school ready or willing to 'trade up' to something 'better.' Another part of it is the commonality of experience. Only a fellow law student can truly understand what you are going through every day, and it takes a very strong and very sympathetic non-lawyer significant other to stand by you when they can't begin to know how demanding your studies actually are.

---

[136] At Cornell, virtually every non-marital relationship that a first-year arrived with was a long-distance relationship. Your mileage will vary based on the city you choose for law school and how close it is to your significant other.

Complicating matters for those attempting to plan around a nasty breakup is a corollary to the proximity issue: being close does not necessary make things better, though it more frequently helps than hurts, at least in staving off local competitors. Being close doesn't mean visiting sometimes. It tends to mean either living together or being there every weekend. The problem is that, no matter where the people may be living, the couple will simply not have as much time to spend together as they did before, and no amount of love or determination can make the first-year schedule more controllable. The schedule is supposed to be overwhelming. A relationship only enhances that feeling, and the lover sometimes becomes the unwitting sponge for frustration created by the law school.

Marriages are the bright spot in this discussion. Though they were unquestionably temporarily strained, marriages typically survived the process unscathed, and the first year's stress level was the worst that it ever became. Married folks were never the targets of sexual predators and typically avoided the dorms and parties, the places where most of the juicy stuff took place. A spouse who wanted to stay out of the dating pool did so without any interference. Marriage tended to dictate some of the professional choices people eventually made, but it did not impair their ability to excel in classes.[137]

Such was not the case with engaged people, however. This was, for me, the single most disquieting component of a hugely disturbing set of otherwise predictable behaviors – though it can be assumed that men will hit on women and vice-versa, and that some people will inevitably break up with boyfriends or girlfriends no matter what the dating pool is like at school, I was amazed at the casualness with which people treated marital engagements. Call me old-fashioned. An engagement ring was not only not a bar to sexual advances from one's fellow law students, but also apparently did not prevent some people from accepting those advances. Wild stories spread of engaged people who cheated on their soon-to-be-spouses, in some cases ending the engagements, and in others, never revealing the infidelity and getting married anyway. Again,

---

[137] Single mothers and women with small children frequently took on tasks that would have challenged even people without such significant outside obligations. One classmate was pregnant throughout the first semester, gave birth during final exams, and brought the child to classes several times during second semester – though following her example is probably not the easiest way to spend one's first year of law school, she proved that it could, in fact, be done. Another classmate, a single mother with a young child, ran for and won elective office in a high-profile student organization with five-day-per-week responsibilities, and did an outstanding job in her position; still another classmate on rare occasion brought her young son to classes when day care didn't work out, and even the professor didn't mind – her son behaved wonderfully and stayed quiet. In my experience, there were no examples of parents who took on additional work and failed, however, not many parents were willing to take on the extra work.

proximity did not necessarily help here: one person was rumored to be living with her fiancé at night while dating a classmate during the days.

The gloomy portion of this section at a close, a few of the brighter spots of love, first-year style, deserve some attention, as well. Many people met their future spouses, bridesmaids and best men during the first year of law school. Some of the longest-lasting relationships were those that started during the first year. And those couples who mutually wanted to remain committed universally succeeded in remaining so. The only question was whether grades would or could suffer as a result of keeping a relationship together under very different circumstances from how it had started.

And for those who aren't so interested in the love dimension of the equation, plenty of people found that there was plenty of sex to be had during the first year, too. The stresses of law school lead to plenty of opportunities for random 'hook-ups,' drunken debauchery and weird opportunities for coupling. There were stories left somewhat unverified of late-night trysts in secluded parts of the library, private study rooms, and a scene at a gorge next to the law school that would have made even former President Clinton smile. The first year does some freaky things to people sometimes.

Though hooking up and short-term relationships are matters of personal preference and choice, the dark side of casual involvement with classmates is the reputation factor. No matter what you're actually doing in your spare time, there's a likelihood – magnified in smaller schools, but present at even larger ones – that other people will know about it, or some twisted version of it. Personal reputations matter, both in law school and in the careers that follow, and the person you treat with respect or disrespect may well be a person who is later randomly asked to evaluate your eligibility for an award or possibly a job. Karma is alive and well in the practice of law, though it often operates in mysterious ways.

P.   EXTRACURRICULAR ACTIVITIES

With all that's been said already on the demands of the first-year schedule, one might assume at this point that there's no time to engage in extra-curricular activities. To some extent, that's true. Finding other things to do within the confines of a law school's walls is typically not the first thing on the mind of a person with five hours of reading left to do after classes every night. However, some law students – and perhaps especially the typical, type A-personality (workaholic) students, thrive on never-ending social and working lifestyles. Some even find extracurricular activities a relaxing break from the formal, structured demands of classes.

Most law school student organizations do not expect heavy first-year membership, and in my experience, few made recruiting pitches early in the first semester – they knew their pleas would fall on deaf ears. But most organizations welcomed first-year participation when they could get it, and first-year students who became involved were often front-runners for leadership positions in those organizations during their second- and third-years.

The typical student organizations you remember from undergraduate institutions generally appear in law schools, too: Cornell had a collection of ethnic, religious and cultural organizations ranging from the Asian American Law Students Association (AALSA) to the Latino American Law Students Association (LALSA), and interest group organizations such as the Briggs Society of International Law, the Environmental Law Society, the Federalist Society, the Science and Law Student Association, and the Women's Law Coalition.

Each of the aforementioned organizations typically drew a handful of first-year members. Some organizations are, by their organizational purposes and charters, closed to first-year students: these are typically limited to so-called law reviews and journals, special student-run legal publications with traditionally competitive membership policies. At Cornell, the *Cornell Law Review* was the oldest student journal at the school, followed by the Cornell *International Law Journal*, the *Cornell Journal of Law and Public Policy*, and the *Legal Information Institute Bulletin*. First-year students who enjoy writing therefore typically either joined the student newspaper, which at Cornell was titled the *Cornell Law Tower*, or the faculty and alumni periodical, the *Cornell Law Forum*. Few, if any first-year students considered starting their own organizations during this time.

One other major student organization tends to vary somewhat from school to school: Moot Court. At Cornell, Moot Court is a student-run, entirely optional organization which enables interested students to participate in a competitive series of mock trials against other students. The trials at Cornell were, at their earliest stages, judged by upper-classmen, then by faculty, and in the very final round, by a panel of three visiting federal judges – typically respected appellate court judges who acted out the role of the U.S. Supreme Court for purposes of the contest.[138] Second- and third-year students write the factual scenarios and legal issues to be tried. First-, second- and third-year students participate in the competitions, some of which are solo, while others let students set up two-person teams. The victors win modest cash prizes and considerable bragging rights; Moot Court champions receive school-wide acclaim and special attention from law firms. Moot Court also offers opportunities to travel to external competitions, the locations of which can be quite exciting. Notably, some schools mandate universal first-year student participation in Moot Court, or at least a single competition; Cornell does not do this, but has its own

---

[138] Other schools' moot courts engage a larger number of actual sitting judges; Ithaca happens to be somewhat further from large courts than other cities.

separate similar system of encouraging oral advocacy.[139]

The temptation to involve oneself in student organizations is tremendous for many law students: if nothing else, the supposed resume-enhancing benefits of membership are incentive enough to consider involvement. Apart from the functionalist approach, many law students were overachievers in college and just loved to be involved in as many student organizations as possible; slowing down now seems hard to consider.

In reality, however, those reviewing legal resumes – unlike those who read your undergraduate materials at law school application time – may not focus much on your extracurricular activities unless you're in one of two types of organizations: a student-run law journal or Moot Court. If your undergraduate life was divided amongst every optional organization under the sun, now's the right time to stop – your resume will draw more skepticism than admiration when hiring time comes around. My personal advice would be to stick to those groups that both truly interest you and merit the loss of your precious free time. Though it varied from person to person, not a single interviewer ultimately asked me about my membership on the *Tower*, or my work with other student groups. But on the other hand, consider that there is definitely functionalist value in networking within these organizations with like-minded people – it's a good thing to have friends – and some people find that these parts of their resumes are conversation pieces when other parts look anemic.

I've left out only one type of student organization here, and that's student government – at Cornell, we had the Cornell Law Students Association (CLSA). Not to trivialize student governments, but like other non-journal and non-Moot Court organizations, their value is dramatically reduced in the legal profession from its already questionable value to undergraduates: people run for positions, including slots to represent their class before the law school faculty or all law school students before the university's faculty, but they tend to have few responsibilities and very little impact. More so than as undergraduates, people frequently don't even bother to vote in the elections at all.

The reasons for this are numerous, but boiled down to a snippy little reality: everyone knows that these elections were just popularity contests when they were high schoolers and undergraduates, and as graduate students, few really care who plans officially-sponsored law school parties or represents student interests to the faculty. At Cornell, at least, the faculty was known to more or less ignore student concerns, and no representative was going to change that.[140] Those who did vote in these elections tended to do so as

---

[139] This system, the winter Legal Methods program, mandated oral argument and legal brief writing in the relatively smaller confines of a classroom.

[140] To engage in a gross generalization that turns out to be largely true, law school faculties are notoriously unresponsive to student concerns, owing typically to a conservative, traditionalist approach deemed "wise" by senior lawyers – if it's not grossly broke, don't

negative votes to keep aggravating people out of offices, rather than elect especially interesting people to those offices.[141] Representative positions will differ in importance from school to school, but my personal conclusion is that they're not the best way to use one's free time as a law student.

Q. PREPARING FOR FIRST YEAR, FIRST SEMESTER EXAMS: OUTLINES AND THE CLOSE OF CLASSES

In law school, grades take on an immediate importance unlike those of any other graduate or undergraduate experience you've had. You have one exam per class. No papers. No mid-term. Only a modest chance of class participation influencing your grade. And therefore one test, taken on one day, determines your entire score for an entire semester.

Of the four non-paper classes in my first semester, each seemed like it was roughly equally likely to have a difficult final exam. If any class seemed masterable, Torts was it. With a friendly professor and interesting material, that class seemed a likely "A" for a dedicated student... but then, many people thought that it would be their best exam, a mix of overconfident and appropriately confident people. The exam was set to have a mix of multiple choice and essay questions, the former a rarity in law school. But both our Torts professor and Contracts professor had reputations for very thorough tests. Contracts had a similar format to Torts, but would not test on material that stuck quite so naturally in the brain.

Con Law and Civ Pro seemed set to be the nightmares of the semester. Rather than a three- or four-hour long in-class exam, our Con Law professor decided to give us a full-day take-home exam that had to be typed and submitted in person on time. Though the class wasn't impossible, it seemed hard to guess what we would be tested on, or how. And Civ Pro had always been the worst of the bunch in every way; our professor had a reputation for

waste time thinking about fixing it. This sort of mentality, perhaps pioneered by the faculty of Harvard Law School, has been mimicked by law faculties elsewhere in the country, to universal detriment; Harvard's unresponsive administration ultimately found itself ranked worst in the country in National Jurist and Princeton Review surveys, and was finally forced to change some of its unpopular policies. See Seth Stern, *Harvard Law Changes the Pace of its Paper Chase*, CHRISTIAN SCIENCE MONITOR, October 24, 2000, available at http://www.csmonitor.com/durable/2000/10/24/fp13s1-csm.shtml. Regardless, few law students believe or care that one of their classmates might be the next great student leader, and some students even actively oppose activist representation. As Harvard weathered decades of complaints from students without change, some believe that activist students are wasting their time. At Cornell, student government was the last remaining candle for those who thought political campaigning had a bright future in the legal profession.

[141] The great irony is that students often looked down on people who tried too hard to win office, so enthusiasm was actually seen as detrimental to one's chances as a candidate.

terrible, long essay exams that touched upon many major points from class. And I personally didn't even have all of the most notoriously difficult professors. One or two were reputed to test on material far outside of class discussions, but typically, only material from class discussions and readings were fair game.

For better or worse, law firms and student journals consider your initial grades despite the incredibly awkward first-year testing procedures, the incredible performance pressures, and whatever other personal stresses and experiences you might be having during exam time. The only relief in sight is the promise of a vacation, albeit a short one, when exams have finished.[142] So you work your ass off until exams have ended, take a break, and then return for more punishment soon thereafter.

The unchanged first-year exam process historically has inspired enough fear to result in a bizarre phenomenon – many law schools now offer special lectures on how to take final exams,[143] along with a single simulated but short practice exam some weeks prior to the real thing.[144] Your actual professor grades the simulated exam. Scores are frequently very, very low; almost humorously so. Both the classes and the practice exam are optional, but attendance tends to be very high. Some people prepare hard for the practice test to see just how far preparation gets them. Some go in without preparation to see whether they can get away with what they did as undergraduates, something I was shocked to see people try again years later.[145] Very, very few who take the practice exam cold will repeat that experience for the real final exams, and those who do are typically people with photographic memories or another transcendent method of memorization. I personally found the practice exam useful; I prepared pretty well for it and received a better-than-average but still not stellar grade, which inspired me to prepare better for the real thing.

No one believes that the first-year examination and grading process is fair or good. Everyone acknowledges that it survives chiefly because of tradition and because a suitable replacement has not been demonstrated to be superior.

---

[142] The ABA's hour requirements force Cornell and other schools to have exceptionally short inter-semester breaks for first-year students, such that the first semester typically ends only days before Christmas and the second semester begins in early January.

[143] Some schools even offer optional courses in how to prepare outlines for final exams, frequently taught informally by upper-class students or legal writing professors. These classes are good, if time-consuming ways to learn some of the ways that successful students outline for examinations. But as different types of people succeed on exams through different methodologies, these sessions also inspire some people to follow techniques that won't work given their unique personal needs.

[144] As mentioned earlier, BAR/BRI also offers first-year review lectures, which despite their expense and huge inconvenience of fitting into your law school "free time" schedule, apparently really help people who sit in on them before or during law school.

[145] See Chapter 11, Section C.

The result, at many schools, has been the imposition of a two-step system for issuing grades and then blindly remedying procedural unfairness. That system is a uniform set of first-year exams administered to all of a school's first-year students on the same days with equal opportunities to study and prepare, and a grading curve that 'normalizes' the scores along a statistical Bell Curve – a formula which allots specific 'normal' numbers of A's, B's, C's, D's and F's based on certain statistical probabilities. Those professors who are inclined to fail 'too many' students are thus prevented from doing so, as are those who are inclined to acknowledge the A-caliber work of "too many" of their students.

At Cornell, the curve had been a 3.0 curve for many years, when students complained repeatedly that grade inflation at other schools was making a 3.3 student from elsewhere artificially appear superior to a 3.0 student at Cornell.[146] The law school faculty, in a rare recognition of market realities, adjusted the curve to a maximum 3.3 in response.[147] Thus a B+ is the statistical mean score that professors are supposed to aim for. Grading distributions are published twice annually so that scores can be reviewed. Most professors are widely known to give out huge numbers of B+ scores and only modest numbers of higher and lower grades. Others are more selective. Few, when confronted with specific questions as to how a grade was reached, can ever quantify the absolute distinction between an A- and a B+ exam: the most common refrain is that the curve is unfair and forces tough decisions to be made. And grades are very, very rarely changed.

A handful of schools have rejected the use of letter grades for first-year students, though other schools are not likely to follow. Among the alternative methodologies' proponents is Yale, which has moved to a "honors/pass/fail" system, but in the legal employment market's present reality, few other schools can meaningfully adopt this sort of system. The presumption is that every Yale graduate is all but guaranteed employment regardless of her or his grades, and therefore, if you're good enough to get in, you don't need to have great grades. Adopting such a system, however, can easily lead to a certain lack of motivation that many law schools and employers would find distressing.

Lacking grades can also lead to complications in the law journal selection process. Recruiting for student-run law journals typically depends, at least in

---

[146] Grade inflation has also been the norm, amazingly, with virtually every major school in the Ivy League save Cornell. A recent article in the Boston Globe stated that 90.8% of Harvard 2001 graduates, 51% of Yale graduates, 25% of Columbia graduates and 20% of Stanford graduates received honors at graduation. See Patrick Healy, *Harvard's Honors Fall to the Merely Average*, BOSTON GLOBE, October 8, 2001, at A1, available at http://www.boston.com/globe/metro/packages/harvard_honors/part2.htm.

[147] But notably, the "maximum 3.3" means that 3.3 is the highest an average should go, not a minimum. Professors are encouraged to hit around 3.3, but can go lower without fear of discipline.

part, on automatic or nearly automatic admission for students with grades in certain percentiles of their classes. The *Cornell Law Review*, for example, long employed a policy that automatically extended invitations to those whose first-year grades placed them in the top 10% of the class, a "grading on" policy that was only recently modified. Cornell's other two law journals traditionally automatically extended offers to people in the top 25% of their classes. Other schools have similar systems. The prestige of membership, in part, is derived from the continued selectivity of the organizations.

So grades and curves are here to stay, however imperfect, as is the first-year exam process. Exams begin shortly after the final classes of each subject. Cornell historically had a "reading period," a one-week break after classes to prepare for exams, but recently discontinued the practice. Though some people start earlier, most first-year students therefore spend four weeks prior to exams – generally starting at the latest by Thanksgiving, if exams are scheduled for mid-December – writing outlines. As explained briefly before, outlines are students' attempts to create cogent, compact understandings of massive amounts of course material in free-standing documents.[148]

Outlines are important because law professors generally do not structure material neatly; it's the student's job to read cases, learn from classes (and perhaps treatises), and then determine "the law" from what they've read and heard. If students can't figure it out alone – a completely normal circumstance, by the way – tables of contents from subject-specific treatises will provide the right structures, and students plug in-class case law into the structures.

How this works in practice is the following: you read three cases from three different states dealing with a specific issue of contract interpretation. All three cases are from approximately the same year, and all three contain the same type of facts, but come to completely different conclusions. In class, your professor will not say that any of the approaches are wrong. She'll briefly mention that one of the cases, decided in Iowa, tends to be the one used by most states when deciding this specific issue. Then she'll mention that the California approach is used by a significant, but lesser number of states. And that the New York approach, the oldest of the three, is no longer used, even by New York. The Iowa rule thus comes to appear in your notes as the "majority rule." The California rule is the "minority rule." And the New York rule is the "old rule," and "no longer good law."

Your outline is a skeleton based on majority rules, noting minority rules where they exist and making brief mention of outdated, traditional rules. Essay exams typically ask you to apply majority law unless otherwise requested, and

---

[148] If you begin with a structure suggested by a treatise – not your text book – and start to develop your outlines at the very beginning of the semester, you'll save yourself a lot of time and stress right before exams.

you'll only be otherwise requested when your instructor is tricky or when your law school is based in a state where a minority rule applies. You typically get extra points for mentioning the outdated rules and why they no longer apply, but only if you first mentioned the current correct rule(s) of law.

Outlines serve three purposes. First, they help students to build foundational understanding of more than just isolated laws – they create and reinforce the 'big picture' that truly is 'the law' you wanted to learn when you came to law school. Second, they give you a means by which to usefully compare your understanding of the law with that of others, including professionals and – if you're careful – other students.[149]

a typed outline with handwritten addenda; larger samples appear at Appendix D

The third point is most important. Many professors allow you to bring your outlines into exams – the so-called 'open book' exam format. Professors offer different types of open book exams, each based on a psychological theory. Some professors believe that, due to the incredible amount of class material that's been discussed, no amount of open-book knowledge is going to save you come exam time. You'll either know it or you won't know it, they think, so they'll allow you to bring whatever you desire, including commercially sold outlines and anything short of a computer. Others operate on a closely related

---

[149] Old outlines from past students tend to float around, serving as good and bad references for unsuspecting neophyte lawyers. Be careful when relying on someone else's outline, especially if it's someone you don't know and trust. On a related note, most professors allow you to work on outlines collaboratively with other classmates, in order to best understand the material come exam time. Generally, you'll probably learn the most by outlining each subject on your own, but if you want to work with other people, be confident in advance that they will not neglect their portions of the work.

but opposing assumption: since nothing is going to save you, you shouldn't be allowed to bring anything (closed-book), because you might just bring something that disadvantages other students; these professors typically cite the existence of commercial outlines and the wealth disparities of students as a primary reason to exclude materials. Some even go so far as to prevent students from bringing their textbooks, which presumably everybody owns.

Most professors take an approach in-between these extremes. Commercial outlines are prohibited, but any self-prepared documents are allowed. This can be a good thing, as commercial outlines typically contain something or another that your class did not, or outdated law now addressed properly in your class. Relying on a commercial outline is done at your peril. Your textbooks are permitted if not required in some way for the exam.

The number of closed-book exams actually given in my law school experience was tiny, and for good reason: a closed-book exam of any sort is an entirely unrealistic way to test any member of the legal profession,[150] and it can lead to incredible personal stresses for first-year law students.[151] Practicing lawyers always rely upon books when coming to conclusions. Any real lawyer who worked purely from memory would be sued for malpractice and sanctioned by any state bar – you must always look up the current state of the law before presenting an answer about it. Additionally, those gifted with photographic memories would be at a distinct, and truly unfair advantage. An outline provides a more or less fair playing field: everyone gets the same time to research and prepare a working document for use in the exam. When panic sets in, you have something outside of your malfunctioning brain to consult.

The length and nature of outlines varies from person to person; some people prepare 100-page typewritten outlines, whereas others use 15-page handwritten outlines.[152] Typically, those who wrote long outlines also created indexes and tables of contents of some sort or another. And after all of my experiences, I can tell you a little about what worked and didn't work for me.

---

[150] Only one professor gave a closed book exam during my first year, first semester: my Civil Procedure professor. Sadly, this was a subject where having an open book exam was almost necessary. Her reason for the closed-book exam: she had tried a limited, textbook-only open-book exam and had believed that people had made notes in the margins of their textbooks. Regardless of the motivations, preparations for that closed-book exam were especially hard.

[151] Especially during the first semester, first-year students have almost no idea what to expect from a law school exam – no amount of reassurance will make the average first-year think that he or she has read and memorized enough. Forcing closed-book exams upon first-year students invites people to make excessive attempts to memorize details of questionable importance, and the result is that many people become either atypically anti-social or temporarily downright bizarre during exam season.

[152] While it can vary from class to class, my rough estimate is four to five pages per credit hour at a minimum, 35 pages per credit hour, maximum.

Keep in mind the fact that I'm a writer, and don't mind writing long, book-like documents. You're reading one right now, and I wrote this on my vacation. And I'm telling you that I think that huge outlines are next to worthless for exam-taking purposes. The longer they are, the worse they are. It's the exact reason that so many professors permit unlimited open-book exams; the average freaked-out law student in the first semester brings five or seven books in, including commercial outlines, treatises, friends' outlines, his or her own outlines, and textbooks. Commercial outlines and treatises can be outdated or incorrect. A textbook may well not explain the lesson you were supposed to have gathered from class discussion. By the time a three-hour exam has ended, none of the books has helped and you've spent all of your time flipping pages instead of writing. And only writing gets you points.

In my experience, a good outline has gone through three stages. The first is the initial authorship – a bit long, rough, and inaccurate. You go through this stage as much to really learn and understand the material as to create something to use later. The second stage is verification and simplification, cutting the size down and finding mistakes. Here you've building your recollection up and also fixing the errors you inevitably made, cross-checking your own outline against a commercial outline to see who's right and why. The third stage is the digest and table of contents stage, where you get at least a decent sense of where everything is located and create a simple road map for exam-time reference. This stage may lead you instead to create a shorter outline that you bring in to the exam; such is not always a great use of your time but it depends on your personal comfort level with the materials.

Regardless of the format you use, each class outline you create should serve a single purpose: to help you understand, to the best practical level, all of the major and minor themes addressed in that class, and how they fit together in a bigger picture. At some point in the creation of an outline – assuming you're not rushing to scrape it together only hours before your exam[153] – you typically have a moment or two where you realize just how much you've actually learned during the semester, and if you've had a good professor, you start to appreciate just how far you've really come. And the professor typically knows it, too; en masse salutes to the students for their hard work and performance in class are commonplace on the last day of class. And every law school class in my experience then ends with a thunderous round of applause for the professor, who typically exited the room to hear clapping following her down the hallways back to her office. These final moments of class were

---

[153] Last-minute preparation – starting four days before an exam, not four hours – does work for some people, and as the semesters passed, seemed to me a better alternative than starting outlines a month before exams. But doing this from the start is a dangerous, if not highly foolish road for first-year law students to walk.

amongst the events that most shaped my perceptions of the law school experience as one of tremendous, stressful learning coupled with great camaraderie and deference to skilled authorities on the law.

R. EXAM DAYS AND CHEATING SCANDALS

If only the last day of classes could be the end of the semester. Exams are the major thing stopping people from having entirely exhilarating first semesters of law school.

In the days before exams, the first-years' stress levels had reached heights comparable perhaps to soldiers about to ship out to war. Many former nicotine addicts had resumed their habits and assembled together outside, anxiously creating clouds of smoke in the chill of early winter. Caffeine consumption fueled private late-night study sessions, close friends stopped talking with each other – except for brief breaks to discuss study problems – and an eerie general panic gripped the entire dormitory. People weren't just wondering whether they would have a chance to make law review. Most people were hoping or feeling that they would pass, nervously praying that they'd be better than average, and secretly wishing they would be in the top 10% of the class when it was all over. Tension inside the law school dormitory and library was palpable. Some people just disappeared for several days at a time; a rumor had it that people had been disciplined a year earlier for leaving school to cram at a hotel before exams. The desire to be better than average or top 10% was driving almost everyone into frantic cramming, as well as last-minute writing and re-writing of outlines.

The outline you bring in with you to the exam combines with what you've got in your head to result, hopefully, in a passing or better grade.[154] You typically prepare an outline so that it's in final or near-final form the night before an exam, then show up for the exam either first thing in the morning or immediately after lunchtime in the afternoon. Our four first-semester exams ran Monday-then-Friday, Monday-then-Friday for two weeks. The mornings before exams, my head was a mess. I had dreamed about the subjects during the nights after cramming them during the days; I woke up before my alarm clock because I was so panicked that I would miss an exam. And this was common.

I participated in exams just like every other first-year student, standing in the crowded hallways before the exam rooms opened up, looking for a good seat where I wouldn't be especially distracted by other people, and setting out everything I was allowed to bring to the exam – pencils or pens, stacks of paper, and textbooks. All of the nervous discussion in the room ended abruptly the moment the proctor closed the door and announced the beginning of the

---

[154] If it gives you any comfort, few professors actually fail students; most give bottom performers technically passing, but dismal grades instead.

exam session. "This is the examination for Torts, taught by Professor Alighieri, for last names listed H through N." My closest friends were not in my alphabetical bracket – this was a room full of people I sort of knew, but didn't feel too close with. Once students had picked up stacks of questions and blank answer pages, the time was announced and the actual exams began.

Every in-class exam day after the first was pretty much the same: three straight hours of reading, analysis and writing, hopefully in that order. Some people attempt to determine in advance how much time they have to complete each section; others just work and work and hope that they'll be done on time. Even for fast workers, it's generally a scramble to complete everything before time is called.[155] And it's all-engrossing while it goes on. I remember looking up from my papers for the first time after one of the exams and seeing my eyes attempt to refocus on the fact that there had actually been a room surrounding me the whole time I was working.

Not that it was easy for my eyes to refocus. To illustrate just what exam time can be like, I developed a massive eyelid infection that swelled one of my eyes closed in the week before exams began – the most critical time for last-minute preparations. The show still had to go on, as far as I was concerned, and there wasn't going to be any note accompanying my grades specifying the nature or severity of my impairment to prospective employers. To its credit, the law school offered to let me delay my exams by several days until the illness cleared up – I could have taken my exams during the Christmas break. But I couldn't think of spending even another day at the law school after the demanding first semester, and wouldn't dream of giving up a day of vacation.

The most memorable part of exams happened completely outside of the testing rooms, and bears discussion at least in part because I can't write it off as random or infrequent – something similar happened during the next year's first-year exams, too. The day before the first of our exams, Torts, a couple of people from my section were making no secret of the fact that they claimed to be in possession of something special: multiple choice questions and answers used in our professor's previous exams. In the name of friendship, they offered to share their good fortune with people from our section; I declined and was not especially happy about the situation.

You might remember that Cornell, like many other schools, placed most but not all of its previous exams' essays on file for review. It did not place its multiple choice questions on file. This point should be illuminating on several

---

[155] Far fewer people, in my experience, finished law school exams than undergraduate exams before time was called. There was also no direct correlation between those who finished early and those who received above-average grades – these people were merely confident, not necessarily excellent – but there was definitely a strong correlation between those who did not finish each section and those who received average or lower-than-average grades. Time budgeting is a skill one should develop, at latest, before finals start.

levels. First, law school exams can contain more than just essays – the only thing that you'll almost never see from undergrad exams is a 'short answer' or 'fill in the blanks' sort of question. Professors sometimes claim that they'll use 'short answer' questions, but tend to want two or three paragraph mini-essays as responses, not single sentences or phrases. There's no point to shooting off three-word buzzword answers in the law, generally. Second, professors have reasons for not publishing at least some of their essays and all of their multiple choice questions. Some professors re-use the materials verbatim. And third, professors by their omission of these materials are aware that people might somehow otherwise come into possession of them and thereby undermine the credibility of the exam.

The "somehow otherwise" in this case was alleged to be one student's upper-classman boyfriend who, according to the rumor, had memorized multiple-choice questions from previous examinations and passed them along to his girlfriend for 'study' purposes. In an attempt to relax stressed-out law students, the professor had used cartoon character names in his multiple choice questions: one of the most memorable questions referred to the Road Runner and Wile E. Coyote of Warner Brothers fame. And the students apparently came into possession of this, and other previous questions.

My Torts class had approximately 100 students, thirty-some of whom might have had access to the 'practice' questions, knowing or not realizing that they were about to re-appear on the exam. Cornell, like other law schools, depended on its "Honor Code" to expose and resolve the problem, which meant that if someone knew that they or other people had access to actual questions, they should have reported it.

After the exam had ended, the professor got wind of the problem, and called suspected students in for questioning. Word of the problem began to spread around, and discussions with widely differing conclusions were taking place all around the law school; some thought that the students were clearly guilty of the offense, while others who had themselves been exposed to the materials quietly said that they'd had no idea that the questions would actually appear. Another group cast blame entirely upon the professor, who they argued had little else to do all year besides repeat the same lectures he had given last year and could have at least taken the time to create a new exam.

The situation was an embarrassment for all involved, and whatever sanctions might have been taken were never made public – but generally if disciplinary action had been taken, people would have known about it. One would have thought that, at the very least, the situation would have prompted the administration to put out a cautionary "hey, it's time to change your questions" letter to all professors.

But the next year, something similar happened, this time in the first year class's second semester Property exam. The professor, a beloved and charismatic lecturer who had been asked to visit and teach at several other schools, had the misfortune of giving an exam at Harvard, which apparently published the exam online without his permission. Diligent students researching the professor found the materials on the Harvard web site, used them as study materials, and then showed up for their exam – only to discover that all of the questions were the same.

To the credit of the student who initially had discovered the Harvard questions, he interrupted his own exam, went up to a proctor, and told him exactly what he believed was going on – his words apparently were, "sir, I'm not sure, but I think that I might be cheating on this exam." This sort of behavior is not only commendable, but incredible: to interrupt your exam and take time away from completing it is something almost no one would do in law school, say nothing of inviting possible repercussions. And you lose out on an opportunity to score an easy A for one of your first-year grades.

The school, after conducting a bizarre survey to determine whether people would admit that they too had seen the web site, opted to offer a pass/fail grade instead of a letter grade on the exam. This may well have been the most useless solution conceivable, and lent credence to those who had previously suggested that administrative laziness, rather than poor student judgment, was to blame for the problems with first-year exams.

There's a reason these situations merit attention: European students claim that cheating on law school exams is shockingly commonplace overseas, and if these two stories are any indication, American schools are not immune to such problems, either. But the difference between the American and European models is seemingly profound: cheating is so hugely frowned upon in American law schools, both by administrators and by hard-working students, that on the rare occasion that it happens, the perpetrators have very little chance of getting away with it. Resentment and exposure of those who break the rules is typically most likely amongst those who followed the rules most strictly. And the consequences for cheaters can be profound: instant expulsion from law school and marks on an academic record that will make it very, very difficult to receive a license to practice law in any state in the country.[156]

---

[156] In an extreme but true example of the impact of cheating on a law student's career, one student was recently accused of visiting several of his professors' secretaries after final examinations were administered, changed his examination answers after they were graded, and resubmitting the answers for higher grades. When one of the changes was discovered, the student received a retroactive failing grade in that class, his future employer was informed, and his transcripts were permanently marked with explanatory notations for inspection by bar authorities. For the sake of slightly higher grades, this student essentially undid three years of law school and any prior evaluations of his moral fitness to practice law, say nothing of the damage to his employability and reputation amongst his peers.

Without trying to sound like a public service announcement, it's fair to say that cheating in law school is not only a losing proposition, but one which will cost its rare perpetrators far more than it's worth.

S.   JUST A MATTER OF TIME: WAITING

Once exams have ended, the rest of the experience is half about waiting and half about trying simultaneously to forget all about the experience while remembering only as much as is necessary to do well next semester. A law school traditionally erupts in celebration at the end of exams, and people typically gather for one last night together before returning home quickly to their families for the holidays. At Cornell, the post-exams night is generally replete with one night stands, plenty of drinking, and very little discussion of the contents of the exams themselves.

There are two camps of thought on exams: those who want to talk with friends about their responses to questions, and those who have no interest in discussing things. It helps to be sensitive to others' desires where idle talk might not be appreciated; many people beat themselves up in the fear that they've missed major issues or mistakenly analyzed ones they found.

Truth be told, professors frequently say that the exams are so packed with issues that no single 'right' answer exists. Assuming that they're really reading the exams, which some people doubt on occasion, they're looking as much for a lawyerly way of thinking as a set of specific phrases and conceptual discussions to appear. You could safely miss something a friend found and still do well on the exam; you can also reach opposing conclusions on the same set of facts and both receive good grades. Lawyers reach opposing conclusions every day; that's what they're paid for. And thus discussion of exam answers afterwards can be safely educational without damaging your ego.

But no one really knows what their grades will be for several weeks: first-year students tend to hear first, if only because they are back in town before upper-classmen get back. And after these first exams, I didn't know of any person who was ready to predict his results, either. Because of the grading curve and the entirely unknown variables of so many new people taking exams for the first time, the most confident answer I heard was that "it all depends on how everyone else did."

T.   PUTTING THE SEMESTER IN PERSPECTIVE

With the end of the first semester comes a major turning point in the lives of those who have survived - though they're not far enough yet to have earned "I climbed Mount Everest" T-shirts, they're six months closer to being lawyers than most people will ever be. And this has unexpected consequences.

1.   The Socialization of Lawyers: Changes From the Inside

You may well notice that you've gone through some psychological changes by the end of the first semester. Among the more intriguing parts of the legal education experience is the one you're least likely to recognize – the process of formally and informally learning actually changes your behavior. While I can't deny that this is true, I debate the severity of it with friends, some of whom view the change as more profound than I do.

Law school has, as its goals, the reduction of one's intimidation by big concepts, frightening people, and bad situations; like the military, law school offers a boot camp for common obstacles. Perhaps its primary goal is to teach students how to 'think like a lawyer,' namely, how to use a systematic process to analyze situations, generate possible alternative conclusions, and choose one that seems like the best reasoned of the bunch. Though I didn't realize it while it was happening, many professors pushed students to ignore obvious answers to questions and take positions that they did not agree with. The challenge was to look beyond your own feelings, the critical skill possessed by most lawyers.

At the end of the first semester, you're likely to be at a point where you can't just blindly agree with another person's thoughts or take the obvious route to a conclusion. You start to rethink and find exceptions to everyday things you used to find simple and clear. Your vocabulary changes to accommodate the terms you hear in classes every day – things that your family and old friends would never say and mightn't understand if you explained, things that you may not fully appreciate yourself. And you start to see yourself in a different light, and question who you are and what you're worth, particularly when you've been humbled by Socratic dialogues and forced to uproot yourself fully from your old life. You make friends with law students and talk incessantly about the law. Someplace in there, the old 'you' may get lost.

The products of this educational process, some have said, are hardened, argumentative, egotistical people who doggedly pursue their own agendas in highly rational, but cold ways. My own perspective is less severe. People gain confidence. They learn how to hold their own in debates. They make fewer blind choices without considering alternatives. But they don't lose their emotions nor gain a need to argue if they didn't have it before. The only negative consequence I personally noticed was that for some period of time, being forced to think in the alternative all the time made it difficult for me to take day-to-day solid positions of my own. I became far less polar on many issues, and it took some time to re-define what I actually believed, and how much I could bend without betraying the values that were still important to me.

The most profound positive change that I noticed was that I had become more efficient and precise in dense reading material and conversations. Several hours of textbook reading became 45-minute or one-hour long chores by the end of the first semester. The books and assignments hadn't changed; I had.

Friends have also suggested that the trained lawyer is, over time, a skeptical and critical reader and consumer, one who challenges rather than accepts. This much I think is true of most of those who go through law school, and the first signs definitely appear during the first year. But it's not true of all, nor is it always awful. A critical mind is one thing; a critical person is another.

At some point, it becomes hard to remember where the line really stood between who you were before law school and who you became thereafter. Law school exposes you to people who have more than a fair chance of becoming lawyers, judges, and other types of successful professionals. Whether one changes because of the experience, because of the company they keep, or because they want to change remain unanswered questions in my mind.

2. The Broader Implications: Changes From the Outside

You'll also notice that people look at you differently as a future lawyer. People will start to ask you legal questions when you least expect them – at the dinner table, at social occasions, and so forth. Your 'stock' socially begins to rise, if only a little, because you are suddenly becoming potentially useful to people who otherwise might not have needed you as a friend.

And you will be left again to wonder what sort of lawyer you're going to become, especially considering that your grades might be telling you something about your supposed aptitudes. On this point, it's probably a good idea to wait a bit before coming to hasty judgments about your abilities. If most of history's greatest figures had let their fates be decided by formal scholastic evaluations, Einstein might have been sweeping floors and Walt Whitman might never have penned poetry. Great people never let schools determine their future success.

But if there was a subject that you really liked and did well in, you might have an inkling about your future career path at this point. And extracurricular activities of some sort, including Moot Court, might be giving you a similar sense of where you want to be going or what you want to be avoiding. This is not too early of a time to make positive decisions about your future. It's probably just not a good idea to make negative ones quite yet.

If you're lucky enough to have done well after your first semester, there are benefits that go beyond just receiving a list of scores to share with your family. Some schools offer a certificate or other award to the recipient of the single highest grade in any given class and section; Cornell Law issues these as "Excellence For The Future" Awards in conjunction with the Center for Computer-Assisted Legal Instruction (CALI), and some students unexpectedly receive cash prizes or scholarship awards in addition to certificates and pats on the back. Further-looking first-years might also consider their class rank, eligibility for future *cum laude*, *magna cum laude* or *summa cum laude* designations, and, of course, the prospect of joining a law journal. But let's hold off on all of that – just for now.

CHAPTER
4

TAUGHANNOCK FALLS, TRUMANSBURG, NY, WINTER 1999
REFERENCED IN TWILIGHT ZONE EPISODE "THE MIDNIGHT SUN"

A. The Forge

Those reading the book chronologically will recall a previously mentioned concept: law school as a catalyst of human conversion. I raise the point again not just for page-flippers, but also because the start of the second semester was when I personally began to understand what was really going on in law school.

The first semester of law school is, for most people, a mix of confusion, exhaustion, and exasperation – it is by design overwhelming and stressful, and has been that way for decades if not centuries. Certainly some experts have contemplated a lighter first year; after all, law school was once a two-year program, and for some time didn't even require an undergraduate degree. If these things could change, so could the difficulty level of the first year, right?

No. At least, that's the strong prevailing view. The average legal education has been made longer and harder to get into, not easier or less stressful. Why? It's not just because there are so many people interested in the law, or because law has become increasingly specialized. Rather, it's because lawyers and law professors alike continue to believe that the real-world gravity of the practice of law demands that soon-to-be-professionals receive an early and catalytic 'wake up' call. Something needs to happen to make a lasting impression upon relatively young people that the matters they will handle are potentially going to result in the deaths or bankruptcies of their clients if they fail, and sometimes even if they succeed. And something needs to make them realize that the profession demands a much higher caliber of day-to-day creative thinking from its functionaries than virtually any other occupation out there – the law is an active thinker's vocation, and few legal matters are properly handled by blindly duplicating forms that worked out successfully for a previous client.

Your first year, and especially your first semester, are as much about training you to think and work efficiently as about helping you to recognize if not memorize the manner in which laws operate. Discipline is borne of stressful conditions, not cakewalks, and thus you are pushed, and pushed some more – until you either sink (like a tiny minority) or swim (like the vast majority). Few people leave law school less organized, disciplined and competent than they entered it, and those people leave it before graduation.

So it is at some point near the end of your first semester or beginning of your second that the experience begins to make a whole lot more sense, and you begin to get your bearings. This realization is itself cause for celebration.

B. Social Realities of the Budding Lawyer

The return to law school after your break may or may not be an event you'll look forward to. For most people, however, the opportunity to see law school friends will itself be motivation enough to come back, and many people will have stories to share about their first 'vacations' away from the grind.

Unfortunately, the rigorous mandates of the American Bar Association set practical limitations on the length of time between first-year semesters. As a result, first-year students typically return to school one or two weeks before upper-classmen, and therefore have much less of an opportunity to travel or enjoy an extended, meaningful period of relaxation when they need it the most.

Paralleling other schools, Cornell used to hold a several-week-long "winter program" for its first-year students between the first and second semesters, mandating that first-years use their winter "break" to participate in a formal program similar to Moot Court. Each student spent the cold Ithaca winter preparing oral and written arguments against a classmate for a mock legal debate, to be judged and graded by an instructor. Small changes in the ABA's policies and Cornell's legal writing program led to retention of most of the substance of this requirement while dropping the school's mandate that it take place in winter. First-years still give up a portion of their winter break, but today the extra time is just used for extended legal writing assignments.

People therefore have a little more time to relax before returning to school, and you will probably hear that people used that time to sleep. A lot. Rarely do people ever work over the break, at least in part because there's too little time, though occasionally people get started a little early on their initial second semester assignments; that's true law school-style overachievement in action.

Most students also use the break to spend time with people they were forced to neglect during the semester. Sometimes this can be among the most emotionally difficult times for a first-year law student, as it can be a period of ending a relationship, patching things up with a spurned lover, or starting with someone new. It can also be one of the best times someone has had in many months, as it may be the right time for a married couple's two-week vacation or an extended frolic with a new someone special met at the law school.

But it's also the case that the first semester foreshadows the later realities of a lawyer's life. While in practice, a lawyer's typical hours run from early in the morning to after dark, and it is thought – if unverified – that rates of divorce and other marital troubles amongst lawyers are higher than average. No matter how committed the lawyer may be to her family, she may never have complete predictability or control over her schedule again, and any understanding family must be able to recognize the challenges and realities of a lawyer's existence.

A surprising consequence of the first-year schedule for some people (including me) is a decreased capacity for real down time, which may or may not manifest itself during this first break. It's hard to transition smoothly from being constantly under the gun to having no set agenda on a vacation; I know that it took me a few days after every semester to 'calm down,' as family members put it, and stop needing to work all the time. Many people I know felt as if they had lost their ability to rest, and just needed to have something to do, even if it was just reading a book. Sitting in silence was not an option.

And other people, of course, will emerge from the semester relatively unchanged. Is this a bad thing? That depends. If the person came to law school highly disciplined, very smart and incredibly lucky, he probably doesn't need to change much in order to become a successful law student or lawyer. But if he arrived either lazy, uninformed or unlucky, it's probably best that those sort of tendencies are exorcised before another exam period passes, say nothing of the bar exam following at the end of the third year. It is, in fact, possible to waste the law school experience. If you didn't find the first semester to be life-altering, there is some possibility that you're on the track towards a relatively less transformative legal education than some people receive.

C. THE WINTER CHILL: WHEN FIRST-YEARS RETURN EARLY

At the end of my first semester,[157] Cornell was still transitioning its legal writing program, and was about to use the winter break for the very thing I had dreaded the most about law school: a short, appellate-style oral argument against another student lawyer, to be performed in front of a judge. Actually, probably two judges. I spent much of my abbreviated break nervous that I was about to return to school for this specific event. Unlike my other classes, even including Civil Procedure, which I had convinced myself to feel positive about, this was not something I could make myself want to do. I was going to be done as soon as I possibly could, and I was never going to do it again.

Every school's mandatory moot court was different – lucky for me, it turned out that Cornell's format was among the least onerous.[158] Though students had no choice over the topic, their judges, or their opposing counsel, the judges were a legal writing instructor and a teaching assistant,[159] the topic was something we were largely familiar with from our legal writing work earlier in the semester, and the opposing counsel was – surprise – someone who had a

---

[157] A number of schools still have winter moot court programs, and those that do not use one of two alternative systems: they either integrate the moot court requirement into the second semester, or allow students to choose between the moot court program and a more vigorous program in legal analysis – the latter a recognition of the prospect that some students have no aspiration to argue before judges. Even if you share my mentality and presently want nothing to do with courtrooms, don't rule out a school just because it has a mandatory moot court program – at least, not until you've read this chapter.

[158] Some schools, for example, require students to participate in an extended competition on a brand new subject that conceivably might continue for several rounds of argument; we were only required to participate in a single argument, and there was no second or third stage to which "winners" would advance.

[159] At Cornell, only Legal Methods had teaching assistants. Typically the teaching assistants were bright upper-classmen with closed lips, so we didn't need to worry about being judged by people who would tell the whole school about a poor performance.

decent likelihood of not wanting to do this mandatory trial thing, either. The proceeding would take place in the school's dedicated moot courtroom, but there would probably not be an audience of any sort. Best of all, though participation was mandatory, our presentation would not be graded.

The concept was, in retrospect, simple. Our legal writing class had focused on an emerging defense to murder known as Battered Child Syndrome (BCS), a theory which essentially gave a youthful killer a defense to a murder resulting from persistent and severe child abuse. We had written memos on both sides of the case – some supporting the release of confessed murderer 'Kyle,' others attempting to jail him. We had to clean up a specific memorandum on BCS we prepared in the first semester, expand it a bit, and prepare to discuss both the facts of the case and a couple of critical legal issues within the memorandum.

This presentation wasn't all that bad, but at the time, it seemed like a major challenge: first, we had to take a side and either defend a patricidal teenager or prosecute the teenager who appeared to have been abused, and perhaps badly, by his father. The facts were written with just enough support and ambiguity that either attorney could craft the facts into a powerful story. Recognizing this, you had to come to grips with the fact that you couldn't take both sides. You had to try to either nail him or free him. I personally opted for prosecution. I adopted the position that murder is murder, and that while I could understand that a child would want to attack an abusive parent, I believed that if Kyle, a frequent runaway, had the chance to run again, he should have done that instead of killing his father. Everyone had their own rationalization; mine matched the facts of the case and the contours of the law.

We spent the weeks between semesters cleaning up the memorandum, which was the only graded portion of our advocacy work, and preparing in bits and pieces for the trial. Picking names from a hat, I was randomly assigned to argue against a nice classmate who wanted to be a litigator, but this wasn't a problem; no grade and no audience took the heat off, and she seemed every bit as nervous as I was. Neither of us was aggressive, and that made everything a little less stressful. But both of us felt as if we needed to be prepared enough not to embarrass ourselves in front of the judges.[160] We couldn't prepare together,

---

[160] One of the important lessons you learn in the first year of law school, and even more in moot court, is appropriate behavior for litigators when dealing with judges: attorneys must display deference and yet speak directly to the judge's questions without being intimidated. Oral arguments at court may be your single opportunity to convince a decision-maker that you're right and counter an opponent's evidence that you're wrong. A good litigator is conversational, not lecturing, and treats the court as a stage from which his performance should be respectful and respected. For history buffs, the relationship between judge, attorneys, and spectators is visually and figuratively defined by the Bench (the elevated seating area from which the judge presides over the courtroom) and the Bar (the physical gate separating the attorneys from the spectators).

so we talked only briefly to establish that neither one of us was going overboard with preparations. We drew a relatively early date on the calendar of trials – all of the people from our class were doing them at roughly the same time – and that meant we'd be finished early. It wasn't going to be as awful as I had feared.

When the trial date came, both of us were there on time, and relatively well-prepared. We were dressed in suits, carrying vague written notes, and nursing butterflies in our stomachs. When it was my turn to talk, I felt incredibly nervous, despite the fact that both the building and the room seemed empty but for us, our two podiums, and the judges. It was a moment where I could hear my own voice as if I was an outside observer and wasn't in command of it. I just wanted to be done with this day so that I could get on with my life.

But then something really weird happened. I had gotten out only a few sentences when some random maintenance guy walked into the room, right in the middle of my opening statement, and started moving cables and audiovisual equipment around right in front of me – in fact, standing literally in between me and the judges. He was apparently oblivious to the fact that he had interrupted not only a class in session, but moreover, a mock trial in session. I stopped for a moment and asked the judges whether I should continue. The guy finished picking up his cables within another 30 seconds, still oblivious, and left the room. If I had been an observer, and not a participant, I would have probably been laughing at the ridiculousness of the situation.

The experience had an unexpected consequence. In the instant that the guy completely interrupted me, it seemed as if the worst thing that could have happened – a bizarre interruption in my presentation – had happened. And it wasn't my fault. I had responded appropriately, and had somehow forgotten most of my nervousness. When the judges stopped me mid-sentence to ask questions, as they always do during real and simulated oral arguments, I just answered them normally, as I would have had I been talking with two people in any other room. Then my still-nervous classmate sped through her case and we were finished. I had faced my greatest fear in law school and survived.

I met with my instructor several days later to discuss the memoranda and the results of our hearings. She told me that our session had been amongst the best she had seen, and that my personal presentation was in the top two of our class. The other top presenter, a great speaker and nice guy, later became chancellor of the school's real Moot Court board. I never did another oral argument. But I realized that if I had to, I could. I just had to stop being nervous. And pray that the maintenance guy would walk in and interrupt me again.

CHAPTER

5

PEACE TOWER, CORNELL LAW SCHOOL

A.   LAW REVIEWS AND JOURNALS

> **"In the past, I've heard some people say,**
> **'make love, not *Law Review*.'**
> **I say, 'why not do both?' "**
> *Senior law professor to first-year students,*
> *approx. one year before*
> *Law Review selected new members*

As it turns out, first-years are only the most conspicuous people to arrive back at school early; a small number of upper-classmen toil in offices during part, if not all of the winter break, locked into fixed production cycles for student-run publications such as law reviews and journals. At some point near the start of your second semester, you'll likely receive your first official orientation explaining the role of these publications, the general concepts behind which have been briefly explored already. Now is the time when you'll be ready to learn about them in depth.

"Making law review" is one of those phrases that you may hear before attending law school but never truly understand until you're actually there; this is especially and unfortunately true if you are a family member of someone who is invited to join.[161] To 'make' law review typically means to earn one's way into the most selective student organization at a law school, one that publishes a socially important type of periodical. I hesitate to discuss the benefits of membership before the responsibilities, but for many people, this section wouldn't be worth reading unless we took the subjects in that order.

It can fairly be said that those who make law review typically find it much easier to get job offers than those who don't, and as many law professors and judges were once involved in law reviews, student members tend to enjoy at least a modicum of extra respect from these people. Professors know law review members' names, and in some schools, because of the heavy demands of journal production schedules and their widely acknowledged importance to the profession, law professors give a little extra slack to editors – when editors need access to class notes, not at grade time. Thus law review membership can benefit your career and, in some cases, your scholastic life.

But now we need to step back for a moment and understand what a law review really is: it's one of several legal journals published by students at a law

---

[161] Family members think of journal membership as similar to membership in any undergraduate or graduate school club, though there are far fewer similarities between the concepts than there are differences. With the exception of those who have been through law school, it seems all but impossible to convince others of the larger importance of journals, and journal membership.

school. More precisely, a legal journal is a periodical dealing exclusively with the law, edited by second- and third-year law students. This definition is important in several ways. Legal journals are different from medical journals in that students edit them, rather than practitioners, yet they carry roughly the same importance within their respective professions. Legal journals, like medical journals, publish articles by scholars and practitioners on a quarterly, bi-monthly or eight-times-annually basis. They typically resemble small books in size and shape, rather than magazines or newspapers, and their articles are densely packed with oblique legal writing and footnotes. A school's 'law review' is typically, but not always, its most prestigious legal journal.[162]

Law journals are generally not meant to be of direct interest to the general public, and thus they are not full of pictures, nor do they have pretenses of attracting huge audiences. But it's not the size of the audience that matters, it's the quality. Articles in journals are written by professors, judges, lawyers, and journal members, those people who are most likely to influence the future development of the law. Notably, however, professors, judges and practitioners typically have no role whatsoever in managing these journals, which traditionally pride themselves on autonomous management by students.

Typically, second-year members join on as 'associates' and have the opportunity to 'elevate' to become editors if they successfully complete an extended series of assignments which generally runs throughout the majority of the second year. The assignments consist primarily of proof-reading, Bluebooking, and editing 10-30 page long sections of articles chosen for publication by the journals, and secondarily of writing a Note, a student-authored article,[163] for possible publication. Proofing normally takes roughly a week per assignment and involves verifying literally every word on a page in some way or another, as well as suggesting rewrites and formatting changes to improve the article's quality. Note writing typically takes six months and guarantees law journals that they will have content of some sort with which to fill their pages, besides the articles written by professors and practitioners.

If none of this sounds exciting to you, you're not alone. Journal work takes a lot of time and demands a lot from one's reading, writing, and editing skills. But it pays dividends, both to your resume and to the legal community. You will do the world of legal thought a service by writing a Note and editing articles read by practitioners and academics. Though the process is tedious at times, it prepares one well for the life of a junior associate at a law firm, both by exposing you to diverse areas of the law and by honing your legal document

---

[162] Other schools use the name "Law Journal" rather than "Law Review" for their flagship journals, including Kentucky (Kentucky Law Journal), Mississippi (Mississippi Law Journal) and Yale (Yale Law Journal).

[163] See Chapter 7, Section N.

production skills. And journal articles are widely available to judges and practitioners, meaning that well-reasoned articles and Notes can help real people to understand and improve complex and problematic areas of law. Under rare circumstances, you may write or work on something that is read and cited by the United States Supreme Court – hopefully, favorably – or plays a part in resolving a bad law or an incorrect legal interpretation.

Besides the 'law review' or 'law journal,' most schools have additional 'secondary' or 'specialty' publications focused on specific topics, such as international law, public policy, intellectual property law, entertainment law, and the like. The names, quantities, and quality of these secondary publications vary tremendously from school to school, and in some cases from year to year with the interest levels of new personnel.

Most journals have competitive membership practices; in other words, you can't join a journal just because you want to work for it – you somehow have to 'earn' it. Law reviews are typically the most difficult to join – at Cornell, and most other schools, an offer of law review membership is nearly automatic if your first-year grades place you in the top 10% of your class, and the highly competitive results of a challenging writing competition determine whom else will receive offers. Admission practices vary for other journals; one of Cornell's journals extends some offers in a parallel fashion to those of the *Law Review*, but with lower grade and writing competition score cut-offs, while the other both uses lower numeric thresholds and allows students to join by working hard for the journal even if they failed to get on through grades or the contest.

Statistics from ten of the country's top law schools might give you an idea of your chances for journal acceptance. As you'll note, an average of 16% of students will be accepted to the law review (or other top journal), and most schools offer several secondary student-run journals.

TABLE 5-1	LAW REVIEW AND JOURNAL ADMISSIONS STATISTICS					
School	*Number of Students Per Year*	*# of 2L Students on Law Review*	*% of Students on Law Review Per Class*	*Total Law School Student Population*	*Total # of Students on Law Review*	*Total Number of Secondary Journals*
Harvard	540	45	8%	1620	90	8
U. Virginia	362	32	9%	1080	60	7
Georgetown	450+125	53	9+%	1600	106	8
N.Y.U.	400	43	11%	1200	87	6
Columbia	340	45	13%	1020	90	13
U.C.Berkeley	270	45	17%	810	90	9
U. Chicago	175	30	17%	525	61	3
Cornell	185	37	20%	555	74	3
Yale	185	50	27%	555	101	5
Stanford	180	50	28%	540	100	6

A certain thought pattern tends to be common amongst students faced with various law journal admissions opportunities. Initially, students who see a list of the various journals typically tend to gravitate towards one name or another based on personal interest. At Cornell, I knew from the name and my political science background that the *Cornell Journal of Law and Public Policy* sounded more focused on subjects of personal interest than did the *Cornell International Law Journal* or the *Cornell Law Review*. Moreover, I knew that most of the personable upper-classmen were on the *Journal of Law and Public Policy*, and not one of the other two journals. So early on, my thought was that it would definitely not be so bad if I wound up working for the *Journal of Law and Public Policy* and not the *Law Review*.

"We're not elitist. We're just elite."
One year's newly-elected
Law Review Editor-in-Chief,
introducing Law Review in a somewhat
criticized presentation to first-years

Law reviews are really another story altogether. They're almost universally considered prestigious, but depending on the school may also carry several stigmas – some are accused of elitism, some have memberships packed with obnoxious brainiacs, and some work their new inductees to a point of incredible exhaustion.[164] From school to school and year to year, you may find these stereotypes accurate or somewhat exaggerated, though there may be at least a little truth in each of the stereotypes. For members of law reviews especially, the second year of law school is often comparable in difficulty to the first year of law school, whereas for members of other journals, it's typically nowhere near that rough.

But despite subject matter preferences, virtually everyone eventually comes to think the same way: you really don't turn down a law review's offer if you receive one. The selectivity alone makes it a club worth joining, even with the consequences of membership. And membership unquestionably has its privileges. Many people rightfully see it as a meal ticket to easier job interviews and offers of employment in the future. A handful of people correctly see it as an almost mandatory step towards a career in legal academia. But the thing that many people ignore is that law reviews teach their members an enhanced set of critically practical legal reading, writing, editing and Bluebooking skills that they may not receive in any formal law school course. Law reviews tend to do all of these things better than secondary journals, if only because they publish

---

[164] Perhaps not surprisingly, these rumors parallel the scuttlebutt about America's large law firms, which often draw their talent from such student organizations.

more frequently and demand more of their associates. You get worked hard, but you learn more. That's the way it often happens in the legal profession.

So law reviews tend to become the top choice of law students, regardless of their issues; only under the rarest of exceptions do people decline a law review's offer, or even have to think about whether or not to accept it. Some people believe, therefore, that secondary journals by necessity are lower-caliber organizations with less value or prestige. That much is neither necessarily nor entirely true. It depends on your school, and more importantly, on the people who staff the secondary journals. A well-run, focused secondary journal can be every bit as influential as a law review, though it happens only occasionally, and then typically at schools that offer educational specializations coinciding with the foci of the specialized journals.

There is little doubt, though, that specialized journals tend to have more problems than law reviews, both in recruiting and retaining their membership. People have been known to join secondary journals just long enough to use them on their resumes for interview seasons, and then drop off of the journals when the workloads increase. This is far less likely to be the case with law reviews, despite their heavier workloads. And some journals are forced for practical reasons to extend offers to candidates whose interest level or ability to handle journal work may well be considerably lower than those for law review and other journals' members. This is especially the case at smaller schools, and where the total number of writing competition participants is low.

Finally, it can also be said that membership on secondary journals carries less weight in the job interviewing process than law review membership does. Though otherwise outstanding candidates had no problem getting top jobs even if they were not *Law Review* members, an otherwise average candidate did not benefit significantly from membership on a secondary journal. Contrast this with the otherwise so-so candidates from *Law Review* who at least sparked interviewers' interest with that fact alone.

Cornell also had a fourth journal-like publication that deviated significantly from the other journals' practices: the *Legal Information Institute (LII) Bulletin*, an online, student-edited portion of the nationally famous LII web site.[165] Recognizing that it would have recruiting problems if it competed against the printed journals or used a writing competition to screen entrants, the LII instead conducted face-to-face interviews of candidates before the other journals even considered extending offers – in fact before second semester exams. It made offers based on demonstrated interest and interviewees' willingness to commit to LII work regardless of whatever their grades or writing competition results turned out to be.[166] And they paid for their work through modest school

---

[165] See http://www.law.cornell.edu, Chapter 5, Section G, and Chapter 10, Section D.
[166] Some students, in fact, came to hold positions on both the LII and another journal.

stipends. The *LII Bulletin* is a major exception to the norm of law school journals, on many levels. Few schools have anything like it.

Every law school will have its own methods for explaining its journal membership policies and competitions, but the experiences of Cornell's various journals offer at least a glimpse as to what you might be told to deal with. Receiving high grades (top 10% of class after first year for *Law Review*, top 25-30% for other journals) is one way to earn a journal invitation; writing competitions are the other way. At Cornell, the three printed journals hold a single annual writing competition authored by members of the *Law Review* and separately graded by teams of members from each journal. The competition would start literally minutes after the conclusion of second-semester final examinations, and have a deadline for submissions precisely three weeks later.

Students would be asked to produce a single document, no more than 30 pages in length (maximums of 15 pages of writing and 15 of footnotes), called a Case Note, on a topic to be determined by the *Law Review* and disclosed only at the start of the competition. The only materials one could use were ones provided in a packet one could purchase from the *Law Review*,[167] and specified supplementary sources such as a dictionary and the BLUEBOOK, the same tools members would later use in editing. No outside research would be permitted.[168] Any violation of the rules was a violation of the school's Honor Code.

Though the prospect of doing a 30-page paper immediately after exams wasn't appealing to most people, writing competition participation was entirely optional. If you're not interested, or too tired, then don't compete. Those whose grades were high enough at the end of the first year would receive journal offers automatically.[169] Competition entrants could also submit a short additional 'personal statement' designed to encourage diversity of *Law Review* membership based on socioeconomic factors; other journals were free to consider the statements, but did not.

If you're interested in learning more about different journal policies, you can visit journal web sites and look over their constitutions, by-laws, and in some cases, articles.[170] My own survey of other schools suggests very strong

---

[167] At a nominal fee (~$15), which is waived upon a showing of financial hardship.

[168] This differs from some schools' writing competitions, which focus as much on research as on writing and editing. These schools have participants pick from a list of pre-selected topics and then find their own materials to write about.

[169] This has changed in recent times for the *Law Review*, not the other journals; you must now compete if you desire to join the *Law Review*, at least at Cornell. Other schools vary.

[170] The *Cornell Law Review* site is available at http://www.lawschool.cornell.edu/clr. The *Boston College Law Review*'s membership information is available at http://www.bc.edu/bc_org/avp/law/lwsch/reviewmember.html, and its articles can be viewed at http://www.bc.edu/bc_org/avp/law/lwsch/bclawrev.html. New York

parallels between the Cornell experience and those of other places, though Yale is amongst rare exceptions to the 'standard' admissions methods because of their unusual first-year grading practices.

B.   GRADES: THE END OF THE WAIT

One of the other major things people expect (or dread) upon their return for the second semester is the distribution of first-semester grades. Generally, students have them in hand before journals hold their informational meetings, but the topics appear here out of chronological order because grades take on a heightened importance when you understand the profound consequences grades can have upon journal membership.

I had a tough experience waiting for grades and ultimately receiving them, but my experience was probably no worse than anyone else's. Based on the fact that I had been sick during exams and was, after all, a typically hapless first-year, I had no idea what to expect. Like everyone else, I waited and waited for several weeks, and when I returned to school, there was a large white sealed envelope waiting for me. Inside the envelope were two pieces of paper: one with my grades, the other with a list of the only three approximate percentile rankings Cornell publishes.

Percentile information is considered important by employers, but some schools have for better or worse opted not to get overly specific in their disclosures. This is as much a tacit admission that grades are not entirely fair as a statement of belief that minute percentage distinctions between people are not an appropriate means to judge their suitability for employment, despite the fact that schools carry GPAs out to four decimal places. I think such realism, though unevenly acknowledged, is a good thing.

Cornell publishes only a top 10% number, a top 30% number, and a top 50% number. If your GPA is higher than any of the three numbers, you know generally where you stand in the class. If it's lower than the 50% number, you know only that you're in the bottom half of the class, but not where. This is somewhat useful, somewhat sneaky. It's hard to know if you're in the top 25% of your class, a frequent cut-off for many firm jobs. But for those in the bottom 50%, there's a cloak of anonymity that masks the potential for one to be in the 'bottom 10%' of the class; no one really knows for sure, so employers might still consider you a viable candidate no matter where you fall, mathematically.

My first semester number placed me around the top 30th percentile, which, as the old maxim and my high expectations had it, made me part of the

University's law review admissions and membership information may be viewed at http://www.nyu.edu/pages/lawreview/joining.html, and its articles at http://www.nyu.edu/pages/lawreview/issues.html.

'disappointed 90%' of the class. On the one hand, I felt bad because I thought that I had done better than I had, and felt, of course, that I might have done better if I hadn't had an eye infection during the final stretch of preparation. On the other hand, top 30% definitely had me in the running for both good employment and possible *Law Review* membership in the future. It was nothing to be disappointed about in the abstract, especially considering that it was my strongest first semester, in raw GPA numbers, of any school I had ever attended.

C.   The Social and Emotional Impact of Grades

As hard as it may be for outsiders to understand, receiving law school grades is a challenging experience in and of itself, especially during the first semester, when they tend to come as a shock to most people. There are two primary dimensions to the challenge – though the emotional one is more important, we'll get the social one out of the way first.

Naturally the stresses of the semester lead students to bond as friends and confidantes, and one of the biggest topics of curiosity – at least for a while – is what grades people received. It has the potential to become the stuff of rumors and open gossip, and often does, depending on the people involved. And the grades you've received may or may not impact the way other people treat you, depending on the school you attend and the company you (hope to) keep.

One of the more memorable moments of my time at law school was the day when grades came out and people filled the hallways near our registrar's office, collecting and opening their envelopes. Virtually everyone wore huge, fake smiles both before and after looking at their grades, trying to appear calm and happy, and the most common refrain when people asked one another about results was a generic "I feel good; I did really well." But the people who put on the biggest positive show were often those who'd had the worst first semester. Hours later, only some would admit to friends where they stood. Others kept quiet and their grades never became obvious to others.

There were many, many disappointed souls. Many shed tears, and many seemed to be ending the dreams they'd possessed of being at the top of their class. It was an unfortunately perennial component of law school life, one that repeats with each new group of first-year students. But each person eventually reaches some level of comfort with his or her performance.

A building full of mostly quiet hallways was the experience of my class. Two years later, the scene was somewhat different. One member of the new first-year class walked the halls of the law dormitory building telling anyone and everyone how well he had supposedly done. For weeks, people could not stop talking about what an obnoxious ass he had been. There will always be a disappointed 90%, or at least a 'very disappointed' 75% (below the top 25%) and a 'mildly disappointed' 15% (at the bottom of the top 25%). The difference is primarily in how the top 10% act.

It's probably a good idea not to discuss your grades with anyone, no matter how well or poorly you did. Doing well only earns you the respect of similarly situated people, and the scorn of others. And if you have a huge ego that constantly needs to be fed by knowing others respect or fear you, have confidence that your in-class performances or other social interactions most likely signaled the level of your skills to your classmates. And if you've done poorly, there are similarly plenty of reasons not to let it be known to others. A stiff upper lip is always useful in the law; now is a good time to perfect it.

There are two distinct emotional phenomena that take place when people receive their first semester grades: some people slump and others turn up the heat. People slump either when they are depressed about missing the top 10% or become complacent wherever they were. Their second semester grades stay the same or even fall because they don't work as hard when other people decide to kick up their performance a notch to make up for past mistakes. Some people turn up the heat even after doing well the first semester; these are the so-called 'gunners' who are persistently angling for top grades and the respect of their professors.

It is, in fact, entirely possible for a person to completely reverse course after having a tough first semester. But fixing a bad first semester requires commitment and a realistic, objective understanding of what went wrong. It also requires a review and appreciation of the previous exam answer mistakes that were made, either in person with the professor or independently. And the result of this can be very positive when dealing with potential employers, too: sometimes seeing the dramatic change is clear evidence that you're the sort of person who, like everyone, makes mistakes, but you figure out what's wrong and deliver results when it's important.

Having said all of this, it should be noted that while grades matter when seeking employment, they are not necessarily determinative of one's future success in the legal profession. Though many successful lawyers, judges and law professors have impressive resumes, just as many strategically omit any reference to grades, and others freely admit that their grades were unrelated to their later real-world successes. One of our most successful professors, for example, confessed that he had done poorly in the very class he was now teaching – and teaching very well – but that he had learned from his early mistakes and turned himself around. There are numerous similar stories floating around about well-respected judges and attorneys.[171] Be proud of your good grades, but don't let your bad ones get you down.

---

[171] The story of U.S. District Court Judge Sherman Finesilver, as just one example, may be read at http://63.147.65.175/scene/husted1114.htm.

D. BURN-OUTS AND DROP-OUTS

There are also less positive attitudes people can take on when they receive disappointing grades: I'll call them the "burn-out" and the "drop-out," though they're variations on the same theme.

The burn-out, in his own mind, can't do any better than he did first semester; he gave it his all and there's no reserve left from which to draw fuel. What's really going on in the burn-out's head is a conscious or unconscious admission of exasperation – that he can't conceive of working any harder. But one thing you tend to learn from law school is that good performance is rarely a matter of working harder; rather it's about working smarter, managing your time better, and learning how to acknowledge your mistakes. A burned-out student makes the mental determination that he is tired out and going to coast on whatever performance he can muster up, and give nothing more to the law than that. He may or may not, at some later point, change his mind.

A drop-out is a despondent burn-out, one who thinks not only that his performance will never improve, but also that the only realistic option is to abandon the study of the law altogether. You'd be surprised to see how well some drop-outs are actually doing, in relative grade or performance terms, when they decide that things are irretrievable: some drop-outs were doing a lot better than people who stayed in. Sometimes the problem is merely mild depression mixed with exhaustion; sometimes it's a much more severe psychological obsessive-compulsive issue that, from several stories I've heard, can play out with very weird consequences.[172] One percent appears to be a statistically accurate approximation of the number of people from each class who will drop out for one reason or another.

Bear in mind, of course, that for those who are truly unhappy,[173] transfer to other schools is always an option. For people who believe transfer to be necessary for their happiness or sanity, transfer is probably the best choice, so long as they understand in advance the impact that the decision may have on their later professional careers. Such transfers typically are from better-known schools to less demanding ones closer to family, friends, or other 'comfort'

---

[172] Some might automatically assume that "weird consequences" means "suicides," but in truth, suicides are far rarer at the law school than they are at Cornell University as a whole. One LL.M. student from Japan, apparently feeling considerable pressure to earn perfect grades, committed suicide during my time in law school, and one J.D. student attempted suicide while in a clinically diagnosed state of depression years later. Most people go through law school without knowing anyone who gets to this level. Though the percentage of people exhibiting career-ending mental problems during the first year is truly small, the percentage of life-ending mental problems is even smaller. Students are typically far more inclined to drop out and/or break down than to attempt suicide.

[173] Transfer is, of course, an option for those who did really well; however, this typically happens at the conclusion of the first year. More on this in Chapter 7, Section A.

factors. If this is both acceptable and necessary, it's the right thing to do.

E. NEW CLASSES, OLD CLASSES, AND THE PROSPECT OF ELECTIVES

Putting the last section's gloom aside for the moment, we'll assume that you're part of the 99% of first semester students who remain for a second semester at their original law schools. There's good news: the second semester will be more manageable than the first, and there will be new classes, too.

Though there are differences between schools, the courses offered in the second semester of the first year are fundamentally similar no matter where you go. At Cornell, Criminal Law (Crim Law) replaced Torts, and Property replaced Constitutional Law. Civil Procedure, Contracts, and Legal Methods continued for second semesters. At other schools, Con Law appears for the first time in the second semester, and courses such as Torts and Property last for two semesters. The differences depend largely upon what the faculty of each law school concludes is the best overall program to prepare students for real lawyering, which in some cases matches the emphases of a given state's bar exam.

Some schools have only a single semester of Contracts; Cornell only recently expanded from one to two.[174] Most schools have two semesters of Civil Procedure and two semesters of legal writing; Cornell only recently moved to a second semester of legal writing, in the process jettisoning a formerly mandatory legal philosophy class focused on jurisprudence. Schools will rarely require a second semester of Constitutional Law or mandate that first-year students take Evidence, which essentially parallels Civil Procedure, but applies solely to the introduction and use of evidence in courtrooms. As many law school graduates never step into courtrooms or argue constitutional cases, Cornell makes these subjects optional and offers them to upper-classmen.[175]

Though as a general rule, first-year students don't get to choose classes until they're ready to start their second years, some schools allow 1Ls to choose one or more elective classes.[176] As the table below demonstrates, Yale is

---

[174] Cornell's Contracts class is one contiguous survey of the world of contracts, but it would more usefully be thought of as a first semester in traditional concepts in first-year contracts law, and a second semester of "contract remedies," similar to a class called Remedies offered at many schools and tested on some state bars. Whereas the first semester lays out the general principles establishing who has and has not done wrong, the second semester focuses more on what sort of compensation is available when wrongdoing has been established.

[175] However, most students will eventually opt to take Evidence, which appears prominently on every state bar exam.

[176] Though electives decrease the uniformity of experience for first-year students nationally, it does give 1Ls an early opportunity to chase after their personal interests outside of the core curriculum. And it also gives 1Ls their first chance to do something that they might otherwise only think of starting during the summer – solicit recommendations about good

amongst the most permissive in this regard. By comparison, the University of Connecticut Law School mandates that every student's single second-semester elective class come from a select list of "statutory or regulatory courses."

TABLE 5-2	FIRST-YEAR COURSE SCHEDULES ACROSS THE NATION									
School	First Semester/First Year					Second Semester/First Year				
Arizona	Contracts	Intro to Legal Process and Civ Pro A	Con Law	Torts A	Practice Lab	Crim Pro[177]	Property	Introduction to Legal Process and Civ Pro B	Torts B	Legal Analysis, Writing and Research
Connecticut	Contracts	Civ Pro	Intro to Con Law	Torts	Lawyering Process + Winter Moot Court	Crim Law	Property/ Intro to Con Law	Statutory/ Regulatory Elective	Contracts	Lawyering Process
Cornell	Contracts I	Civ Pro I	Con Law I	Torts	Legal Methods I	Crim Law	Property	Civil Procedure II	Contracts II	Legal Methods II
Duke	All core classes (Civ Pro, Con Law, Contracts, Crim Law, Property, Torts) alternate semesters by section, while Legal Analysis, Research & Writing spreads out over two semesters.									
Florida State	Contracts I	Civ Pro	Property I	Torts	Legal Writing and Research I	Crim Law	Property II	Con Law I	Contracts II	Legal Writing and Research II
Iowa[178]	Contracts and Sales I	Criminal Law I	Property I	Torts	Intro to Legal Reasoning	Civ Pro	Property II	Con Law I	Contracts and Sales II	Legal Bibliography
Stanford	Contracts	Civ Pro	Criminal Law	Torts	Research and Legal Writing	Con Law I	Property	Research and Legal Writing	Electives (2-4 courses)	
Texas at Austin	All classes (Civ Pro, Con Law, Contracts I, Contracts II, Crim Law, Property, Torts, and Legal Research & Writing) alternate semesters by section									
Virginia	Contracts	Civ Pro	Criminal Law	Torts	Legal Writing	Con Law I	Property	Legal Writing		Electives
Yale	Contracts	Procedure	Con Law	Torts		Crim Law	Electives			

Despite the small differences between schools, two things are for certain: regardless of where you go, you're highly likely to continue your legal writing class and at least one, perhaps two of your first-semester core classes in your

teachers and classes from upper-classmen. Additionally, some law student associations publish cursory guides to professors and classes that may well serve as at least a good initial point for decision on optional classes; such guides might be useful to have in hand before you even decide to attend a law school.

[177] Whereas Criminal Law focuses on substantive criminal law, Criminal Procedure focuses on procedural law, and frequently upon several critical U.S. Constitutional Amendments that bear upon the rights of the accused.

[178] Iowa chooses one small section course from the list each semester and adds additional writing and analytical components to that class.

second semester. You'll have at least two, perhaps three entirely new classes to enjoy, and brand new professors for those classes, as well.

For many people, including me, the second semester's Criminal Law turns out to be a perfect replacement for Torts. The concepts are very similar – mental state, action or omission on the part of the defendant, and injury as a result. So are the stories – Crim Law is a series of stories, sometimes shocking, infrequently amusing, mostly about people injuring other people. And then there are the stories where people laugh even when they're not sure if they should be laughing, like during the classic case when someone posing as a doctor convinced a woman that she had a life-threatening disease that could only be cured if he personally delivered a medication via an injection from his penis. The subject matter, like criminal cases shown on television, can become very salacious and bizarre.

Our Criminal Law class was interesting in another way, too: it was our first opportunity to learn from a visiting professor. Such experiences typically turn out one of two ways: the professor is visiting because she's established and fantastic, or because she's established, not fantastic, and looking for other work. Our new Crim Law professor was an exception to the general rule: James Hale was an unestablished recent Yale Law graduate with little teaching experience. But he had been Editor-in-Chief of the *Yale Law Journal*, worked for a Presidential candidate's most recent campaign, had clerked after law school as a clerk to a U.S. Supreme Court justice, and been hand-picked for a shot at teaching by an outgoing Dean of the law school. All by the age of 26.

The class was a learning experience for me on two levels. First, I learned a lot about criminal law, and loved the subject. Crim Law is the class where you learn about the different types of crimes – typically starting with murder, moving to rape, examining conspiracy and attempted crimes, and considering other issues that the professor believes are most important. Over the course of one or two hundred cases, you start to understand the reasons why famously accused criminals have been convicted or freed on certain charges, and more. But this class had a second, non-academic lesson for me, as well. I also learned a lot about the human difficulties faced by law professors. I'll come back to that in the next section.

Our other new class was Property, which is in no way similar to the Con Law class it replaced in our schedule. Property is hard to describe because it's an odd mix of so many different legal principles, all of which revolve around real estate, personal property, and the means by which people or the government may acquire or dispose of each. Property is not so much about interesting stories as it is about legal theories and concepts; what stories there are typically contain puzzling family fights over parcels of land, paintings, or the like. There is a very strong likelihood that a class such as this one could get tedious. But my class got really lucky.

We had the pleasure of taking Property as taught by Professor Franklin, who was a legend around the law school for several reasons. The advance word on the class was that his former students all loved him, and that was a very good sign. It turned out that he was among the most gifted lecturers at the law school, if not the best; his understanding and explanation of the material was fantastic, and he also did not have a need to unnecessarily crack the whip in any way. This meant no Socratic Method for our first time in law school, and no gratuitous piling on of readings just to pile them on. Rumors suggested that he was angling for the position of Dean of our law school, and had been offered a position at another prestigious school should his quest for that office fall through. Within days, it became apparent that we had a bona-fide superstar on our hands. Property lectures were always interesting, becoming the highlight of any day of classes – and that meant a lot considering that it met four times a week and the cases themselves were nothing to write home about.

Substantively, then, the new classes were a pleasant but mild change from the ones that preceded them. The biggest change I noticed in the second semester was that my quality of life, and attitude from day-to-day, changed considerably, at least in part because these two classes proved to be as enjoyable as they were educational.

F.   THE FEAR FACTOR

Regardless of your schedule, one thing will be certain: the second semester, while not technically easier than the first, will most certainly be more predictable. By this point, you will know at least generally what it takes to juggle five tough classes, including random legal writing assignments.

In fact, something weird might start to happen if you have the same professors for your second-semester classes as your first – you may notice that you're no longer feeling cowed by the godlike figures whose acts of breathing, staring and speaking intimidated you just a semester before. And the realization that you no longer feel intimidated is a very, very important feeling. In the legal profession, there's something to be said for a lawyer who adroitly stands up for herself and her client in front of a menacing judge: that's a 'good' lawyer. You begin to develop this sort of ability as you make your way through the second semester and gradually, if not completely, lose your fear.

This can be a dangerous change in attitude for some people. Like it or not, fear is a significant motivator in almost any first semester of law school, and sometimes losing your fear means decreasing your motivation to study, or overestimating your knowledge going into a new situation or class. Either of those things could leave you open for a big embarrassment if you get zapped by the Socratic Method one day. My second semesters of Contracts and Civil Procedure led me down this dangerous path; I found my mind wandering sometimes in class and didn't push myself quite as hard during the semester as I should have – keeping up with readings was not enough. Other people went further down the dangerous road, using their laptops to play games of Solitaire and – on exceedingly rare occasion – literally losing consciousness in class. I might not have put pressure on myself, but some classmates were definitely taking the second semester much more or less seriously than the first.

On some level, I was beginning to feel as if I could focus on the classes I enjoyed, namely Criminal Law, Property, and Legal Methods, and coast through the others. At this moment, I can't explain this mistake beyond to suggest that I probably had burned out a little on Contracts and Civil Procedure after my first-semester exams,[179] where I had pushed myself but not received the A+ grades I was imagining; but perhaps I was also just becoming more comfortable at the law school. Chalk it up to a lack of fear in either case.

Another element of the lessening of the fear factor was the presence of a professor I could identify with. Professor Hale was, like Alex Spitzer from my first semester, someone who wanted you to call him by his nickname: Jim. As someone nearly fresh out of law school and only as old as some of the members of the class he was teaching, Professor Hale had a hard time getting the respect he deserved, even from an audience that was accustomed to behaving itself in every other first-year class. And his mastery of the material, while considerable, lacked some of the presumptuous polish of our more experienced professors. There's definitely something to be said for a little or a lot of white hair on a law professor. He tried to make up for it by giving off tough guy vibes in the first couple of weeks of class, but that was easy to see through: he was a nice guy, likeable enough to have recently been elected to head up a top-flight law journal by his peers, and smart enough to have clerked on the Supreme Court.

Professor Hale's background, and his lack of white hair and pomp, were among the reasons I showed up at his office one day after class. Every professor maintained pre- or post-class office hours at the law school; many were famously difficult to speak with, and some circumscribed their on-campus presences to narrow windows that dissuaded people from forming lines, which they often did anyway.[180] In truth, I didn't care too much about any professors'

---

[179] If I learned any lessons, they were to take second semesters of classes at least as seriously as I had taken the first, and not to expect final exams to be even vaguely cumulative. Moreover, any first-year student should enter second-semester classes feeling 100% grounded in any two-semester subject, because you will need to know enough from semester one to be able to handle semester two. I was personally called on to discuss a case from semester one on the first day of the second semester of Civil Procedure. It wasn't a good feeling.

[180] Some people were known to be office hour hogs, showing up every day after classes to ask all sorts of questions inside and outside the scope of the material. This group of "hogs" primarily included the gunners and other people who were eventually to become the top

office hours during my first semester.[181] The class that I found most perplexing, Civil Procedure, had an intimidating enough professor that I didn't want to draw extra attention to myself. But Professor Hale was different, and my reason for showing up at his office was different. This was a guy with an interesting background – he had clerked for a federal court and worked in politics, two things I was personally considering as post-law school options. I didn't show up because I wanted to talk about Criminal Law. I showed up because I wanted to know what his life before Cornell had been like.

And he was surprisingly quite willing to talk. We talked for a while about the things he had done – the Supreme Court clerkship, he explained, was the ultimate power rush – there was no position one could hold in a lifetime, he asserted, better than writing opinions for the Supreme Court.[182] Without a trace of ego, he alluded to a well-known phenomenon of post-clerking depression amongst former Supreme Court clerks, resulting from the fact that most believed that there was nothing they would ever do in their lives that could outshine such prestigious clerkships. This, he explained, was where he was right then in his life. Teaching law would be a good follow-up, but there would be a sense of emptiness – he didn't have a wife or girlfriend, Ithaca was a small place, and his chances of being invited to teach permanently at Cornell were very unclear. He, like the previous Dean, was a conservative amongst an increasingly liberal-leaning faculty, though they were by no means the only right-leaning people in the administration. The Dean had left the school shortly after extending Jim

---

10% of the class, but it also included a handful of people who legitimately didn't understand material and wanted to talk through an issue or two. People used the office hours as much to brownnose the professors as to legitimately discuss class issues, and this is one of those pointers that I can give you, even though I never would have done it myself: spending time with professors after class, so long as you're not an annoyance, is a sure-fire way to prime yourself for later clerkship and job-hunting success.

[181] If you truly feel as if you need to ask the professor a question – and this is, in fact, a completely reasonable way for any student (and especially a first-year) to feel, do not hesitate to stop by the professor's office. Whatever fear of the professor you may have can be dispelled by sitting down for a few minutes, really thinking in advance about the specific question or questions you want to pose, and limiting your inquiry to that which you've prepared to say. If you're afraid of being asked difficult questions by the professor in return, or drawing attention to yourself, there's good and bad news. The bad news is that either of these things is likely to happen. The good news is that you probably can handle the extra attention – that's part of law school. If, after all of this, you still feel uncomfortable talking with a professor, pose the same question instead to a trusted classmate or two.

[182] Judicial clerks are ghostwriters for judges; they submit drafts of opinions based on a mix of their own legal reasoning skills and the judges' philosophies. To write for a Supreme Court justice is to have a good shot at rendering the very final word on proper interpretation of a given law.

Hale an offer to become a visiting professor, and as the political scene looked at that moment, there weren't going to be a lot of other people lining up to push for him to join the faculty permanently.

This was my first peek behind the law school's Oz-like faculty curtain, and I wasn't sure that I liked what I saw. I considered myself an unaffiliated political moderate, and never loved hard-core right- or left-wingers, but it struck me somehow as entirely inappropriate that someone would be more or less likely to be offered a job – either initially or permanently – based on one's politics rather than teaching ability. It was unclear to what extent the political factor had swung once in Jim's favor, and now against him, but there definitely was somewhat of a growing undercurrent of discussion amongst those in the know that the faculty was becoming increasingly politically polarized. The consequences of this would not become clear for many months.[183]

G. An Aside: Lexis and Westlaw

Most of the second-semester was dominated by daily, time-consuming class readings, with breaks to check E-mail, eat meals, and go out once in a long while to the movies. Legal Methods papers were most to blame for making life unpredictable. Friends in my section were able to balance assignments and class work, but friends in other sections were overwhelmed by heavy appellate briefs and oddball assignments. It was hard to convince people to go out except on Friday nights, and I was all too ready to go back and study some more when the options in Ithaca were otherwise so limited. A lot of this time was spent doing case research and paper rewrites for my Legal Methods class.

The legal writing program at Cornell began to place increased emphasis on computer-assisted online research during the second semester, and as there's no better place to discuss the topic, we'll take it up here.

Though there are less expensive options, online legal research in the United States is dominated by two different research tools you'll learn about during law school: one is called Westlaw, and the other is called Lexis-Nexis, or sometimes just Lexis.[184] Each offers a more-or-less complete collection of judicial opinions, statutes, constitutions and other legal materials, all of which will be necessary for you to investigate in some way. The proper searching of these huge databases is somewhat complicated, however, mastery of these services can save both you and your future clients untold quantities of otherwise wasted time and money. Most legal employers will expect that you have been trained in using these services, in addition to poring through stereotypically old, dusty law books – the 'old-fashioned way.'

In a nutshell, when you want to determine the current state of the law on

---

[183] See Chapter 7, Section H, and Chapter 10, Section D.

[184] Among the options is the Legal Information Institute (LII), described at Section A.

any given subject in any given geographic location or jurisdiction in the United States (and beyond), you will at some point need to consult Lexis or Westlaw, if not both of them. In class assignments, you'll probably start by looking for applicable statutory law – the laws written by elected legislators and carried to votes, then executive signatures – and afterward moving on to read what judges have said on the subject.

But Lexis and Westlaw have a lot of other things to offer law students. You can get access to a vast collection of treatises, course outlines, and law review articles through these services. And believe it or not, because they want to win you over as a future customer, they give you virtually unlimited access to their premium services for free during the time you're in law school.

Your other option, of course, is to learn how to sift through the old law books in a library and determine what is or is not valid law. This is achieved via a complex system of verification that now generally winds up requiring a final cross-check of Lexis or Westlaw anyway. You'll generally spend at least part of your legal writing course learning how to do the old-fashioned book searches, but online access continues to grow in importance and prevalence and for law students, the advantages of using Lexis and Westlaw are innumerable.

H.   One Necessary Distraction: Making Your Summer Plans

Like it or not, law school constantly forces students to think about their futures –starting in their very first year. "What will you be doing next?" is one of the constant questions facing law students at least informally; if your school has a career office, you will probably hear the question formally around the end of your first semester, as the school wants to let you know what to do to maximize your chances of summer employment. For most students in the midst of the first year grind, "next" means tomorrow, and no one wants to think about planning something for four or five months from now. But the planning of one's legal life continues to demand thought and some preparation.

First-year students typically have four ways they can spend their post-first-year summers. The first is to do nothing and relax. The second is to work for a law firm. The third is to work for a professor or judge. The fourth is to study in a summer program. In tight economic times, you should skip option one.

Clearly, after the stresses of the first year, everyone's top choice would be to take a long vacation that starts as soon as possible. But for most people, and especially the ambitious ones, this isn't likely to happen. Writing competitions have to be completed, and finding some form of legally-related summer employment is perhaps even more of a popular pursuit; working at a McDonald's is not going to do anything to help your resume or future career. Most people seek jobs either with law firms, judges, or professors.

Law firms typically interview first-year law students for summer positions starting in late December, shortly before or after the time grades begin to trickle out of some law schools. As a general rule, they do not conduct on-campus interviews for first-year summer positions. You must somehow make your way to their offices at your own expense, and many people choose to do this during their winter break period. Yes, it's possible to interview for a position without having received your grades, but the firm will want to see the grades when you get them and will likely make its final decision only when it can base it somewhat heavily upon them. It is not at all unusual for a student to have a fantastic interview only to be rejected later based on an arbitrary grade cut-off.

The interview process will be discussed at much greater length later,[185] but a few details of particular interest to first-year students merit attention now. Summer employment of students by law firms is very expensive for any firm, so the number of spots is limited, especially so in harder economic times.[186] Firms are not keen to hire too many first-year students, as their work product is not especially useful or worth passing along to a client without major revisions, and because students frequently seek employment elsewhere during their second-year summer. For the sake of estimation, even a large firm's office may bring on two first-year summer associates at most; rarely more.

Therefore your chances as a first-year are best if you express interest early, have strong ties to the city where you're looking for work, and can show up in person for a scheduled interview looking sharp and talking smooth. This means having at least temporary use of a suit and a calm, pleasant demeanor, while expressing a level of interest and knowledge in the specific firm you're interviewing with. To increase your chances of securing a job, you may also look at the firm's list of associates and partners to see if any are alumni of your undergraduate or law school, and if so, mail or e-mail them to express interest.

Getting a job with a judge or professor over the summer is considerably different from the firm experience. Typically you'll have to meet with the judge or professor in person to discuss your interest in working with them, and this is more frequently done informally than formally as a first-year student looking to 'summer clerk.' Knowing the judge personally prior to law school, or having some tie to her, is a major door-opener. Having a good in-class experience with the professor you target tends also to help your case, though some schools have seemingly open interview calls for 'research assistants' for professors where you submit a letter of interest and go from there.

Law firms can pay handsomely for your summer work; unpaid firm internships are today uncommon. Professors tend to have modest budgets, if any, to compensate students for their summer work, and judges typically do not

---

[185] See Chapter 9, Section A.
[186] Summer programs at law firms are a high-cost means of attracting quality talent early in a law student's career, and securing that talent for future employment. First-year students are perceived to be less likely to return permanently to a summer employer than second-year students, and so law firms hire fewer of them.

pay for summer clerk work at all. In any case, the most valuable rewards one gets from these experiences are experience and resume-building credentials.

The final way some people spend their summers is in non-remedial 'summer school,' or Summer Institutes, as some schools call them. Cornell, for example, is one of a number of schools offering international 'study abroad' programs that combine law school-caliber class work with study settings outside of the United States. The Cornell program is offered in Paris with ties to the Université Paris I Panthéon-Sorbonne; other schools have programs in London, Berlin, and Vienna, as well as other major cities across Europe and Asia. At Cornell, you can earn a maximum of six credits (spread over three two-credit courses) for your summer class work, which are later applied towards your diploma.

The summer course may be the best option for those who wish both to travel and to spend the summer doing something productive. Applications are typically due several months before the courses begin, which is generally at the beginning of July or thereabouts.

Finding housing, both for the summer and for the upcoming semester, is another decision you'll need to make around this point. You might remain in your first-year apartment, or seek housing with law school classmates,[187] or decide to go solo in a brand new place. In my experience, law students tended to enjoy living with each other more than other graduate students, with whom many first-years had found themselves placed somewhat randomly by the university's housing office. The hard pace of law school life doesn't mix well with the leisurely, party-friendly atmosphere enjoyed by business and other graduate students.

After my own first year, which was spent in the law school's dormitory building, I considered living either with other law students or going solo, ultimately opting for the latter when I found a great one-person apartment.[188] Other friends moved into two- or three-person apartments, sometimes exclusively with law students, sometimes with significant others.[189] As with the initial housing choice you made before starting your first year, your decision here is an entirely personal one, and will likely be shaped most strongly by the

---

[187] Before you commit to an apartment, be careful to consider whether you or a given classmate might transfer out of the law school.

[188] Though it was not a factor in my deliberations, one of the interesting issues that comes up with law student roommates is the potential, albeit over-exaggerated, for litigation between classmates if things go wrong. Of our 180-person class, I heard only one story of a roommate who sued another during law school, but it was under highly unusual circumstances. Regardless, the inconvenience was profound.

[189] Moving in with a boyfriend or girlfriend during law school can be a mixed blessing. Consider whether you're really interested in subjecting yourself to the risk of a messy break-up and move from the apartment part way through the year.

experiences you've had during the first semester, and the housing options available at your price range immediately before the second one.

I.   A GASP OF FRESH AIR AND A RETURN TO THE RUMOR MILL

For months, the law school seemed like a minimum-security prison: we could go outside, but never get away for long. During one spell, Ithaca's winter trapped most dormers' cars in the student parking lot, and it took a vehicle the size of my SUV just to get out of it. The bridge to Collegetown was caked with snow and ice, and it often seemed a better idea to stay indoors than plod through whatever unfortunate weather might await beyond the law school's dorms. From January to March or April, rain or snowy slush awaited those who walked to school or parked in Collegetown. It barely made a dent on my life. I was used to snow, having lived in Buffalo for so long, and even the aggressive bar-hoppers in my class weren't going out that much at this point. Small in-dorm or apartment parties were the extent of the action for a while. I felt surprised on the few occasions when I caught a rare glimpse of sunshine from a vantage point outside of a window, rather than inside one.

When April came, the clouds lifted from the law school both literally and figuratively. Our legal writing program ended earlier in the semester than our other classes, bringing a much-needed several weeks of breathing room before exams. It began to feel as if we were actually going to make it through our first year after all. People – especially first-years – started to venture outdoors in the afternoons to play Frisbee and touch football, and at night resumed visits to Ithaca's not-so-exciting bar scene. The law school's favorite haunt, a dirty little dive called The Palms, began to pick up again. A few funny stories made their way around the school every weekend.

One of the more interesting stories had to do with Professor Hale. Students held a party after a law school event called Cabaret – a chance for students to show off their talents for live performance and place bids in a series of charity auctions.[190] In an attempt to meet people and stave off the boredom of Ithaca nightlife, he had appeared briefly at the post-Cabaret party and mingled until it became evident to all involved how weird it was. Some people found the story funny; I understood the situation well enough not to appreciate the humor in it, and to empathize somewhat with the loneliness inspired by Ithaca. A story later circulated that he was dating an upper-class student – someone who he wasn't teaching. I wasn't so sure how I felt about this one.

Romance in law school is a tricky thing. I'd had my eyes open for the entire school year and didn't see anyone quite right for me. But I was increasingly becoming aware of the allure of law students, especially attractive ones, to single professors. During the first semester, Professor Alighieri had

---

[190] For more details on Cabaret and its sponsors, the PILU, see Chapter 7, Section I.

taken class time to deny a virulent rumor that he had invited a number of the law school's best-looking first-year women to his office to discuss their thoughts and feelings on the law school experience – or, at least, he denied that he had invited them because they were good-looking. They were just supposed to have been a random sample from our class. After all, the professor was married, one male had been invited, and so on, went the story.

Law students were prime material for young professors: smart, self-motivated, and interested in the law, just as the professors were. This same rationale applied to student couplings; many people felt that only a law student could understand the problems another law student was having, and there was such commonality of interests between most law students that it was never a surprise that people got together. By the end of second semester, there were numerous established couples who had met at the law school. Rumors of professorial intermingling with students tended not to be confirmed.

Gossip was also spreading about another established law school couple, but one that was not quite so well-known – one of the school's high-profile professors and his long-time girlfriend, a professor who was then teaching at another law school. Apparently, the professor's girlfriend had been invited the year before my arrival to teach a class or two at Cornell as a visiting professor, and had been met with such widespread complaints from her students that she was not invited to return. But, as the story went, the high-profile professor had pulled strings, and she was going to come back and teach another set of classes in the upcoming year – a fact which disgusted many of the students who had suffered through her previous lectures. Blind student deference to the wisdom of the faculty was eroding, if only slightly at first.

Another faculty decision was somewhat less controversial. Late in the semester came word that Professor Hale wasn't going to be returning in the fall – something that disappointed but didn't surprise me. No one on the staff was there to champion his cause when the outgoing dean left the school, and some students hadn't enjoyed his class as much as I had.

But visiting professor decisions turned out to be the least provocative ones made by the faculty near the end of the second semester. In a shock to virtually every concerned student at the law school, the dean search had ended with a faculty vote in favor of an outside candidate. Professor Franklin, our beloved Property professor, had charmed students, proposed an aggressive plan to revitalize critically needy aspects of the law school's infrastructure, and seemingly bested all of several competitors for the law school dean's position. In a series of interviews with students and faculty, three other candidates, including a quiet but friendly Cornell Constitutional Law professor and two outsiders, had hardly registered on the students' maps.

The faculty picked the outside candidate who was quietest during his interview with student representatives. Known to his peers as a conciliatory consensus-builder, the new dean was a man who had presented students with no specific agenda for the future, but was believed by the faculty to be someone who could talk through issues and heal the deepening political rifts in their ranks. He was a marked contrast with Professor Franklin, who was somewhat of a firebrand and represented the sort of institutional change a more concerned institution might have rapidly embraced.

Professor Franklin's rejection felt like a dramatic slap in the face, but it was entirely consistent with the legends of law school administrations: students' preferences come someplace far down the list. Some people thought of writing angry letters to the student newspaper, but few went as far as to touch pen to paper. The rumor that haunted the law school for the final weeks of the semester, and even for months thereafter, was that Professor Franklin was upset by the decision and now exceedingly anxious to pursue the other opportunity he had been offered by another school. Some people doubted that he would even stick around to administer the final examination for his class.

J.   SECOND SEMESTER EXAMS: HAS ANYTHING CHANGED?

From many vantage points, the second semester is what you decide to make of it – a big change from before. Near the end of the semester, some people were ready to start protests over the school's second invitation to the poorly-received visiting professor and the appointment of a mild-mannered dean. Predictably, most people were too focused on upcoming exams to care much, if at all. As had been the case at the end of the first semester, the end of the second saw professors walk out of their classrooms to rounds of applause, and students retreat hastily to the library for their final stretches of studying.

By the time second semester exams roll around, you're certain to know a little about their general format, whether you'll need to do more to prepare (such as extended reviews of old exams on file), and what areas you can review to optimize your performance. More importantly, you'll now have less of a sense that every single thing you read or heard is going to appear somehow on the exam; you'll begin to get a sense of what materials your professors believe to be especially important and can focus your energies upon them.

And yet though all of this is true, the second semester still retains some of the first semester's crapshoot characteristics: no matter how good you were at predicting your grades as an undergraduate, you'll never really be sure how well you did on these exams until you get your grades. At least you won't have to get them in person with everyone else; because the grades come out during the summer, you'll receive them in the mail or access them via the Internet.

In anecdotal experience, the general trend amongst people I knew was to hover around or drift slightly upwards or downwards from the same GPA throughout law school. Very few experienced major spikes unless they both committed to and effectively executed major lifestyle changes after a tough first semester. Those who only generally desired to do better and worked hard typically improved, but not dramatically. And those who did not desire to do better often maintained grades, but in other cases actually fell – sometimes surprisingly hard, other times gradually over the remaining semesters.

Second-semester exams were like the first: long, challenging, and unsettlingly uncertain at the end. Again students walked out without a sense of what their grades might be,[191] though by the end of the exam stretch the previous semester's top 10% were just starting to get a sense that things were not going to change much. Criminal Law's exam introduced a new type of question: two of the four essays dealt with 'policy' issues, asking not so much for traditional issue spotting as the student's analysis of what was missing or over-aggressive in a given proposed law and what would have to be removed or added to make it conform conceptually to existing legal norms. It was another interesting intellectual twist on the standard law school exam question, and one that I enjoyed.[192] Unfortunately, policy questions were never to become a significant part on my other law school exams, though some other schools' exams were reputed to place a greater emphasis on policy.

Again, all of the exams except Civil Procedure were open-book; that exam, however, switched for its first time ever to a half multiple-choice, half

---

[191] My own second semester grades dropped only modestly – by a tenth of a point or thereabouts. And this, despite the fact that I had no eye infection to contend with. But I scored my highest grade of the first year during the second semester, as well. Admittedly, although I wasn't expecting my grades to be lower overall, I had definitely not stressed myself out studying as I had in the time prior to first semester exams, and I was probably at least a little too comfortable walking in to a couple of exams with less than a comprehensive knowledge of their "big pictures." If I had it to do over again, I would have spent more time going over the new material and sketching out the new "big picture" for Civil Procedure, in particular, and probably Contracts as well – both classes which had continued from the first semester to the second. Those grades were the lowest I received in law school, though I had given both classes a fair share of effort during exam prep time. My lesson for this semester: never be complacent with your first-semester knowledge of a two-semester subject. While I was falling behind in two classes, other people were clawing their way upwards after harsher first semesters.

[192] My highest grade was the one I received in Criminal Law, a subject I had loved while hardly expecting or angling to receive a top grade. Interestingly, my grade in Crim Law seemed to have touched on an odd truth about law school, particularly present because of the curve. Almost everyone I knew had complained incessantly about Crim Law throughout the semester and during exam preparation time, because our young professor hadn't been as seamless and clear in his lectures as some of our other, more skilled lecturers. People complained up until exam day that they were confused by the material; by contrast, I made efforts both to understand the professor's style and make sure that the material made sense by the time I entered the exam. And my grade was surprisingly high, a reflection of the maxim that when your school has a forced grading curve, it's not how much you know that determines your grade, but how little everyone else knows.

essay format that was riddled with small mistakes. It was an exam that people walked out of with plenty of complaints. But these complaints were quickly forgotten amidst celebrations of another completed semester, and this time, we had really accomplished something: we were no longer 1Ls.

K. JOURNAL WRITING COMPETITIONS: WHETHER, HOW, AND GRADING

1. *Whether*

By the end of the second semester, especially the final grueling exam stretch, you'll be very much ready to go off and start doing whatever you've planned for the summer. But for most people, there will be yet another hurdle to tackle: the journal writing competition mentioned earlier in the chapter.

At most schools, the writing competition begins immediately – and I mean literally immediately – after the last of the second semester exams has ended. Outside of the *Law Review*'s business office, the center for coordinating the competition at Cornell, lines of people formed only moments after our last exam, all waiting to collect their so-called "competition packets."

The big question, of course, is whether you really need to participate. And the answer, thankfully, is no. You can completely skip the writing competition under one of two circumstances: if you have no interest in writing for a journal,[193] or believe that you will have such stellar grades that one of the journals at your school will invite you on regardless of whether you participate in the competition or not. You'll need to check to see whether the journals at your school have such policies, and then check yourself to be sure you're not delusional about your chance of prevailing under such a policy.

With that said, and overachievers aside, there are plenty of people who decide after the first year that they cannot imagine spending their second and

---

[193] You might have no interest because you have better options, or because nothing thrills you about journal work. While you may justifiably avoid participating in a journal if you are planning to be active in extracurricular moot court, you shouldn't dismiss journal work entirely unless you have some other excellent extracurricular activity up your sleeve. Under some circumstances, moot court participation can be just as beneficial as journal membership, depending on your school, personal aptitude for competition, and the type of law you hope to practice. Wannabe litigators typically benefit more from moot court membership than transactional attorneys. But few other activities compare with journal work or moot court participation on legal resumes, and in practice. The single student in my class who had previously graduated from medical school, for example, would have stood out in virtually any resume pool he entered, because his skill set was so incredibly useful to certain types of law firms. Similar attention accrues to those with graduate degrees in areas specific to their future employers' practices.

third years working for a journal.[194] This is totally understandable. The first year is terribly stressful, and journal work is rightfully reputed to make the second year just as taxing, though in different ways. Of my class of 180 students, approximately 110 (61%) entered the writing competition. You can add perhaps 10 to that number as an estimate of those anticipating that their grades would automatically earn admission to a journal regardless of doing the writing competition, and count the remaining 1/3 as 'not interested.'

Guessing that you'll get an offer to join a journal anyway is a tricky proposition. First, you need to know what the grade cutoffs are for each organization. Then, you have to have stellar grades in your first semester. And finally, you need to be confident enough as of the last day of exams to bet that you'll repeat the phenomenon again. Most people on the margins thus tend to participate in the writing competition anyway.

But if you don't participate and you do get an offer, you earn bragging rights of a sort – but not the kind wise people brag about. One of the factors leading Cornell's *Law Review* to mandate that every candidate for membership complete the competition was the perception of a class disparity between those who 'wrote on' and those who 'graded on' without writing. So if you attend another school and know you graded on, try your best to take only quiet pride in your accomplishments, lest the policy change.

2.   How

Though there are major differences between various schools' journal writing competitions, there are some issues that commonly come up. One is the time allocation issue, and this is something you should plan around if possible.

The Cornell writing competition lasted three full weeks when I took it, and was reduced to two full weeks in the subsequent year. Every new Board of Editors is allowed to determine the subsequent year's competition length, but the general trend has been to keep the competition reasonably long, but also not too long. You need time to churn out a decent product, but three weeks of writing is time that could and must, in some people's cases, be spent working to support a family or pay off debts.

It helps to know as far in advance as possible how much time you'll need to set aside for the writing competition; however, journals often do not solidify

---

[194] There are people who have no interest in the work, people who have no desire to give up their free time, and people who just generally have no idea of what benefits journal work may have for them. If by this point in law school you're in one of the former two categories, forget about journal work so long as you can live with the possible consequences to your career. See Chapter 9, Section A. If you don't know how important the benefits will really be for you, speak with some journal members at your school and get a sense of whether they felt that they got anything out of the experience. Don't avoid participation just for lack of knowledge.

dates until some time after they elect their new Editors. You might therefore have to wait until April or May to know for certain, which means that if you're hunting for a job, you need to try to keep your start date flexible until the competition dates are made firm. If you can't be flexible, give yourself three weeks plus whatever time you need to physically change apartments.

Your actual success in the competition will to some extent be dependent on how well you manage your time, and how much of a load of materials your school's journals will attempt to pile on you. And they will, or at least should, make it tough. A good writing competition attempts to provide a significant enough challenge that really good work stands out from the bad, and although it is frequently said that the aggregate quality of the materials submitted is "astonishingly bad," there's enough difference to separate out wheat from chaff.

How does a person make their work 'good?' Let's start with the objectives. A typical writing competition asks students to prepare one thing: the so-called case or scope note, which looks at a recent case and compares it in some way – left to your discretion – to past cases, explaining their similarities and distinctions. Some schools offer you a choice from several fountainhead cases, while most others give you only one. Most schools also use a 'closed universe' format, giving you all of the materials and banning the use of virtually any others when working on the competition. Some schools just give you a choice of cases and tell you to write something based on whatever you can find.

In both types of exercises – the open and closed universes – the way to succeed is the same: you have to write something that looks like the notes that the journal already publishes. And that means you should, at some point significantly before the competition, understand the structures and formatting of real law review notes. They are not like magazine articles or op-ed pieces for a newspaper; your opinions are only modestly important. They are generally about the history and importance of case law, statutes, and scholars' opinions.

Then adapt what you've generally learned about law review articles to follow the specific directions given to you by the people holding the competition. You'll no doubt, for example, have a page limit, so don't try to write something as long as the yawners that make it into real law reviews. Most importantly, make your piece stand out by going a little – and I mean a little – outside the norm of law review writing by giving your note an interesting title, a snappy introduction and a quick conclusion. Grabbing the reader's attention is always a good way to succeed in a writing competition.

There are a couple of other pointers that everyone needs to understand. BLUEBOOK citations matter. Learn how they are normally used in a journal article before you attempt them yourself. Aim for roughly six to ten citations to the materials per written page of text. Finally, do one or two last-minute proof reads of your submission before sending it off. It's hard to meaningfully check your work when you've been mired in it for so long – I know from experience –

but you need to be sure the final version has no rough edges readers will note.

Cornell is one of only a handful of schools to employ a second supplementary component to its writing competition – a recently-introduced 'editing competition.' An editing competition is designed to parallel the real-life work that would be done by associates, namely, taking a short segment of an already-written argument and checking it for mistakes. While use of the BLUEBOOK is necessary for the writing competition, it was really brought into play in the editing competition, where finding citation errors was a task at least as important as discovering typographical and pagination problems.

But be careful. If your school uses both a writing competition and an editing competition, it might not be wise to divide your time equally or even close to that – at Cornell, the *Law Review* weighted the editing competition 20% versus 80% for the writing portion, and another journal weighted it only 10%; the third apparently did not consider it at all. While it would be a mistake to write it off entirely, you might not treat the editing competition with the same level of anal attention you give the final draft of your writing competition piece.

The skills that are tested by the two competitions are intended to be practical ones: whether you can do the work expected of journal associates, namely editing articles and writing a note. Those who come closest to the real thing in the competition are nearly drafted, so be careful what you wish for.

Some schools, and some journals, add one last element to the writing competition: a personal statement. Cornell's *Law Review* is the only journal at Cornell to take a personal statement into account; the goal is to enhance organizational diversity by allowing applicants to disclose life-shaping personal hardships or experiences, which could include, but were not limited to, economic, racial, ethnic or gender-related hardships.

Without launching into a defense of the personal statement initiative, I'll say only that I think it is quite likely to help a person earn admission to a journal that takes the statement into account. Moreover, I felt and still feel quite comfortable with the *Law Review's* guarantee of anonymity and security for the personal statements, such that students who endeavored to share personal experiences were not outed for doing so. So if a personal statement option exists at your school, consider doing it. It generally can only help you, and won't hurt you; moreover, it may be as easy to complete as regurgitating and updating something you wrote as a law school application essay.

3. Grading

The fundamental downside to the writing competition is the reality of its administration: students run the competition, handle the grading, and thereby pick the winners of the competition. While I have personally not heard of irregularities in the selection process, they are of course conceivable, and if you suspect something is drastically wrong, you should take the appropriate steps to investigate and report the apparent problem.

But in most cases, the schools leave the process untouched, as spotty as it might sometimes be. Well-run journals know just how fallible the grading process actually is, and have instituted checks on the process, such as multiple anonymous graders and grading, reconciliation sessions where unusually high or low grades are discussed prior to finalization, and formal grade recording processes vesting final responsibility in the editors-in-chief to set standards. For the most part, these procedures fix the problems I'm about to mention. But they're not perfect checks on an imperfect system.

As mentioned earlier, those who will be grading your writing competition submissions are students. Unlike those who grade bar exams, who are paid a tiny bit of money for every exam they read, and those who grade law school exams, who are typically paid a lot of money, students get nothing for grading your writing competition materials. It is quite likely that they will actually be working for someone else during the summer, most likely a law firm or professor. And they may spend very little time actually looking at your work. A rare few may spend no time at all on it; the proverbial 'throw the papers down the stairs and the ones that fall to the bottom get A's' situation.

The stories of writing competition grading are tragic even for those who go in with the best intentions. Many graders delay and save all of the reading for one day, and then have to sift through 10-12 separate submissions in a full or half day. I'm not just speaking of my classmates, by the way; I've observed this much and worse from coworkers at a large law firm who represented a wide swath of well-known schools. And worse yet, this sort of behavior comes from people who would bitch to high heaven if they believed that their own papers were given such little attention by professors, though their own writing competition papers were likely given similar attention by their peers.

This does not in any way reduce the advice shared earlier in this chapter. Write well, try to catch their attention, and follow the model provided by other law review articles. If you might only get five minutes of someone's attention, make sure they remember you positively in those five minutes.

In the end, the process typically works out – in part because of the checks on the problems mentioned above, and in part because many people simply burn out during the writing competition and turn in legitimately poor work products. Those who succeed are the ones who follow through on their commitments to do well in the competition, and thereby demonstrate their interest enough to stand out. Though there will always be a person or two who clearly deserved, for one reason or another, to be on a journal that he or she was not accepted to be on, this is a rare complaint, and deservedly so.

STUDYING ABROAD: SUMMER INTERNATIONAL LAW CLASS AT
COUR DE CASSATION (FRENCH SUPREME COURT

Your post-first-year summer can be one of two things: an important career-building opportunity or a much-needed chance to relax. Even more than was the case in the second semester, the summer will be what you make of it, but if you want to work, it will mostly be what you *are permitted to* make of it, because someone has to hire you in order for you to actually get a job. And then they have to like your work.

Though it's tempting to discuss the various vacation options that one might have after the first year has ended, I can't in good conscience recommend a true vacation as a step towards success in the legal profession. But under the right circumstances, you might be able to get pretty close to a vacation by enrolling in one of the summer study programs offered by a number of law schools around the country, in conjunction with other law schools around the world. As a practical alternative, I'll also briefly discuss what you might expect if you succeed in getting a summer job, either with a professor, a judge, a public interest group, or as a 'summer associate' at a law firm. Depending on the place where you work and the type of work you'll perform, your labor in one of these positions might even draw a paycheck of some significance.

A. SUMMER STUDY PROGRAMS

As of this writing, the options for summer legal study abroad are numerous.[195] Eighty-five of the over 180 ABA-accredited law schools have international study programs, which are typically called Summer Institutes, a prestigious name which belies their potential for relaxation. Students can enroll in courses of study as challenging or mildly taxing as they desire; many schools offer the option to enroll in as few as one credit or as many as eight credits of classes. Few courses start as early as mid-May; most start in mid-June or the beginning of July, and end no later than the early part of August.

Several schools offer summer institutes in three or more cities at once – among them, the University of San Diego,[196] Temple University,[197] and Tulane University.[198] Most participants will only go to one city per summer, but the rare individual will do more. The University of San Diego (USD) Law School offers courses in Barcelona, Dublin, Florence, London, Oxford, Paris, and Moscow at prices ranging from $1,850 to $2,750, depending on the number of credits and excluding food and housing. Temple offers courses in Athens, Rome, and Tel Aviv at prices from $2,220 to $2,600, and Tulane has classes in Montreal, Cambridge, Paris, Berlin, the Greek Isles, Jerusalem, Siena and Amsterdam at

---

[195] A complete list of the options may be found at http://www.abanet.org/legaled/studyabroad/foreign.html.
[196] See http://www.acusd.edu/lawabroad/ and http://www.acusd.edu/usdlaw/islp.html.
[197] See http://www2.law.temple.edu/page.asp?page=summerstudy.
[198] See http://www.law.tulane.edu/abroad/.

prices from $1,650 to $4,177.50. Most schools offer programs in only one or two cities per summer, and those cities tend to be the same from year to year. Cornell offers an annual program in Paris,[199] Duke has programs in Geneva and Hong Kong,[200] and Pace has an annual program in London.[201]

It shouldn't be too hard to locate a program, either offered by your law school or another one, which offers law school courses in a setting you'd like to visit during the summer time. Advertisements for summer study programs were plastered all over the walls of our student center, and could also be found in the pages of free law student magazines. Because of its course offerings, location, and convenience of admissions, I chose the Cornell program, which is taught in Paris and consumes the entire month of July.

There are several considerations that one should take into account before committing to a summer study program of any sort. First is the aggregate price, including airfare, housing, and program costs – the program prices above include only tuition, not books, necessities, or any of the numerous travel expenses you'll have to deal with.[202] Second, transferring credits from your summer program to your law school may, in some cases, be difficult. Do at least a little research with your law school's career office before you make any commitments. And third, you'll need to determine whether the program's usefulness outweighs its consequence – namely that you won't be able to work during your first summer. While an international summer program proves to be a very good discussion point in second-year job interviews, it probably doesn't carry the weight of competitively-sought employment. But then, the market for first-year employment is so small that study abroad will probably not be held against you by an employer. In terms of prestige, having a job with a professor at a good school is probably better, but going to a well-respected summer program shouldn't hurt you, either.[203]

It's worth considering all of these things, but that doesn't mean you have to be disturbed by them. I personally would never think twice about picking my summer program again, because it turned out to be extremely important to my

---

[199] See http://www.lawschool.cornell.edu/international/Paris/default.html.

[200] See http://www.law.duke.edu/internat/summerInstitutes.html.

[201] See http://www.pace.edu/lawschool/london/brochur5.html.

[202] Finding housing may be the single most difficult part of planning a summer abroad. Students pursued options ranging from youth hostels, dormitory buildings, and living with family friends, to renting apartments and even making month-long arrangements for hotel rooms. It helps to make contact with people you know in the country (even through the grapevine) and begin the housing search as far in advance as possible.

[203] The summer programs at these schools tend not to be especially competitive, either in admissions or in class atmosphere. They can be a good way to get a good school's name onto your resume and have a relatively collegial legal study environment, if either of these experiences has earlier escaped you.

law school experience – and my life overall – in a few key ways.[204]

First, I had the opportunity to travel to Europe, something that I had wanted to do for years yet had never managed to accomplish before. The summer program in Paris offered a convenient excuse to spend a couple of weeks in advance trekking through other Western European hot spots, so I used Eurail railroad passes to inexpensively visit Berlin, Vienna, Zurich, Vaduz (Liechtenstein), and Belgium, then arrived in Paris just in time for the Summer Institute to begin. During the Paris program, groups of people took weekend outings to Barcelona, London, and beyond; I formed a London group and visited the Loire Valley as part of an official Cornell-sponsored trip. It's hard to explain just how much I enjoyed the summer strictly on the basis of my travels, and how much it broadened my perspective on the world.

Second and of equal importance were the friends I made during the summer – these were some of the best friendships I developed through law school. The Paris program brought me in touch with great people from a number of different schools, some of them international, and there's still a loose network of communications in place between the summer program participants. And it also introduced me to people from Cornell that I had not met during the two relatively less relaxing semesters that had come before. When it comes to forming friendships, there's nothing in the world like being able to hang out with people in a city like Paris,[205] where there's cheap wine aplenty and all sorts of attractions to let you make the most of all your free time.

And most people do have free time, even during weekdays. Though the courses are challenging, they are by no means as taxing, generally, as standard first-year courses – mostly because you only take two (or a maximum of three) courses at a time. You're advised beforehand that taking three classes will result in a less than relaxing summer,[206] and thus the only people who do it are those in joint degree programs who desperately need the extra credits to graduate.

I personally took two classes for four total credits: International Litigation and a class called Free Speech and Minority Rights. International Litigation turned out to be a minor-scale nightmare – it was literally almost entirely an

---

[204] It goes without saying that you reduce your future class burden by as many credits as you're willing to take on during the summer, something I knew at this point but didn't fully appreciate until my second and third years of law school. I've never met the person who would mind having a slightly less stressful second or third year.

[205] I assume that the same holds true for many European capitals, though the atmosphere may not be quite so loose elsewhere. Try your best to talk with previous Summer Institute participants before you commit to a given school's program; you'll get a better feeling of what it's actually like before you go.

[206] Those who chose to take three classes were definitely hurting by the end of the summer, and most expressed regret that they had blown their summer abroad by working themselves too hard.

unexpected reprise of the second semester of Civil Procedure, but taught by three different professors, two Americans and one from France. The Americans were decent; the French professor wasn't. If I had known that the class was going to rehash already-discussed themes of jurisdiction, I would never have signed up for it. Free Speech and Minority Rights, by contrast, was excellent. It was partially an exposure to the international side of First Amendment concerns – a subject I hadn't learned in Constitutional Law – and partially a discussion of international human rights treaties. It was in this class that I first encountered and really enjoyed Professor Benjamin Glazer, a noted First Amendment scholar whose classes I would later come to take en masse at Cornell.

There were other course options, as well, each with an international theme ranging from finance to tax. Business courses were clearly dominant in Cornell's program, but it should be noted that other schools' international summer programs may have similar offerings, or they may instead focus more on litigation or philosophical courses and less on themes of interest to transactional attorneys. Those interested in international programs should consider several programs before deciding on any single school's offering, and choose a city where they can feel comfortable for a month or more of classes.

Though my summer program was great, those looking for greater prestige have other options. If you're looking to seriously add a discussion point to your resume, imagine participating in a summer program with lectures by a sitting Supreme Court justice. Tulane University and St. Mary's University School of Law have succeeded in luring Chief Justice William Rehnquist and other noteworthy justices to participate in their international lecture programs; Penn State's Dickinson School of Law has attracted Justices Ginsburg, O'Connor, and Scalia. Not all summer programs will be relaxing, and for certain, the expenses involved with international summer programs may well put them out of reach, but the benefits of participation are unmistakable.

B.   LABOR AND RESEARCH

All of this is not to say that the first-year summer cannot be entirely different and still be incredibly valuable. It definitely can be. Working for a professor or a law firm is the most common other way to spend the first-year summer; only a small handful of people go off to work for judges during this time. You also have the option of working in the public interest, positions which tend to be perennially open to those who seek them.[207]

---

[207] The National Association for Law Placement (NALP), discussed in greater detail in Chapter 9, Section A, notes in its guidelines for law firm employers that "[t]here has been a long-standing tradition that the first year summer be used to engage in public service work or to take time away from the law altogether, and while the practice of having first year students work in private law firms provides additional employment opportunities to

As briefly discussed earlier, getting a job with a professor is typically at least a modestly competitive process – at some schools, the professors put out a formal notice of some sort that they are looking for 'research assistants,' and the presumption is that enough people will apply that they'll be able to pick and choose the best candidates. You either submit a resume and statement of interest to the professor, or know the professor beforehand and informally ask if you might be able to work with her or him. The research assistant's work over the summer typically involves locating and checking over materials related to a book, article, or other project that the professor is presently working on.

Depending on the professor, this could be a nine-to-five job or something more or less demanding. And the work may or may not be interesting: find the right professor and you might pore over issues that fascinated you for a lifetime; find the wrong one and you might review stuff that presumably no person in his or her right mind would ever care about. Realistically, true legal scholarship is so infrequently interesting to students that your chance of getting a great assignment is small; just bear in mind you're not doing it for interest so much as experience. If you like both your professor and the material, feel lucky.

The benefits of working for a professor are clear: you become experienced in a form of legal research – though digging for materials is probably not the most practical research one can learn – and if you do well, you can wind up with a favorable recommendation to use on resumes and in future endeavors. Some professors are personable enough that their research assistants go on to become lifetime friends and colleagues, though this is certainly more rare than typical. And some research positions pay a stipend, albeit modestly, to insure the continuity of one's work over the summer.

Those who might give strongest consideration to professorial rather than firm employment are those contemplating judicial clerkships immediately after law school. Letters of recommendation are herein at their most useful, and professors often have personal ties to judges that can open other doors. But it's also worth noting that you have to be prepared to work pretty hard during the summer to get a good recommendation from a professor. Treat the summer as serious employment so that you don't have problems seeking future jobs.

If you really want to work during the summer in an academic setting and cannot find a professorial opening, another option worth considering is work for your university's office of university counsel, which handles legal matters for your school. This option, which is typically open to law students from any year, gives you a bit more hands-on experience working with practical matters than

some students, such experiences should not be valued or emphasized inordinately." NALP, Principles and Standards for Law Placement and Recruitment Activities, available at http://www.nalp.org/pands/pands.htm. Though this tradition is not emphasized quite so much nowadays, it apparently accounts for the less-than-critical importance of doing something important with your first-year summer.

working with a professor, but is not as glamorous as working for a law firm. For those seeking the most practical private-sector first-year summer experiences, law firm employment is about as close to the real thing as one can get. Depending on the firm and your personal situation, you might be doing work similar, if not identical to that being done by practicing attorneys – albeit issues with a bit less gravity and modestly diminished expectations of professional perfection. And in most cases, you will be compensated for your work, and rather handsomely. It's no wonder, then, that the process of finding first-year summer employment is so competitive.

As it turns out, once you get the job and show up for the first day or two of orientation, your life as a first-year summer associate is somewhat confusing.[208] On the one hand, you're so fresh out of your first-year classes that you barely know what to do at a law firm or how to do it. For the first time since graduating from 1L status to 2L status, you begin to feel just like a 1L again – overwhelmed and uncertain. On the other hand, the experience isn't a lot easier when you're doing the same sort of work for the first time as a second-year summer associate. Struggling through the work, learning as you go, and maintaining professional composure are all just as important during your first-year summer as they will be in your second-year summer, despite the fact that you come to your job with a lot less experience with the legal subject matter.

These struggles take on greater weight because the objective of the typical summer program, at least in the mind of the law student, is to receive an offer to return to work at the firm after graduation. For first-year summer associates, eligibility to actually receive these offers differs from firm to firm. Many firms never extend offers to first-years. Some will tell you up front that they don't extend employment offers to first-years, others will only let you know as much after they've seen your work product all summer, and still others have such a policy but make exceptions in unusual situations. The norm is not to extend offers. Small firms tend to be the ones that make exceptions for especially outstanding first-year candidates, though in good economic times, very large and desperate firms may also extend such offers. One common compromise is a policy against extending offers to great first-year performers, coupled with a warm invitation to come back next year to work there again.

The major differences between first- and second-year summer practice are that by the time you've completed your second year of law school, you have at least some idea of what sort of work you'd like to be doing when you're finished with classes, and therefore, you should be demonstrating aptitude when you're doing it at the firm. At the end of your first year, you've only learned the basics and quite likely have not been able to attend a single class

---

[208] The experiences related herein are those of close friends with whom I've discussed, and in some cases personally observed the first-year experience.

you've chosen for yourself. Even if you have, you probably have no idea what sort of work you ultimately want to do, and you may well be wondering if you really want to be a lawyer at all after the first year of law school. No one expects great performance from a first-year, but surprises are always welcome.

Rest assured that firms understand the uncertainties in your mind and generally, though not universally, accommodate your speculation. Many firms allow summer associates to 'rotate' through given 'practice areas,' so that you can sample a little bit of the different kinds of work a firm handles. Typically, practice areas are broken down into 'litigation' and 'corporate' departments, with specialized groups that handle only specific sorts of matters for the firm – 'labor and employment law,' 'intellectual property,' 'divorce and family law,' 'securities regulation,' and 'corporate taxation,' amongst other possibilities.[209]

You'll ultimately choose an employer that has at least one practice area of personal interest. But for now you'll go generally to a place with two or more options that seem at least potentially interesting. This means that you'll probably avoid a firm specializing exclusively in 'corporate taxation' if you're looking to work on the appeals of death-row inmates.

Those desiring such work, however, tend not to look for jobs at law firms – rather, they often pursue 'public interest' Jobs. People working in the public sector can choose one of several types of careers – criminal prosecution work for district attorneys' offices, criminal defense work for the indigent through public defenders' offices, and other work in local, state, or federal governmental offices' legal departments. The offices of some federal agencies have competitive programs for summer and permanent placement – the Department of Justice is among the most prestigious. While some public sector jobs are hard to get, others - especially at the local level - tend to be less competitive and thus good fall-backs for those who can't find law firm jobs for their first summer.

Depending on your personal preferences, public sector employment may be strongly preferable to working for a law firm, and thus you can adjust your priorities here accordingly. Traditionally, some form of work in the public interest was seen as an appropriate way to spend the first summer, though as a practical matter, if you're considering future work at a law firm, it is probably easier to approach a 2L summer law firm job if you've had some sort of practical experience during the 1L summer.

For many reasons, perhaps the all-around best public sector job is the opportunity to work for a judge in what might be called an externship by schools and a clerkship by judges. Judges may not solicit resumes from first-year law students, however, so personal ties of some sort to the judge in question tend to be useful in obtaining these positions. As with all clerkships, state and local summer positions are easier to get than federal ones, though

---

[209] See Section D, Table 6-1 for a list of areas of specialization.

your future employability will certainly benefit from any clerkship you do.

C. LAW REVIEW AND JOURNAL ANNOUNCEMENTS

One of the biggest events of the summer (and law school itself) for those who participated in the journal writing competition is the announcement of the results. Depending on the traditions followed by your law school's organizations, the only announcement might be something privately received by you in the mail – or the absence of such a something. Or your school's organizations may release lists of people receiving offers, and post the lists in some public place. At Cornell, these events would typically take place around the end of July – sometime around the 20th of the month.

Traditionally, my law school's organizations sent out letters, and expected to receive acceptance or rejection responses within a very short time – several days or a week at most. The various journals' letters, if any, would be mailed out on the same day, and you'd make your decision about journal membership based on the 'best' invitation you received. However, as a good number of Cornell Law students were in Paris classes when the decisions were reached, and it was impractical to send us letters and request responses from overseas, the administration in Paris did something unusual – it posted all three journals' lists on a wall and let people gather around to see the journals they had made.

The Paris administration did this without an announcement that it planned to do so; perhaps the practice was so common at other law schools that no one even considered Cornell's standard policy of grade privacy. But everyone I knew had been talking about the impending decision for a week or two before that, and the curiosity level was high. At that moment, many people were hoping that they'd be on *Law Review*, and a few claimed, inaccurately, that they wouldn't bother with any journal if *Law Review* didn't make them an offer.

The lists weren't up on the wall yet when rumors started to make their way around one of my classes – a friend who had apparently seen one of them came up to congratulate me, and tell me that I had been accepted to join the *Journal of Law and Public Policy*. As Cornell's youngest journal – founded in 1992 – *JLPP* was the journal that typically had the nicest group of members, the people I would most have wanted to hang out with in my spare time. And the subject matter, as mentioned previously, seemed the most specifically interesting to me. So I was happy to hear the news, but also wondering what, if anything, I would discover when I saw the other lists on the wall.

I'd heard about *JLPP* before class began, and as everyone knew the lists were being posted as we were sitting there, the rest of the class passed as slowly as any in our lives. The moment class ended, we rushed out into the hallway of the Sorbonne to see the lists; the final one was just being taped up. Two lists were long – maybe 20 names a piece. A third listed only five names. People were edging their way in at the sheets to see where they stood. Some people seemed to be experiencing their first moments of vague pleasantness, others vague unhappiness. Eyes were desperately scanning for names.

My eyes first hit the *International Law Journal*'s list. My name was on there. Then the *JLPP* list. I was on there too. So I had two journals to pick from. And then I saw the *Law Review* list.

My name was on that one too.

Suddenly I was feeling very excited. I think the word "wow" might have quietly escaped my lips. But massed around me were all sorts of people in a throng, and I realized from the list that only five people from the Paris program had made it onto *Law Review*. I was surrounded by people who had seen my name, and not theirs, on that list. Some had not seen their name on any list.[210] None of my friends in Paris had made *Law Review*. And while I felt only vaguely uncomfortable at that moment, I wasn't prepared for what came later.

A group of six or seven of us went to lunch together shortly after the news came out. On the way out the door, I had located friends from other journals, and people I hardly knew who were on the *Law Review* list, and offered my congratulations. As we began to walk to lunch, I could hear a slightly acidic tone in the words of the people I was walking with – they began to ask questions like, "so now that you're on *Law Review*, I guess this means that

---

[210] Notably, this was not necessarily the end of the line for those interested in journal membership: students in the LL.M. program or the International Legal Studies area of concentration could apply to the International Law Journal separately with other writing samples and resumes, or could take on low-level assignments from the Journal of Law and Public Policy to "work on" to that journal, amongst other options. The downside of these alternatives: you won't become a member until it's almost too late to note your participation on your resume. As each school's journals will vary in post-competition admissions practices, you might want to research these back-up options in advance – and hopefully not have to use them.

you've got your golden ticket, eh?" and "gee, I wonder what journal's offer you're going to accept." But mostly there was an uneasy extended quiet thereafter, and at lunch the subject came up only briefly. I could tell that there was resentment in the air, and it was really my first dose of it since coming to law school – this was the first and only time I recall people displaying disturbance at someone else's achievement. It hurt that in this case, it was mine.

And inside, I felt really wounded, which was an odd thing to be feeling right after winning acceptance to a school's most prestigious organization. Though I've never been the bragging type, I had a definite sense that this accomplishment was something that I really couldn't discuss with any of my friends, and that I would mostly have to keep bottled up inside.[211] No friendships were lost as a consequence of the *Law Review*'s offer – this thankfully wasn't even likely – and honestly, I think there would be something wrong with either me or my friends if that had happened. But there is no doubt that some people harbored at least a hint of lingering bitterness about the general subject of *Law Review* for the rest of the time they spent in school.[212]

Not being able to discuss it with friends was one thing. My real problem was that I couldn't share the experience meaningfully with those who were closest to me: my parents. We kept in touch through E-mail and sometimes the telephone – this was one of those occasions where an extended phone call from France was appropriate. But as my parents weren't lawyers, and didn't have close lawyer friends, they had no concept of what it meant to be accepted onto a law review, as an academic honor, as a tremendous new responsibility, or as a future professional credential. There was no celebration. The only people who understood what had happened were my classmates.

In summary, I explained to my parents that being asked to join a school's law review is close to the highest honor one can receive, based on its selectivity, its reputation amongst academics and practitioners, and its practical importance to the legal community. And I explained that, as a result of this acceptance, I would be living a second-year experience similar to my first-year experience: plenty of work, more than most people would tolerate, without a lot of time for fun and relaxation. And finally, I explained that in exchange for accepting the responsibilities of membership, the benefits to my resume and future professional career were likely to be substantial. Though it is not a golden ticket, it is certainly something that tends to make firms look past your GPA.

The story would have been much the same if I had accepted the offer of another journal instead, except the benefits and consequences of membership

---

[211] Regardless of the little I said about it, the journals published their finalized new membership lists to the entire school near the beginning of August, and word spread amongst those who were interested.

[212] One especially competitive person, whose similarly competitive girlfriend made *Law Review* when he did not, appeared quite disturbed for a considerable time thereafter.

would have been somewhat muted. Associates with the other journals do not typically work as hard or as much as those on the *Law Review*, something that is certainly true at many, if not most other schools. And associates on secondary journals do not get the same resume benefits – though they definitely receive a measure of respect from employers for participating in journal work, employers tend to look more closely at their grades and other factors. In a good economy, many firms ignore the grades of law review associates at top-ranked schools altogether, though top law firms continue to consider both their grades and other personal factors, if perhaps less strictly than with other candidates.

To some extent, I think that this amount of detail is about as much as friends and family outside the profession want to ever really understand about a journal or law review: the publications themselves are so dense as to be unreadable by the general public, and the organizations tend not to hold widely-publicized social events.[213] A law review is not a public organization in the way that a glee club or volleyball team is public. So suffice it to say that you work very hard, and perhaps leave it at that. Your family, like mine, will probably take one look at a law review issue and say, "that's very nice." Only you will realize just how much time and effort you've had to put into it.

And the first signs that you're working hard will be immediate. Joining a journal typically means that you'll return to the law school one or two weeks before everyone else does in the fall – perhaps even earlier than the first-year students. This gives your journal's 'board of editors' time for an extensive orientation on your new position as an 'associate,' a junior editor who is assigned to read and fix articles submitted for publication by professors and other students. And you'll notice the other changes in your upcoming schedule: in addition to whichever classes you take, you'll now have journal assignments due either weekly, bi-weekly, or at some similar interval.

And most likely, even after completing the writing competition, you will be required to write a second, more extensive Note, which this time will most certainly discuss a legal subject area of your choice. The *Law Review* advised us to consider possible topics immediately after receiving our letters of acceptance. If you're really looking to get ahead of the curve, now's the time to search Lexis and Westlaw with such key phrases as "circuit! w/5 split" or "case w/5 first w/3 impression," restricting your timeframe to the last six months or less. This will give you a heads up on novel legal issues, and ones that have recently led to disagreements amongst federal courts. While this is by no means the only set of topics you can choose from, it's a good place to start.

---

[213] Except for symposia, which are some journals' annual assemblages of noted professionals and academics for discussions on select topics. Contrast this with the typical public events of other organizations, such as marches, telethons, and public performances which family members might witness or be a part of.

D. THE "WHAT SORT OF LAWYER DO I WANT TO BE?" QUESTION, REVISITED

1. Reflection

At some point during your post-first-year summer, you'll have to choose your second-year classes, and that is the right time for a modest amount of reflection on a previously mentioned issue – what do you really want to do with your law degree? As the first year of fundamental classes has ended, you're now faced with your first real opportunity to chart your own destiny in the law, and for the first time you'll need to seriously start thinking about what sort of law you might want to practice. Perhaps you'll base your thinking on some measurement of what subjects you've been enjoying and not enjoying.

You don't need to have your mind made up on a career path yet, but for some types of careers – criminal prosecution and defense, for example – it helps to get started as soon as possible on courses such as Evidence, and Criminal Procedure,[214] assuming that you didn't take these courses during your first year. A three-year law program is too short to consider as an opportunity for rampant exploration of tens of classes, and unlike undergraduate colleges, many law schools have strict limits on your ability to continue your studies after three years: law school cannot become a four, five, or six-year lifestyle. You enter with a class, and only with rare exception graduate without them.

In this age of rapidly-changing professions, some people use the summer as a time to figure out what sort of legal career they're going to start out with, especially if they're not planning to maintain the same career for several decades. Though they don't drift from concentration to concentration while in law school, lawyers frequently and for many reasons drift from legal career to legal career over the years.

The possibilities from which people can sample in the first summer are dichotomies. Students' most popular distinctions are 'big firm versus small firm,' 'in-house counsel versus law firm associate,' 'law firm associate versus solo practitioner' and 'public versus private sector.' This essentially means that a person who really hates the idea of working as one lawyer in a huge, thousand-person law firm might consider sampling big law firm life for a summer, or perhaps even for a few years of practice. Similarly, those who hope to work as criminal defense attorneys in private practice often start their careers working as

---

[214] As briefly mentioned in the previous chapter, Criminal Procedure is the counterpart class to Criminal Law, a subject that may not be required by your law school but yet will likely still appear on your bar exam. The class can either be taught from its broadest perspective, in which case it focuses upon U.S. Constitutional issues such as due process, searches and seizures, and a criminal defendant's Miranda rights, or from a more narrow perspective focused on a given jurisdiction's code of criminal procedure. The former class parallels Constitutional Law, the latter class Civil Procedure.

prosecuting district attorneys so that they can learn all of the tricks that will be used against them one day.

A cross-over of special note in challenging economic times is the so-called 'litigation to corporate/transactional work' switch. It's unusual for a person to start out as a courtroom attorney, litigating cases, and significantly later switch to something like drafting contracts and negotiating deals. One person typically does not do both sorts of work, at least at medium- to large-sized law firms: you choose one or the other, and then specialize in it, unless you're planning to work at a small law firm as a general practitioner, personally handling whatever matters might come through the door. Thus while the specialist's life enables her to do only what she finds particularly interesting, it tends to become routine, and while the general practitioner gets to dabble in whatever she wants, it's hard to find a firm that will employ her.

Some of the other market realities, as they now stand, are unfortunate.[215] It's difficult to transfer from a solo practice or an in-house counsel position to a huge law firm, but not the other way around. And it's harder to come from the private sector into the public sector than the other way around, in large part because of salary disparities. These sorts of issues tend to increase demand for big law firm jobs and the relatively few truly prestigious public sector jobs, as they're viewed as career stepping stones rather than places to spend a lifetime.

And thus, brilliant maverick solo practitioners typically began their careers at well-established law firms. Tomorrow's star defense attorneys spent their first years of practice helping to put people in jail. And if you're going to work for a huge law firm that does a little bit of everything, you have to expect that you yourself will only be doing one type of thing. The professional challenges of practicing attorneys are many, indeed. So for your first summer, consider where you might want to be next summer and the years thereafter. Then think about trying something completely different, first.

2.   Upper-Class Scheduling: General Comments

For many law students, the summer will be the time when you pick classes for your fall semester, which means re-opening your school's course catalog, reading descriptions over, and then praying that the course is actually being offered at a time when you can take it. You might not have glanced at the course catalog before law school, so take a moment to familiarize yourself with

---

[215] I say this is unfortunate only in the sense that with such mobility appears to come a greater tendency in the profession to commoditize lawyers and spend less time training them or appreciating them for their individual distinctions. This is a result of the suspicion amongst senior attorneys that their juniors are likely to pack up and go elsewhere several years down the line, regardless of how much time one spends trying to build them up, or give them freedom to develop a unique practice. But that is another issue for another time.

what else the school is offering besides the mandatory first-year agenda.

Every school reduces the number of mandated courses dramatically after the first year; flexibility in fulfilling set requirements is so common as to be universal. These post-first-year requirements take three forms: mandatory participation in professional responsibility classes, completion of a generic upper-class writing requirement, and 'highly recommended' but optional classes in several specific subjects. "Professional responsibility" courses are the legal profession's extended terminology for ethics classes. Every lawyer must take at least one class in ethics before leaving law school. Writing courses are similarly mandatory; every lawyer needs to complete a post-first-year writing class of some sort before graduation. And the highly recommended classes differ from school to school; most focus on a handful of subjects considered useful to subsets of the practicing legal community, and those that appear on the bar exam of a given school's state.

Putting aside these requirements, it's important to remember that in all likelihood, you will have no more than four semesters to learn whatever you really want to formally learn about the law. Everything after that will be learned on the job as you go. So during law school, you have to pick courses that interest you the most, and not put things off for too long – a course you like might not be taught again before you leave.

This is also a good time to ask upper-classmen for their advice on courses and teachers, if you haven't done that during the previous semester. A subject you might really enjoy could, potentially, be taught by a fantastic teacher; it does happen, however, that a great subject is being taught by a dud.[216] Many people believe that in law school, you choose classes based on the professors who teach them, rather than on the subject matter. So choose wisely.

And also bear in mind that the first semester of your second year carries a responsibility that goes beyond journal work and course work: job interviewing. Many, if not most schools understand this fundamental reality of upper-class life and schedule classes such that few, if any courses meet on Fridays – this gives you the opportunity to go out of town or do job interviews during the business week. In law school, avoiding Friday classes is a typical part of second- and third-year existence; when you're not interviewing you'll use the extra day to complete journal assignments. So don't pack your schedule too heavily. By then, even undergraduate overachievers will know what first-year life was like, and may well be reluctant to relive the experience.

---

[216] Two courses of particular interest to me were being taught by a tenured professor whose inappropriate behavior was so notorious that he had been banned from teaching first-year classes. The stories of his behavior were so widespread that many people shied away from taking his upper-class courses; those who did, out of interest in the subject matter or under the impression that the stories were untrue, were stunned by just how bad the classes actually were.

3.   Upper-Class Scheduling: Specific Options

Though you'll be permitted to take as many as seven classes per semester, you will probably average five, and in a light semester will only take four. This means that you'll most likely have roughly 20 elective classes over the course of your two upper-class years. Some schools offer academic credit for journal work and moot court participation, as well, which might further reduce the number of classes you would ultimately elect to take.

While it would be misleading to suggest that your law school is likely to have quite as broad a selection of course offerings as the ones laid out in the following table, the purpose of this listing is more limited: it should give you a sense of just how broad the study of law can be, and might even help you choose a school that offers classes similar to the ones you find interesting on these pages. Over the 22 categories and hundred-plus classes represented here, you'll see virtually every field of law you might ultimately hope to study; just be aware that while many schools attempt to offer at least one course in each category, few schools will offer this much depth in any given specialization.

TABLE 6-1	THE LARGE LIST OF MODERN LAW SCHOOL ELECTIVE SPECIALIZATIONS
Specialization	*Course Names*
Admiralty Law	Admiralty; Collision Law & Limitation of Liability; Marine Insurance; Personal Injury & Death; Regulation of Shipping and Commerce. These courses deal with the separate body of laws dealing with activities and events that take place at sea, off the shore of a given country.
Alternative Dispute Resolution (ADR)	Arbitration; Dispute Resolution; Mediation; Negotiations. These courses teach strategies and techniques that can be used in situations when litigation is being avoided (and litigation situations before the fact-finder reaches a verdict) to resolve conflicts between parties.
Antitrust Law	Antitrust; Economics of Regulation. These courses look at laws and theories governing anti-competitive corporate practices.
Commercial Law	Bankruptcy; Commercial Law; Insurance Law; Payment Systems; Secured Transactions; and some Uniform Commercial Code (UCC) courses. These classes look at rules governing business dealings and the winding up of companies that have run out of money.
Constitutional Law and Theory	Civil Rights Legislation; Constitutional Law & Political Theory; Constitutionalism and Social Progress; Death Penalty in America; Legislation; Public International Law; Separation of Powers; The First Amendment; The Religion Clause of the First Amendment. These courses take broad or specific looks at parts of the United States Constitution and related court decisions.

Specialization	Course Names
Corporate Law	Corporations; Corporate Finance; Funding of High-Tech Startups; IPO's & Acquisitions; Mergers & Acquisitions; Securities Regulation; Venture Capital. These courses cover everything from the creation of businesses to the sale, purchase, and issuance of stocks and debt, to the mergers and acquisitions of businesses by one another.
Criminal Law and Procedure	Capital Punishment Clinic; Corruption Control; Criminal Procedure; Death Penalty in America; Evidence; Organized Crime Control; Philosophy of Criminal Law; Post-Conviction Remedies. These classes cover specific areas of federal and state criminal law, from the theoretical to the concrete, and from the statutory to the procedural.
Entertainment and Sports Law	Entertainment Law; Sports Law. These classes cover contract, labor, tort, and other issues related to professional entertainers.
Environmental Law	Biotechnology Law; Environmental Advocacy; Environmental Law; Natural Resources Law; Pollution Control; Regulation of Toxic Substances. These classes deal with different dimensions of environmental law, including the hot-button tort issues of toxic substances and modern genetic biological contamination.
Ethnic, Gender, Racial and Religious Law	African-Americans & the Supreme Court; American Indian Law; Biblical Law; Civil Rights Legislation; Immigration & Refugee Law; Law & Violence Against Women; Race Relations; Reproductive Issues Law; Sexuality, Gender & the Law; Women & the Law. These courses deal with a wide variety of race, gender, ethnicity and religious issues.
Family Law	Children and the Law; Children, Parents, & the State; Family Law; Juvenile Advocacy; Juvenile Litigation; Law Guardian Externships; Law & Education; Law & Violence Against Women; Senior Law; Trusts & Estates. These classes handle every aspect of law from the rights of children, spouses, and senior citizens to the development of family inheritance plans.
Health Law	Law & Mental Health; Health Care Law; Health Care Practice. These classes guide students through modern regulations and changing laws dealing with health care issues.
Intellectual Property Law	Copyright & Digital Works; International Protection of Intellectual Property; Intellectual Property Strategies; Intellectual Property Transactions; Internet & Software Issues in Patent Law; Patent Practice & Prosecution, Trademark & Unfair Competition; Trade Secrets. These classes deal with the various disparate subjects of modern intellectual property law.

Specialization	Course Names
International and Comparative Law	Admiralty; Comparative Corporations; Finance & Banking Law; Comparative Labor & Employment Law; Comparative Law; E.U. Law; Int'l Business Transactions; Int'l Commercial Arbitration; Int'l Energy Transactions; Int'l Human Rights; Int'l Litigation; Int'l Taxation; Legal Aspects of Foreign Investment in Developing Countries; Roman Law & Modern Civil Law Systems; U.N., Elections, & Human Rights; U.S. & E.U. Antitrust Law. These classes tackle disparate areas of international law; omitted are the individual classes for specific national laws you might imagine.
Labor and Employment Law	Employment Discrimination; Employment Law; Injured Employee Compensation & Tort Remedies; Labor Law; Sports Law. These courses survey laws governing employer/employee relationships and common issues in employment situations.
Litigation	Advanced Civil Procedure; Civil Advocacy; Civil Litigation; Conflict of Laws; Criminal Procedure; Evidence; Federal Courts; Remedies; Trial Advocacy. These courses deal with the nuts and bolts of litigation, including procedure and practical trial skills.
Legal History and Theory	American Legal Theory; Constitutionalism & Social Progress; History of the Common Law; Jurisprudence; Law & Social Change; Philosophy of Criminal Law; Theories of Law & Theories of Film. These courses look at abstract, academic dimensions of the law.
Public Interest Law	Civil Rights Law; Discrimination Law; Employment Law; Family Law; Government Benefits Law; Immigration Law; Poverty Law. These classes come from the other substantive areas, and converge here because of the broad applicability of so many areas of practice to the public interest arena.
Regulatory Law	Administrative Advocacy; Administrative Law; Communications Law; Energy Law, Environmental Law; Federal Offshore Oil & Gas Law; Public Utility Regulation. These courses offer an introduction to the "fourth branch of American government," administrative agencies which pass regulations to fill gaps in Congressional laws, and the procedures used when pushing regulatory change.
Tax Law	Corporate Taxation; Federal Income Tax; International Taxation; Partnership Taxation; State & Local Taxation; Tax Practice & Procedure. These classes focus on different areas of tax law.
Technology Law	Bioethics; Computer Law; Internet/Cyberspace Law; Telecommunications Law. An emerging cluster of courses, these classes deal with life sciences, computer science, Internet law and other increasingly important technologies.
Tort Law	Advanced Tort Law: Defamation & Privacy; Injured Employee Compensation & Tort Remedies; Products Liability. These classes expand upon themes initially explored in first-year tort law.

This list is not intended to be exhaustive, but should at least suggest some of the possible types of courses you might want to take. There are plenty of others, including clinics, seminars, and externships, that depend upon a school's flexibility, specialization and staffing in a certain area of law.[217]

Even with a less comprehensive set of classes than the one above, my only problem during scheduling was trying to find a way to fit the classes I wanted into a workable schedule. My school somehow managed to place three or four of the most interesting classes per semester in the exact same time slot or a slot that conflicted with another class only one day per week, but thereby fatally. Why were such scheduling problems so common? Part of the problem was the pressure to avoid early-morning classes,[218] and schedule as few classes on Fridays as possible. First-years had to put up with morning classes; only with rare exceptions would upper-class professors show up first thing in the morning.

It would be an understatement to suggest that I didn't get to take all the classes I wanted during law school, and especially not during my first elective semester. Part of my problem was advance planning; I typically planned semester-by-semester, starting *after* the first year rather than coming to law school with a schedule that would transform me into the lawyer I hoped to become. Though I cannot recommend that you avoid my mistake by choosing an interesting area of specialization in advance and then sticking to some pre-law school plan of how things should be, I will admit that there are advantages to being single-minded. If you are among the lucky few people who stay consistent with their original legal visions, then you will likely be satisfied just by picking a school with plenty of classes and faculty for that specialization.

But even if you, like me, suspect that you might not be thrilled with your vague and tentative current interest in specialization, there is an option better than just crossing your fingers and hoping that the school you picked somehow manages to schedule classes to your liking: pick a law school ahead of time that offers both a wide variety of courses and a large number of courses during any given semester, rather than spacing out slim pickings over three or four semesters. You're most likely to be satisfied during law school if you can choose a place in advance that frequently schedules more than a handful of

---

[217] Aside from generalized rankings, U.S. News and World Report also ranks the top law schools in seven areas of specialization and one non-specialization category: Dispute Resolution, Environmental Law, Health Law, Intellectual Property Law, International Law, Trial Advocacy and Tax Law are the specialties, Clinical Training measures opportunities for hands-on work outside of classroom settings. While U.S. News' rankings don't include all of the various areas of law listed in the table above, these rankings should offer some additional guidance on the schools you might pick, and thus the classes you might take.

[218] Note that although I've heard of rare people who managed during law school to create class schedules that had no courses on either Mondays or Fridays, I never attempted this myself; the most I attempted was to avoid really early-morning courses after my first year.

classes in several potential subjects that interest you. As a corollary point thereafter, be sure that the school doesn't just pack its course catalog full of interesting classes that are only offered once every three years. The alternative is to plead with the registrar's office to do a better job with scheduling. My frequent requests to see course times changed fell entirely upon deaf ears.

Another alternative that will depend upon the school you choose is the possibility of attending non-law school classes for law school academic credit. Many schools permit upper-class law students to use a very limited number of outside class credit hours towards their diplomas; your interest in actually doing this will depend on the classes that are offered, the ones you can fit into your schedule, and your personal comfort with the idea of diluting your pure law studies with something else. Language courses and 'fun' courses tend to be the most popular class options outside of the law school.

4.   In Summary

By the end of the first-year summer, though students need not have decided precisely what sort of law they hope to practice after graduation, they definitely should begin to focus upon subjects of potential career interest. With only two years of elective coursework and limited scheduling options at most schools, students are at a distinct advantage if they think and plan ahead, though flexibly enough to escape from once-appealing elective specializations that turn sour. Early explorations of schools' specializations and course offerings will enhance one's opportunities to choose from a variety of interesting electives when the time comes.

A.   THINNING OUT THEIR NUMBERS

The difference between the start of the first and second years could not have seemed more profound when I arrived back in Ithaca: the first year brought everyone in on the same day and marched everyone around the school in lock-step, all to churn out uniform products at the end. By contrast, as the second year started, my classmates were coming and going from the city at totally different paces, each on a schedule tailored largely for personal benefit.

By the start of your second year of law school, one of two things will have happened. If you're in the majority, you'll be back at school comparing summer stories with your friends. If you haven't kept in touch with everyone through E-mail, you'll start to hear details about the professorial, law firm, or public sector work experiences people have gone through, and perhaps you'll even have a few of your own stories to share. And you'll be a hell of a lot more comfortable at your law school than you were only a year earlier. You'll be ready to stand on the other side of the hazing line, telling first-year students the stories that will scare them into working like crazy.

If you're in the minority, you'll be at a completely different law school, starting almost fresh as a transfer or visiting student. Transfer students have an especially tough time of it, regardless of their previous academic records. As a general rule, because of the competitiveness of law school grades, transfer students moving up in the *U.S. News* law school rankings are not allowed to bring over their grades from whatever institutions they attended. Upwardly mobile transfer students are typically in the top 10% of the schools they leave, and thus allowing a bunch of people to come in at the top of a new class would be at least inequitable, and at most tantamount to inspiring a revolution amongst existing students.

Transfer students also have to deal with social issues. If they're doing well when they transfer, they choose to take a risk on a completely new place while leaving whatever friends they've made at one law school, say nothing of giving up an enviable class standing. It's socially difficult to make up for the bonding that most of their new classmates have gone through in the first-year, but after a few months have passed, most have met new people and made solid new friendships. Some find themselves sought after as prime dating material – fresh faces minus 1L anxieties and drama. And while it is going to be difficult for the transfer student's grades to be as high at their new schools as they were wherever they left, it is also possible for a transfer student to seriously mop up at a new place. Most students capable of upward transfer have a shot at honors.

There will also be people who transfer for other reasons. While a significant number of drop-outs act immediately after the first semester, some people brave out the year and then leave once they've received their second-semester grades. And there are people who have family or other personal crises that demand either leaves of absence or complete withdrawals from law school. Exercise appropriate discretion when attempting to contact people who have left law school without a trace; there might be something going on that's different from what you expect.

Visiting students are in an entirely different category. Though somewhat uncommon, the practice of studying temporarily at a place other than your first law school draws a handful of people every semester over the second- and third-years. There are at least nine formal 'semester abroad' programs for those who desire to study in Great Britain, Japan, Australia or New Zealand,[219] and students may alternately petition their law schools for the right to individually participate in classes at other schools in the United States. The most common reasons that people become visitors are to study the laws of another jurisdiction,[220] or to be closer to family or friends for a short time; the former reason is a good method to expose oneself in advance to subjects that might appear on another state's bar exam, and to enhance one's resume for employment in a specific location. Approximately five percent of students went for a semester of study outside the law school, though most do this in either their fourth or fifth semesters of law school. Interviewing and journal obligations in the third semester keep most people around.

People in the returning majority of the class will typically be surprised at some of the people who have disappeared, whether permanently or temporarily. While our class lost almost every one of its most pompous people via permanent transfers to other schools, we also lost a few people because of geography alone – they wanted to be closer to their spouses, fiancés, and, in Ithaca's case, civilization.

B.   THE FIRST LAW SCHOOL PARTY OF THE YEAR

One year earlier, I had entered law school knowing almost no one and having almost no concept of what was about to take place socially. A lot had changed since then. I had made a number of good friends, and thanks to my

---

[219] For a current list of summer programs that have already been approved, see http://www.abanet.org/legaled/studyabroad/semester.html.

[220] In addition to the joint-degree programs resulting in two courses of study at a single school, Cornell and several other U.S. schools offer "cooperative" joint-degree programs with foreign law schools that result in the award of two separate law degrees. The Maitrise en Droit is a four-degree program yielding a J.D. and French law degree; the M.LL.P. (Master of German and European Law and Legal Practice) is a four-year program for a J.D. and German law degree. Students in these programs spend half of their time in the United States, and half abroad. As these programs are not well-advertised, and have different language requirements, you will need to do a bit of research to determine whether a school has a good program and whether your own background suits a given school's offerings. A decent starting place is the ABA's listing of cooperative programs at http://www.abanet.org/legaled/studyabroad/cooperative.html.

summer in Paris, I was more relaxed, and despite the impending start of *Law Review*, I did not want to spend every waking hour buried in books. Moreover, as second-years, my friends and I were entirely conscious of the fact that a new group of first-years was about to arrive on the scene, and just like the year before, upper-classmen were going to pounce on the best and brightest first-year women as soon as they had a chance. In the last weeks of our summer program in Paris, three of my closest friends and I had decided not to give our third-year brethren that chance. Actually, we wanted to beat them to it.

So we did what any red-blooded American men in Paris would have done under the circumstances. We planned a party.

We decided to invite the whole school – more accurately, we would put up posters and then place personal invitations in the student mailboxes of the first-years, and most of the second-years. If we had enough mailers to go around, we might give them out to a few of the third-years we liked, but not ones who were on the prowl. The idea was simple: be first on the scene, and if possible, define the scene. We would not only hold our party first, but pre-empt the aggressive third-years by dismissively titling our party "The First Law School Party of the Year." If they wanted to try and hold something, they'd have to conflict with us, either in fact or in word.

My friends dreamt up the details of the party. I designed the posters. A good party, I thought, needs a mascot like Spuds McKenzie, Bud Light's classic Official Party Animal. We needed a party animal that women would flock to join, and we found our mascot. Our classmate and good friend Eric Sprague was a larger-than-life, jovial guy whose name had already become synonymous with "amusing comments," "booming voice," and "weekend binge drinking." He was not an alcoholic, but he played the role pretty well.

He was therefore a natural for the theme we conceived: we parodied the well-known "Got Milk?" advertisements with our own phrase: "Got Beer?" Though Got Beer? jokes and photos would later appear in magazines and television shows, ours was the first. I photographed Sprague wearing a beer-frothed mustache, and sporting a shirt labeled "Join the Bar." We thought of picturing Sprague with a bevy of bikini-wearing law school beauties, an ode to Spuds and the one-time master of modern propaganda, former real estate mogul Tom Vu, but ultimately decided against it. Sprague was instead superimposed, beer mug and bottle in his hands, against the backdrop of the Swiss Alps, a photo I snapped during my summer tour of Europe.

The posters were destined to become collectible, and did. Talk of the party spread around the law school like wildfire, and Sprague became known by the new first-years as "the 'Got Beer?' guy," a moniker which brought smiles to faces for the rest of our days at the law school. But the party wasn't for a week, and it wasn't the only thing going on in our lives – far from it. We had come back to town early to start our journal orientations, and to get ready for our new slates of classes. Some people were beginning to interview already for their second-year summer jobs. And other people wouldn't be back until days after the semester had officially started, for one reason or another.

C. JOURNAL OBLIGATIONS

With the exception of the fact that you'll be choosing classes for yourself, the biggest change in your schedule as a second-year student will be the addition of journal work to your routine – assuming that you opt to participate.[221] And if you wanted to participate but weren't extended an offer, that doesn't mean the end of the line for you – many new journals were started for the same reason,[222] and there may well be the opportunity with at least one journal to work your way on through labors in the second year.

Journals typically use the first week or two before the start of classes to immerse their new junior editors, commonly called associates, in general instructional sessions and their first real assignments. Classes consist of formal introductions to the use of editing symbols[223] in cleaning up articles for the journals and discussions of the journals' editorial boards, production processes,

---

[221] It's worth mentioning that transfer students, under some conditions, may be able to involve themselves in journal work, too. Some journals offer separate transfer student writing competitions or other means by which transfer students can earn their ways on.

[222] At one point, some disaffected people at Cornell talked about starting a parody journal, but nothing came of it.

[223] The editing symbols are typically called "proofreading" or "editing" symbols. Samples of the symbols are currently available at http://www.m-w.com/mw/table/proofrea.htm, and http://www.colorado.edu/Publications/styleguide/symbols.html.

and important policies. The junior editors are supervised by at least three layers of other editors, starting with Note and Article Editors, climbing to Managing Editors and possibly Executive Editors, ending always with the Editor-in-Chief. As an associate, the first things you learn will likely be similar to what you're about to read, but coupled with some free beer and pizza or a barbeque paid for at the journal's expense.

Orientation may be the first time that new associates learn why their second-year schedules are going to become crowded. And as mentioned earlier, journal work won't be easy. Depending on the number of associates on your journal, and number of issues it puts out, amongst other factors, you'll be handed stacks of 10-30 typewritten pages which need to be read over, checked for any conceivable type of error, Bluebooked, and either mildly edited or largely re-written. Different journals, and even different editorial boards of the same journal, will have entirely distinct aggressiveness standards when fact-checking and editing publishable articles. You may well have to devote a considerable number of hours to doing a single assignment.[224] And you'll most likely complete your first assignment just in time to start classes.

You'll also hear some of the journal's initial suggestions and expectations for the authoring of your student Note. A Note is similar in concept to the writing competition piece you previously submitted, but longer and more detailed. More importantly, you will be responsible for insuring that your Note is on an original topic – and this is a major challenge. You choose a possible topic for your Note, and then go through a process known as pre-emption checking by searching Lexis and Westlaw's databases to verify that no one has written already about the same subject. You're expected to repeat the pre-emption check several times through the writing of your Note, which will take a number of months, and are supposed to rewrite around the conflict or start a brand-new Note if someone else publishes on the same topic before you finish.

Notes are important to your journal for one reason: they typically comprise 35-50% of a given issue's content, and therefore need to be dependable – a weak flow of possible Notes to choose from means that issues could fall behind, diminish in quality, or lose content altogether. And Notes can be important to students, too: it's typically quite prestigious to have your Note selected for publication by your journal, and something that you list on your resume. Of course, not everyone writes something they want to see published. Sometimes people write just because they must do so to remain on the journal,

---

[224] Coupled with the well-known importance of journals to the profession and to the reputations of law schools, the heavy time commitment has led many schools, but not necessarily the majority, to offer academic credit (or, rarely, cash payments) for journal work. Cornell is amongst the schools that refuse to offer credit despite requests from law review editorial boards, though one of its journals (*LII Bulletin*) does offer modest stipends.

or because there are academic advantages to doing so.[225] So even if you never publish it, the Note isn't entirely a huge drain on your time. But your journal will likely lay out an aggressive timeline for draft submissions that will make it seem that way for a while.

Taken together, the editing assignments and Note-writing processes have the potential to consume as many as 10 hours a week, but fewer for participants in most secondary journals. Some journals have other requirements beyond editing and Note-writing, though: they may require handfuls of people each week to write 'abstracts,' summaries of entire articles in short paragraphs that precede each Article and Note. Others require some obligatory 'on standby' time, whereby associates are made to stick around in the *Law Review*'s offices during a pre-arranged one or two hours every month, just in case some low-level grunt work comes up.

Journal work will, at worst, leech away at your free time every week or so throughout the first semester, and for half of the second semester. If this seems like too much to you, remember that there will be plenty of benefits to compensate you for the hours you've lost – some academic and experiential, others tangible when you're searching for a job. If you get lucky enough to have a decent group of people to work with, the work won't be so bad. And you'll still have plenty of time for social events – more, for sure, than in your first year.

D. On Falling in Love, and Cycles Thereof

In case you're wondering, the "Got Beer?" party was outrageously well-attended. Held at the apartment of three of my classmates, the party filled up their place and flowed out onto their front lawn, with as many people hanging out outside as inside. Attendance from 1Ls and 2Ls was outstanding, and 3Ls made more than a token appearance – we estimated total attendance in the 350-400 person range out of our school's total size of over 540 people. The music roared, and we all had the chance to mingle with the new 1L class, just as we had wanted. It was a great way to meet people.

But it actually wasn't our first time seeing the 1Ls. Many of us had been introduced informally at the annual pre-semester Happy Hour, which we learned was open to all 1Ls and those upper-class students who chose to serve as mentors. Mentors signed up with different agendas: some were there to act as friends and advisors, others were there to 'get in good' with the new first-years. Others didn't sign up at all; the life of a mentor wasn't right for everyone.

---

[225] Though some schools won't offer academic credits for journal work, these same schools sometimes allow students to apply their Note-writing work towards completion of an upper-class writing requirement. Cornell used to permit this, but has changed its policy.

As first-year dramas and traumas are so predictable,[226] many people wanted to avoid vicariously re-living their first-year nightmares, and becoming sources of outlines, advice, and sympathy.[227]

The same second-years shuddered at the thought of dating first-years; many repeated the law school's common and only half-teasing mantra that "the age difference between first- and second-year students is like dog years." Especially at the beginning of the semester, it really does seem that way.[228]

But other people, including me, don't mind the gap quite so much. The first-year experience is a rite of passage, and although few people want to re-live it, there can be advantages to doing so. First, you can make some good friends who aren't members of your class. Second, if you're acting in a mentoring or advising capacity, you can help someone avoid some of the mistakes you made and suffered through. And third, if you want to and can adequately act in a tutoring capacity, you can brush up on subjects that are virtually certain to come up repeatedly when you take a bar exam and begin the actual practice of law.

I signed up to mentor a first-year student despite the fact that the person who had signed up to mentor me never showed up or introduced himself – a rare experience, I was told. Another second-year informally took my 'mentor's' place, and had been so valuable that I wanted to be there for someone else. The Law Students Association matched mentees up with mentors who were hopefully from their undergraduate schools. I met my mentee at the Happy Hour and learned that he was a self-assured guy from my old alma mater – besides a few small questions, he said that he had a complete handle on the material and didn't need advice. This experience was also atypical, though we bumped into each other occasionally and talked about relatively trivial issues.

But something else happened when I attended the Happy Hour: I met *her* – the woman I would date for the rest of my time in law school, and thereafter. I'll be the first to admit that I've never believed those movie sequences where time slows down and a person's whole world focuses in on a stranger from across a crowded room, but it happened to me that day. A tall, stunning redhead with long, flowing hair, she had the look of a model and the grace of a

---

[226] This was a conscious attempt to get away from one of the legal profession's best-known cycles: students becoming teachers, mentees becoming mentors.

[227] While this may not be the most charitable attitude, some people are justified in adopting it. Depending on the first-year student in question, requests for outlines in particular can be overwhelming.

[228] The age difference seems more profound between people starting these two years than one can understand beforehand; every year, second-year students remark that the new class of first-years looks like kids. I've actually observed this over four separate repetitions of the cycle, and it always happens. The second-years truly aged during their first year, and the first-years have no idea what they're about to get into.

princess. (Call me corny, but it's true.) The message which ran through my brain was stated in the form of a compelling choice: the person you're seeing over there is likely to become very important in your life, and you should absolutely introduce yourself to her, unless you want to regret it forever. Despite my prior dating history, I'd never had that feeling about another person.

Thus compelled, I introduced myself to the stranger I saw across the room, something I literally had never done before and haven't done since. Her name was Heather, I learned; she had just graduated at the top of her class from the University of California at Irvine. I'm sure I came across as awkward, especially to someone who had clearly been approached before by interested suitors; it helped only somewhat that I knew her 2L mentor from our summer in Paris.

And I learned, over the course of a couple of days, some things that made this particular person very different from the typical beautiful woman who came to our school. She lived a clean, healthy lifestyle, and wasn't dating anyone or engaged when she arrived. These were qualities I liked. She loved Ben & Jerry's Coffee Heath Bar Crunch ice cream. Wow. She was also very serious about doing well in law school. I liked this, too. And she therefore was not looking for a boyfriend. This part, I didn't like so much.

But I shouldn't have been surprised. By the first week of classes, she was, as expected, knee-deep in the drama of typical first-year life, just as shocked by the experience as every other first-year and struggling to keep up with the workload. She had double-majored in college and had graduated as class valedictorian with a summa cum laude in political science and magna cum laude in psychology. Yet like me, and like everyone else we have known, she was overwhelmed, sleepless, and not looking to add more time commitments to her life. Meals had become her only breaks from classes and studying; an experience I knew well. While I will spare you the details of our courtship, we used those meal breaks to go out for coffee a few times, and dinner once or twice before we actually started to date.[229] Those who had warned against dating a first-year were right to assume that it wasn't going to be easy, but wrong to assume that it wasn't worthwhile.

Watching Heather start her first year, I had my earliest sense of just how much of the initial law school experience is the same for the majority of law students. Like eyestrain that demands glasses. Sleepless nights. Heartbreak over grades, no matter how well you do. And daily challenges, even for the best and brightest people, those born to be lawyers, and those who later succeed.

---

[229] It was initially through my experiences with her and her classmates that I learned how many of my own experiences had been typical, and which had been more unique to me. Heather later became a mentor to incoming first-year students, during both her second and third years as one of two residence hall graduate community assistants for the law school's dormitory. As a result, we both spent plenty of time surrounded by first-year students, and the confines of the law school and its dormitory.

Because it's all so predictable, law schools know well in advance how many of their students will experience given sorts of social adjustment problems, mental and/or family issues, and other seemingly 'unusual' problems. Over time, even the unusual problems are understood to be part of a law school cycle; they turn out to be unusual only in the sense that they affect relatively few people each year, not that they have never happened before.

Law schools also know that second-year life will calm down dramatically for most students – including and perhaps especially married ones. Despite the continued demands on a second-year student's life, married and otherwise involved 2Ls often have a lot more time during that year to spend with their loved ones, and though it's unlikely that the second year will be a time when married couples can 'fall in love again,' it is definitely a time when they can plan a semester or year away from the law school together in different surroundings – perhaps during the even less stressful third year.

E. BEGINNING THE SECOND-YEAR LIFESTYLE: STRATEGIC CLASS AND INTERVIEW JUGGLING

**"At law school, the first year they scare you,
the second year they work you,
and the third year they bore you."**
Well-worn maxim of legal education,
As repeated by law professor to his upper-class students

As well-known and oft-recited as the maxim above may be, it's not necessarily accurate in modern American law schools. "They" was supposed to refer to professors, but most modern law students find that professors work them the hardest in the first year, not the second. In fact, for people without journal obligations, second-year life can be considerably less stressful than the first, though tough classes, journal work, job interviews and social events can more than fill your time if you let them.

Though so much of the law school experience is predictable, and therefore controllable, one thing seemed perpetually beyond the administration's ability to handle: upper-class scheduling.[230] Class sign-ups were perennially late, drop-add periods inexplicably short and confusing, and dissatisfied students continually complaining. Prerequisite classes inevitably conflicted with one another and each semester's standout classes often had waitlists of over a hundred people. Some students felt compelled to resort to guerrilla tactics, such

---

[230] Even in a school that denied elective classes to first-year students, it was apparently too difficult to balance a schedule with roughly 30 upper-class daytime elective courses spread across more than thirteen classrooms, seven hours a day, five days a week.

as signing up for twice as many classes as they wanted, in the hopes that half would actually pan out. As a result, it was highly unlikely that any student would get many, or even some of the classes she wanted.[231]

In theory, the second year will be your first chance to pick a bunch of personally interesting topics every semester and pursue them. Practically speaking, I became satisfied when I could conjure up a decent mixture of courses strongly recommended by the law school as part of their "core curriculum," and other courses that actually interested me. Cornell considered four non-first-year classes to be part of their core curriculum – Administrative Law (Admin Law), Corporations (Corps), Evidence, and Federal Income Taxation (Tax). The recommendations meant that the courses were not mandatory, but that a wise student should take no fewer than two, and probably three of the courses.

These courses are paralleled by similarly optional, but recommended classes at other law schools – some schools phrase their recommended curricula as drawing from practical "statutory and regulatory law." As mentioned previously, the concept behind the recommendations is this: not every lawyer has a broad law practice, so forcing all future transactional attorneys to take Evidence is as problematic as forcing all future litigators to take Tax. Law schools continue to recommend the courses to give future attorneys breadth of exposure, hoping that some will take both classes anyway.[232]

Each semester, I aimed to get one core class out of the way, with the exception of Tax. Though I was not sure at this point what sort of law I hoped to practice, I knew that I wanted nothing to do with tax law. Your decision-making process may well be similar by this point; if you don't know what you do want, at least know what you don't want. The remaining courses ranged in my mind from at least interesting to necessary.

Admin Law essentially walks you through key court decisions on the scope of Congress' and the President's abilities to delegate certain powers to federal agencies, and various situations in which agencies have acted properly and improperly within the scope of their authority. As the course focuses upon key Supreme Court and federal Courts of Appeal decisions, Admin Law is a close parallel to first-year Con Law, though its coursework tends to be a lot less touchy-feely than the Con Law material can become in the hands of some

---

[231] Administrators apparently threw up their hands and refused to remedy the problem, compounding it by introducing the law school's first computerized sign-up process – in 1999. This should serve as somewhat of a lesson about law schools – unlike business schools, they tend to be considerably behind the times in technology, and in some cases, even fail to offer modern conveniences.

[232] Most people will, for better or worse, take just the classes they think they need. Good friends have come to regret this when they've found themselves unexpectedly reassigned by their new law firms to completely different practice areas.

professors. This class generally has nothing to do with civil rights, a woman's right to choose, or free speech – it's entirely an examination of the Commerce Clause, judicial review and federalism principles in practical, day-to-day use. Admin Law is the archetypical course on "regulatory law."

Corporations is the archetypical course on "statutory law." Though there are 50 separate state corporations codes, Corps generally focuses upon majority law – primarily and specifically Delaware's state corporations law – which is thought to be the country's most advanced body of statutory and judicially-created business law. This class teaches you the legal requirements for creating and operating a corporation, the legal differences between corporations and other forms of business entities, and the most noteworthy legal difficulties corporations have run into over the years. If you have to think of Corps as a parallel to a first-year class, it's most similar to Contracts, but far less abstract.

Evidence is neither regulatory nor traditionally statutory. It's a class that focuses upon the Federal Rules of Evidence, which like the Federal Rules of Civil Procedure were originally derived from the common law -- the best practices and precedents of state courts dealing with issues that come up in trials. The Federal Rules of Evidence deal strictly with the introduction and use of evidence in courts, a seemingly narrower field than Civil Procedure that somehow manages to have just as many rules to memorize. Evidence, however, is an optional class, which instantly reduces the largest factor that made Civil Procedure so intimidating – its compulsory status.

And Federal Income Taxation is entirely about the federal personal income tax code. Tax introduces students to the legal side of the tax code, including its most common and interesting deductions and the practices of the Internal Revenue Service, the agency that polices the code. Corporate taxation is left for another course, as are international tax codes and the state and local tax codes. Tax classes, more than any of the other recommended classes above, become more or less tolerable depending on the professor who teaches them. These are classes in which charismatic or humorous presentation matters at least as much as the subject matter.

Why would I skip Tax? Some people enjoy the course based specifically on the fact that they like their professor and find the material easy to learn from that person. They urge others to consider taking tax and other seemingly bland subjects, as they might turn out to be fascinating. But I've heard an equal number of horror stories from people who never really learn the material because they dislike the subject matter. Personally, if Tax wasn't mandatory, I wasn't about to subject myself to it voluntarily, especially given that tax laws are threatened by dramatic changes so often.[233] By contrast, no one is going to

---

[233] It seemed especially risky to undertake the study of the tax code in an election year, given that politicians repeatedly pledge to scrap it for a flat tax. I've also observed that

scrap or dramatically change modern administrative law jurisprudence, corporations law, or the Federal Rules of Evidence any time soon. There were two other ABA-related academic requirements I needed to consider, too. One was universal to ABA-accredited schools – every school must require its students to pass a course dealing with legal ethics, also known as Professional Responsibility (sometimes abbreviated PR). Though students could pick PR courses from the selections offered by their schools, most of the classes look the same from the outside – the major difference between classes, like Tax, turns out to be the instructor. PR courses had a bad reputation at Cornell because the instructors were said to be less than enthralling; students repeatedly waited in line for visiting professors to arrive, then filled their classes to capacity. The other requirement involved legal writing coursework. When I started law school, graduation required two-upper class courses in writing, or one upper class writing course and a separate Note for a journal.[234]

After much angst over my schedule, I came upon a workable but not thrilling 13-credit semester – I wanted a light first half of the year so that I could focus upon law review work when I needed to. In the 'subjects that interest me' category, I got one class: Copyright, one of the iron triangle of key intellectual property subject areas I had decided that I wanted to study. In the 'subjects that only sound sort of interesting but have a fantastic teacher,' I picked my former Property Professor Franklin's Trusts & Estates class,[235] which had a great reputation and was both a New York and California bar exam subject.[236] Then I decided to get my Professional Responsibility course out of the way by taking a totally unknown class called Negotiating the Ethical Minefield with a visiting professor. Finally, I reluctantly picked up the core class Evidence, despite the fact that the best-known professor wasn't teaching it that semester. I took it solely because it fit into my schedule. Other classes I wanted either conflicted or weren't being offered.

---

even trained professionals who enjoy tax law and accounting never claim to be able to master the tax code, a fact which limited my confidence in my own ability to master it.

[234] Based on improvements in the first-year legal writing curriculum, Cornell later dropped the second writing requirement for upper-classmen, but not until I had already taken a writing class to satisfy the requirement.

[235] Thankfully, Professor Franklin had not left immediately after he was denied the school's deanship, though rumors circulated that he was still looking elsewhere.

[236] Depending on your confidence with a specific professor or subject, taking four-credit classes can be a good way to boost grades during the second year. Trusts & Estates seemed like a sure-fire winner at the time because it had a great professor and was also a four-credit class, and because it was likely to appear on the bar exam. See Section F. Trusts & Estates goes by similar names (including "Wills & Trusts") at other schools.

F. IS THE BAR A FACTOR?

Though I didn't realize it at this point, I had signed up for three courses that were testable subjects on the California Bar Exam.[237] This is as good a time as any to address two different schools of thought on taking classes in anticipation of your bar exam: some people think that you should take as many bar-testable subjects as possible during law school, while others think that you'll pick up as much as you need to know in a post-law school bar review course.

My personal take is that you'll be best served by taking most, but not necessarily all of the courses that will be tested on your state's bar. Your school may not even offer courses for some of the bar subjects, a situation much more likely to occur when you attend a law school in a state other than the one where you will be practicing.[238] Some of these classes will probably be more hassle than they're worth.[239] And if you're not sure which state bar you'll want to join, then look at the subjects your possible state bars have in common and take most of them. I'm not recommending this strategy because I think you will actually memorize and retain everything for an exam two years away; the only value this has is that you'll learn enough during law school that, when the bar comes, you won't freak out from all of the new material you're being shown.

And this is because the 'don't bother taking all of the classes' people are largely correct, at least in my view. Speaking from personal experience, BAR/BRI's popular post-law school bar review class does teach you everything you need to know for a given state's bar exam, so long as you keep up with the material. And sometimes, the more that you remember from law school, you'll be surprised to find that it's harder to learn the material in the unique manner that a given state's bar examiners will test it. This is counterintuitive, and you may doubt it even when you hear people saying it, but it's true. Or at least, it was true in my case and those of people I know. Regardless, my recommendation stands. You're better off taking some of the courses and knowing most of what the bar is about to ask than avoiding the classes and

---

[237] I especially had no way of knowing that these subjects would, in fact, later appear on the extended essay portions of my bar exam – evidence, professional responsibility, and trusts each came up.

[238] It's hard for people to predict where they may ultimately practice. My personal decision took into consideration economic trends and the locations of my families, friends, and possible future spouse, factors which are quite common. If you can choose a law school in the city where you will ultimately practice, you increase your chances of getting a job and being able to take bar-relevant classes. Law schools tend to conform their curricula, at least on some level, to even the more random subjects that appear on the bar exam.

[239] Even if you're taking Montana's bar exam, where you could possibly get tested on water law and worker's compensation, the exam *might* ask only one small question on workers' compensation. Is it really worth taking a whole class just to prepare for that?

hoping to learn everything two months before the exam.

Having said that, there are some law school classes which are more likely to be useful than others for bar preparation purposes. Forty-eight of the 50 states share the same multiple-choice questions for every bar exam – a standardized portion of the test called the Multistate Bar Exam (MBE). The MBE always tests six subjects: Constitutional Law, Contracts & Sales, Criminal Law & Procedure, Evidence, Real Property, and Torts. Most of these are first-year classes, but you can consider picking up the ones that aren't as electives.[240] Of the key elective classes offered at most schools, all 50 states test Trusts, Estates and Wills independently or collectively, subjects that you'll learn in a Trusts & Estates class; 47 of 50 test Corporations, and at least 27 of the 50 test on Professional Responsibility, the latter a misleadingly low number.[241] By comparison, only 19 of the 50 state bars test on tax subjects, and only 14 of the 50 on Administrative Law. Unless you plan to practice in these states or find the subjects interesting, they're not classes you need to consider.

G.   THE SECOND-YEAR CLASS EXPERIENCE

During one of the very first classes of the second year, a professor repeated a maxim of legal education that we heard a few more times before graduating: "at law school," he said, "the first year they scare you, the second year they work you, and the third year they bore you." The phrase is old and well-known, but more importantly, it's only partially true.

There's no doubt that the second year is lower-key than the first in four ways – you take the number of credits you want, you don't have to take classes that are as difficult, you are unlikely to be as overloaded with assignments, and there are less likely to be in-class Socratic experiences. Whereas virtually all of my first-year professors used the Socratic Method, very few of them used it in my second or third years. This needn't have been the case, however; part of it was just the luck of the draw in class scheduling. Some professors were reputed to work upper-class students as hard as the first-year professors had. Those who wanted to take classes in this sort of environment had the option to do so; I personally opted to steer clear of professors who had such reputations, as I believed that interviewing and law review responsibilities were going to be more than enough stress to handle every day.

---

[240] In fact, all 50 states test Evidence, making it a de facto must-take class in law school. Though 49 states test both Contracts & Sales and Criminal Law & Procedure, the subject names are mildly misleading – the "Sales" portion, derived from the U.C.C., is very easy to pick up during bar study, as is the small amount of "Criminal Procedure" that appears in the MBE questions. Taking elective classes for these subjects is not advised unless you find the material interesting in its own right or useful to your future planned practice.

[241] See Section H below.

My single Socratic class of the semester was Evidence – a class taught by an actively practicing, highly intimidating federal prosecutor named Chuck Graber, whose daily classroom persona placed students in the grips of a tooth-pulling cross examination. The professor knew his stuff, but insisted that he would teach the course in a way that we would find maximally useful in real practice, because only some of the 60-plus Federal Rules of Evidence ever "really" got used in the courtroom. Each class, he would call one or two people for the entire class session, and typically would keep on poking at people who clearly hadn't prepared adequately for the class. The professor even told students that they had to seek his permission in advance to miss classes, a draconian step that even first-year professors had never explicitly requested. Some upper-class professors at other schools insist on a similar practice to maintain attendance; it was rare at Cornell.

Professor Graber contrasted markedly with the other Evidence professor, Aldo Rizzoli, who was much beloved by his students and alternated teaching the class during other semesters. Grandfatherly but quick-witted, Professor Rizzoli had also been a successful courtroom attorney at one point. Now he taught at Cornell during the academic year and did well-known and widely-respected Evidence lectures for a bar preparatory course. His law school class similarly focused on preparing students for the bar exam, not the courtroom. In retrospect, and even as I was somewhat aware at the time I signed up for Professor Graber's course, I should have taken Evidence with Rizzoli.

At the completely other end of the spectrum on all levels was the class I took on copyright law. Taught by the Harvard-educated Professor Paul Lewis – a respected professor now renowned for his knowledge of the Internet and copyright issues – this class was far more of a zero-energy experience: students could clearly get away with not attending, not preparing, and actually, not really even understanding the material for most of the semester. It was a first for me in law school, but similar to classes I had taken before Cornell. If Graber's version of Socratic was overly aggressive and interrogatory, Professor Lewis's version was academic and confusing – he posed a never-ending series of questions which were frequently unanswered, mostly led to other questions, and seemed to be put out there solely for the purpose of showing just how little of the possible universe of future copyright problems had been explored by the year 1999. It was unclear whether Professor Lewis intentionally left issues open-ended to compel students to seek their own answers, or for other reasons.

Despite the class structure, the subject matter of Copyright was amongst my favorite material in law school – it's the primary set of federal rules for protecting various tangible forms of human expression, including everything from books, poems, short stories and magazines to photography, architecture, microprocessors, ship hulls and software. The class teaches you why copyright law doesn't protect ideas, concepts, or facts, and how a copyright is different from a patent and a trade mark. It is one of the foundational classes in intellectual property law, which is a modern extension of classical, tangible property law that offers protection for intangible creations of the mind.

In part because of the meandering lectures, Copyright became a teach-it-yourself subject, and lacked even a textbook.[242] Moreover, it was my first law school class to have both a final exam and assignments due during the semester. In a hokey, 'I love computers way too much' fashion, Professor Lewis had set up assignments to be read and completed online, where there were inevitably server connection issues and you were never sure if your answers were actually being read. On the bright side, the final exam had a huge collection of topics from which you could select the questions you desired to answer. If only all of law school, and life for that matter, was like that exam. I knew that I would enjoy copyright law going in; when I was finished, I thought that I probably wanted to practice it in some way later in my life.[243]

Trusts & Estates was exactly what I expected when I signed up for it: a class dealing with the legal methods of holding property and controlling its future disposition. Touching upon the laws of trusts and wills, as well as the lawyer's special responsibilities when creating trusts and wills, Professor Franklin, true to his reputation and previously demonstrated talents in first-year Property, delivered a series of fantastic lectures that other professors might only have given on days when they were in rare form. His were the classes that people dream about when they first hear about law school – oratory filling a room; large, important concepts becoming clearer in your mind just through hearing someone talking, and learning something useful every day that might benefit you and your family sometime soon.

Participation was voluntary and largely uncoerced, and the subject matter made complete sense as it was taught. Unlike Copyright, which I took out of pure, strong interest and left every day feeling confused (until I re-organized around outlining time), Trusts & Estates was taken with modest interest and I finished every day feeling well-informed and confident. It's amazing what a difference a given professor's style can make.

---

[242] Instead, we had a big stack of cases retrieved from free sources on the Internet – a pet project of the professor.

[243] Interestingly, Copyright was one of the only classes I took in law school where the male-to-female ratio was decidedly skewed in favor of male students; in fact, all of the intellectual property classes I attended were seemingly less attended by women, though the ones who were there tended to be seriously interested in practicing intellectual property law after graduation. Most of my classes had a seemingly equal balance of male and female students, though there were a handful of classes which frequently had female enrollments outstripping the male ones, such as Family Law, Feminist Legal Theory, Feminist Political Thought, Health Law, Law and Mental Health, Sex Discrimination and the Law, and Women and the Law.

H. PROFESSIONAL RESPONSIBILITY – THE NEW ETHICS

My fourth class of the semester fulfilled one of the law school's few upper-class mandates: completion of a course in ethics. The first word that comes to the minds of many non-lawyers when they hear "legal ethics" is "oxymoron;" even law schools now refer to ethics as "Professional Responsibility." It's easy to believe the classic lawyer stereotypes – some think that the legal profession is all about evasiveness, helping people get away with crimes, and shading the truth. Yet law students are universally trained in the critical provisions of several separate codes of ethical standards that have been adopted by states to regulate the conduct of practicing attorneys. The standards are strict, frequently non-flinching, and subject lawyers to the strong threat of professional discipline if violated. In the worst circumstances, disciplined attorneys may permanently lose their licenses to practice law and suffer other serious consequences.

Law students must know key provisions of the ethical rules before they will be permitted to join any state's bar – a requirement enforced by the American Bar Association's mandate of ethics classes, then reinforced by each state's mandatory testing. Students are tested on ethics from one to three times before they may join a state bar. One could be at the end of an ethics class, another during your state's bar exam, and a third someplace in-between the other two.

Thrice annually, the National Commission of Bar Examiners[244] offers the third type of examination, called the Multistate Professional Responsibility Exam (MPRE) and required by 45 of the 50 state bars.[245] Not only must you take the MPRE, but you also need a score of at least 75 out of a possible 150 points; 15 states require scores as high as 85, and the recent trend has been for the standards to increase. By comparison to first-year exams, the MPRE is reasonably demanding but not first-year-exam-caliber – it's a two hour and five minute test with 50 standardized multiple choice questions. There is no essay component. The average score is roughly 100.

At the moment, you might be wondering whether to practice instead in one of the five states that don't require the MPRE – Connecticut, Maryland, New Jersey, Washington or Wisconsin. They test ethics on their bar exams, instead. Many other states test ethics both on the MPRE and then again on the bar. There's simply no way that a prospective lawyer can get around ethics testing, regardless of what the general public may believe.

Professional responsibility training is universal, but not uniform. Many schools offer multiple courses dedicated to legal ethics, any one of which can

---

[244] See http://www.ncbex.org/tests/mpre/mpretxt.htm#General for additional information on the MPRE.

[245] Two states, Connecticut and New Jersey, will accept a grade of C or better in an ethics course instead of requiring a MPRE score.

satisfy the ABA's requirement. Typically, in addition to requiring either papers or the taking of a final exam, the courses generally prepare students for the questions that will be asked on the national MPRE exam as well. But to fully prepare for the MPRE, students typically either study for a short period of time on their own or take an abbreviated BAR/BRI lecture.[246] In either case, you wind up slightly beyond the scope of most classes and have to study the Model Code of *Judicial* Ethics, a subject dealing solely with the conduct of judges.

Professional responsibility courses at my school had a somewhat checkered history. The school's highly respected, older professors of legal ethics also had bad reputations -- some bored their students to death, others were unnecessarily prickly. Cornell's best-known ethics course, Lawyers and Clients, was widely regarded as a terrible experience just waiting to happen to unwitting second-years. I was advised by upper-class friends to find a way around taking courses with the resident faculty, and instead signed up for the first visiting professor I could find. I took a big chance when I signed up for a class called Negotiating the Ethical Minefield with a visiting professor, Stephen Bear, whose name and history were at that point completely unknown to me. But anything seemed a better option than taking a class where I would either fall asleep or become the target of weird professorial behavior.

As it turns out, Professor Bear was a practicing attorney at a firm in Philadelphia, and more interestingly, was a member of the American Bar Association's committee on the drafting of new legal ethical rules. He fit into the visiting professor category of 'established and fantastic;' despite the fact that he flew back to Pennsylvania to practice law every day of the week when he wasn't teaching us, he seemed to be looking for a more academic lifestyle. As an author of one of our textbooks and former managing partner of a major law firm, Professor Bear had the rare combination of practical experience and academic interest in a subject that makes a visiting practitioner great.

He was also a more human character than any of the professors I'd dealt with at the law school at that point. Despite the fact that he was so up-to-date on the material that he was handing us draft proposals of new ethics rules only days after they were drafted, he took pains not to be intimidating in his mastery of the material. And though he called on people every day and riddled the class with interesting questions, he taught in a manner completely different from his Socratic contemporaries. His questions led us to understand some of the most challenging contemporary issues in legal ethics – areas that experts disagreed about. And he showed us, better than did most professors, both sides of philosophical arguments, while allowing us to take our own positions on them.

---

[246] The lecture lasts for part of a day and consists of walking students through the completion of a 50-some page, fill-in-the-blanks outline mixed with sample questions. It's not rocket science, but it does the trick.

Each class would begin with one hypothetical situation drawn completely at random from the professor's broad list of topics, and then move to a second hypothetical during the second half of the class. Responding to each hypothetical required a mix of common sense and recollection of the rules we had read in preparation for the class. In the process, we learned the biggest rules of professional responsibility – those governing confidentiality of discussions with clients, situations constituting the unauthorized practice of law, and resolution of multiple-client conflicts of interest – while working through situations that actually came up in Professor Bear's practice. We also learned about the attorney's legal obligations to candidly disclose certain bad facts and adverse law to courts and other proper authorities, and how to politely deal with opposing attorneys. And, of course, we learned the distinction between professional discipline and a suit for legal malpractice. Not all courses are taught in the same manner as the one I took, but almost all of them cover the same materials.

Professional responsibility is an important topic for law students, and one that under the proper conditions, can be as well-taught and interesting as the best of your other classes. It is unquestionably more practical than most courses, as it mandates certain day-to-day behavior of all lawyers, not to mention that you will be tested on it so many times before becoming a lawyer. Though you'll re-learn the material in time for the bar, any course you take will be a good first exposure to the general principles every lawyer needs to know.

There was another unexpected component to this class: I bumped into Professor Bear a few times after he left Cornell, and always found him to be exceedingly friendly and overwhelmingly interested in helping me, or other former students, get good answers if we were ever confronted with ethical questions we didn't know how to address. Far from the negative lay presumption of the questionable lawyer, Professor Bear embodied the legal profession as I have most frequently seen it: strongly concerned with doing right and helping other attorneys to do so, as well.[247]

I.   RECONSIDERING STUDENT ORGANIZATIONS

Student organizations typically come to play a much larger role in the lives of second-year students than they do for first-years. The second year will be the time when you join the clubs that sounded interesting during the first year, and at some point in your fourth semester, you might consider running for elective

---

[247] This dovetails into another example of law school administration irony: the school was in need of a new ethics professor to replace a retiring faculty member, and though Professor Bear had hoped to return to the school to teach again, and did such a spectacular job when he was there, it did not request his return.

office in those clubs.

Law student organizations can be as interesting or as limited as their members make them. As was probably the case in your experiences prior to law school, some student organizations benefit from and are inspired by great leaders and ideas. Among the most stable organizations at Cornell was the Public Interest Law Union (PILU), a group of students devoted both to personal careers in the public sector and also to raising funds to help others pursue similar employment. With the tremendous disparity between public and private sector salaries, organizations such as the PILU help to bridge the salary gap by securing funding from outside sources to supplement the salaries of students who do public interest work over their summers or thereafter.

PILU held an annual event called Cabaret, which for fundraising purposes interspersed an auction with a series of on-stage student performances. Cabaret offered musically- and dramatically-inclined students and professors the chance to perform before a large audience, and also placed many interesting products and services up for auction – including meals, golf outings and bike rides with professors and deans, items and services donated by local stores and restaurants, and a small collection of student-produced goods and services, as well. The event was typically quite well-attended, enjoyable, and impressive. It was amongst the only opportunities people had to see their classmates all together and dressed up outside of classrooms and job fairs.

Other such opportunities were the Cornell Law Students Association's two dances – the fall semester's Semi-Formal and the spring season's Barrister's Ball. Though formalwear was optional, most people came dressed up in impressive suits and dresses, danced a bit, drank a lot, and had a lot of fun in the process. These events were typically held off-campus at a local hotel or nightclub that could accommodate 400-500 people. Annual Halloween and Thanksgiving events were typically held, as well, but were lower-key and less-attended.

By contrast, we didn't see a lot of student rallies, marches, or protests, which might surprise those who view the legal profession as a breeding ground for antagonism. Even those organizations with social agendas – including the conservative Federalist Society, the liberal Women's Law Coalition, and the non-aligned Science and Law Association – tended to hold meetings, organize petitions, and infrequently sponsor events open to the law school community.[248] The Black Law Students Association and Latino American Law Students Association held bake sales to raise money for dances. During outbreaks of

---

[248] An example of the activities of these organizations was the Women on the Walls project, a fundraising drive to place portraits of important female lawyers in the hallways and atrium of the law school. The project was sponsored by the Asian American Law Students Association, Black Law Students Association, Cornell Law Students Association, Environmental Law Society, Latino-American Law Students Association, Native American Law Students Association, and the Women's Law Coalition.

violence in Northern Ireland, the Irish Brehon Law Society organized a happy hour. This isn't to say that students lacked for political agendas – to the contrary, groups of students went off to Bosnia and Israel during flare-ups in both places – but people did not often wear their affiliations on their sleeves.

On a single occasion, a student acting outside of any formal organizational structure did something that was to become the talk, and mostly, the contempt of the entire school. The student, who came from a conservative religious background, authored an extended essay purporting to reveal a genetic basis for the professional inferiority of women. He submitted copies of the essay to members of the faculty, and another copy to the student newspaper. The paper published the essay – probably as an exercise in free speech – a decision which came to infuriate virtually everyone at the law school. Students received the paper on a day set aside as a special visiting day for recently accepted prospective female students; a possible coincidence. Though the essay generated both an extended, positive discussion on the subject of gender and an unparalleled submission of response editorials to the newspaper, the effect on the law school's visitors was never fully ascertained. Whether they appreciated it as the first step in a debate or found the content offensive enough to avoid the otherwise decidedly pro-female campus is open to question.

The student newspaper turned out to be a great avenue for student expression during the second year, though participation continued to wane because of organizational difficulties. Several second-year students authored columns for the newspaper, and other students contributed news stories, photographs, editorials, and letters to the editors. Other organizations also sprouted up to promote creative expression during the time I was there, too: a poetry, photography and short story magazine was published infrequently, and the student organization SOLATA formed to promote theater and the arts.

Some people, of course, preferred to stick entirely to journal work in their free time. And yes, there are additional opportunities for some associates to get even more involved in journals' affairs. Many journals sponsor annual symposia or lectures on topical subjects related to their specialized purposes – a symposium is essentially a gathering of scholars who attend panel discussions on a common subject and present papers. As examples, the *Stanford Law Review* developed a lecture series on First Amendment and Copyright issues, and the *Harvard Journal of Law & Technology* recently featured a symposium on Technology, Freedom and Control in a Digital Age. Though the attendance at lectures and symposia varies dramatically from year to year, subject to subject and speaker to speaker, each event requires a staff of editors and associates to manage the logistics and speakers. Similarly, journals often organize annual formal banquets for their members, and additional people are needed to make sure these events run smoothly.

Somewhat atypically, the *Law Review* during my second year set up three separate committees that a person could join – an Elections Committee, an Admissions Committee, and one called the Academic Credit Committee. The first committee met once or twice only to discuss potential recommendations for changes in the elections policy, and essentially did nothing. The Academic Credit Committee efficiently drafted a request to the law school's administration to extend academic credits for journal membership, which was considered and then rejected by the faculty. These two experiences were wholly outstripped by the Admissions Committee, however, which proposed some fundamental and far-reaching changes to the journal's admissions policies, and won their approval over the course of two separate votes of the journal's membership. Committee work has the potential to pay off in important, but less obvious ways than participation in lectures, symposia, and other functions.[249]

J.   DATING UPDATE: THE AGE GAP NARROWS FOR SECOND- AND THIRD-YEARS

While much has been said on the topic of first-year/second-year dating, a related theme has been ignored: if some second-years won't date first-years because of the 'dog years' difference in age, what happens to the risk-adverse upper-classmen when first-years become second-years? The answer is that the dog year stigma ends and increased dating begins.

This was demonstrated several times during the second year, frequently at social events when third-year students realized that the former first-years had now 'matured' enough to be fair game. The result was that a number of third-year students started to date second-year students, and some of the relationships quickly became serious. Other third-years, of course, had never minded social involvement with first-years, and a couple of third-year men became somewhat notorious for showing up at the first-year dormitory to visit girlfriends. Third-years were universally faced with a dilemma, however, which was the classic light at the end of a tunnel that turns out to be a train: law school was soon to come to a much-needed end, but since no one stayed in Ithaca after graduation, any new relationship with a second-year would become long-distance within two semesters and require at least another year to resume in

---

[249] Need a journal member participate in any of these optional activities? Not really. A few of the people later elected to high leadership positions on my journal participated in one of the optional committees, but most participated in none of them. When I was an associate, my editor-in-chief proposed the maxim that law review editors only begin to get good at their jobs right before they are replaced by a new editorial board. From my vantage point, those most active in a journal's committees, yet lacking more, will not be elected to its offices. The best advice I can give a journal associate considering a future leadership role is to work hard, do excellent work, kiss ass so gently as not to leave a mark or be seen doing it, and make very few if any enemies.

person. Any new relationship with a first-year would require two years to continue in person. Third-years cited these as primary reasons to avoid dating people from other classes, at least if they had long-term relationship ambitions.

I had understood this from the start of my second year, and felt that if I didn't meet someone early on, I would probably not want to get involved thereafter. Even though we had 'officially' started to date by the beginning of her second semester, Heather and I both understood from the start that a clock was ticking on our relationship – either I had to look for jobs with her in mind, or vice-versa, and preferably both of the above. This is challenging, if not patently unlikely to happen in a nascent relationship given second-year interviewing timetables, and it worked out for us only because I assumed that things might become more serious, and that we might survive a one-year separation when I completed my third year. These were tough assumptions to make, and I think that they're not especially common ones.

Another interesting phenomenon was the second year's breakdown of the formerly cohesive section identities people had acquired during the first year: for the first time, all of the sections mingled, and that led to some surprising introductions of students who hadn't even met during the first year. One second-year couple met at their journal orientation, and were engaged to be married within literally a month of their first date.[250] Numerous less serious couplings were reported, as well.

Some people, however, were thoroughly tired of seeking dating opportunities within the law school; our class was small, the possibilities were limited, and a good number of people were still unconvinced that they really wanted to be romantically involved with other law students. The second year is when most of the disenchanted began to look elsewhere, starting with joint business school-law school social functions and panning out across the range of other graduate students. While the total number of people who found matches outside of the law school was relatively light by comparison to those who found something inside, this was a viable option for those who wanted it.

Far more common were matches made through friends of friends. The second year offered plenty of opportunities and time for visitors to travel to Ithaca and stay with their friends at the law school, and a number of visitors found themselves inquiring and inquired about by law students. Other couples were introduced outside of Ithaca while visiting a law student's family or friends in a larger city. Something about the second year just brought out a need for companionship in people.

---

[250] The suddenness was eclipsed only by the second-year student who became engaged to a first-year student within weeks of the start of the first semester. Both couples, incidentally, are married now.

K.   GETTING BACK IN TOUCH WITH THE WORLD OUTSIDE

Looking outside of the law school wasn't just the pursuit of those who wanted to date; it tended to be the active pursuit of any person with five free minutes to rub together. This was as much a social thing as it was a practical one; people wanted to play some golf, do some real shopping, and travel to see friends and families outside of Ithaca. One's wanderlust tended to be limited only by a given day's workload. And, interviews aside, some people wandered far more than others.

Developing oneself past the limitations of the first-year existence is likely to be an important component of any law student's life. And this development takes many possible forms.

One piece of it is returning to doing the little things that might not have been convenient during the first year – reading newspapers and watching the news to see what's going on in the world around you. This might be as much for business as it should be for pleasure; it's important at a minimum to understand what sorts of conditions are presently prevailing in the market for legal services. For example, if you were hoping to work for a dot-com upon graduation and the market is showing signs of collapse, it's definitely to your advantage to be aware of the practical limits on your employment prospects. Unless you expect a rebound, you might be better off with some bankruptcy, employment law, or tax courses. If you hope for public sector work, it similarly might be useful to know what sorts of issues are traditionally or politically hot and not in the jurisdiction where you're hoping to work. Focusing your coursework on environmental law might not be as lucrative in a Republican political climate as it was in a Democratic political climate.

If you haven't already done it, you also need to develop some sort of real life for yourself outside of school, giving you something to fall back upon when you're later working long hours in an office. Sports, exercise, family, or other cerebral pleasures might be your personal antidote to long days spent poring over paperwork; whatever floats your boat, spend some time doing it.

Some of these outside interests might spark you to take classes you might not otherwise have considered – if you enjoy writing, you might take a class in copyright law; golf or football, a class in sports or entertainment law, and so on. And this needn't be limited to law school courses if you have the option to sign up for classes outside. More importantly, your interests are likely to form the basis for the friendships you build both in law school or the office. It's hard to keep good relationships with people based solely on conversations about your classes and work. Cultivating other dimensions of your personality and lifestyle is one key to later professional success.

L.   DO YOU HAVE ANY PASSION LEFT FOR THE LAW?

Amidst all this discussion of other topics besides classes comes a difficult question: with everything else that you could be doing, is there any passion left inside you for the law? This is a question that sometimes proves tricky for second-year students, as there can be a lot more opportunity for self-reflection after the hectic first year has ended. Self-reflection might lead to deeper commitment to the law, or a sense that the law isn't what you thought it was before you arrived at law school.

Be careful to separate your feelings for the law from your feelings for your classmates. If you enjoy both the people and the profession, you're in great shape. But there are many people who find elements of the second year personally troubling, and more often than not, it's the behavior of fellow students, not the law or the professors. One noteworthy but morally ambiguous example was an antagonism between friends that started during a mock negotiation session. In a group of students, one student was quietly asked to play the role of the disruptor during the negotiation. Another student was quietly asked to be the conciliator. When the disruptor went fully into his role, the conciliator exploded with fury because her friend was doing his job, and because she could not bring peace to the group. Was the conciliator turned off to the concept of negotiation? It's hard to know for sure, but the two former friends did not talk again for the rest of law school. Similar bitterness between people – often arising from their training as lawyers – emerged now and again throughout the second and third years.

If you're feeling disillusioned with the law as a second-year, now is the right time to revisit whatever inspirational fountainhead you developed before law school, during the first year, or perhaps during the summer, and try to remember just why it is that you're here. Stay focused on your goals and stay as true to your original vision as possible; you will be thankful when you graduate.

M.   A SECOND YEAR'S SECOND SEMESTER

It took three semesters of law school before I began to feel as if I knew generally what sort of law I might want to practice. If there was any coherence to my life before and during law school, it was that I had been continually fascinated by both the law and technology, and had increasingly felt that a career of some sort in intellectual property (IP) law might be my calling. For the uninitiated – as I was, before law school – IP law consists of several primary and secondary subjects. The primary subjects are copyright, patent, and trademark law. The secondary ones are lesser-known areas such as trade dress, idea protection, domain name rights, and trade secrets.

But as with several other areas of legal specialization, intellectual property law was still in a transitional growth phase when I began the application process to law schools, and in all truth, I did not even know what the profession had named what I hoped to do. Cornell, like many other schools during the Internet boom, was rushing to add new courses to satisfy student interest in various forms of IP law; it had only two course offerings when I arrived – Copyright & Digital Works, and Patents & Trademarks. And those courses were also the only offerings available during my second year of law school.

Like Copyright, which I had taken and enjoyed during the previous semester, I was very much interested in trademark law. But for practical reasons, I was less interested in patent law – unlike every other type of law, those hoping to actually practice patent law without supervision must have at least an undergraduate degree in a hard science,[251] and must also pass the completely separate "Patent Bar" before they are officially allowed to draw up or litigate patent documents on their own.[252] My undergraduate coursework and degree didn't qualify me to formally practice patent law,[253] but neither of these prerequisites mattered if I was interested in trademark and copyright law.

But as mentioned before, the field of IP law was still in its growth stage, and if I wanted to study trademark law at Cornell, it seemed that I would have to take a combined course dealing with both patents and trademarks. And as I discovered when I attended the course, the patent material received a disproportionate share of attention – so much so that one semester later, the school unexpectedly split the course into two separate ones and hired a new professor to teach trademarks, which was renamed "Trademarks and the Law of

---

[251] Hard sciences include engineering, biology, or physics, amongst others; political science, behavioral sciences, social sciences and mathematics degrees don't count. For a complete list of qualified hard science backgrounds, see http://www.uspto.gov/web/offices/dcom/olia/oed/index.html.

[252] The Patent Bar is presently offered twice a year (April and October), and application deadlines are roughly three months in advance of each date. In total, the exam consists of 100 multiple-choice questions split between two three-hour morning and afternoon sessions; you pass if you score 70/100 or higher. The total fee for the exam, not including preparatory materials, is $350.00; Patent Bar review courses range from a very low-end $250 to a very high-end $3400. It should be noted that many firms employ attorneys who have passed the Patent Bar and may therefore legally supervise the work of attorneys who have not passed the Patent Bar; this loophole enables even those without science backgrounds to get involved in patent work, at least at a junior level. But attorneys who haven't passed the Patent Bar cannot open their own patent practices, nor can they get involved in some of the higher-level activities of patent attorneys. Those looking to practice patent law exclusively should therefore have a science degree before coming to law school, or pursue one immediately thereafter.

[253] Bachelor of Science degrees typically automatically qualify their recipients to take the Patent Bar; in the alternative, a significant number of hours of chemistry, physics, biology, botany and/or engineering coursework can also qualify a person to take that exam.

Branding." Students who had registered for the prior class were deemed ineligible to take either of the newly independent Patents & Trademarks classes.

It became increasingly clear during the Patents & Trademarks class that intellectual property was my legal calling – particularly the trademarks materials, which dealt with the federal and state protection offered for symbols, logos, and slogans, and the limited exposure we had to trade dress, a related concept dealing with unique product packaging and store decoration. If I didn't love the patent material, I at least found it interesting. Copyright law protects tangible expressions. Patent law protects certain types of novel ideas. In recent years, patent law had dramatically expanded both in the United States and internationally, and covered everything from classically inventive devices to ways of doing business and – especially interestingly – software.

There was, therefore, some apparent overlap in copyright and patent law, an issue that I came to properly understand as the class went on. The software code as written lines of computer instructions would be protected by copyright law – the unique functionality of the software might be protected by patent law. The same was true of a business plan; the written document containing the plan would be a copyrighted work, and any novel idea within the plan might be patented. Like Property before it, the various legal ways in which you could view a single piece of paper, let alone a business plan or complex piece of software, kept me interested for the entire semester, and made me wish there were other IP classes to take.

In the absence of other IP course offerings, I signed up for several other subjects that interested me – I had really enjoyed Torts, and had heard excellent things about Products Liability, a class which focuses entirely upon injuries caused by the manufacturers and stores that sell defective products. I initially signed up for the class because Professor Jack Harrison was reputed to be friendly and good-natured, which was unusual considering his importance – he had just literally finished co-authoring part of the groundbreaking Third Restatement of Torts, which was the American Bar Association's definitive "model code" for state legislatures to follow in enacting new tort laws.[254] His words would, in effect, serve to tell legislators what the country's courts' best tort practices have been. Consumer protection has always been among my most favorite subjects outside of law school, so this class seemed a natural.

Perhaps not surprisingly, Products Liability is an advanced course in tort

---

[254] Restatements of the Law are highly debated collections of "model law," essentially what results if you put a bunch of experts on a specific subject into a room and ask them what would be the single best way to rewrite existing laws. Simply put, they look to the existing laws of the 50 states and "restate" the best laws for your consumption. In actuality, the experts debate for years and eventually churn out a single document that resembles a constitution, only every rule within it contains a large commentary as to the debates that surrounded eventual adoption of that rule.

law, and could confuse those who found the original class on torts perplexing. With the famous exploding Coke bottle case as one backdrop, it delves into some of the subjects which torts glosses over – how courts can decide that users broke or misused the products rather than using them properly and being injured by defects; the modern ways to assign liability to parties who both were at fault for selling a dangerous product; and identifying just what makes products truly dangerous. Like Torts, cases ranged from amusing to gruesome, a state of affairs exacerbated by Professor Harrison, who had been a part of so many products liability trials that even the gruesome had become amusing.[255]

Another follow up to a first year class was Constitutional Law II: The First Amendment – a natural class for me given that I had enjoyed both Constitutional Law and my summer course in Free Speech and Minority Rights. Some schools require two semesters of Constitutional Law, usually devoting one to the First Amendment, which is not a bad idea considering that many bar exams threaten to test somewhat extensively on the subject. Cornell made the class optional, and allowed only one teacher to handle it: Professor Glazer, with whom I had wanted to study again after my first year's summer.

More than any other class at the law school, The First Amendment really illustrates the most dramatic differences between the lay perception of law school and its reality. To the outside world, say the phrase "First Amendment" and see what responses you immediately receive – "freedom of speech," "freedom of religion," and "freedom of the press" are likely to be amongst the first you hear. And typically, people believe that in America, these freedoms are absolute – there cannot be any restriction on an American's freedom of speech, or practice of religion, or a newspaper's ability to say whatever it desires.

Law school classes almost universally deal in exceptions to widely-held rules. This particular class is fascinating in that the concepts are so well known and yet so largely misunderstood. And at the same time, if asked the right sorts of questions, even people with absolute views on censorship, religion and the press can intuitively be led to understand why none of these freedoms are, in fact, unlimited, and at the end they will typically agree that it is for the better.

Take, for example, the freedom of speech. It's right there in the text of the First Amendment, which has been reprinted innumerable times over the past two hundred years and most likely appears in a book you own, even if you don't realize it. That makes it about as well-publicized as any law can get. Yet, contrary to the most widely-held belief about free speech, you are not legally allowed to say literally anything you want. You could be jailed if you organized

---

[255] This was another class where uneasy laughter followed the presentation of a subject in a certain light – who really thinks, for example, that bottles of baby oil need huge warning labels that read "not safe to drink?" But then, when you think of the circumstances that might have occasioned such a warning, the specifics are more tragic than amusing.

a rally and, in a speech, told other people to pick up assault rifles and follow you immediately to the office of a local politician. You could be sued if you intentionally lied about a private citizen and damaged his or her reputation. And you might be subjected to the death penalty if you were a CIA agent and communicated top-secret information to another country's spy agency.

This class, like many in law school, illuminates just how far you can go, in speech, religion, and beyond, without running afoul of properly drafted state and federal laws. What it does not typically do, and what lay people might most expect such a class to do, is involve heated discussions between students over protests they've attended and experiences they've had where the cops seemed to unjustifiably tell them to disband and move along or be arrested. That is the stuff of undergraduate classes and extracurricular discussions, not law school. The distinction between a law school lecture, where you learn what the law is, and an undergraduate class, where you wax endlessly about how you wish the law was, is brought most sharply into focus here.

This does not say that law school is completely devoid of opportunities to express one's opinions. Another class I took during the same semester was Constitutional Law and Political Theory – a seminar. And seminar classes in law school, unlike lectures, are designed at least in part for active student discussion. If you're asked to speak in a lecture class, the professor is asking you to tell the class what he or she is thinking. If it's your turn to speak in a seminar, you're generally being asked to say what you're thinking. And the latter request, as it turned out, was somewhat of a problem for me in this class.

Scheduling difficulties at Cornell were the norm, as mentioned earlier in this book; between the school's unusually late registration process[256] and its repeatedly botched attempts to introduce computerized registration, course selection was a nightmare – as was the drop/add period if you got into a class and didn't like it. During my second semester, I tried to juggle the addition of two classes – Patents & Trademarks and a seminar in a specialized criminal law subject (Organized Crime Control), but growing pains associated with the computer bungled up my schedule. I couldn't get the crime seminar, and needed to find something to add at the last minute, so I tossed in Constitutional Law and Political Theory. Like Constitutional Law II, it was being taught by Professor Glazer. And my girlfriend had raved about the work of some of the theorists that were to be discussed – John Stuart Mill and John Rawls amongst others. I had no great love for political theory, but I figured that it couldn't be that bad. And it would let me to satisfy my second writing requirement.[257]

---

[256] First class sign-ups came only weeks before the start of classes, creating huge, unresolved backlogs of students for virtually every seminar.
[257] The first was about to be satisfied by my mandatory completion of a Law Review Note.

Well, I was wrong – it could be that bad.[258] And it turns out that a seminar may well be the worst place for a person to be totally disinterested in the subject matter, especially a seminar where every student is required to orally present his or her thoughts on each week's readings, and submit a weekly list of three questions or thoughts on the readings prior to the start of the class. Though the class had Constitutional Law in the title, it no more resembled either of the other Con Law classes than had, say, Property or Torts. Every class was a look at another political theorist, typically polar left- or right-leaning ones, and a discussion of everyone's views on whether that theorist was right, wrong, brilliant, short-sighted, or whatever. And you had to pay enough attention both to participate every week, and to write one of your two final papers in a manner that somehow addressed most of the theories from class.

The final class of the semester was one that I chose solely because it was a recommended core offering – Administrative Law. And after taking it, I understood both why it was recommended and how underappreciated the topic traditionally has been. When you really stop to consider it, administrative law is likely to be one of the most important subjects a practicing lawyer can learn about. It's an important enough area of law that several modern U.S. Supreme Court justices specialized in the topic before coming to the Court.

Why is it so important? Because the study of administrative law essentially answers the question, "what happens when Congress and the President are too busy dealing with big problems to handle the billions of small ones that come up each day?" The answers derive from the concept of the administrative agency and the delegation of legislative and executive authority. No one thinks for a moment that the President personally hunts down stock market cheats, even though the President is charged with faithfully executing the country's laws against insider trading and market manipulation. And few people think that Congress right now spends its time deciding exactly how much of a tax to place on goods traveling by train from Alabama to Texas, even though Congress has plenary power to regulate and tax interstate commerce. The President and Congress entrust federal agencies with the powers to supervise and make minor rules regarding the stock market, transportation, the environment, and dozens of other areas of everyday life. This is the subject matter of admin law, and as lawyers can spend a lot of time dealing with these

---

[258] Though I've said it before, you should seriously look at the description of a class in the course catalog before signing up, and that's especially true if you're going to be signing up at the last minute and won't be able to drop the class. This class proved an exception to the otherwise strong rule that a good professor can make it easy to learn even the most boring subject matter. While I largely believe in that rule, it's equally true that if the subject truly bores you, not even the best professor can make you feel interested in it. This class was one of only three in my time at the law school that I really regretted signing up for.

agencies, it's highly practical to learn about it in law school.

I can only think of one reason to skip the class: if you have a compelling reason to avoid the professors who teach it at your law school. In truth, there is no reason that administrative law needs to be taught by sticklers – unlike most areas of the law, the Supreme Court has recent taken unusually strong measures to create straightforward administrative law standards, including the 800-lb. gorilla case *Chevron*,[259] and a disproportionate amount of class time is wasted discussing how much of a mess existed before. Yet professors who gravitated towards administrative law tended to be pushier and more demanding than even first-year professors, and the result was that a highly useful and relatively clear subject became a confusing mélange of lapsed precedents and question marks. Admin Law became one of only two classes in law school that I felt compelled to supplement with a hornbook,[260] but when I did, the mess was almost entirely resolved. As only fourteen states currently test the subject on their bar exams, you can most likely avoid the class if you have a good reason.

N. RESIDUAL DEMANDS OF THE SECOND SEMESTER, INCLUDING EXAMS

As a whole, the second semester of the second year turned out to be a good one for me. Despite my 15-credit course load, the pressures of *Law Review* and the demands of a new relationship, my GPA jumped up to its highest level since starting law school. Yet there were some interesting speed bumps along the way.

One was my *Law Review* Note. While I won't tell you that it was insanely difficult to write, it did in fact consume quite a bit of time. Like all Notes, mine required plenty of research – both to find a topic and then to develop it into something that could stretch for more than 40 pages. Beyond the initial selection of a topic, which would have created problems had I chosen the same topic as another associate,[261] each topic also required continued pre-emption checks on Lexis and Westlaw to be sure that no other journal had recently published something on the same subject. If one had, I would need to start again; this happened to one or two of my classmates during the process.

The topic patrol wasn't nearly as challenging as the writing process. If I

---

[259] Chevron U.S.A. v. Natural Resources Defense Council, 467 U.S. 837 (1984). A hornbook series I came to prefer over the others was recommended by friends – West's NUTSHELL SERIES, a narrative format explanation of the current state of the law. I have little doubt that the ADMINISTRATIVE LAW AND PROCESS IN A NUTSHELL guide was critical to making sense of the materials I learned in class.

[260] The other was first-year Civil Procedure.

[261] If two or more people selected the same topic, they could either flip a coin to see who kept it, or try to find different ways to approach the topic.

wanted to graduate from the associate ranks of the journal to the editorial ranks, a process called 'elevation,' I would need to at least generally follow a submission calendar for several successive drafts of the Note. An associate could only become an editor if she successfully completed a Note and achieved a minimum average score for all of the weekly or bi-weekly editing assignments. Adherence to the Note draft submissions schedule was optional but strongly recommended; I personally followed it.[262] My final Note was submitted on time and earned me elevation.

Another speed bump was an unexpected consequence of Cornell's course registration system: only days before my Patents & Trademarks exam, I was informed that I had never been properly registered for the class. This, despite the fact that I had personally met with the professor the first week of the semester to get his permission to add the class; the registrar had kept me signed up for the similarly-named Parents, Children, and the State. After a hastily-arranged meeting with a dean, I was permitted to take the exam, eliminating a last-minute stress that was not especially welcome.

And the final speed bump was one that probably should have been anticipated in any 2L-1L dating relationship – exam-time stresses. Plenty of stories made the rounds as to how people dealt with their stresses during exam times; suffice it to say that Heather and I went through our share of tense moments, because we had different study habits and could hardly find time to relax during the weeks leading up to exams. What will work for other couples will be entirely a matter of trial and error, but it's safe to err on the side of keeping an appropriately healthy distance from your loved one during exam times, unless he or she expressly wants you around. The two of us enjoyed each others' company much more when we could talk during breaks or go out for dinner than we did when we were both trying to study.

As a whole, second-year exams were substantially less stressful than first-year exams.[263] It wasn't because the subject matter was less difficult, but rather because the sense of uncertainty as to testing methodology, time constraints,

---

[262] Perhaps half of the associates did not follow the optional guidelines, but every associate submitted a Note on or before the final deadline. At elections, Note Editors revealed those who had not followed the guidelines, but criticism was muted if the Note was excellent.

[263] Though my grades increased, I did not push as hard as some classmates. One of the more remarkable was a woman who, after working for a secondary journal, took advantage of a *Law Review* policy that automatically extended admission to second- or third-year students whose third- or fourth-semester grades were near the very top of the class. As a result, she was one of only a handful of people in history to simultaneously hold membership on two journals at once. Though this may sound enviable, it probably took more work – and was harder to explain to law firms – than just writing onto *Law Review* in the first place. People who worked on only one journal or Moot Court describe the second-year as equally demanding as the first. Two activities? Even worse.

and other issues continued to decrease each semester. At some point during the second year, I decided to change my outlining strategy: I had realized that the material I remembered best was that which I had studied during the semester but reviewed aggressively only shortly before the exam. The final four days before an exam thus became my most important outlining periods.

And I also realized that forty or fifty-page outlines weren't helping me much – I began to boil down my courses into ten- or twelve page, handwritten outlines that I could actually use, or even shorter typewritten outlines. Each outline included a table of contents and references to relevant parts of my class notes and textbook, which I brought along just in case. I would go over the outlines one last time right before exams to add missing points that just wouldn't stick in my memory.

The new outlines worked pretty well. In the first semester of my second year, only one of my exams rattled me – Professor Graber, in addition to having a prosecutorial classroom demeanor, also had a reputation for writing Evidence exams that were shockingly difficult. It was very difficult, true to the rumor, but virtually everyone thought so. The interesting thing was that by comparison to Trusts & Estates, a class with a mixed multiple-choice and essay examination, the grading result was typically the same though the exam experiences were totally different: both classes had huge B+ curves, one because almost everybody felt comfortable with the subject and did well, and another because almost everyone felt uncomfortable with the subject and did poorly. It was another demonstration of the problems wrought by grading curves.

As a general rule, things were never again as bad as they had been during the first-year. The final exams for Copyright and Negotiating the Ethical Minefield were both relatively friendly essay tests with very sufficient opportunities to demonstrate my knowledge of the subjects or lack thereof; so were the second semester exams for Con Law II, Patents & Trademarks, and Products Liability. Truly oddball final exams, and closed-book exams, were becoming a thing of the past. The remaining two second semester classes, Administrative Law and Constitutional Law & Political Theory, required final papers rather than final exams, another factor which considerably decreased my stress level and need to generate extended outlines. And when all of my exams had ended, there was no writing competition to worry about, or other school-related concern for a number of months. Now I just had to show up for my first day of law firm work.

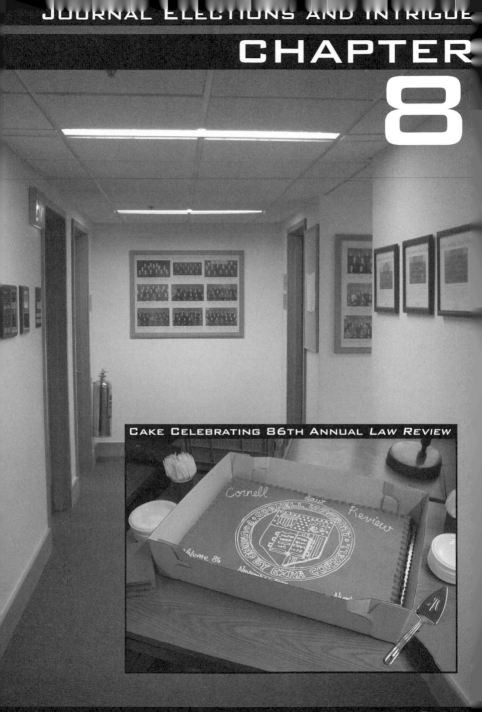

CAKE CELEBRATING 86TH ANNUAL *LAW REVIEW*

Parents and friends of law students, consider yourself warned: this chapter may not be worth your time to read. In fact, some prospective and current law students might themselves skim or skip it, at least on a first reading, because it deals with an aspect of the law school experience that's not mandatory, and comes if at all relatively late in a law student's life: once near the end of the second year, then again near the end of the third year.

Despite the fact that journal membership is not required at American law schools, there is little doubt in any law student's mind that participation is somewhat less optional for most of those who aspire to elite post-law school employment. When seeking jobs with judges, recognized law firms or cream-of-the-crop public agencies, journal membership of some sort is everything but necessary to put your resume on par with your competition.

There are a few fragments of the law school experience that the general public has heard about: the terrible first year, the concept of law review, and the fact that there is an editor-in-chief of a law review. To someone on the outside, and even to your typical practicing attorney, you get a little credit for getting into law school, another boost for getting onto law review, and major, major kudos if you become editor-in-chief. For law reviews at least, and perhaps other journals as well, the editor-in-chief mythology lures a disproportionately high number of people to seek the office regardless of their visions, skills, or interests in the actual work required for the position.[264]

The truth of the matter within the legal profession is that your resume has a good chance of standing above others if you can get yourself elected to any high office on your journal – and though journals typically only have six or seven 'high' offices, there are a number of additional offices that carry their own measure of prestige, as well. But winning elective office on a journal can be almost as challenging as earning your way onto that journal in the first place.

This chapter has been set off from the rest because it has the greatest potential to vary from year to year, school to school, and organization to organization. Journal elections are held behind closed doors and no individual will be privy to more than two of them – once when her class stands for election in the second year, then once when her class is replaced in the third. The experiences described herein are the product of personal inside observations and many discussions with people from other journals and other schools, and may prove more or less useful depending on the competitiveness of your school, class, and journal.[265]

---

[264] Even for the general public, the difference between someone being an "editor" of a journal or "editor-in-chief" is not completely clear.

[265] As a broad generalization, it can fairly be said that electoral competition is particularly fierce on a school's flagship journal – a Law Review or Law Journal – and less intense on others. Similarly, the competition tends to be greater at higher-ranked schools, though the difference between schools is far less pronounced than the difference between journals.

A. REFLECTIONS OF A LAW REVIEW ASSOCIATE

My personal experience with law review as an organization was not the usual one. I came to law school from a publishing background, having worked as a columnist and even as a magazine editor-in-chief before setting foot in any graduate school. Before I had even read a law journal or started law school, journal membership struck me as an opportunity to stay involved with the writing, editing, and publishing of interesting articles. To be frank, I was perhaps overly enthusiastic and somewhat naïve. I loved to write, and loved to read, and figured that law journals were basically magazines for lawyers.

As a newly-accepted student, I signed up for three-year subscriptions to all three of Cornell's printed journals, and actually made efforts at first to read them. And when I learned that the journals were 100% student-run and entirely antiquated from a technology standpoint, I really hoped to bring my knowledge of professional editorial policy, as well as computerized layout technology, to improve upon whatever assets a journal already had in place. Full of ambition because of my positive experiences with journalism, I was ready to lead before I even knew which organization I would be leading. At that point, I prayed that I would just be invited to join one of them.

Even on my first visit to the law school, months before I had accepted Cornell's offer, I found that the mystique surrounding the *Law Review* was considerable. Walls of the hallways leading to its offices were decorated with formally-attired membership photographs, taken annually over the journal's nearly 90 years of history, similar every year but reflecting the very different compositions of the journal during years of American change: the law school's historically early admission of women, a staff of only five people during World War II, a member donning ethnic head dress during the 1970s, a dog in one photo, and so on. First-year students routinely stopped to glance at these collections of photographs, commenting on the names they saw – including current professors, noted practitioners, and family members of students. Many recognized that, perhaps, they might one day become part of history.[266]

At the most public end of that hallway was a collection of small offices that were occupied by the *Law Review* – one office for the Editor-in-Chief and two other important editors, another office for the Articles Editors who worked hands-on with some of the most important pieces that were to be published, a

---

[266] This isn't to say that the other journals were entirely lacking in organizational mystique, but as the *Law Review* is at Cornell, as at most other schools, the oldest student organization on campus, it receives a disproportionate share of attention from new students. Other journals and student organizations have nearby offices with less ornamental trappings; Moot Court's photographs, placards and other decorations lined the hallways leading to the school's moot courtroom and adjacent 'practice training' classrooms, and inspired their own degree of excitement in hopeful litigators.

separate 'reading room' that could hold perhaps 15 sitting people at a time, and an office for the secretaries of all three printed journals. The message of the portraits and the offices together was clear: the *Law Review* is an important part of both the school's history and present mission, and its editors are given preferential office space to carry out their duties.

When the writing competition had ended and I was invited to become a *Law Review* associate, I felt exceedingly excited. The prestige, in truth, was only a minor concern; I was mostly enthusiastic because I believed that there was a real opportunity for me to be a part of something ancient and yet progressive. For years, *Law Review* members had taken seriously the task of authoring and publishing articles of legitimate social value. While it was hardly as widely read as *U.S.A. Today* or *The Wall Street Journal*, there were certainly good chances that our articles would influence the thinking of judges, including those on the United States Supreme Court.

And I pursued my work as an associate with quite a bit of fervor. When the Editor-in-Chief, Cheryl Lester,[267] set up entirely optional committees on admissions policy, election policy, and the drafting of a request for journal members to receive academic credit, I signed up for all of them. We had assignments almost every week for months, and a Note due early in the second semester. I turned in all of my assignments on time and spent incredible numbers of hours working on them. And I made sure that all of my Note drafts were properly submitted.

My attitude extended to my communications with other associates. Several people groused loudly about the quality and quality of the assignments we were given. I bit my lip rather than complain if something seemed askance, and spent many hours talking privately with Cheryl about things that were being done, and could be done, to further improve the journal – both during committee meetings and elsewhere. Still enthusiastic and optimistic after months of hard labor, I saw a need to get things done and tried to be diplomatic about doing them.

B.   EARLY POLITICKING

But true change at the *Law Review* was hard to come by, for two primary reasons. First, as is the case in many organizations, its editorial board was overwhelmed enough by simply running the journal as it was, and no matter how right a change seemed, if it took too much time or energy, the effort wasn't deemed worth it. Second, change of any sort was a hard sell for a significant fraction of the membership; law reviews are often populated at least in part by 'play it safe' traditionalists who weren't interested in taking risks. Even when the

---

[267] Editor names and modest biographical details may have been changed.

'safe' population is numerically smaller than supporters of change, the 'safe' crowd can become quite vocal.

Though it wasn't entirely obvious to outsiders at the time, the six dominant members of the editorial board had a fractured working relationship. These key players were not necessarily friends outside of their offices, and some of their meetings could be surprisingly contentious. Some strong personalities with inflated egos and limited social skills were only somewhat counterbalanced by people with more social grace and self-control. Being friends with one editor therefore did not necessarily endear you to the others, but it rarely hurt, either. Taking sides on a politically sensitive issue, however, could be suicidal: one person strongly opposed changes to the journal, while another had equally strong desires for fundamental change.

Rumors and speculation regarding prospective candidates for election began in February and formal lists of candidates were created in March, both processes more the work of candidates than current editors. People could either nominate themselves or be nominated by others to run for office; sometimes a particular editor would approach several worthwhile associates and encourage them to run for a specific office, typically their own, if they had not expressed interest. Every potential candidate seemed to have his or her own approach to appearing interested or disinterested in seeking office. Some people announced their candidacies early and immediately;[268] those who announced early became known quantities and subsequently received little attention. Otherwise qualified people who remained ambiguous about plans or disclaimed interest in running generated plenty of speculation, which sometimes eventually led to the sort of populist support needed to win offices. Hell, if disinterest worked for George Washington, why not use it in a journal election?

Despite the fact that there was an Elections Committee, associates knew very little in advance about what the elections would entail. Everyone had heard, correctly, that elections tended to consume an entire day and required – for the sake of maintaining quorum – near-full attendance of the entire membership of the journal barring extreme and unusual personal circumstances. Thereafter, a candidate needed a simple, 50.1% majority of all votes in the room to win an office; as the numbers of 2Ls and 3Ls in the room were roughly equal, a unanimous vote of one class's members would have been nearly enough to push someone over the edge. The room was to be closed to the public and professors, family members, and anyone not on the journal – no one else could be admitted.

---

[268] These people, interestingly enough, tended not to prevail at election time; they gave detractors the greatest opportunity to sully their names, and entirely avoided what some other candidates intentionally cultivated: popular movements to see themselves 'drafted' for the offices.

While almost everyone knew that candidates left the room after delivering speeches and responding to questions from the audience, only some people were aware that earlier elections had been plagued by negative sniping at certain candidates after they left the room. Having shown up as an associate for the single meeting of the Elections Committee, which was sparsely attended by editors, the only thing I could gather from the experience was that the editors in attendance were hoping to limit the negativity they'd experienced the year before. Surprisingly, these experienced, seemingly disgusted editors later turned out to be the worst offenders in the upcoming election; rather than bettering themselves, they just wanted to dish out what they had gotten the year before.

C.   POSITIONS AND HIERARCHIES

At this point, it's worthwhile to briefly explain the editorial structure of a journal so that it becomes clear why, if at all, people might consider running for positions. As was discussed earlier in this book, a journal has associates – typically 2Ls – and editors – typically 3Ls. Only two formal hurdles prevented *Law Review* associates from becoming editors: the successful completion of all of their assignments and the editorial board's decision that their completed Notes were 'publishable' by the law review's standards.[269] A meeting is held once annually for the current board of editors to 'elevate' the associate class to editor status, shortly after which the journal holds its elections to replace all of the specifically titled editors with new people. Those who elevate and are not elected, or not running for election, become 'General Editors' and have modest ongoing involvement with the journal during their third year.[270]

At the top of every law review food chain is the Editor-in-Chief, but from there, different journals have different structures. The *Cornell Law Review* has four Managing Editors, a Production Editor, and a Senior Note Editor who together comprise the upper echelon of the Editorial Board. Yale's *Law Journal* has two Executive Editors and two Managing Editors at the top, but many more types of editors below. The *University of Texas Law Review* has a highly specialized board, with a single Managing Editor, Chief Articles Editor, Administrative Editor, Book Review Editor, and Chief Notes Editor. Other schools have similar structures to these models, most with a handful of managing editors, some with a Senior Articles Editor, and so on. The essential job descriptions are as follows.

---

[269] Other journals may have slightly different policies, but these requirements are by far the most typical.

[270] The General Editors category is the most variable category from journal to journal – the responsibilities of this group change somewhat depending on the journal, especially if a school offers academic credit for third-year participation. At Cornell, no credit is offered, and the editors have almost no responsibilities.

The Editor-in-Chief (EIC) is simultaneously the final decision-maker on all major internal journal decisions, and the most cognizable face the journal displays to the outside worlds of faculty and students at the law school.[271] Like the rest of the upper echelon of the Editorial Board, an EIC typically puts in an incredible number of hours, enough that professors universally tolerate and accommodate these editors' class absences. The EIC personally approves each of the journal's final printed pages, signs off on its business decisions, and handles any administrative issues raised by associates.

Managing Editors (ME's) typically have the hardest jobs in the journal: they are responsible for hand-checking every word, piece of punctuation and footnote that appears in every issue, and in some organizations spend more hours working on the journal than perhaps any other editor – even the EIC. In some journals, they are collectively the second most powerful types of editors in the organization; in others, they are trumped by one or more Executive Editors, who can do many different jobs but essentially handle most of the day-to-day administrative judgment calls that other journals leave to their ME's and EIC's. A Production Editor or Administrative Editor manages the journal's calendar and coordinates the work of associates for various other editors, and a Business Editor, if there is one, generally deals with advertising and other contracts on behalf of the journal.[272] Depending on the journal, the school, and the personalities involved, some of these editorial positions may not exist or may have less importance than in other organizations.

Rounding out the upper echelon of editors are positions that tend to vary from journal to journal: either the Senior (or Chief) Note Editor (SNE), who happens to have heightened importance at the *Cornell Law Review*, or a Senior (or Chief) Articles Editor, who has prominence in other schools' journals. At Cornell, the SNE is responsible both for creating the annual Writing Competition, and helping to coordinate lower-ranked Note Editors, who in turn arrange the development and selection of associate Notes for eventual publication. A Senior Articles Editor is responsible for directing the work of several Articles Editors, who choose for publication and edit those articles written by and submitted to the journal by professors and practitioners.

At Cornell, the only other editors are a Book Review Editor, who commissions reviews of books; Symposium Editors, who develop annual

---

[271] The *Stanford Law Review* is among several that have used the business title of President for their highest-ranking editor rather than the traditional publishing title Editor-in-Chief.

[272] Business Editor or Business Manager positions typically handle only meager advertising and financial affairs. Many journals are funded entirely or in substantial part by their law schools, and as such their editors have little meaningful control over their budgets. Other journals control their own budgets, and handle financial matters ranging from advertising to the hiring and firing of staff-level personnel. Business Editors typically serve as student coordinators on these sorts of issues.

symposia and help to edit symposium issues; an Internet Editor, who manages the *Law Review*'s web site and perhaps online editorial policy; and most recently an Admissions Editor, who helps to direct admissions policy and assists in authoring the annual writing competition. Other journals have Publications Editors, Research Editors, Essays Editors, and on and on. These editors are typically in the lower tier of the editorial board, attend fewer meetings, and most often have little say in the day-to-day affairs of the journal.

D. COMPROMISING YOUR CHANCES

Even though I had tried to get an advance sense of what the election was going to be like, few editors could generalize about typical election procedures or climate, perhaps because at that time they had only attended one such event – their second election, where they selected their replacements, would be their last. When the day actually came, I therefore felt very uncertain of the format and appropriate tact. Walking into the giant classroom that was allocated for use in the election, I carried the naïve and optimistic belief that proposals for positive but moderate changes would be welcomed by both the outgoing and incoming classes of editors.

It turns out that whereas the outgoing board, for purposes of creating a legacy and continuing its own policies, has a considerable interest in influencing the outcome of the elections, members of the incoming board have their own opinions on how things should be done. And herein you find the critical friction or tension of journal elections: candidates cannot openly criticize any but the most universally despised policies of the previous board without incurring the wrath of existing officeholders.

At the same time, law review elections aren't as bad as the shallow popularity contest elections held by undergraduate student organizations. To succeed in a law review election, you need to have avoided making major enemies on the old board, and need to have at least some solid, respectful acquaintance-class relationships with a few vocal people from the departing class. The elections are largely about selecting officers who simultaneously have respectable academic backgrounds, decent stage presence, strong records of journal participation, and no major enemies on the journal. And I personally believe that you need at least three out of the four to win an office.

Perhaps the easiest way to make enemies or limit your prospects, even at the last moment, is to use an election-day speech as a platform to criticize any aspect of your experience. This must be interpreted broadly; saying something as simple as "law reviews publish articles that even law review editors don't enjoy reading, and we should change that," a true statement if there ever was one, was enough to subject one articles office candidate to near-crucifixion during the elections. Note that this wasn't a direct criticism of our specific law review. It wasn't a criticism of any specific person. And most people, perhaps a sizeable majority, agreed with it. But it wasn't *universally* believed. All five outgoing articles editors were hugely upset by the comment. And their opposition alone was almost enough to torpedo the exceedingly well-qualified candidate's eligibility for office.

Like all organizations, law reviews consist of people. And these are people with the dangerous combination of fragile egos and enough power to modestly influence their successors. Only editors who clearly abused their power or made great mistakes of judgment will be ignored in the process of electing their successors; the norm for key offices is to give at least a public airing and perhaps slight deference to the opinions of outgoing editors regarding who they think would make good successors. Though there is plenty of opportunity for further debate and discussion amongst other people, it was clear that people who lacked strong opinions of their own tended to look to these key officers to see who they believed merited support.

But this doesn't mean for a second that outgoing editors get to directly choose their successors. As one might guess, the upper echelon editorial positions – especially the office of Editor-in-Chief of the *Law Review* – are seriously contentious ones. Some people who by their own admissions were unqualified pursued the office solely because they said they would have felt remiss if they hadn't made a modest effort. And these candidates, along with many people who express great actual interest in and talent for the position, typically don't have a prayer.[273]

The great irony of the electoral process is that, repeatedly over the years, those who most strongly assert their interest in high offices are frequently denied those positions because they seem overly eager, or dare to take difficult stands on issues, while people who give off an air of modest disinterest and say little about their plans for office frequently win. And that's what happened both in the elections for my class of officers, the subsequent year's elections when we were replaced, and the year thereafter. Winning EIC candidates repeatedly displayed a quiet competence and took the least aggressive positions; those who were opinionated and passionate seemed to turn off the majority of voters. But disinterest wasn't enough. The other requisites for victory were calmness, relatively high average scores on assignments, and completion of a good-quality Note for publication. And there was little question that the EIC winners had at least the respect of the outgoing editorial board, if not an active supporter or two.

---

[273] It should be noted that, due to the importance of and contention for the EIC position, elections for that office alone tend to take hours.

E.   ELECTING YOUR REPLACEMENTS

Though Cheryl Lester quietly encouraged me (and perhaps others) to run for her office, she later appeared to have a favorite potential successor – another widely-respected, bright woman with similarly impressive credentials. Few of the other top officers had approached possible candidates, but some of the Note and Articles Editors had made comments to suitable replacements. In the days leading up to the election, it also became clear that one especially sly person – a true resume-polisher – had been buttering up an officer or two at the last minute in hopes of winning a high office. Several people had made more general sweeps of the membership to try and round up votes.

The election started early in the morning and quorum in the room was quickly established. In anticipation of spending the entire day in the classroom, a huge variety of snack food and drinks had been laid out on tables in the back. Voting would take place in an order specified in the *Law Review*'s By-Laws, beginning with the EIC and proceeding through the most senior members of the editorial board. Candidates for each office would make speeches, then participate in a group question-and-answer session, then leave the room so that people could discuss the candidates and vote.

EIC candidates spoke first; even the most composed was a little nervous, and the least composed were downright shaky. Cheryl's favorite was clearly a serious contender, delivering a speech on her vision for the journal and repeating her commitment to it. Others enunciated visions, as well, ranging from the specific to the incredibly general, and one or two people offered no vision at all. The question and answer session passed without major incident, and the candidates were asked to leave the room for the discussion period.

Though the voting was close, Cheryl's favorite was torpedoed by people who might be considered her ideological enemies – like the outgoing EIC, Sonya Gonzalez was outspokenly liberal, but unlike the diplomatic EIC, she had brushed a few people the wrong way. The winning EIC candidate was equally bright, had enunciated no clear vision for the journal whatsoever, and had not made any serious enemies anywhere at the law school. He was a hardworking guy who seemed largely apolitical;[274] the room had been won over to his side after someone had raised concerns about Sonya's activism.[275]

---

[274] In the following year's election, he proved so apolitical as not to even offer a hint as to whom should succeed him, but one candidate won easily with clear backing from other members of the board – particularly certain Managing Editors. The winning candidate that year was supported by Cheryl's former favorite, who along with a similarly liberal friend had been elected MEs.

[275] It should be pointed out that the election of an EIC is followed by an interesting change in the air of the room; when candidates for other offices had left the room and no clear consensus was being reached, incoming EIC's were occasionally asked the question as to

Because they are so technically demanding, Managing Editor positions often go almost automatically to the people who have the highest assignment scores – almost regardless of their personalities or other qualifications. The person elected EIC had one of the journal's top scores, and Sonya had another; she was an automatic choice to become a ME, and he would have been had he lost the EIC slot. To generalize, ME's tend to have one of three personality types consistent with their high assignment scores: they're either abrasive sticklers, reserved and quietly brilliant, or activist and outgoing in a way that had ironically knocked them out of the running for EIC. Any of these personalities could win a ME office, but the anti-social personalities tended to win over the outgoing ones. And if you're wondering how abrasive or reserved people could get enough support to win, and outgoing people could somehow lose, this is the heart of the intrigue of this chapter. Some of it was that people tolerated odd behaviors from MEs, because a certain quantum of anti-social behavior is expected from people who would run for positions with such crushing workloads and tedious labor. But at least as much was attributable to weird things that happened during elections to bolster or scuttle candidacies that respectively seemed either doomed or guaranteed when the process began.

Those weird things, I will suggest, were part of minor-league conspiracies – small groups of people who knew enough in advance to anticipate some of the problems their anti-social friends might have in the election. And while it's fair to assert that these groups never had the destruction of an outgoing candidate as their primary objective, they would not have a problem shooting someone else down to see one of their friends win. This was possible because of the makeup of the *Law Review*'s electorate: one-half of the editors were 2Ls who likely knew the candidates personally or knew of their reputations, and one-half were 3Ls who were unlikely to know more than the candidates' names and published assignment scores. The 3Ls explicitly relied upon the 2Ls to appraise the outgoing board of the personal strengths and weaknesses of the candidates, and a convincing, positive, unopposed testimonial about even the worst candidate could sway enough 3Ls to win an office on the first ballot.

Case-in-point: one of the candidates in the first ME election was an activist with high assignment scores, shot down for a ME position because a few people in the room unexpectedly claimed, in a cruel twist on the candidate's fatherly, coaching nature, that he was too pedantic. Those doing the shooting were promoting the candidacy of a friend with a similarly high assignment score but a well-established reputation for obnoxious behavior, which behavior they knew they had to address and explain away before anyone made a negative comment. The obnoxious candidate won because his friends had organized a

---

whom they'd prefer to work with, the first sign of deference to the new Board's wishes. The answers would typically sway at least some people in the room.

drive to get him in and deemed him "mellowed," and the "pedantic" candidate lost because he didn't have supporters in the room ready to rebut the accusation; the candidate himself could not be there to speak on his own behalf and answer his accusers. Those who were early to master this format reaped the spoils of the election.

But lest 2Ls believe that they alone, through manipulation of under-informed 3Ls, could control the outcomes of the elections, it should be noted that the outgoing editorial board had one set of powers extending even beyond hinting at their own personal choices. After candidates left the room, three or four Board representatives spoke 'authoritatively' about the candidates' organizational performances: the Senior Note Editor or Note Editor commented on the quality of their Note submissions and final draft, while the Production Editor and a Managing Editor discussed their assignment scores and 'typical' comments they had received. A negative comment from any of these people might reduce a candidate's viability, and it was clear in both of the elections I witnessed that while a consistently excellent performer could achieve serious credibility just by having worked quite hard, the editors went out of their way to put the shine or the shaft to people they liked or disliked.

One ME candidate, Tara, received abnormally strong support from an outgoing board despite admitting in her election speech that she had detested the *Law Review* for the entire first half of the year. She explained that she had experienced an epiphany and was now very excited to be running for an office. She received support from both an outgoing Managing Editor and an incoming one, who both took pains to explain that although Tara's production scores had been very low, her second-half production scores were so high that she would have been competitive with any of the top candidates in the field. Explain the logic of bolstering Tara over the 'pedantic' person who had consistently outperformed Tara throughout the year, and had demonstrated strong commitment to the journal while Tara was still detesting it. There was no logic; it was entirely personal politics. Tara, the epiphany candidate, won high office.

Like the 2Ls who primarily wanted to see their friends win, only rarely would members of the board attempt to screw up other people's candidacies, but it happened: those who criticized the board in their speeches were later described in less than favorable terms by the board when they left the room, sometimes quite unfairly and dishonestly. And if you're reading this and thinking that one negative comment begets another, the point should be made here that candidates should not be knocked for identifying problems and pledging to fix them. Sad is the organization with such a fragile institutional ego that those who audibly strive to improve it are crushed for daring to question its present state of perfection.

Thus, oddly, those who suggested bold, thoughtful ambitions for a given office were often rewarded with lesser offices instead. Qualified but outspoken candidates for EIC often found themselves winning ME slots or lower Note Editor or Articles Editor positions, as their allies in the room would trot out the repeated and somewhat predictable suggestion that "the fact that she was willing to run for EIC indicates just how great her commitment is to the journal."[276] But the fallacy of this suggestion is manifest from the fact that some people ran for higher office knowing they hadn't the slightest chance of winning it, and that the prospect of winning a powerful and interesting office such as EIC was in many cases unrelated to the commitment to doing the insane amount of technical, tedious work required of ME's; this latter problem also held true for other mismatches of offices. Yet friends would drag out this argument on behalf of candidates for virtually every office until the point at which someone in the room eventually rebutted it.

That argument was raised repeatedly, in part, because the candidates themselves often seemed somewhat dispirited after losing their first election. Having stood before everyone and given their speeches, and then lost, they now had to walk back up to deliver a second or third speech and proclaim that this later office was, in reality, the one that they really wanted to hold. Even giving the speech was tough; there is something humbling and strangely silencing about losing the first office you go after. Friends who made pitches for candidates outside of the room were often the same people pushing them to continue in the running after they'd lost an office or two that they were seeking.

Some losing candidates for EIC also ran for the position of Senior Note Editor, and such is also the case in journals with Executive Editor and Senior Articles Editor positions. These positions, like the office of EIC, involve some degree of administrative control over the journal and offer more than just the prospect of never-ending copy editing work for their winners. The sly resume-polisher tried to run for the SNE office, but was denied election by a skeptical crowd; this tended to be the result for any sneaky candidate who thought he could pull the wool over people's eyes at the last minute.[277] Interestingly, winning candidates for the SNE position never, in my experience, enunciated improvements they wanted to make while in office; there was no special reward for people who demonstrated knowledge of a position, or even had stopped to talk with the current office holder about what the job entailed.

One position that seemed to have no overlap whatsoever with the other high offices was the Production Editor office, the person who keeps the journal's calendar running on time, which while critical to the journal's success

---

[276] This thinking actually wound up securing high offices for some people in each election, but when a candidate had behaved in any manner that attracted negative attention, it wasn't enough to save him. Notably, men (and not women) were typically the ones attracting negative attention.

[277] Depending on the nature of the previous behavior of the person seeking an office, election would either be entirely denied or limited to a significantly lower office.

and high on the masthead tended not to secure candidates with strong leadership ambitions. In one year, only two people ran for the office. A qualified and obviously committed candidate with a reputation for surliness lost out to a very friendly but less clearly ambitious candidate who promised, nonetheless, that she would do her best. And she ultimately did a fantastic job. The position was uncontested in another election, largely because no one was really excited about the office, and won in yet another election, somewhat ironically, by someone who didn't even show up for the voting.

Losing candidates from all of the aforementioned higher offices ran for, and enjoyed a disproportionate advantage in winning, Note Editor and Articles Editor positions. By having run for higher offices, these people qualified almost automatically for the 'commitment already demonstrated' award of a lower office that some people had advocated earlier; again, this was unfortunate for those who had decided intentionally to run only for a very specific position. And this was especially a shame considering that people who overestimated their candidacies would not receive the office they really wanted, but received preferential treatment for other offices, whereas those who were realistic about their prospects and wanted only one office often became second in line.

Frankly, some people were much better suited to standard Note Editor and Articles Editor positions than more senior administrative positions, and many candidates themselves knew this to be true. The time demands for top offices were more than many people wanted to bear; in a later election, for example, my girlfriend didn't want to give up her entire life but wanted to have some continued role in the journal, so a Note Editor position seemed perfect for her needs. Some people who otherwise might have been good candidates for Senior Note Editor were either not leaders, as the position somewhat demanded, or were so aggressive that they would have alienated the junior Note Editors had they been elected to head the office.

At the point at which these offices went up for election, however, people weren't thinking quite as straight as they had been earlier; five or more hours had passed, including a short lunch break, and some degree of pragmatism was beginning to be heard in the room. People were no longer interested so much in the best candidates as finding people who seemed to have enough popular support to win quickly. Candidates themselves were losing steam, especially those who had run for earlier offices. Three-time losing candidates, qualified for each of the offices they'd sought, were showing signs that they would not bother to try again. And some in the room sought to cultivate last-minute candidacies by their friends, occasionally to keep an unsavory candidate out of office, otherwise to at least create a contest for an open office.

The Book Review Editor position, like the far more important Production Editor office, was typically uncontested. But the fact that it was so traditionally unimportant, yet continued to exist as an elective office, drew one interesting candidate each election – in each case, someone who had sought no other offices and wanted only to be responsible for that one job. And these people won without serious dissent of any sort. Once elected, the Book Review Editor position left only a handful of people without elected offices. These people, for the most part, had not sought offices and either had good reason to do so or harbored personal reservations about running and exposing themselves to the political process. Only one or two people who had continued to seek offices until the end had walked away empty-handed.

F. ON NEGATIVITY AND APPLICABILITY TO OTHER JOURNALS

One of the biggest concerns people had going into elections was the possibility that things might get seriously negative during the discussions after candidates left the room. Before I had even witnessed an election, Elections Committee members had spoken openly of the fact that, once the candidates left, the atmosphere in the room just devolved into personal trashing – almost for sport. But we had an editor-in-chief at that point who was committed to keeping things running relatively quickly and hopefully without resort to such negative comments, and her initial words on election day led to a quelling of at least some fires before the process began. The goal was, she explained, to focus on the positive reasons people should be elected rather than fixating on negative discussions or reasons to deny people offices.

Yet, as mentioned before, the most vocally negative people were those who had decried the negativity of the earlier election, but even though there were some serious mischaracterizations of candidates and a handful of arguably inappropriate comments, the elections went pretty smoothly – depending on one's perspective. Some could reasonably see the elections as tragic from the standpoint that those elected often lacked passion for their offices, but over time, I've come to believe that that's what people on a law review expect – not activism, but competency. Viewed from that light, the least appropriate comments related to Sonya's personal politics, which were not so much attacking her politics as questioning her prospects for turning the EIC's office into a den of advocacy, and one Articles Editor's suitability for office considering his supposed disrespect for the articles the journal had been publishing in the past. There were at least elements in each of these criticisms that one might deem worthy of discussion.

Though the electoral experience of the *Cornell Law Review* might not be entirely typical of others, I'd venture to say it's probably pretty close to the way other journals work. But there are identifiable differences. Generally, secondary journals take less time to elect their officers: half-days, rather than full days, tend to be adequate to complete all requisite elections. And this is because secondary journals often have a different problem with their offices: sometimes there aren't enough people interested in filling them, and it's more a matter of finding a single candidate for an office than picking among different ones.

The similarities are in the tone of the elections themselves: they're frequently at least modestly personally critical, which is the primary reason some people opt not to run for offices. Our law review was able to keep the mood largely positive, with the result that some candidates lost only because no one discussed them at all rather than saying negative things about them. But the unofficial sunshine constraint also had another effect: it inhibited some of the critical thought that otherwise might have scuttled under-qualified people from running, let alone winning. As an example, a candidate for Production Editor with a notoriously poor record of timeliness might not have run if he or she believed that someone might bring it up. Under these rules, someone in that position could both run and win.

It seems fair at this point to state that journal elections in the future would be best conducted in an atmosphere which identifies, up front, bona fide occupational requisites for each of the offices, and limits debate on candidates to discussing those requisites. Many journals achieve this, imperfectly, through trial and error over years of conducting elections. Those that have not should consider adopting measures to insure that the only people discouraged from seeking election are those who are patently unqualified, by their own measures, to hold a given office.

G.   General Editors and Appointments

Those who either opted not to run for office or ran and failed became General Editors, the journal's official title for those editors lacking constitutionally specified ongoing responsibilities. General Editors were an interesting mix of personalities: some were people who either legitimately lacked the time to continue in active journal roles or just claimed to lack the time, and others were the sorts of people who preferred to complain about problems on the sidelines without taking responsibility for fixing them. A few were people who were genuinely put off by the types of people elected already, and a rare one or two were people who, from an outsider's perspective, had no reason but self-imposed limitations to preclude them from having won high office. A noteworthy example of the latter case was one person whose name was floated by friends as a candidate for a ME office, and whose assignment scores were through the roof, but who tearfully declined even to deliver a speech or subject herself to what might come when she left the room.

There were, thankfully, still opportunities for interested people to serve as titled editors of the *Law Review* even if they hadn't been awarded offices in the election. The Editor-in-Chief has broad powers to appoint general editors to specific titled positions, and traditionally, the offices of Symposium Editors and

Internet Editor were appointed positions. I was interested in the Internet Editor office and successfully sought appointment by my EIC shortly after he won election, and Symposium Editors were appointed some weeks later. Responding to subsequent concerns raised by an Admissions Committee, the next EIC created a new office for an Admissions Editor via appointment. Vacant elective offices on the journal could also, in some cases, be filled by appointment rather than election, and a couple of General Editors came to fill open Articles Editor slots when elected office holders vacated the positions.

General Editors maintained only limited roles with the journal in their third years. Other than attending infrequent meetings of the complete board – typically two over the course of an entire year – General Editors had no real responsibilities and could relax for the first time in years – so long as they graded at least a handful of summer writing competition submissions. If they chose to join committees, they could, but otherwise, they were free and clear.

H.   THE IMMEDIATE AFTERMATH

What most tantalized me when I was an associate were the stories of what happened immediately after elections: outgoing editors surrendered to incoming ones their keys to the *Law Review*'s offices, gave them 'turnover binders' prepared gradually over the course of decades, and essentially, in one fell swoop, handed entire responsibility for the journal's publication over to a totally new group of people. Though the *Law Review*'s editors' offices were not the most exciting rooms at the Law School, there was certainly at least a bit of mystical aura given that these were the places where generations of journals had been edited. And one could only guess as to what a new EIC must be thinking, besides, "oh no," when she is handed the binder of notes and reflections passed down from so many of her predecessors. I personally found the whole prospect exciting, but my predecessor had no turnover binder and no great words of wisdom when I took office.

The responsibilities of new offices are unquestionably considerable, even for a journal that was running entirely on schedule – if not a bit early – as ours was when turned over to us, and then when we turned it over to our successors. There are still major issues to decide early on – what articles and Notes to select, what dates to choose for submissions and publication, and how to hold an upcoming banquet, a formal photo session for posterity, and yes, the writing competition for first-year students that's expected to start only a month and a half later. There is plenty of work to be done.

Some journals don't engage in precisely the same abrupt sort of turnaround as ours did. One journal ran enough behind in production that its editors continued to work for months after they were replaced, just to catch up. And even the *Law Review*'s outgoing editors made themselves available in an entirely informal capacity to consult on an as-needed basis with their successors – consultations, however, are traditionally expected not to be significant or time-consuming. For the most part, however, the day after elections is literally the official end of one class's involvement and the beginning of an immense amount of work for a brand new group of people.

I.   LONG-TERM ELECTORAL IMPACT

With all of this talk of elections, it's easy for an outsider to ask, "what's the big deal? And why does this merit its own chapter?" The answers are important yet concededly unlikely to ever make a dent on the average parent, spouse, or other non-law student reader.

For the layman, the answer is that elections offer prestige. Page through the biographical details law firm web sites provide on their practicing attorneys, and if you notice one extracurricular item that has traditionally always been present in a lawyer's biography or resume, that item would probably contain journal membership details. It's like military service: few who have served would ever omit that fact. The average attorney's web biography, say nothing of their official Martindale-Hubbell professional listing, notes four things about their life as a law student: the law school she attended, whether or not she received an academic honor such as cum laude, then the name of the journal he or she served on, and finally the editorial position he or she held. There are few professional credentials that say as much about a person as "Editor-in-Chief, Law Review," though some journals perhaps unintentionally allow some pop culture blurring of this by allowing their General Editors to be called Editors. The average reader would probably think that "Editor, Law Review" is the same as "Editor-in-Chief;" only people within the profession know differently. Other positions, such as Managing Editor, Executive Editor, and Senior Note Editor, tend to generate stronger employer interest in candidates than they'd have received without those offices; junior Note and Articles Editors also get their fair share of extra respect during interviews, as well.

There are also more subtle benefits, as well. While the law school's general populace is more than modestly interested in the results of the election, and in fact the news makes its way from student to student all throughout the day, professors are surprisingly keenly interested to discover the results. In some cases, professors actually know the election results and begin to congratulate students before the students' friends find out. Why? Some of the professors were themselves members of law reviews, but that doesn't entirely explain the interest: many professors hope to see their articles published, and hopefully without major hassles, by the new editorial board. And professors extend, for many reasons, significant deference to law review editors – particularly those who show up bleary-eyed for classes the day or two after elections.[278] Even prickly professors offer a modicum of respect to the new editors.[279]

Admittedly, with all this talk of offices' associated perks, it's easy to lose sight of the reason I first discussed when I opened this chapter. With an election comes the opportunity to fundamentally change and improve the journal. The right people, under the right circumstances, could really fix a journal's problems,[280] and might even make a fundamental change in the types and quality of articles that get published. One of our Book Review Editors took a position previously viewed as low on the totem pole and elevated it significantly by successfully working cooperatively to increase the number and quality of book reviews published in the *Law Review*.

But I have to be candid and perhaps a little cynical here: the strong belief that I possessed after elections was that change and improvement were never really the major interests of the larger voting populace on my journal. As I've probably overemphasized by now, the most passionate candidates were reduced to roles in which their enunciated goals appeared out of reach, and dispassionate, disinterested candidates won offices. Even the aforementioned Book Review Editor elicited some laughter when he enunciated a legitimate interest in doing something positive with an office that no one else wanted. The only time I ever heard of any journal strongly embracing a mandate for change was when a crisis of some sort existed – a poor record for on-time publication that needed fixing or some personnel crisis that could only be fixed by an earthshaking change. One specialized journal responded to a tyrannical prior administration by building a single, well-liked slate of candidates for election and holding what was, in essence, a short exercise in collective affirmation of the slate. But it took tyranny to bring everyone together to find a solution, and the only change sought was 'no more tyranny,' not a broader mandate.

This isn't to say that a journal, armed with the right people, couldn't make really positive changes even in the absence of a mandate. It's just difficult to accomplish. Journal members serve as peons for one year and executives the next, with no ongoing accountability for their decisions save their personal reputations. And since almost every decision is collectively reached, there is plenty of opportunity for finger-pointing if something goes wrong, so no one is especially worried that he or she will shoulder blame for a failure. Early ambitions of 'doing something new' quickly give way to feelings of

---

[278] This may include offering public congratulations at the beginning of a class, or private congratulations after class, a prolonged respite from Socratic interrogation, or an understanding with implicit permission when the new editor needs to miss an unusual number of class sessions to complete law review assignments.

[279] Some professors go even further. One brought his attractive daughter to a law review-sponsored event, then introduced her and seated her next to the new male EIC.

[280] Of course, new people could also really mess up a journal, but that's another story.

overwhelming existing responsibility, mitigating even progressive editors' hopes of accomplishing anything big. Well-conceived and largely executed proposals to update our computer systems, online publishing capabilities, and the like were all scuttled when key people couldn't be bothered to follow through at the last moment because they had other things going on. And one year's plans quickly became the next year's glossed-over pages in the turnover binders.

You might conclude from all of the above that the route to winning office is to demonstrate a high degree of commitment to the journal, generate vague but not transparent signs of competency to hold a given office, and restrain one's mouth about journal affairs at all times prior to actually taking office – even during the elections themselves. Once you win, you can do – or not do – whatever fits your needs at the time. As Machiavellian as the approach may be, this may well be true today. But as a writer, former law review editor, and persistent believer in mankind's potential for improvement, I will not tell you that this is the way things *should* be. Editors sitting for election should have researched the offices they seek, and should be asked to enunciate forward-looking visions for those offices. The privilege of editing a journal should not fall to the deliberately stealthy, nor merely to the vaguely competent, having slipped away from those with the courage to research and take positions on important but potentially divisive issues.

Of course, every school and every journal within each school will have its own unique set of people and issues, so my personal perspective on the way things worked will no doubt differ in at least some ways from what you ultimately experience. But I feel confident in asserting that a read of this chapter should at least give you a general sense of some of the issues important to understanding law review and journal elections, as well as their consequences.

DOWNTOWN BOSTON, MA

IRVINE, CA

STATE STREET BANK

DKNY

Bloomberg

CLEVELAND, OH
NEW FEDERAL COURTHOUSE

NEW YORK, NY

A. INTERVIEWS

1. *Why You're Interviewing*

There are different schools of thought regarding the purpose of law school. A small group of people think that law school is an educational experience like any other field of graduate study, and that completion of a law degree need not necessarily lead to legal employment.[281] Most people, however, believe that law school is a stepping stone to employment as a lawyer, professor, or similar practitioner, and as such, one chooses a law school both to learn and to have the maximum chance of securing future employment.[282]

The key to understanding the interviewing process is to know, in advance, that you are coming to the present legal job market at a strong disadvantage if you start your job search after graduation from law school. Most top-ranked schools advise their students to begin their search for post-graduation employment during the start of the second year of law school, creating a two-year window for the job search. If this sounds odd in any way, the process will appear more sensible when it's mentioned that law firms, amongst other legal employers, prefer to have an opportunity to meet you and see your work product before they hire you on as a full-time employee. So you chase a summer job in order to get a job after graduation.

As was the case for the first-year summer, several types of summer legal jobs are open to second-year law students: positions with firms, judges, and professors. It's atypical, however, for a second-year student to spend his summer doing a summer study program; it happens, but most law students try to use the second summer to get practical, hands-on experience of some sort.

Most law firms refer to their student employees as "summer associates," a title which deftly makes the young lawyer wannabes feel like lawyers while avoiding an important fact: they are not. Law firms generally divide themselves into three types of practicing attorneys – associates, partners, and "of counsel." All three, with rare exceptions, are fully licensed to practice law.[283] Summer associates do not, by simply obtaining legal employment, have the right to act in ways that would make them appear to be lawyers. All of their actions must be fully supervised by practicing attorneys at the firms they're working for, and

---

[281] Options for these people are discussed later at Chapter 10, Section H.

[282] Though hiring statistics vary dramatically from boom to recession periods, the graduates of top national and local schools tend to be more insolated from recessionary hiring problems than lower-ranked schools, even where their grades are numerically less impressive than stars at the lower-ranked schools.

[283] Law school graduates cannot sign court documents and require special supervision until they have been sworn in to a bar; however, law firms typically admit them into their 'associate' ranks immediately after graduation.

they cannot hold themselves out to be lawyers when dealing with the public.

The modern title of summer associate replaces "summer clerk" or "summer intern," titles that tend to persist at public sector jobs and smaller firms. All three concepts are the same – you will always be heavily supervised, and you're only there for the summer – but summer associate sounds more prestigious than "clerk" or "intern." And as the latter name best suggests, you are, in all three positions, still supposed to be learning. Firms do not typically expect perfection from their second-year summer associates, but they do set very high standards and expect to see a high level of competence displayed, especially when the economy is poor and they can afford to be picky about whom they hire. Every summer associate has the same goal: to receive an offer of later employment, regardless of whether or not she intends to actually work at the firm.

Firms therefore, perhaps obviously, expect that people in such junior and tenuous positions will display the type of behavior appropriate to securing a full-time job. Like the first-year summer associate, the second-year summer associate is therefore expected not to do really stupid things.

But first, you need to get the job. The general chronology of the job search can be divided into four steps, two of which are discussed together below.

FIRST STEP	SECOND STEP	THIRD STEP	FOURTH STEP
You or School Contacts Employer	Attend On-Campus Interview or Job Fair	Attend Call-back Interview at Employer's Office	Work During Summer, Attempt to Receive "the Offer"

2.   Seeking the Job

Along with four classes and *Law Review* came another commitment that tends to overwhelm the schedules of second-year students: job interviews. These interviews are the primary doses of real life that students experience in-between heavy quantities of academic legal work in law school.

Unlike much of the subject matter of this book, interviews will vary dramatically from school to school, and person to person. In descending order of importance, the factors that generally make interviews easier are: attending a highly-ranked or regionally prominent school, being personally well-ranked in law school GPA, personally securing interviews you couldn't get on campus, and having a great, social personality. And the factors that, conversely, tend to make your life harder are attending lower-ranked or regionally unimportant schools, having a poor GPA, not being a self-starter in getting independent interviews, and having an anti-social or quiet personality. Once you've chosen a law school, at least one of these factors becomes beyond your control; it becomes imperative to actively work to avoid the others.

One additional factor of slight importance is your selection of courses. Interviews start and end for most second-years during their first 2L semester, and thus, you'll only have grades for your first-year classes – and perhaps the summer. As your first-year schedule is pre-determined, it's unlikely that you'll be able to pick many classes by interview time that will impress interviewers. You will seem serious about litigation if you sign up for evidence, trial advocacy, or another litigation-specific class; similarly, business courses will help you seem serious about transactional work, and specific classes will help for other specializations.[284] While it will no doubt help in your interviews if you have selected courses that reflect the interests you state in those discussions, law firms do understand that students are still exploring options in the early semesters. Grades are far more important than the classes you've selected.

Interviews take place in a number of different settings. Some students mail or cold-call employers on their own to seek individual interviews, but many schools operate full-time career offices year-round and make aggressive efforts to help students find second-year summer and post-graduation employment.[285] They often schedule so-called 'job fairs,' sometimes in conjunction with other law schools, where multiple employers take over rooms at a hotel and conduct several days of cattle-call style job interviews.[286] Cornell offered job fairs in most major cities in the country, but put perhaps the most time into its New York and Washington, D.C. fairs, as the majority of each year's graduates wound up working in one of those places. At larger schools, job fairs are coupled with on-campus interviews (OCI's) to create the vast majority of interviewing opportunities for students interested in future employment.[287] These interviews are conducted under guidelines promulgated by the National Association for Law Placement (NALP), which attempts to limit the occurrence of unreasonable

---

[284] Most of the appropriate classes for various practice areas are obvious just from their names, such as environmentally-themed classes for those who hope to practice environmental law.

[285] They also generally offer at least token assistance to first year students who seek summer positions, though they tend not to spend lots of time on this.

[286] Your school may hold an 'interview workshop' to offer students a general introduction to the 'do's and don'ts' of job interviewing.

[287] At smaller and lower-ranked schools, job fairs and OCI's are the exception, rather than the norm. Rather than showing up at your school, employers may expect you to come to them. Interested candidates typically write letters and E-mails, make telephone calls, and work their social connections to find employment – difficult and frequently unsuccessful mechanisms that tend to result in rejection-to-interest rates of 100:1.

behavior by both employers and job candidates.[288]

Regardless of whether you or your school schedules the interviews, there is a staggering collection of American law firms to choose from. As a starting point, over 1,400 firms are listed in NALP's DIRECTORY OF LEGAL EMPLOYERS, an annual 1,800-page book organized by state, then by city, then alphabetically by law firm name within each city. Each firm typically receives a page per office, and a number of firms have several offices. Once you've selected a state and city for your job search, however, the book only hints at the answer to your most important question: will you feel comfortable with a firm? The NALP guide provides only statistical data, such as firm size, office size, ratios of partners to associates to staff, and bare information on previous years' summer hiring – such as how many summer associates there were, and how many received offers. These are among the most important factors to consider, but your search should definitely go deeper, and perhaps broader as well.

For depth, it would be worth your while to look for outside opinions on firms, including those provided by upper-classmen from your school and ones publicly available through law firm rankings. Word of mouth at your school will probably bring you up to speed on the latest trends in legal employment, but if you want to supplement local gossip with regional or national information, several web sites publish rankings, firm-related stories and rumors. Vault's website generally sticks to rankings and statistics, but has gossipy message boards;[289] Law.com publishes stories and rankings in association with *American Lawyer* magazine and *The National Law Journal*;[290] and FindLaw's Infirmation.com is best-known for its rumor-filled message boards.[291]

But notably, these sites tend to focus on bigger, well-known firms, many with national or international aspirations – firms often known as "BIGlaw" within the profession.[292] Reading web sites may lead you to focus

---

[288] For more information on job interviewing under the NALP guidelines, see http://www.nalp.org/pands/index.htm.

[289] Vault publishes The Vault 100 each year, ranking the country's top 100 law firms online at http://www.vault.com/hubs/507/hubhome_507.jsp?ch_id=507. They currently also sell an extended version of the guide in book form.

[290] The lists and rankings section of Law.com is currently found at http://www.law.com/career_center/lists_rankings.html.

[291] Infirmation's famed Greedy Associates Boards, which you can currently find at http://www.infirmation.com/bboard/clubs-top.tcl, are discussion groups organized regionally and by certain areas of specialty. Infirmation also provides salary and other statistical information on firms in an easy-to-search format.

[292] BIGlaw firms receive disproportionate attention because of their well-known corporate and litigation clients, huge profits, and larger-than-local levels of influence and employment. They typically demand more working hours from their associates, and compensate them better than smaller firms could. However, the BIGlaw lifestyle isn't for everyone, and in fact, many young associates tire of it within six months, and either

disproportionately on salaries and prestigious names rather than your day-to-day quality of working life or ability to actually practice the sort of law you will enjoy. Some BIGlaw firms have reputations as 'sweatshops,' where young lawyers toil into the wee hours of the morning under abusive partners, only to return scant hours later for more and more work. Others work hard to offer better lifestyles for their employees, and a few firms have earned their way on to *Fortune* magazine's "Best Companies to Work For" list.[293] You can broaden your search past BIGlaw firms by searching phone books or NALP listings for a specific local area, and you will further deepen your understanding through actual conversations and interviews with the smaller firms.

Ultimately, interviews are an important part of learning about firms that also want to know more about you. If you schedule interviews on your own, you will probably have a chance to see the firms with your own eyes when you speak with their interviewing attorneys. The climate of an office and behavior of attorneys and staff other than your interviewers will probably say as much about a firm as the interviewers themselves. At larger schools, however, you are unlikely to sit for an initial interview at the firm's offices; rather, you'll be one of many people in line at a student job fair or OCI.

In both job fair and OCI interviews, each prospective employer occupies a single room of either a hotel or school, and applicants knock on the door of the room at a previously scheduled time to spend 20 or 30 minutes talking with one or two attorneys about their firm.[294] You're generally responsible for handing each firm your transcript, a resume, and a writing sample.

The primary difference between job fairs and OCI's is that students are responsible for all of their own costs in getting to job fairs, whereas they can attend OCI's for essentially the cost of a business suit, some resume paper, and a few missed classes. Perhaps 'few' is an understatement. Students often sign up for as many interviews as they can get.[295] It's hard to avoid missing classes for

---

remain within BIGlaw firms for three years while paying off debts or leave before that. Others avoid BIGlaw from the beginning.

[293] The list is currently available at http://www.fortune.com/lists/bestcompanies/index.html. Be careful, however, to confirm how up-to-date the list actually is, as some companies receive awards and then drop the policies that received so much attention.

[294] The interviews can be creepy, wildly interesting, or very difficult to judge. There are many reasons for this, almost all of which are beyond the scope of this book.

[295] While you want to schedule a large enough number of interviews to have a good chance of getting more than one offer of employment, you also do not want to be indiscriminate in signing up to speak with various firms. Some filtering process is necessary, beyond just geography; this is a point at which it definitely helps to have at least some focus about what you'd like and not like to do during the summer. The NALP directory lists the practice areas a given office of a firm contains, such as "tax law," "securities law," "litigation" and "intellectual property," specialties mentioned in this book. After going through the previously discussed "what sort of a lawyer do I want to be?"

interviews, and the only consolation is that second-years can afford to do so.

Some second-year students, including and especially those who have problems with any or all of the aforementioned four key points, wind up looking for jobs in another way: essentially searching on their own for other opportunities, writing interview request letters to law firms or other employers,[296] and traveling at their own expense to interview with those employers who express reciprocal interest. This process can become expensive and somewhat discouraging. Students frequently attempt to schedule multiple interviews on a given trip to minimize their expenses, which law firms will normally not reimburse. And the rate of reciprocal interest is low – even in good economic times, sending out twenty letters might net a single positive response, unless you have a personal tie to the firm or can otherwise make a very strong case for your personal interest in a given employer.

Rejection letters are, in fact, the norm – both after mailing out resumes, and again after you've gone through your scheduled interviews on campus or at a job fair. Amusingly, three friends papered the walls of their shared apartment with their collected letters, which often shared language verbatim or possessed other strong similarities; the firms' collective disinterest in unsolicited applicants at some point loses whatever personal sting it might have had.

Just to give you a heads-up and hopefully negate in advance any feelings of rejection letter stigma you might harbor, the typical rejection looks somewhat like this:

> "Mr./Ms. Candidate:
> Thank you for your interest in our firm. Despite your impressive credentials, we regret to write that with so many qualified candidates for the limited number of positions in our summer program, we cannot further pursue discussions with you at this time.
>
> Best wishes for your future career.
> Truly, Jack A. Smith, Esq."

---

routine in your mind once more, it helps to rule out firms that have no practice areas that could conceivably interest you, and place highest priority on those with something that catches your eye. And be conscious of the fact that just because one office of the firm specializes in something, does not mean that all of its offices practice that sort of law. Make sure that the office you are targeting does the sort of law you might want to practice.

[296] If you're in this boat, start with the aforementioned NALP Directory, available for students' free access in printed form at most law schools, and match it against Martindale-Hubbell's guide to registered American attorneys, found at http://www.martindale.com. With these tools in hand, you can target specific attorneys at NALP-listed firms, focusing on background factors that are similar to yours.

The 'nice' firms may add a sentence to indicate that your resume is being kept on file in the event of a change in the firm's near-term hiring needs, or a sentence to suggest that you re-apply next year. Rarely, firms send out letters even shorter than the one above. One such actual sample of efficiency reads:

> "We are in receipt of your letter dated October 7, 2000 regarding an associate position with our firm. Unfortunately, we do not have any positions available for someone with your qualifications.
>
> Thank you for your interest in our firm."

Thirty-nine not-so-friendly words may be a record for letters of this sort, but no firm should be proud of such curtness. Notably, this latter letter was authored by a staff recruiter who was not herself a lawyer, which may explain the apparent lack of empathy for a young law student's feelings.

3. The "Call-Back"

I discuss the rejection letters first because they are so common. If a firm is interested in talking more with you, one of several events will follow your initial letter or personal contact. Most often, you'll receive a telephone call personally inviting you to come to visit the firm on a "call-back interview," at the firm's expense. This means that you'll be responsible for arranging travel to the firm and securing very short-term overnight lodging, for which you will be recompensed.[297] And if you include your telephone number on your resume, you might well receive a phone call; this means that you have to be at least largely professional whenever your telephone rings. Much less frequently, firms will indicate their interest in a call-back interview via a letter or E-mail, and even less frequently, a firm will offer you a call-back immediately at the end of your OCI or job fair interview with them.

During the peak of the 1999-2000 season economic boom, a tiny handful of firms gave their interviewing attorneys the authority to make employment offers during first time on-campus or job fair interviews. In truth, I personally felt somewhat uncomfortable when I heard about this. No matter how great your initial interview has been, rare is the stability of any long-term commitment made solely on the basis of a 20- or 30-minute meeting – in my view, at least. I viewed with great suspicion the firms that would consider this.

The flip side of distaste for over-eager firms is that you need to be prepared to deal with the more common occurrence – a half-day call-back interview.

---

[297] Some firms will cover the expenses up front.

When you arrive at the firm, typically in the morning or early afternoon, you shuttle through the offices of multiple attorneys, speaking with each of them, during which they try to determine whether or not you fit their office's 'good candidate' mold. Smart firms tend to place candidates with smart, interesting, and sociable attorneys who won't frighten prospective new employees away. By contrast, you'll know just from visiting other firms and meeting their chosen representatives that you wouldn't want to work there.

Though it depends a lot on the firm, there's a good chance that even getting a call-back interview is a presumption in your favor – it costs time and money to fly you out, so if you're invited to a call-back, you're probably being checked for a personality fit more than anything else. Relax, be friendly, and don't say anything memorably stupid or obnoxious. Optimally, if you have the prospect of securing multiple offers, your goal is to minimize the impact of interviews on your schedule, while also having enough options if possible to make a good choice among firms.

What are your chances of actually succeeding in securing a job after going through all of these steps? Rough estimates suggest that, in boom times, summer placement appears to be quite high – 90% and up for students at top 20-ranked schools, 60% and up for students at top 50-ranked (first-tier) schools, and 40% and up for students at second-tier schools. But in recessions, the numbers become much less impressive, and even top first-tier students struggle to find work. Smooth on-campus and call-back interviews probably make all the difference in avoiding hard job searches for most law students.

4. My Own Experiences

Part of the problem with choosing a New York State law school, even a good one, is that there's at least a presumption that you'll want to interview for jobs and ultimately practice in New York City. Though that was true for at least half of my classmates, nothing could have been further from my mind. Even before the threat of terrorism, I never felt comfortable in the city, and the idea of working there for even a three-year stretch gave me chills.[298] So when Cornell announced that its first job event for incoming second-years would be held at a hotel in New York City, I hesitated to go. I assumed that the interviewing firms would be New York-based, and it didn't help that during scheduling I was in still in Europe and having trouble communicating with the law school's career office. I wound up writing off the New York job fair, which some of my

---

[298] New York City firms are almost universally branded with 'sweatshop' reputations, a perception most of the firms struggle mightily to avoid. According to widespread stories, the typical New York law firm job experience is a three-year, back-breaking dawn-to-dusk-to-dawn job at a firm that recognizes that you are likely to go elsewhere, and therefore treats you as temporary in all material respects.

classmates attended right before classes started in Ithaca.[299]

I hadn't missed many employers that I would have wanted to interview with, but I did lose out on something my friends experienced: a mad rush on virtually any law student with a pulse. The economy was still in the stratosphere and firms were scheduling hundreds of call-back interviews or making offers on the spot – people without social skills, good grades, or other assets were returning back with three or four different opportunities to choose from. And the interview season was just beginning. Had I wanted a job in New York, I would have had one, even though I had never sat for a legal interview before. *Law Review* associates were averaging six or more offers a piece.

Instead of New York, I considered interviews in Chicago and Washington, D.C., possibly elsewhere depending on the circumstances. The possibility of spending part of my summer in California came up, but I didn't give it a lot of thought – the Los Angeles job fair was reputed to be one of the school's least impressive, with low turnout from major firms, and it was not going to be worthwhile for me to pay my own way out to Los Angeles to interview with firms I had never heard of. I didn't know it at the time, but my chances there would probably have been dismal at that point anyway; I had no previous ties to California, something that firms typically look for, and it was hard for me to muster up enthusiasm about going to work in Los Angeles, either. I'm just a suburban sort of guy.

Chicago and D.C. seemed like better bets, though, and Boston seemed like a possibility. I had lived briefly in Chicago and had friends in D.C.; both cities were also close enough to my family to be good options. So I scheduled OCI and job fair interviews with firms in both cities. On a lark, I signed up for the Boston job fair, too, though I felt a lot less certain about my chances there. I hadn't even visited the city before, though I had wanted to see it for years.

The interview sign-up process turned out to be the deciding factor in my attendance at these job fairs. Following the steps of my classmates, I submitted my name to the career office with lists of firms I wanted to interview with. I was then randomly assigned interviews with some firms via a computerized selection process, and placed on a wait-list for other firms' interview slots that might open through student cancellations. As I learned perhaps too late in the game, if I submitted the names of 10 firms, I might be assigned interviews with four of them and wind up wait-listed on the rest. And of the rest, I might actually secure an interview slot with one or two more.

When I signed up for Boston and Chicago and was confirmed only for a total of two or three interviews per job fair, I gave up my interviews at those events, too, but on much more defensible grounds than I had done with the New York City ones. It just wasn't cost effective to fly into places with few

---

[299] But see Chapter 10, Section B for another take on the New York job fair.

opportunities, and ones reputed to be unlikely to actually happen.[300] By contrast, I successfully scheduled at least six interviews in Washington, and picked up an open slot at random when I arrived. That was a trip worth taking. So, in summary, I would attempt to secure a job by attending a number of on-campus interviews, then travel to D.C. for the job fair, and have a bunch of other OCI opportunities before reaching a final decision.

My first on-campus interviews went well enough. Held during the first few weeks of classes, they were essentially the same experience over and over: sign up for a whole bunch of interviews, spend a little time researching the firms the night before their interviews, and when the 20-30 minute interviews came two or three in a row, have a piece a paper with brief notes on what makes each firm special to briefly scan when moving from interview to interview. Each interview offered an initial moment of anxiety at the very beginning, when the door to the interview office was still closed and the previous interview was running over in time – students were responsible for knocking on the door even if they could hear people talking inside. I would typically knock, the conversation would continue, wind down within a minute or so, then a student I knew would walk out, and I would be invited in.

I didn't spend a lot of time thinking about the interview process before I started going to them; had I researched 'how to interview,' I would have known that there were a bunch of typical interviewer questions and goals that I should expect to be focused upon meeting in kind: interviewers were primarily interested in seeing how I interacted with them, and wanted more than anything to see the conversation 'flow,' but they would also try to ask me to name and discuss some of the previous employment challenges I'd had, and wanted to see me demonstrate specific interest in their firms. I came pretty well-equipped for the specific interest part. Based on studies of the NALP guide and the web sites of the individual firms, I typically came into the interviews knowing what was special about each firm and the specific offices I was looking to work in. It also helped to know something about the people who were about to interview me before I walked into the room, such as the areas of law they practiced, the schools they attended, and the office they were coming from;[301] interviewer information often had to be researched on the day of interviews because last-minute interviewer changes are so common.

But, in all honesty, there were some things that I just couldn't have understood at that point that would have increased my success rate even

---

[300] It was said at the time that Chicago firms preferred graduates of Chicago law schools and that Boston was a very hard city for outsiders to crack.

[301] Sometimes a single interviewer flew out; often interviews were conducted by two-person tag teams. If the team came out from the same office, it seemed to be likely that the firm was only seriously interviewing for that office; if each member came from a different office, the firm was more likely to be recruiting more widely.

further. First, I had an entirely incorrect understanding of the structure of large, multi-city firms. I generally picked firms that had offices in both Chicago and Washington, or some other combination of cities I could work in, and expressed my interest in working at whichever office I could. I was sincerely equally open to the prospect of working in either city; if I had picked a job in either place, I would have been happy there. It was natural for me to honestly convey my interest in both places at once. But it was totally wrongheaded.[302] Even large firms with multiple offices want candidates who are only interested in a single office – open-mindedness is not an advantage here.

Similarly, even though I was just starting my second year, and had no experience with elective classes, I didn't know quite what I wanted to do after law school. I hadn't ruled out litigation completely, despite the fact that it would be the courtroom law I had really never wanted to practice, and I didn't know a lot about how transactional corporate law – the traditional opposite of litigation – actually worked. I hadn't worked for a law firm yet and did not want to commit to doing a sort of work that I would hate.[303] Many of my classmates were in the same boat, but would walk into interviews and state "litigation" or "corporate/transactional" when asked for a preference – this was the right way to do it.[304] Originally, I succeeded in interviews with firms that did not require their first- and second-year associates to pick a specific practice group, and with

---

[302] Firms consistently liked to see a commitment to a given city, as opposed to a general interest in working in a geographical region of the country. Even if they claimed to be recruiting firm-wide, they typically sent attorneys out from the offices that actually intended to fill empty spots; this meant that if a national firm with offices in 16 cities sent attorneys from only their Boston and Los Angeles offices, they were typically only looking to act on candidates expressing interest in those cities.

[303] It's important to know at this point what the life is really like for a junior associate in litigation practice, and this requires two understandings – first, that there are firms with so-called "general" or "complex" litigation practices, and other firms with specific litigation practices for given types of law, such as "Intellectual Property Litigation," "Product Liability Litigation," and the like. Second, few large firms will actually let young associates make court appearances (and will therefore be interested but not overwhelmed by the knowledge that you hope to take Trial Advocacy and other practice classes); most are looking for people who have strong interests in the federal or state rules of civil procedure, evidence, and the specialized area of law in which you hope to practice. It's somewhat easier to know what corporate and transactional practices are like: if your interest skews towards business law classes, and you want to be involved in multi-million dollar deals, you pretty much understand the corporate practice. Letting interviewers know that you either have a business background or are signed up already for business law classes is critical to demonstrating interest in corporate interviews.

[304] Though what's 'right' depends on a number of factors, my strong feeling is that the average law student increases her chance of receiving job offers by stating a preference, so long as the firm has openings in that practice group.

firms that had very limited practices that I found especially enticing.[305] Over time, I learned just how important it was to state one of these preferences, and when I did, my success rate increased across other types of firms.

Something weird happened during the interview process, though: my city flexibility took me in an unexpected direction. One of the giant firms I interviewed with, Smith, Crutcher & Reeves,[306] had offices literally across the world. I interviewed with a Cleveland-based attorney for positions in the firm's Washington and Chicago offices, and the attorney took an instant liking to me – based on my background and interests, he asked if I would be willing to come and interview with his group in Cleveland. My initial reaction was tentative but polite; I let him know that I was really interested in Washington or Chicago, but that I would be open-minded to seeing Cleveland. In truth, I was somewhat surprised and flattered that the attorney seemed so interested in me on a personal level, which disposed me to a heightened level of open-mindedness. His response was that I could come to Cleveland, which I would love, and if I still wanted to interview with the other offices, he would set me up with the interviews. The firm sent out a letter days later asking me to visit Cleveland.

Several other interviewers took a similar liking to me: one from a Boston-based firm that had a strong corporate practice and liked my high-tech interest and M.B.A. background, another from a small Washington telecommunications boutique firm,[307] and another from a larger Washington-area firm where our interview session unexpectedly began when I helped the interviewer find the office he was supposed to be using for the day. The boutique firm in D.C. had so few attorneys that it was barely even a blip on the NALP book radar, but the interviewer and I hit it off. I expressed very legitimate interest in the firm, and he offered me a call-back interview on the spot. He said he would be in touch, and then never called. I took the firm's small size and their lack of follow-up as signs that this might not be the most stable place for me to begin my legal career, and did not make an effort to pester them for the call-back.

Regardless of how they turned out, these 'personal connection' interviews were the most memorable, and I knew that each would lead to an employment offer or call-back within seconds of the start of the interview. There were also positive interviews that had less to do with any personal connection than

---

[305] I did better with firms that specialized in intellectual property, communications or telecommunications law, for example, because I was able to walk in and say, "that's the sort of law I want to practice." The same strategy would have worked for more diverse firms, as well, because they don't care if you have diverse interests – they want to place you into one category, one group of people, not leave you the choice of several.

[306] Firm names have been changed, as well.

[307] Boutique firms are those that are especially small and specialized in one or two primary sorts of law, often consisting of experienced attorneys split off from larger firms during economic crises.

needs-skills fits: a firm with a Washington office had a burgeoning intellectual property practice and I seemed like a good candidate to fill the lower ranks.

For the most part, on-campus interviews went decently. Every day during the first three or so months of classes, classmates would be walking the law school's hallways in full suits and ties, sneaking out of classes with briefcases or binders in hand, and lining up outside classroom and office doors marked only with yellow sheets of paper.[308] The yellow sheets contained each interviewer's list of names of interviewees; you could see as you knocked on each door whom you were about to interrupt.

There was always something odd about walking into a room with a complete stranger and having to tell that person what made you different from your classmates, and hopefully better. I hoped each time that an interviewer would see something in my resume that stood out and made me employable. Many times, it happened. Other times, I had to do a more substantial job of selling myself. The right sales pitch was generally one that explained who I was, how my background proved that, and why my background was the right fit for a practice group the firm was bulking up. If the firm would hire anyone with a heartbeat, my sales pitch didn't matter. If the firm was very picky, my pitch had to be just right, or else they weren't interested.

This wasn't to say that there weren't rejection letters after my interviews: there were plenty. Every law student gets them, and mine were nothing special – the letters seemed virtually identical to one another, generally terse and in many cases amusingly condescending. Expressed in Haiku shorthand, the letters took on pretty much the following messages:

(1) Your resume came;
We considered it briefly.
Good luck finding work.

(2) We think we're special.
You don't seem as cool as us.
You can't join our club.

(3) We like your skill set,
But we have enough like you.
Try again next year.

---

[308] Interviews took place both in spare rooms at the law school and in reserved rooms at a campus hotel, which as part of the undergraduate hotel management school was used as a convenient venue for such events.

(4) Please feel no sorrow.
We can't accept everyone;
Your classmate beat you.

(5) We can't all get jobs.
You may find it difficult,
Look somewhere else, soon.

(6) Many people write me,
My replies bring them sadness;
If they stop, I will.

(7) Thank you law student,
We received your envelope;
It made us laugh hard.

Well, maybe the last one is a bit severe, but the real letters aren't much better. The only stand-out of the bunch caught my eye only because it came from a large British firm that I hadn't even contacted – apparently they had mass-mailed rejections to all of my classmates, as well. This event happened early enough in the job hunt – actually, before most of my interviews – to entirely reduce the psychological impact of rejection letters upon me. When I had good news, I had good news, but the bad letters weren't so bad.

My interviews with major firms in Boston, Cleveland and Washington were all good learning experiences, and amazing experiences overall. In each case, the firm not only paid my way to and from their offices, but put me up at a deluxe hotel in a swanker-than-swank room. I opened the doors of my Boston hotel room to find a chilled bottle of champagne and a complimentary kit of expensive snacks.

I was met at the Cleveland hotel for dinner by the attorney who had taken such a shine to me, and in Washington, my accommodations were similarly first-class. Though I found the Washington people friendly, they were just slightly too laid-back for my liking;[309] the Boston people were way too aggressive and money-focused – they spent the entire lunch trying to impress me with the size of the deals they had been working on.

Of all of the attorneys I met, the people from Smith, Crutcher & Reeves seemed just right – smart, friendly, and driven. But then, they were set up to be

---

[309] The Washington firm was the most casual of my top three. As had been the case at my OCI with the firm, I found some of my interviewers not to be especially prepared, faced with huge piles of paper on their desks and telling me half-embarrassedly that they hadn't quite gotten to my resume yet.

that way: the interviewer I had met at my law school had told me in advance that he was setting up my call-back to be a breeze – all nice people. I thought it was odd at the time but didn't give it a lot of thought. I should have. It was just too easy to be wined and dined, then treated with such interest, and not really think about why it was all taking place.

I felt good enough about the offers I received that I stopped on-campus interviewing and began to turn down call-backs, including one in Philadelphia and more in Washington. I would finish the interviews I had on campus only if I couldn't hand them off to other people, and would make my choice from amongst the firms I had already talked with. Though I had missed a handful of classes, my schedule had not been impacted nearly as much as friends who interviewed more aggressively. Juggling classes and interviews had not been especially difficult.

5. Interview Horror Stories

Not all experiences are like my own – many bizarre things can happen during job interviews. The best I've heard are alleged not to be urban legends.

- After knocking on the door for her interview, one student walked in to find her two interviewers engaged in sexual intercourse. She left the room and reported the incident to the school's career officials.
- Many students fail to properly research the firms they are about to interview with, and believe that they can just fake their way through interviews. On several personally verified occasions – though this probably happens every year – interviewers asked pointed questions such as, "so how interested are you in employment law?" to which the interviewing students responded, "not at all, I'd hate to do that." At that point, the interviewers responded, "you're aware, of course, that all our firm handles is employment law." And the students typically responded by apologizing and sheepishly ending the interviews.
- Students have been asked clearly inappropriate questions regarding aspects of their personal lives, such as their racial background, national origin, age, or religion.
- Interviewers have appeared to be in some way intoxicated during the course of their interviews.
- Entire interviews have taken place without ever discussing the firm, the interviewee's resume, or the law, instead focusing upon sports or some other topic.
- Students have been given call-back interviews which are later cancelled at the last minute or otherwise botched because of a mix-up at the firm.

Then there are those interviewing events which seem bizarre, but are actually somewhat commonplace tricks to throw you off. These include:

- Being invited unexpectedly to attend a dinner or other social event being held by the firm the evening after your interview; these events are often used as screening events for call-back invitations. Unfortunate as it may be, you typically must attend the event if you hope to receive continued consideration with that firm.
- Being asked about your greatest weaknesses. You typically shouldn't point to something truly terrible – in other words, Superman would not respond, "when someone takes out Kryptonite, I lose all ability to function normally and become rather unimpressive." Rather, you should briefly describe something generic and not so bad, such as your obsessive focus on the perfection of your work products or your vague concern that you don't yet know everything that you need to know about the substantive area of law you hope to practice one day at the firm.
- Being asked about your least favorite classes in law school. You might want to give this one enough thought that you don't respond bitterly about a subject that the firm or interviewing attorney specializes in, or say anything especially nasty. A good response is something such as, "constitutional law, but only because I didn't get a chance to participate in the class as much as I had wanted."

Finally, there are the female-specific interview experiences – those which are worth sharing despite the fact that they might cause concern for some women. As was the case with the discussion of rare professorial misconduct, gender-based interviewer misconduct is not common and may well never appear in the course of your interviews. It is mentioned only because it has happened in the past, and therefore should hopefully provide warning to those few people unlucky enough to deal with it in the future.

- Male interviewers have made insensitive remarks to female interviewees about the habits of suburban 'soccer moms' and other stereotypes of women that might offend interviewees.
- Interviewers have flirted with interviewees – though this tends to be the case where the interviewer rightfully or wrongfully has some perception of possible reciprocal interest.[310]

---

[310] Sometimes interviewees (male and female) have intentionally used their sex appeal to generate interest at interview time, so this is not a completely clear-cut issue.

Regardless of which sort of horror story you might encounter, it's important to minimize your apparent level of distress, respond as best as you can under the circumstances, and report the occurrence to your school's career office as soon as possible. Your school will know how best to handle such a situation and will hopefully be able to give you some perspective that will at least calm your nerves. Of course, you may also not have to go through any bad experiences, even the commonplace but seemingly weird ones, in which case you will have smoother interviews than most of the law student population.

B.   SPLITTING THE SUMMER: I DID, BUT SHOULD YOU?

Based on anecdotes shared by classmates, I considered the prospect of 'splitting the summer,' which was becoming an increasingly popular if somewhat risky thing to do. Students who 'split' take two summer jobs at two places, work at one and then the other.[311] They hope that one firm or the other will stand out as superior. And they also hope that the superior firm, if not both firms, will offer to employ them when it's all over with. I was going to split the summer between Smith, Crutcher and the Washington firm – roughly half of the summer at each place. Then a thought came up: why not split the summer between two separate offices of the same firm?

This may sound weird, and it probably should: I had really liked the Cleveland firm's people, but I still wasn't so sure that I actually wanted to live in Cleveland. As previously noted, when Smith, Crutcher came for its on-campus interviews, I expressed interest in the Chicago and Washington offices. The senior interviewer had asked me if I would consider Cleveland, too. I agreed, quite naively, and when the firm flew me out for a Cleveland interview, the interviewer told me that his office could line up opportunities in any of the firm's other offices if I was still interested.

So I tried to take them up on the offer; it was either that, or split the summer with the Washington firm. Smith, Crutcher & Reeves had an office in Irvine, California that I decided I wanted to split the summer with. My girlfriend had lived in Irvine, and perhaps this would be a place worth checking out. If Cleveland was so great, I would love it and wind up there. If not, I would be in Irvine, or else re-interview the next fall. I told Smith's Cleveland office that I was considering splitting the summer with another firm, but that I would spend the entire summer with a single firm if I could split between offices. Though I learned that it was unusual for the firm to do it, they skipped doing a second call-back for me in Irvine and let me come to work there sight unseen because of the sway of the people in Cleveland.

And thus I agreed, around December, that I would work for half of the

---

[311] Students never work at two firms simultaneously, because of conflicts-of-interest.

summer in Cleveland, and the other half in Irvine, California. The dates I chose, subject to the firm's approval, were May 22 to July 3 in Cleveland, then July 5 to August 18 in Irvine. I later learned that other people who had arranged to split the summer between two of the same firm's offices had not necessarily been given as much leeway in setting dates. One had been forced to accept only three or four weeks in her second city.[312] Other students had more significant restrictions on their splits – some firms had policies requiring a certain number of weeks in a given office, and a small number of firms refused splits altogether. Sometimes, such policies caused students to lose interest and just try other firms instead.

On some level, I later learned, I was personally defeating the purpose of splitting the summer – if you're a decent and non-offensive summer associate, going with two separate firms gives you greater latitude to get offers from both firms, and moreover, you get to pick from what could be two very different cultures to find the best fit. By picking one firm, I was giving either office the latitude to entirely reject me – and blacken my name with the other office – if I made any major mistake, and increasing the chances that I would find a single firm culture rather than two to pick from. By turning down the Washington firm, I had given myself one less option had Smith, Crutcher & Reeves turned out not to be so great after all.

As you might have gathered, I had no idea whatsoever what I was getting myself into. I sort of knew that, myself, at that point, but there wasn't any book for sale or otherwise definitive way to make more sense of the situation. If other people had survived their first summer job experience flying blind, so would I. At least, that was my theory.

If I had been wiser, I might have spent more time asking former summer associates from my school what they thought about Smith, Crutcher & Reeves and the other firms I was considering. After signing up for the summer, I heard a nasty rumor that Smith often buried its youngest attorneys in warehouses full of papers to review in preparation for massive trials; had I spoken with more people, I would have had a sense as to whether this was true, likely to happen to me, or unfounded. More importantly, I would have had a better sense for the human dimension of these firms – what the attorneys and other summer associates were really like, how well the firms treated people, and so on. There were many questions I should have asked. I just felt, wrongly, that all firms were more or less the same, and that no matter how good or bad it was, my experience would be roughly like that of anyone else I knew.

---

[312] Some of the firms' offices were considered to be more powerful than others, and thus exerted greater pull on interested candidates. This wound up backfiring, however, as students felt as if they were already being manipulated to suit the firms' needs, rather than their own, and thus went in to the summer feeling skeptical about the firms' policies.

C.   NALP AND NON-NALP EMPLOYMENT

Up until this point, this book has referenced NALP as relatively authoritative on the subject of private sector legal employment. The directory is the first place to consult when looking for legal employment, especially when cross-referenced with Martindale-Hubbell materials. Together, these tools help law students locate firms that are willing to commit to NALP's interviewing and hiring guidelines, and those that are not. All things being equal, students should prefer a NALP-listed firm over the alternative.

The guidelines established by NALP attempt to create a uniform standard for the acceptance and rejection of law firm offers, binding both upon students and the firms that hope to hire them. In brief, the guidelines[313] set out two key standards to insure that students aren't holding too many offers open during the critical interview season. First, a student may hold as many offers as she receives until October 15, at which point she must whittle the number down to four. The number decreases again on November 1 and December 1. Second, the guidelines state that second- and third-year students have until December 1 of a given year to accept offers made either by new employers or old employers who made their offers after September 15. These students have only until November 1 to accept an offer made before September 15. This means that students get as much as two and a half months to decide, sometimes less time depending on the circumstances.

To the extent that NALP has helped to create order from chaos, I will continue to recommend its products as an ideal starting place. That does not, however, mean that they are the only place a person can look for jobs.

There are other options in both the private and public sectors. Smaller law firms – those consisting of 20 or fewer attorneys – may not be listed in NALP's directory. You might learn of them through friends, telephone books, television or web advertisements, or Martindale-Hubbell. And public sector employers, such as government agencies, typically do not have listings in the NALP directory. Virtually any government office you can think of has a summer clerkship program of some sort; contacting the right people is generally a matter of searching web sites, telephone books, and any career office materials you might be able to access. Some of the most popular positions continue to be in district attorneys' and federal prosecutors' offices, as well as public defenders' offices. As is the case for first-year law students, judges may be hesitant to open their chambers to random people for summer clerkship positions, so be prepared to use law school career office or professorial contacts, family friends, or a really sharp resume guaranteed to make a positive impression. Pursue this venue at your own risk.

---

[313] Current as of 2002.

D. THE QUEST FOR "THE OFFER"

For most summer associates, clerks, and interns, the 2L summer is both an exciting and perpetually frightening time. On one hand, you're getting your first real exposure to what the legal profession is actually like, and on the other hand, because it's so different from law school coursework, you're constantly concerned about whether you're doing the right thing. And if you're doing the wrong thing, you believe – sometimes correctly – that you will have a hard time being offered permanent employment.

The summer, then, is a quest for "the offer" – the offer of employment to continue after you finish law school. You do your best possible work, act with appropriate decorum in new social situations, and spend a lot of time demonstrating to the firm, your supervisor, or judge, that you are worth keeping around. At the end of the process, you wait to hear whether you met the employer's standard, and generally speaking, if you did, you get "the offer." Smart people continue to seek "the offer" no matter whether they might ultimately turn it down come November or December 1. There is a stigma associated with not receiving an offer, and people typically avoid the stigma to whatever extent they can.

This does not always mean that the process is fair. Some firms are known for extending fewer offers than the total number of summer associates they hired, even after offering vague assurances that quality summer performance virtually guaranteed future employment.[314] Sometimes, the students who don't receive offers tried their best and were the victims of circumstances beyond their control.[315] But sometimes, students do things that any wise employers would want to distance themselves from.

There are quite a few stories, apparently true, that have circulated regarding the types of exploits of past summer associates that have cost students permanent job offers. Many involve alcohol. Many involve sexual harassment or sexual conduct of one form or another. And many somehow involve a summer associate doing something highly foolish in front of the firm's managing partner or other important people. The comment one could make on this is pure common sense; control your alcohol consumption, stay away from sexual situations with other people at the firm (no matter whom), and behave yourself at all times in front of your colleagues, especially your seniors.

One of the most widely circulated stories of behavior leading to denial of

---

[314] Law students typically attempt, if possible, to avoid working for these firms for fear of being in the 'no offer' category; NALP updates its "number of offers-to-number of summer associates" ratios yearly for each firm.

[315] In bad economic times, the number of offers tends to drop, as do the number of summer associates initially hired. Some firms unexpectedly change their performance standards, and others simply make unplanned cuts in their hiring budgets.

an offer involved a summer associate's drunken bidding at a firm charity auction for a meal with the managing partner. Though the auction was being conducted on-stage by someone else, the summer associate rushed the stage and took the mike to personally appeal for both the meal, and an offer of employment. Before losing the bidding, he made enough of a fool of himself that other attorneys pooled their money just to deny him the opportunity. And the firm ultimately denied him an offer.

Other summer associates have had problems involving sexual liaisons with other attorneys, secretaries, and staff members. Some have become involved in drunken altercations in public places, been arrested, and then called the firms' partners to bail them out or get assistance. These are egregious examples, mentioned here solely as a warning for those who might otherwise consider such behavior non-culpable.

For every example of grossly poor behavior, there are other examples of borderline behavior that might – depending on the firm – cost you an offer.

- Repeatedly turning down work assignments.
- Giving off an air of self-importance that says "I'm more concerned about my personal life than this job" to anyone at the firm.
- Getting oneself engaged in controversial discussions with full-time employees or other summer associates.
- Turning in work product that is grossly below the standards set by the firm.
- Missing deadlines of any sort.
- Refusing to work a late night or weekend when the circumstances require it.
- And acting poorly towards firm staff, such as receptionists, assistants, and paralegals.

Then there are ways to maximize your chances of getting an offer.

- Listen carefully to the requirements for the assignment you are given and insure that whatever you submit is thorough and otherwise professional.
- Turn in all of your work on time or ahead of schedule, no matter how ridiculous the deadline. Plan to work late hours and/or on weekends.
- Put aside personal time in favor of firm-scheduled events, especially if your firm gives you hints that specific events are must-attend events.
- Be a team player.
- Respond politely at all times to all requests, even when dealing with prickly attorneys.

- And don't waste time doing things you weren't asked to do; stay focused on the task you were given.

Clearly, there are plenty of blurry lines on all of these items, save the especially egregious ones. It will be up to you, based on your instincts, to decide at what point you say "no more" to piled-on work, or decide to offer your own strong viewpoint to counter a tract issued by a co-worker during lunch. But be aware that the risks you take might cost you an offer.

E.   REAL-LIFE SUMMER EXPERIENCES

Over the past 15 years or so, law students have definitely come to expect that a summer spent with a law firm is going to involve a certain amount of wining and dining. As much as you are selling yourself to the firm as a valuable cog in the machine, the firm is also expected to be selling itself to you as a place where you want to settle down and practice law for at least your first several years, if not longer. One of the paradoxes of legal employment is that the firms that typically try hardest to offer extraordinary summer experiences are those which work their new employees the hardest once they start. But even smaller firms make competitive efforts to offer memorable and pleasant summer experiences. The summer is therefore viewed almost universally as the appropriate time to win you over and convince you to stay for at least a year.

The top New York law firms are reputed to have the largest summer program budgets, and not coincidentally, the highest turnover rates several years afterwards. But for the summer, students typically feel as if they've just won game shows: you'll leave on your first day with bags full of gifts and goodies, and spend the summer attending concerts, theatre performances, sporting events and even occasionally trips to other cities. Some of my classmates went from New York offices to offices in Singapore or Hong Kong at the firm's expense; many others traveled between domestic American offices. You'll frequently hear that summer associates pay only for a total of one or two meals all summer, over the course of 12 weeks or more of employment – the firm picks up the rest, often at fantastic restaurants.[316]

And in good economic times, as odd as this may seem, this bounty is entirely expected of law firms by their student employees. Quality candidates can go anywhere they choose because so many places are looking for talent. Every major firm is in an unofficial contest to see who can impress their

---

[316] But in a contrary example that is perhaps more amusing than useful, one major law firm, concerned about its spiraling summer program budgets, decided to go the other way by developing a "boot camp" that promised to create a tough, glamour-free summer experience for its participants. The flip-side: rather than spending money on meals and events, the firm heavily over-compensated its summer associates on salary.

summer associates the most, and they're doing it to make an early positive impression. Even Lexis and Westlaw get in on the goodies game to win over summer associates: during my summer, Lexis gave away leather bags and held frequent dessert parties, while Westlaw gave away brass clocks and shirts. None of this abundance even takes into account the salaries, which are typically incredible in major (primary and secondary U.S. city) markets and more than reasonable in tertiary markets.[317]

This set-up brings you to my own experiences, both in markets that are typically considered to be secondary – Cleveland, Ohio and Irvine, California. My experiences are contrasted against those of friends who summered in the same cities with different firms, different cities at the same firm, and in several other cities at different firms.

1. Cleveland, Ohio

Like most other firms, Smith, Crutcher & Reeves had multiple possible 'start dates' for summer associates. As I had opted to split the summer, I was forced to start near the beginning of the program, because each of the firm's offices wanted to observe me for a six-week period.[318] The Cleveland office had roughly 40-some summer associates – a high number – coming in three separate waves of 15 people, give or take. Each time a new group would begin, the old group would attend a welcome reception for them at 9am, then leave them to begin their two-day orientation.

I came in on my first day as I did every other day in Cleveland: wearing a Brooks Brothers suit and tie, shined shoes, and a smile that showed that I was glad to be there. Men dressed like me. Women dressed in suits too, but with more feminine touches. We could take off our jackets in the office.

Our orientation was simple: filling out tax forms, learning about the firm's history, hearing about its sexual harassment policies, and so on. Perhaps the most important event was an introduction to the firm's computer systems, specifically its document management software, which would help us organize all of our work for future reference. We were all given inexpensive tote bags with coffee mugs, copies of coffee table books on the firm's history, and on Cleveland's history, a T-shirt, and other small items. This was a decent collection, but friends at other firms bragged that they'd received firm-branded fleeces, high-quality backpacks or bags, and other 'cool' items. By comparison, my girlfriend – a first-year student at this time – had a similar orientation at her

---

[317] Consult the current NALP Directory of Legal Employers for up-to-date summer salaries.
[318] This is fairly typical; you can work fewer weeks only if you're splitting with a firm you've previously worked for. People often do this if they worked during their first summer and still want to consider returning to their first summer's employer after law school.

smaller firm, but didn't receive any free goodies. My firm was at least competitive in handing out free stuff, early on, and by summer associate standards, that was pretty exciting.

The generosity at Smith ended pretty quickly, however. Even with her smaller firm, my girlfriend spent 75% of her lunches at the best restaurants in Cleveland, entirely on the firm's tab. Still, she was on the low end of the freebies scale. My friends across the country reported, almost without exception, paying for fewer than five meals during the entire summer, and eating at incredible, well-known restaurants, besides. This was the norm in bustling economic times.[319]

But Smith, Crutcher & Reeves was different. My meals were generally at my own expense, but were occasionally catered in a conference room at the firm, largely with sandwiches or something similar. I was taken out for meals by the firm perhaps three times in Cleveland. My girlfriend's firm kept free Starbucks coffee and soft drinks on tap at all times; our only free snacks were the ones we had during those catered lunches. And lest you think I am overemphasizing this component of the summer experience, there is no doubt within the profession that people *do* compare these things, and for a reason – this is one of the only ways a firm can win over its summer associates, and if your firm is skimping, that's a warning sign.

What all of the firms had in common, though, was a propensity to spend lots of money on alcohol. Virtually every summer program offered weekly and sometimes more frequent happy hours where expensive inebriation was the norm. If you haven't read it already, it's time to re-examine the discussion of ways you can lose your offer – the number of problems that came as a direct result of these happy hours was tremendous. But law firms, for better or worse, are often fueled by 'play hard' evenings to complement their 'work hard' days, and they show off by picking up extraordinary bar tabs. Several New York firms, in classic braggadocio, allow summer associates to invite their friends from other law firms to come out free of charge to join the happy hours. Many people have stories of outrageous consumption, covered entirely by firm funds.

For many summer associates, the summer was mostly about eating, drinking, and having fun – 'fun' events ranged from cutting out early to see the opening day of a movie to visits to numerous local landmarks and voyages on yachts. But the rest of it was about working. I had perhaps more than my fair share of that. My hours were atypically short in Cleveland – get in at 9:00am and leave by 5:30 or 6:00pm – this is at least an hour too short a day for a normal summer associate. But I work very efficiently, don't spend much time goofing off during the day, and rarely take lunch breaks longer than an hour.

---

[319] One year later, in her second summer – spent in Southern California -- my girlfriend never once paid for a meal and consistently ate at top restaurants.

This, too, is atypical for summer associates, and associates for that matter. I was 'billing' about 6-7 hours a day when I was told that summer associates typically averaged 3-5. Billing is the profession's word for 'time you spent doing things that can reasonably be charged to a client,' such as researching, writing, editing, and consulting with other attorneys on the matter. The time I wasn't billing was being spent almost entirely on non-billable summer program events.

My girlfriend also had an unusual degree of control over her hours during her first summer – she worked from 9:00 to about 5:00 or 5:30. But during her second summer, at a larger firm, she worked from 8:15am to 6:30 or 7:00pm consistently, every day. And she came in on a rare Saturday or Sunday for a few hours, occasionally bringing work home on weekdays. Friends in other cities found 9:00am or 9:30 start times typical, and 6:30 or 7:30pm end times typical, with the occasional weekend or late-night assignment. Many people knew of others who rolled in at 9:45 or 10am, but this was atypical and tended to cast some doubt on one's eligibility for future employment.

The quality of my assignments in Cleveland was mixed. Unlike some people, I arrived with a certain degree of specific stated interest – I said in my interview that I wanted to do Internet, copyright and trademark work, and that was why the firm had recommended Cleveland; most of their intellectual property work was being handled there. But the firm made only shallow efforts to match me with the work they had promised; I would get a 'trademark' assignment only to discover that I would be researching one of the federal rules of civil procedure on a case that happened to be a trademark dispute. But even these assignments taught me something, both about researching and the realities of firm life – you don't always get the work you want. This happened somewhat less frequently to my friends at other firms, but rather consistently to friends at my firm, no matter what the city or what they had specified as their interests. Those who were least dissatisfied were those who had specified no interests going in, and developed no distastes during the summer.

But the assignments that were actually Internet-, copyright-, or trademark-related turned out to be excellent. I had infrequent chances to work with some very skilled attorneys on matters that were helping clients to form businesses or resolve disputes. And my work received favorable comments from attorneys.

Yet when my progress review came along, I still had no idea what to expect – like everyone else at the firm, and everyone else I knew at other firms, you're never quite sure what your performance evaluations will say about you. You're put into a room with two attorneys who have access to your file and comments that were written by the assigning attorneys. My comments were entirely favorable, with the exception of one that apparently was very common for summer associates – "sometimes writes too much like a law review article." And I guess that was merited; I had spent the last year doing just that. There are much worse comments I could have imagined. One notoriously tough partner had even liked my work enough to send it directly to a client without any editing; I was told by others that his approval was a very good sign.

My friends had similar, but not universally similar mid-summer reviews. As a general rule, it turned out that those who made mistakes on projects had heard about it far in advance of their mid-summer reviews. But those who had worked for tough partners and were chewed out on paper at least tended to receive 'everyone knows that the partner is nasty to everyone' comments of understanding from the people conducting the performance review. Stories of bad reviews were rare, especially for people who were more or less 'normal' members of my class. The general rule about a bad review is that if you work hard to correct the problem, and make clear that you're doing so, an offer is still salvageable – unless the firm is setting you up to be denied an offer. This does happen, and unfortunately, there's not a lot you can do about it.

A firm typically tells its associates to put together solid work files early in the program so that the second half is largely coasting. This is somewhat less true for split-summers, who have so little time at offices that they keep pretty busy until the fifth of six weeks. I had been billing long hours consistently since the beginning; by contrast, friends at other firms, and my girlfriend, would routinely be taken out for half-day events by their firms, and occasional full-day events. Her firm always invited me to come along, but of course, I couldn't do that during the week, and my firm didn't have any events during work days. At best, we could attend events after work or on weekends.

On the other hand, I was allowed a courtesy that many firms extend to summer associates who are members of journals – I was permitted to do a little bit of journal work in my non-billable time at the firm. For many second-year summers, this is a time to grade writing competition submissions; as my girlfriend was a participant, I recused myself from judging the competition and instead used my free moments to work on the *Law Review*'s web site. Notably, my girlfriend had delayed her start date at her law firm in order to write her competition entry. Then, while all of my friends were grading over one hundred nameless submissions, she got to spend the summer waiting for the results.

My Cleveland exit interview with the firm was positive, but because of firm policy, inconclusive. Typically, if you split the summer with two law firms, the first firm will either make or deny you the offer immediately after you finish with them. However, if you split between two offices of the same firm, the first office won't make you an offer, in deference to the second office, which wants to see you perform hard for them, too. So despite the fact that I had no negative evaluations, the Cleveland office couldn't tell me their decision.

In sum, I had very mixed feelings about Smith, Crutcher & Reeves as an employer by the end of the first half of the summer. It had lived up to a reputation people whispered about for general indifference to the concerns of its employees, perhaps a result of the huge size of the firm and its summer program, but to an extent masked better by other large firms. I knew that my friends elsewhere had received targeted, interesting work assignments. Other firms had offered purely royal treatment to students, taking them on a daily basis out to the fanciest restaurants around; I knew that I had been paying for most of my own meals and having only occasional, crummy catered lunches. There were compounding levels of disappointment, too. For example, no attorney realized I was leaving until the day or so before I left, despite the fact that it had been scheduled for six months; there were too many other summer associates to concern themselves with.[320] When a few attorneys realized on my last day or two that I was about to go, they called to ask me if I wanted to go out for a final lunch. But the firm had already scheduled one last mediocre catered conference room lunch to celebrate the simultaneous departures of three or four split-summers, so I had to decline and invite the attorneys to that.

I hesitate to even hint that a series of bad lunches became a determining factor in my final employment choice. In truth, they only stuck in my head as a contrast to the supposed strong interest the Cleveland office had in me when they recruited me away from other firms and cities. All of my friends had kept in touch to tell me that they had just spent their days playing golf, their lunches eating steaks and their nights drinking Johnnie Walker Blue Label scotch. I'd spent my days working, my lunches eating with co-workers in the food court of a shopping mall across the street, and my nights either finishing up assignments from the days or hearing my girlfriend talk about the places she'd been enjoying without me earlier. And this was only the summer. Smith, Crutcher & Reeves had a reputation for working people very, very hard once they started there full-time. Finally, Cleveland, as much as it was making a major come-back from its decaying previous history, was still a very sleepy, underdeveloped city – not one where I'd want to live. All of these things were floating through my head as I considered whether I wanted to be at this firm after graduation.

My girlfriend remained in Cleveland when I left for Irvine in early July. She had a month left to work, and I had six more weeks – another, totally separate proving ground. Her next four weeks were a lot like her first ones – friendly people, interesting work, and the typical amount of confusion faced by a first-year trying to do her best on all sorts of unusual assignments. It was interrupted only by a piece of good news – she received a telephone call and letter inviting her to join *Law Review*, which she accepted. And when the summer was over, she had an offer to return the next summer – this was the typical way that her law firm extended its continued interest in a first-year summer associate. Pure job offers for first years are rare at any firm.

---

[320] On the day before I was supposed to leave, an attorney called me up to give me an assignment due in a week; when I told her I was about to leave, she decided that she wanted me to take the project along to Irvine and work on it there.

2. Irvine, California

My second half of the summer was largely unlike the first, despite the fact that I was working at the same firm: Smith, Crutcher & Reeves' operations in two separate cities couldn't have been more different. In Cleveland, I wore a suit every day to the office, arrived and left relatively anonymously, and worked on a total of seven projects – though they were all long ones. In Irvine, I was assigned a total of twenty projects, some quite long, others somewhat shorter. The office had a business casual policy, which meant no suits – fantastic – but also that I needed to buy another wardrobe. Polo shirts and khaki pants were the standard attire. I had walked into Cleveland comfortable with the people and uncomfortable in my clothes. I started in Irvine comfortable in my clothes but not knowing a single person.

Whereas the Cleveland office had hundreds of attorneys, the Irvine office had fewer than 20. No one noticed when people came in or left the Cleveland office. But everyone noticed when you arrived or left in Irvine. The upside of that was the unofficial policy that people would typically not remain at the office after the managing partner left for the day, which was usually between 5:30 and 6:00pm. And few people worked weekends.

The experience was also significantly different because of the sort of work I was doing. Unlike the Cleveland office, which handled corporate and litigation work of every conceivable variety, the Irvine office at that point was solely a litigation shop – all of its attorneys made court appearances and spent their time writing letters, making calls, doing research on past rulings of local courts, and filing court documents. I didn't think, necessarily, that I wanted to be a litigator, but I wanted to try it out and see for myself. And though I had been interested in exploring litigation, no matter what sort of specific law I might be working with, it turned out that the firm was just beginning to build an intellectual property litigation practice in Irvine, which would be a convenient alternative option if I stayed there.

Unlike the Cleveland office, where I had been aggressively recruited and treated at least by some people as if I was highly likely to receive an offer, the Irvine office made me feel like I had something to prove. On my first day, I was led to an attorney's office to collect roughly five massive double-phonebook-sized binders full of cases to review and summarize in capsule form to update an office treatise. Later, with only two weeks left at the firm, I was given the assignment that all new associates dread: an extended off-site document review. This is where you're given huge collections of papers to sort through, search for key phrases or concepts, and summarize your findings for other attorneys. Smart firms typically don't give document reviews to their summer associates, because the work tends to be so mind-numbing and tedious that no one wants to do it, and it's a bad sign for incoming first-year associates.

According to the rumor I'd heard at school, Smith was famous for document reviews. And this particular document review was going to be in a windowless room with multiple filing cabinets and boxes full of stuff to sort. Accordingly, several of the firm's junior associates suddenly became 'too busy' with other projects to work on it, and thus the summer associates were stuck doing it. Because we were off-site working at a client's offices, something we were not told to expect during our time in Irvine, this assignment also meant that I had to repeatedly re-wear the single suit I had carried with me from Cleveland, changing ties and shirts when possible.

The part of the Irvine story that's missing is the list of perks – you know, the things that make all of the hard work worthwhile. That list is missing because there really weren't any. Although it was a satellite office of a large firm, Smith, Crutcher & Reeves apparently felt content to treat Irvine like a very distant satellite – word was that the office's entire summer budget was around $500. When you consider that there were only two summer associates in Irvine, that's still not much money for an entire summer – especially when you consider that all of the office's attorneys were hoping to eat at least once on the firm's dime too. The junior associates couldn't find time to work on document review, but when the firm offered a free lunch, they were first to order the appetizers.

Only a handful of summer events were scheduled for that office, the biggest of which for my purposes was supposed to be a trip to a local miniature golf and air hockey place, near the end of the summer. That event was ultimately cancelled. And a handful of somewhat more interesting events jointly scheduled with the firm's Los Angeles office became uncomfortable to attend when, early on, one of the Los Angeles summer associates made a raunchy, drunken, highly public and highly embarrassing pass at me in front of the hosting partner, some senior attorneys, and their spouses. The situation was one that, at many firms, might well have cost the offending party her offer.[321]

There were a couple of bright spots. The other summer associate in the office was a really great guy. He attended Pepperdine, had a nice girlfriend, and offered an appropriate amount of moral support when situations such as the embarrassing pass went down. And there was one intellectual property attorney in the office who seemed to have really interesting projects and a good personality. I had hoped to do more work for him, but the office's policy of exposing me to as many attorneys as possible kept me plenty busy with other people. Finally, I loved the Irvine area. I had learned about it from my girlfriend, who had received her undergraduate degree from the University of California at Irvine. It was a very safe, highly modern, and pleasantly suburban city close enough but far enough away from both Los Angeles and San Diego. Every day, the temperature was around or about 72 degrees. I had only love for Irvine,

---

[321] Here, it did not. And that was one of the nails in the firm's coffin for me.

though I knew almost no one there.

Though it was somewhat lonely in Irvine because of the small office size, I kept in touch with friends in Cleveland and elsewhere in the country. My friends at other firms would call or E-mail on occasion about the incredible experiences, outings, and meals they were having, and laughed aloud when I told them halfway through my Irvine summer that my big meal on the firm had been at an Arby's drive-thru.[322] There was no doubt that other firms were treating people better than either the Cleveland or Irvine offices; even firms in Irvine offered better. When presented by my law school with the opportunity to sign up for other job interviews and the New York job fair, I did.[323]

At the same time, I was forced to maintain an increasingly uncomfortable smile every day in the office. I knew that I was not being treated especially well, and in some cases was getting the worst that a summer experience could possibly offer. I also knew that if I hinted disappointment, or that I would not likely accept any offer from the firm – especially this office – I might not receive an offer at all, which would look very bad when I subsequently interviewed for a position elsewhere. So I kept working hard, and only once barely let on that I was stressed about the doldrums of the document review.

F. A QUIET MINORITY

Though the vast majority of people I knew had fantastic experiences over the summer, there were a few people who did not. One was the person who had been forced to spend only three or four weeks in her split-summer Smith, Crutcher & Reeves office; as she was unacquainted with the people and the office protocol, her arrival near the end of the summer proved both far too short for her to adjust and similarly far too late to bond with the other people in her summer program. Stories of 'failure to bond' were uncommon, generally, but tended to be more attributable to lack of time than lack of social ability to do

---

[322] Seriously. The other free meal had been at a burger joint. I paid for almost every meal in Irvine, and moreover, because everyone from the office ate together, repeatedly wound up at the same several restaurants - third-rate taco and salad joints.

[323] And I did something that I would probably not repeat, at least in the same way, if I had it to do over again: this meant modestly changing my departure date from the firm. I had to receive formal permission from Smith, Crutcher & Reeves to leave early, and explain why: I politely and honestly explained that there was a job fair being held, despite my very strong feeling that to be honest about my reason might cost me an offer. And I still feel as if, under slightly different circumstances, it might well have done so. My advice to any summer associate would be to determine the dates of your job fairs as far in advance as possible, and even if you think your firm can't possibly deliver a bad summer, leave yourself the option of attending other interviews.

so. Virtually everyone found at least one other person at their firm with whom they had something in common.

Far more frequent was mild discomfort with small aspects of the summer experience; enough to give some people cause to consider re-interviewing, but not enough to ultimately choose another place to work. Slight interpersonal stresses tended to be normal at firms where summer associates shared offices – typically firms make strong attempts not to force this upon summers, but where it happened, productivity seemed to decline modestly as a consequence. Similarly, some people reported mildly uncomfortable situations where they were asked by attorneys either in public or in private whether they would accept employment offers if they were made.

The only horrific experiences I've heard of were ones that had ended in failures to receive offers. Some of these experiences had started out conspicuously bad – such as the firm which gathered all of its summer associates together on the first day to announce that the summer budget had been discarded and that poor business meant that the office was in rough shape. A small handful of other experiences became messy over the course of weird interactions with existing attorneys, and it was frequently unclear as to whether the students or attorneys had precipitated the problems.

By far the most common experience people have discussed, and one that tended to undermine even otherwise decent summers, was an uneasy fit between a firm or practice group's 'culture' and the summer associate. Many firm cultures rely heavily upon alcohol as an evening social lubricant, and numerous people admitted to feeling pressured to drink to fit in with their co-workers. Other firms are what the average person would consider overbearing upon their associates' personal lives, all but mandating attendance at numerous outside activities and consuming most of the few free hours associates would otherwise have to themselves. And a small number of firms, typically suburban ones and ones outside of the country's coasts, tended to be more family-oriented, keep-to-yourself places, where single summer associates found it hard to mix in and meet new people. The issue of fit tends to be one that a summer associate can only evaluate at a distance during a call-back interview, and then in phone calls to attorneys prior to accepting a summer offer.

Most of the 'fit' evaluation is simultaneously done by the student and the firm during the summer; much of the waiting you do while waiting for a final offer of employment seems to be based on the firm's aggregate assessments on this issue. While it seems as if lack of 'fit' between student and firm accounts for a lot of the hiring-time disappointments people face, there are some firms that simply don't care about personality matches beyond work ethic and work product, and some that – at least during the 1990's hiring boom – didn't care about much at all. Receiving an offer was more about having a pulse and a smile than anything else.

G. WAITING FOR THE OFFERS

Like most of my friends, I had to wait to hear whether or not I was going to receive offers – I didn't leave on my last day with that in my pocket. All indications had been positive, but unlike the Cleveland office, the Irvine office had no formal performance evaluation process, so I had never formally heard the words, "you're doing a great job" or "you really messed this thing up." All I'd heard was that if I hadn't heard anything negative, I was in decent shape to receive an offer. And the firm was busy physically expanding its offices to have room for more attorneys, so that was a positive sign.

My hard, muted labor paid off: I received offers from both offices. The only problem was that I had decided that I didn't want to accept either one. I loved the city of Irvine but didn't like how I had been treated by the office there. And I enjoyed the work more in Cleveland but didn't like the city, and didn't like the fact that I felt completely anonymous – it felt highly likely that I could just as easily wind up doing document reviews in Cleveland, where they were reputed to be much, much worse than the ones in Irvine. So I was going to have to re-interview, and come up with a strategy of some sort to insure that I had some options come the end of interview season.

Something I didn't realize at the beginning of my third-year interview season, to be discussed in more detail later, was that this was the point at which I definitely needed to have decided exactly what law I wanted to practice after law school. The second-year summer is the laboratory for experiments to see what works for you and doesn't; unlike the firm where I worked, many firms place new associates immediately in the practice group where they may remain until they leave the firm. Associates who have group preferences are typically accommodated to the extent possible – some firms offer no guarantees – and those who have none get whatever the firm has left. With the exception of the few firms such as Smith, Crutcher & Reeves, where all associates are placed into an uncommitted 'new associates' pool without any specific practice group placements, the luxury of possible practice group choice *after* starting is not left open to third-year candidates. If you're going to re-interview at the start of your third year, you need to be highly specific about what you hope to do and which practice group you will fit into.[324] So if by the end of the summer, you're still uncertain, figure out a way to at least temporarily become certain about your plans when it comes time to re-interview.

One cautionary note, however, on the subject of re-interviewing: as of the

---

[324] The great irony of this situation is that the firm's hiring needs could easily change dramatically between the time of your interview and your actual start date, and if so, the firm will expect you not to complain about forced assignment to another practice area. This happened to numerous friends who declared interest in corporate law right before the economy slumped, turning all of them eventually into litigators.

time of this writing, the legal job market has tightened considerably, and even top 3L candidates are having problems finding firms willing to interview them for post-law school positions. Therefore, to the extent possible, make absolutely certain that you've researched and chosen the right place for your 2L summer, even if economic conditions have improved by the time you're planning.

Whether you should consider splitting the summer between two firms as a hedge against getting turned down by one firm is, at this point, entirely unclear. Conventional wisdom suggests that in a market in which demand for law student talent is greater than the supply, you would do better to split the summer, but where supply outstrips demand, as is today the case, you might do better to commit fully to one firm and give them your all. My own anecdotal evidence suggests that splitting between two firms tends to increase, rather than decrease a person's offer security, but today this will require you to actually find two firms interested in hiring and sharing you for the summer. On that score, I wish you the best of luck.

Join Doug, Steve & Suchir
122C Valentine Place off state near n
9.9.200

EXCERPT FROM **"ABSOLUT LIABILITY"** PARODY POSTER

DESIGNED TO POKE FUN AT FIRST-YEARS' WORST NIGHTMARES

A. BORING OR BENEFICIAL: YOU MAKE THE CALL

If you believe the old maxim, the third year of law school is supposed to be a time when professors bore you. And to some extent, the maxim is understandable; for generations, law school was a two-year program, and by the third year, you should be more or less done with your mandatory classes and there shouldn't be much left that you 'have' to learn. Rather, your coursework is likely to be almost entirely elective, and thus, for some people, boring. Some law students express this sentiment outright: you can spend the third year golfing and relaxing. Such people often claim by the beginning of the third year to have mastered the critical lesson of law school: how to effectively teach oneself any subject, no matter how difficult.

But only a minority truly slack off in the third year; it's one of those things that people brag about but rarely actually do, at least, at competitive schools. A handful of people will use the third year as a chance to get the last vestiges of recklessness out of their system;[325] it's far more common to see 'bored' people use the beginning of the third year for an externship of some sort, or to study somewhere other than at their law school.[326]

For those who stay on campus, the third year can be a refreshing change from the hectic first and second years. It can be a time to peacefully complete the study of an area of specialization, such as business law, with classes that sound most interesting, or try a totally new area just for fun. It might even be the chance to be part of a clinical class where you'll actually get the chance to work on behalf of real clients who actually need your help.

Rare indeed is the 3L who is even close to stressed out or otherwise taxed during the third year. And those people are typically either called law review editors or masochists, if not both. To be a bit more accurate, only a tiny fraction of people are still in 'gunner' mode by the third year, and these are the people with major extracurricular activities or those angling for *cum laude*,[327] *magna cum laude*,[328] or *summa cum laude*[329] designations; some others are either

---

[325] Every year, a number of people anticipating "conscription" into law firm life will dye, shave off, or style their hair in some radical way – this is perhaps a reflection of the dual stresses of the impending end of a 'relaxed' student lifestyle and the impending challenges of taking the bar exam and starting a new job.

[326] See Section C below.

[327] "With honor," frequently restricted to the top 25% of graduating students, but with modern academic inflation of honors, sometimes as many as the top 30% or all students with 3.5 or higher GPAs.

[328] "With high academic distinction," often restricted to the top 5-10% of graduating students under summa cum laude, but sometimes as many as the top 15% or all students with 3.7 or higher GPAs. Note that top 10% students at some (but not all) schools are additionally invited to join the Order of the Coif society for this level of achievement.

driven to work to complete their dual-degree programs or struggle to reach or surpass the 'top-50th percentile' mark in their class.

Is all this last-minute effort really worth it for something such as a percentile ranking or student organization that may or may not even appear on a diploma? Even assuming that personal pride isn't your deciding factor, the practical answer is probably yes. Today, fourth-year law firm associates report that their grades, and sometimes journal memberships, still matter to firms when they try to interview for new jobs.[330] So, as of today, the last year of law school might mean the difference between easier or tougher post-graduation interviews for as many as five years; from where I stand, it's worth considering how best to make use of your final year.

While some might think that it's a breeze to do well in the third year, it should be said that although it's not the toughest year for most law students, it's not likely to be a cake walk, either. First, you're taking the same classes attended by second-years; unlike undergraduate and other graduate schools, law schools rarely require or recommend prerequisites that wind up limiting certain classes to only third-year students. Second, law schools typically design their curricula so as to require reasonably full course loads during any third year, and those professors who are sticklers for attendance will not ease up on third-year students; if anything, they become more aggressive and begin to check seats each day.

Third-years should approach their final semesters, then, with at least some degree of humility. A couple of common traps that third-years fall into are the 'been there, done that' syndrome – acting like a know-it-all in class – and the 'no need to go there' syndrome, which is failing to attend many, if not most of a semester's classes. Cocky third years have found themselves humiliated for speaking obnoxiously in class, and even as recently as my final semester in law school, a couple of students in prosecutorial Professor Graber's Criminal Procedure class found themselves unexpectedly barred at the last minute from taking his final exam because of their failure to attend classes. Both appeared, at least temporarily, to have been prevented from graduating as a result. Don't let yourself fall prey to such mistakes.

That doesn't mean you won't have fun in your third year. There's plenty of time for that. Parties, including Absolut Liability,[331] our successful follow-up to

---

[329] "With the highest academic distinction," often restricted to the top 1% of graduating students or top individual student, but with modern academic inflation of honors, sometimes as many as 5% or all students with 3.9 or higher GPAs.

[330] However, such academic factors tend not to be an issue much after that point in your professional career; only your work product and reputation matter.

[331] As the follow-up to Got Beer?, the Absolut Liability party featured a photographic poster depicting Sprague passed out with a shot glass and Civil Procedure textbook in the law school's library – an ode to the worst possible situation the new 1Ls could imagine.

the infamous Got Beer? party, were very commonly hosted by third-years, and the bar scene in Collegetown found its most stable supporters in the 3L class. But early in the year, you may have other concerns.

B. RE-INTERVIEWING FOR 'PERMANENT' EMPLOYMENT

At the beginning of the third year, a typical law student is in one of two frames of mind: uncertain about whether to accept a permanent offer from their summer employer, or certain that they won't be going there – either because of a lack of an offer or a lack of personal interest. Of course, there are students who feel largely certain about accepting their offers, yet it seems far more common that even the most comfortable people harbor at least a hint of doubt about their firms based on their summer experiences, and at least give fleeting consideration to the prospect of re-interviewing. Even if one sincerely believes at the end of his summer that everything was perfect, there's always a lurking, if minor suspicion that things were too perfect.

Amongst those who were lucky enough to get jobs in the first place – sometimes especially the people for whom interviewing was easiest – re-interviewing is frequently considered, if not actually undertaken. Many such people will schedule several interviews, only to recall just how much they'd hated interviewing during the second year, and then interrupt the process to accept their summer firm's offer. Some of them will go through the interviews but face a very common third-year dilemma – firms simply do not hire many 3Ls by comparison to 2Ls; the number of initial screening interview slots for third-years, even in good economic times, is often one-third or less of the second-year number, and getting a call-back is much, much harder. Firms simply don't want to take a risk on offering permanent post-graduation employment to a person without feeling quite confident that they don't need a summer trial period in order to hire them.

Those who struggled to get jobs in the first place are far less likely to re-interview, even if they're unhappy or moderately displeased with their summer experiences. The employment market looks far less inviting, and even a job at a less-than-thrilling firm looks far better than risking possible unemployment.

That said, I personally felt so disinclined to join Smith, Crutcher & Reeves that I very strongly wanted to re-interview. Even though the economy was starting to look shaky at the beginning of my third-year of law school, there were still a handful of positions open at quality firms. Hiring freezes had not yet started, though they would begin at various firms around the end of my interviewing season. I decided that I would only return to work for Smith if I had no other options.

Having been through the interview process this second time, I feel confident in saying that you can succeed as a 3L interviewee, but that your chances are very, very slim in all but the very best economic conditions.[332] This leads to a piece of advice for second-years: be dually advised to make sure that your 2L interviewing season is as thorough and well-vetted in advance as possible. If you can avoid re-interviewing, you will be much better off for the experience. Two call-backs I went through, and some chaos beforehand, provide the best anecdotal evidence of this point that I can offer.

I started the re-interviewing process only days after finishing my second half of the summer in Irvine. My Smith experience had left me disillusioned enough that I decided to attend the New York City job fair, something I had skipped the year earlier but now believed critical to finding alternate employment. I went to a relatively aggressive set of ten interviews offered at Cornell's New York job fair – aggressive only because I had signed up for virtually any California firm I could find that would interview 3Ls. Some people, generally 2Ls, had actually scheduled over 35 interviews for the three days of the job fair, so I was objectively light-burdened by comparison.

But I found that those ten interviews were among the most difficult ones I had faced as a law student, and friends in attendance said the same thing – interviewers were demanding more specifics about my future goals and asking all sorts of tricky questions about my summer experiences, including the specific types of assignments I had done and the departments I had worked for. A number of interviews essentially became throwaways because I wasn't aware going in that the questioning was going to be so much different from the way it had been only a year earlier. Now most firms wanted to know exactly what department I wanted to be in, and why I would fit in that department based on the classes I had taken and my summer experiences. And all at least seemed interested in whether I had received an offer or offers after the summer;[333] as my firm had not yet informed people, all I could say was that all of my evaluations had been positive, and that I was waiting to hear back.

Moreover, I had to walk the exceedingly fine line of appearing interested exclusively in the interviewing firm while not trashing the firm that had

---

[332] When the economy gets bad, the first positions squeezed are the 3L openings; firms instead want new blood with experience, and seek lateral attorneys from other firms.

[333] Ironically, though it might seem that this question lets an interviewer know whether your last firm found you worth hiring, the question doesn't necessarily help an interviewer get at anything. One of the interesting situations in legal recruiting is the existence of the so-called "cold offer," which is a perhaps predictable result of a profession where reputation means so much; some firms extend artificial "offers" to their summer associates for purposes of helping them survive the "did you get an offer?" question during interviewing. But these offers, it is understood, may not be accepted by recipients. It's the equivalent of a positive letter of recommendation from an employer who decided not to hire you. I heard rumors that one member of my class received a cold offer, but most people either received legitimate offers or none at all.

previously employed me. Though this certainly would vary from firm to firm, I think it unwise to show up for interviews and suggest that you had personality conflicts with attorneys or other problems with the summer experience.[334] I had never had a personality conflict with anyone, but I had a strong suspicion that my working life was going to be miserable as a new associate at Smith. These points didn't seem worth discussion in interviews; others will probably want to have a good but not wholly vicious explanation waiting, just in case the "why precisely are you leaving?" question comes up.

I'd had a much better run during the previous year's interviews: as the job market was beginning to settle into a recession and 3L interviews were getting abruptly cancelled left and right, I didn't get a single call-back from the New York job fair. Rumors were circulating that many firms were imposing hiring freezes. A close friend was one of the rare 3Ls with a call-back, and from the weirdest interviewer at the fair, no less. My friend scheduled the call-back, but days later, after packing his bags and with car ready to leave for the airport, the telephone rang. The firm called to cancel the interview; it hadn't noticed on his resume that he was a 3L until the day before he was supposed to show up.

My own experiences were similar; firms either were interested because they thought I was a 2L, or tended not to pay a lot of attention once they knew I was a 3L, even after I had received offers from both Smith offices. My most memorable call-back experience of the third-year, and perhaps of all time, was when a firm flew me out, got all the way through my interviews, and on the very last one had the hiring partner ask, "so what can I tell you about our summer program?" I responded, "well, as I'm a 3L at this point, I wouldn't be in the summer program." It was as if all the gears had stopped spinning in her head at once. She picked up my resume, re- read it, and fumbled through a few more questions as if she was still interested in me. But it was obvious that she was not. She explained that the firm already had filled all of its slots for the department that I had clearly told the firm was my only choice, and asked me if I would be interested in any other departments. I expressed a mild amount of flexibility just out of courtesy, but knew I would never be coming back to work there. I had a nice lunch on the firm. Got to visit a friend in town. And didn't hear back from the recruiting coordinator for months. The firm eventually tacitly admitted that they'd had to turn me down because they hadn't bothered to closely read my resume before asking me to visit. The whole experience had been a waste of time, except of course for the free meals and hotel.

---

[334] But there is a flip-side to this one, unfortunately. To not be completely thorough in your discussion of your reasons for re-interviewing leaves you open to the presumption, however incorrect, that you were at fault for whatever problems you had with your summer. If you can't just say, "I was groped by a senior partner and felt uncomfortable working there afterwards," the presumption might be that your work product made you receive a cold offer at best.

But I also had a positive interview experience worth sharing. While the job market was tightening considerably, there was one firm I wanted to work for – Bender, Walls & Eddington (Bender), a firm with a very good reputation for treating its employees well and some very strong positive recommendations from a friend who had been working in their Palo Alto office, living the good life while I was sweating all summer. It was a technology firm. It had an office in Irvine, California. And it looked quite perfect given my interests.

Like most other firms, Bender wasn't recruiting 3Ls too heavily. It had made offers to and received acceptances from most of its previous summer class, and therefore didn't have a lot of slots open. So, after my on-campus interview with the firm, and no response – positive or negative[335] – I took a risky shot after consulting with my Palo Alto friend and e-mailed the head of the Irvine department I was interested in working for. The E-mail was short, but expressed that I sincerely hoped to have a chance to interview with him, as he in fact had the exact sort of intellectual property practice I wanted for myself. My E-mail was apparently enough to tip the scales in my favor and get me a call-back. This time, I was flown out to California – for a day. And when the interview started, it was the most challenging I had ever encountered – as I was a 3L, Bender wanted to be sure that I would fit in with the entire department I would be working with, so instead of scheduling one-on-one interviews, I was put in a conference room where members of the group came in two or three at a time to talk with me for a couple of hours. When the firm called to make me an offer, it was the fact that I had been comfortable with the people, and that format of interview, that apparently had led the firm to offer me a job.

And this was an offer I was anxious to accept – Bender had a much better reputation amongst employees than Smith, Crutcher & Reeves, and would place me in the city where I wanted to be, in a technology-focused intellectual property practice. Though the offer came at the very end of the hiring season, it was worth waiting for, and gave me something exciting to do after law school.

C. EXTERNSHIPS AND STUDYING AWAY

There are several options available for students who want to spend time away from their law schools while still earning academic credit. Different types of externships are perhaps the most popular options, and studying away at other law schools is a less common but still noteworthy possibility. Studying away was discussed earlier,[336] but there are some conditions specific to third-

---

[335] This, by the way, was the case with a number of firms – rather than rejection letters, I received no response. My belief is that firms with some level of interest, but uncertainty as to their hiring needs, will simply delay sending positive or negative letters out.
[336] See Chapter 7, Section A.

year students that should be noted: many schools prohibit or strongly discourage students from spending their final semester away from the law school, and you may have other obligations – such as bar registration and preparations for graduation – to consider during your third year. Regardless, consider your fourth and fifth semesters of law school as safe times to study away, and the third semester as the right time to start planning and obtaining permission for any sort of activity outside of your school.

Externships, like studying away, are typically conducted later in your academic career – some externships earn you one course worth of credit, and semester-away externships can earn a full semester's worth of credit.[337] The concept of an externship is that a student learns from the experience of doing something practical, such as working in the public interest, interning for a judge or legislator, or conceivably even working at a law firm, and receives credit – perhaps pass/fail – for her labor. Students keep journals of their work and communicate with a school faculty member throughout the semester, but the content of the educational experience may otherwise be left entirely to those running the externship, depending on how novel the program is. Established externships may be pursued with less interference from the law school; new or untested ones will require the student to explain in advance why the program will accomplish something they cannot learn in existing classes.

Schools often have placed students in externships before, and thereby have a general sense of what a given program will encompass. Judicial externships are essentially semester-long, regulated clerkships with trial court judges combined with weekly classroom sessions for discussion of the experience. Legislative externships involve the drafting of legislation and advanced intern-like work for a legislator that requires particular legal knowledge. Advocacy externships allow students to take on supervised roles as representatives of juvenile delinquents, or poor clients in relatively minor disputes, and other externships let students work for government agencies or non-profit institutions, doing research and writing legal memoranda for credit.

Externship specifics will differ from school to school,[338] and as some schools have fewer externship options than others, it will help to research a given school's possibilities before arriving there. But if you're already at a law school and you discover that there aren't many options available, don't fret – you won't be at any career disadvantage, and you could always speak with your school's administration to see what under-publicized options, if any, are

---

[337] Full-semester externships are often restricted to your third year, and then only to your fifth semester of law school.

[338] The UCLA School of Law has a particularly interesting collection of externship possibilities; a link to demonstrate some of their options is currently available at http://www.law.ucla.edu/Students/AcademicPrograms/externship/externship.htm.

open to you. In the end, though such programs can be interesting and practical, they are by no means a necessary part of the average law student's life, and if you don't wind up pursuing an externship, no one but you will care.

D. A THIRD-YEAR'S WORKLOAD

Semesters away aside, if any time of your law school life can be called manageable, that would be your third year – it can be spent almost as restfully or as intensely as you desire, subject only to your law school's minimum per-semester and per-year credit requirements, though traditionally it is not spent deep in study. With the exceptions of those pursuing joint degrees and people who feel it personally necessary to seek Latin honors or cram in a lot of work, third-year students generally sleep and play better than their younger colleagues at a law school.

Those pursuing two degrees simultaneously are in for considerably different third years than their classmates; depending on the degree, this year may be spent entirely in a graduate school away from the law school, as might be the case with a business degree, or might be spent at the law school taking highly specialized courses to earn an LL.M. of some sort – both options that might otherwise be pursued after completing law school, as well. As a general rule, if a joint-degree program takes four years to complete, the law student will also have another interesting hurdle to deal with: a so-called 'third summer' with the prospect of more law firm summer program interviews and what is in essence merely a reprise of the second-year summer experience. Many joint-degree J.D.-M.B.A. students use one of their two upper-class summers to work in a business setting rather than a law setting; any extended four-year program might instead be used for multiple consecutive law school summers. The extra year provides interesting interviewing leverage for 3Ls who otherwise might be pushed into the highly difficult 3L permanent job re-interviewing scenario discussed above.[339]

1. Developing a Specialization

My personal third year educational experience was neither lightweight nor punishing. I used it as an opportunity to enhance my exposure to the substantive areas of law I hoped to practice: the courses I took were almost entirely discretionary electives in intellectual property, technology and

---

[339] But it also leads some 3Ls to take the patently unwise step of trying to split one of their summers between full-time employment and bar study, a combination of tasks that frequently proves fatal to at least bar passage. This subject will be explored further in Chapter 11, Section B.

commercial law subjects. And they enabled me to fulfill Cornell's requirements for a separate but minor certification – the school's so-called "specialization program" that earned me a document to accompany my diploma at graduation, a certificate of specialization in Business and Commercial Law. Moreover, I hoped to take a course or two outside of the law school, just for fun, as a number of my then-graduated upper-class friends had recommended.

The third-year courses that gave me the final credits I needed towards the specialization certificate were Corporations, a recommended core offering which I took during the first semester of the third year, and Initial Public Offerings & Acquisitions, which I took during the second semester of the year. Corporations (Corps) turned out to be among the most important courses any law student could take. It is a primer on all of the critical aspects of forming and legally managing an American business entity with limited liability, and an introduction to some of the biggest stock and debt issues that most companies face. Corps is a gateway, and thus prerequisite to a large number of other courses, including everything from securities regulation to corporate taxation to secured business transactions.

It had been hard to work Corporations into my second year schedule, when I had really wanted to take it with Professor David Parker, another of the school's perennially beloved professors. Visiting professors taught the class during semesters when Professor Parker was not lecturing, but I waited until slots opened up in his class during my third year. In many ways, Professor Parker was an emotional foil to our Property and Trusts & Estates Professor Franklin – while both were masters of the non-Socratic lecture format, Parker's style seemed to suggest efficiency over comprehensiveness – he wanted to present a clear black letter answer quickly, not a completely argued answer on both sides – while Franklin did the opposite, so you had to learn it all. Parker's direct, business-like approach had earned him a reputation for quick, sharp thinking and a history of publishing second to no one – his frequent law review articles were among the most widely read of any professor at the law school, and like Franklin's articles, very influential. Students raved about both men.

But both professors were known to be somewhat less accessible outside of the classroom. Stories circulated that students had tried to speak with Parker after classes and wound up talking with him at his desk while he juggled phone calls and article writing – all at the same time. One student claimed to have seen him exercising at a local gym while he simultaneously taught himself Italian. Professor Franklin was similarly known to spend a lot of time co-authoring articles and working on a textbook when he wasn't teaching classes. This sort of multi-tasking and intellectual behavior, interestingly enough, was not uncommon amongst professors at the law school; it was one of many signs of the academic caliber of our instructors.

Initial Public Offerings & Acquisitions (IPO's) was an entirely different sort of educational experience. The professor was a relatively young entrepreneur who had graduated years earlier from our school, and was now running an emerging-growth company in another state. He flew in once every week for class, as did several other professors in similar situations, and spent the rest of the week actually conducting the business and legal affairs of his company. This turned out to be one of the largest classes I took at the law school, with perhaps 130 students in total, mixing both J.D. and M.B.A. candidates in one room. This class, like several others, was offered jointly by the business and law schools, and could count towards a law degree, a business degree, and the law school's specialization certificate in business law.

IPO's is a class that can vary dramatically in character during good and bad economic times. An initial public offering is essentially the first point at which a formerly private company begins to allow members of the general public to buy shares and thereby acquire fractional ownership interests. As part of the class typically involves examination of current companies' initial public offerings and dissection of their financial statements, there is a tendency towards IPO-related excitement in economic boom periods and lethargy in slumps. Professors seem to enjoy teaching the class more when there are plenty of juicy new IPO's to discuss.

My IPO's class just happened to coincide with the beginning of a recession and the collapse of the dot com sector – while we were left to discuss the record-setting IPO's that had come only a couple of years earlier, the current news tended to contain only cancellation notices and minor-league public offerings. And at around the same time, investment banks began to lay off their youngest employees and rescind offers of employment to students that had been accepted months earlier; law firms were reportedly preparing to do the same. Those impacted by the tightening economy were sitting together in our classroom as a microcosm of the problems actually affecting the market, and worse yet, all of us had signed up for the class because we had hoped to be able to handle IPO's that were apparently now few in number.

But the other side of the IPO's class is the concept of acquisitions, the subject of the second half of the course and a perfect practical complement. In the real world of law, when IPO's dry up, corporate lawyers are often kept busy because large companies want to acquire smaller companies or their prized assets, and both the large and small companies need people to advise them and draw up agreements. This acquisition process, like the IPO process, is governed by a set of interesting laws and court decisions mandating certain disclosures to buyers and investors. And owing to both the unusual nature of the class – two discrete subjects and two types of students – the class actually offered my first and only law school mid-term exam plus final exam format, and used one exam for each course subject. This came as a relief to many of the law students, who had not seen a mid-term in two or three years.

In addition to this chance to have greater control over my grades, the third year also gave me several opportunities to take classes on the subject of technology, a field of personal interest that was sadly untapped during my first and second years of law school – both for curricular reasons and because the few courses were restricted to small enrollments. In my first 3L semester, I was lucky enough to get into a prized seminar titled Law, Science and Technology, a fantastic discussion and paper presentation course taught annually by an accomplished visiting professor from Cambridge University, Elsa Irwin. Each semester, the course explored the legal dimensions of contemporary topics in biotechnology and genetic engineering, computer science and information technology, and similar subjects. This class was another opportunity to learn the practical implications of some of the intellectual property laws I had spent the past two semesters studying.

I also was able to enroll in the first semester of a brand-new class, International Protection of Intellectual Property, which became the third IP course offering at Cornell.[340] This class, which we nicknamed IPIP, immediately became a haven for all of the IP fanatics who had tapped out the other course offerings and were desperate for any other IP course they could get. It also attracted a considerable number of foreign students from the school's LL.M. program, who had little experience with American IP law but needed credits in 'international' subjects. The professor therefore offered a quick American introduction to each topic, in addition to copious discussions of the international treaties and cases related to copyright, patent, trademark, trade dress, and then-existing domain name law. It was a perfect capstone to what I had learned before, and was taught by another visiting professor – a rising young star named Michael Thompson who had taught at George Washington University Law School and specialized in patent law.[341]

The final technology course of my law school career was one that I had never expected to take, because I never knew about it beforehand – its relative anonymity, in my opinion, revealed a major problem. One of Cornell's greatest and largely unsung assets is the Legal Information Institute (LII), a public domain source of American law which has been available on the Internet since the dawn of its popularization in the early 1990s. The LII is amongst the most trafficked sites on the Internet for legal information – especially consulted for

---

[340] Cornell also rolled out separate Patents and Trademarks classes at this point, but I was, as mentioned before, ineligible to re-take these subjects separately.

[341] Like the other visiting professors I've profiled, Professor Thompson was outgoing, friendly and open with students, and may well have been the best instructor of the group. He had earned awards for his writings on Intellectual Property law and held several prestigious positions after law school, including a federal clerkship with the U.S. Court of Appeals for the Federal Circuit – the nation's top patent court. Also like the others, Professor Thompson angled for a tenured faculty position and did not receive an offer.

applicable law whenever a major legal story breaks in the mass media. Yet despite the fact that it's literally resident – computers, files, and everything – right inside the law school, one would never know from any of Cornell's literature that the LII's founders are both teaching classes.

Legal Information Systems is one of the founders' pet classes. It deals with some of the infrequently considered, but critically important subjects surrounding modern legal research – the trustworthiness of online sources of law, the monopolistic/oligarchic conditions prevailing in the legal information business, and methods for accessing legal information when Lexis and Westlaw are either unavailable or not useful. Positive word of mouth tends to produce small groups of students every semester it's offered, but no one realizes until they're in the class just how important the professor is – he wrote the first Windows web browser, and is consulted by numerous foreign governments on improving public access to legal resources. It's like taking a class with a person of Professor Winter's stature that no one fears, and everyone respects.

2. Leaving With a Bad Taste in Your Mouth

The IP and technology-related courses were, without a doubt, my favorite classes at the law school – the ones I came to covet in my third year schedules. But there were, unfortunately, dark clouds later in the third year, owing again at least in part to the scheduling conflicts produced by Cornell's registration system. Finding few other options, I registered in my first semester for Public International Law, which sounded like a vaguely interesting international class that would fit into a hole in my schedule. In my second semester, I bumped aside another interesting course for Comparative Law: Asian Legal Systems, another international law course. I should have known from the first course never to enroll in the second. And I should have never allowed myself to remain in the second long enough to miss the end of the drop-add period.

In truth, I'm bothered by the thought that I would itemize the problems these courses had, because there are some things about law school – precious few – that I'd almost rather forget. But a true accounting of my law school experience would not be complete unless I explained just what went wrong in these two classes, and I make these statements understanding that though I've verified with classmates that my perspective was widely shared, it is not the exclusive perspective. A handful of people liked each class despite what most people would have said, and what I'm about to say right now.

Public International Law was supposed to be an education in treaties, executive agreements, and other supra-national laws regulating the conduct of states. At the end of such a class, you would hope to understand the overarching principles governing international affairs, such as how treaties are formed, what their effects are, and how they might be altered or repealed thereafter. But instead, this class was at best an introduction to a bunch of seemingly unrelated documents and international court decisions, and in its worst moments, a pure exercise in confusing exam preparation. None of the topics was explained well enough to make sense of a big picture, no systematic method of understanding international agreements was ever enunciated, and no one knew what to study for the exam – or even what it might cover.

Comparative Law: Asian Legal Systems was far worse. Though its title suggested that students might compare the laws of different Asian legal systems, this was a class that never examined a single system of law, let alone contrasted or examined differences between Asian authorities. Intriguingly, this class was being taught by a visiting professor who had spent time in Asia and had highbrow credentials in anthropology, yet this professor belonged to the class of established, but not fantastic visiting professors looking for other work. By the end of the class, which the recently graduated professor pompously touted as being taught in the "Harvard style," we had not learned enough about a single aspect of any Asian legal system to make practical use of a thing we had read or heard. Instead, we had engaged in class discussions of such idiotic documents as the table of contents of a book and articles purporting to explain the comparative anatomies of human society and scattered social movements in several countries. To say that the class was useless to the practice of law, even by comparison to the scattershot Public International Law, is a profound understatement. Several students complained to the administration about the class and the professor. Yet unlike Professors Bear, Thompson, and Hale, the school offered this professor a tenured position on the law school's faculty.[342]

That courses such as these could be so poor was somewhat astonishing, but then, I had not taken many international law courses until the third year of law school. Cornell prides itself on its international law program, in which it offers a full LL.M. program, the opportunity for a certificate of specialization, or just individual classes of general interest, but many people who take the international classes have found them to be distressingly bad. Instructors are

---

[342] The school simultaneously extended a tenured faculty position to another unsuitable candidate, the professor's girlfriend (from Chapter 5, Section I) who had provoked tremendous complaints in the class above mine. If this doesn't make sense to you, several facts might explain the decisions. The Asian Legal Systems professor, unlike the others, had other high-profile temporary teaching offers on the table, including a position at Yale, had attended and organized numerous conferences, and had published many journal articles recently on anthropology and comparative law topics. This gave the impression that the professor was a mover-and-shaker in some demand, which despite their academic honors, prestigious positions, and actual educational talent, the other professors were apparently not. And regarding the professor's girlfriend – well, they got married, and one of the two professors was going to move to another school. That Professors Bear, Thompson and Hale were all superior lecturers was apparently irrelevant in both cases.

frequently accused of poor lecturing styles and poorly structured syllabi, and my own experiences bear this out – neither of these classes had actual textbooks and although each was supposed to be a lecture, both degenerated at the instructors' whims into seminar-like rambling.

Some people feel that the problem with these international law courses is a flaw in the entire system of international legal education. Comparative law, as it often is called, is a much-maligned field of study; its foremost practitioners have struggled for literally generations to shake off accusations of amateurishness and lack of academic discipline. And from everything I've gathered, these accusations are often right on target. With rare exceptions, and then only in the case of truly stellar faculty, it is hard to find a course on international law that actually teaches you anything practical. For this, you need typically to focus on a single country – say, an introduction to French law – rather than something as nebulously titled as an introduction to Asian law. In the French example, you will study one country's legal system and perhaps contrast it with the American one you partially understand. In the Asian example, you may never even look at a single legal system in detail. If you're particularly unlucky, you may well be left with meaningless platitudes on how 'the Chinese constitution just isn't like the American one because the Chinese always change their constitution and don't follow its words in the same way we would.' So if you aspire to study international law, choose both your courses and your school quite wisely; your practical utility as an international lawyer may hang in the balance.

My final course of the second semester was, in the grand scheme of things, a mere blip on the radar screen, but serves as an interesting cautionary tale. One of the touted assets of studying law at a large university is a law student's supposed ability to register for courses outside of the law school curriculum. In addition to enrolling in virtually any course you want, without receiving law school academic credit, a number of "sufficiently rigorous" non-law courses entitle law students to obtain full credit towards their J.D. degrees. The only restriction is that such courses may only constitute a small percentage of your total credits, and thus your legal education.

Under the right circumstances, someone can make a lot of this opportunity. Prior to the advent of law school courses in feminist jurisprudence, a student might have taken similar graduate-level courses in sociology, history, philosophy and other social sciences to develop a similar concentration of knowledge; today's budding entrepreneur might mix in business courses, and so forth. Some people do exactly what I've just mentioned. But typically, two classes at Cornell receive a lot of attention because they're non-academic and yet intensely practical for the day-to-day lives of schmoozing lawyers – a wine-tasting course and a course in preparing gourmet foods. Offered by the school of hotel management, these classes are often booked solid, and the wines course is surprisingly considered amongst the most challenging courses at the whole university, with an astonishingly high failure rate. But people want to sign up for these classes regardless because the subject matter is interesting and complements the academic ivory tower stuff that students otherwise get so much of. Upper-class students had mentioned these classes since my first year at Cornell, and people would randomly walk through the law school in full chefs' uniforms. As an amateur chef who had been waiting anxiously to take the class, I was thrilled when I got into the gourmet cooking course.

The long and short of this story is that the law school's unique course registration system again intervened to destroy my chances of taking a course I wanted, and this time, did so at the very last minute so as to almost completely deprive me of other options. How could this have happened? Though this may not be the case at other schools, the law school at Cornell prided itself on its independence from the rest of the university – so much so that it would not participate when the university instituted an otherwise universal telephone course registration system, or when it later created completely computerized Internet course selection software. The law school finally decided to computerize its registration under a separate and buggy system in 1999. As a result, not only were law students forced to suffer with terrible registration problems for their law classes, but they were also at a unique disadvantage when they tried to register for courses outside of the law school. In this case, the school's computer claimed to have registered me for the gourmet food class, but when I showed up for class, I was denied admittance. I was later told that a bug in the software was responsible. Unlike any law class I could have missed and learned 'on the job' at the firm, I was not going to be able to learn this material at a law firm. Once I started working for a law firm, I probably wouldn't even have time to cook for myself, let alone take a class about it.

Though I already had enough credits to graduate, I was forced to sign up for a one-credit 'supervised writing' course just to meet the semester's minimum credit requirements. I cannot in good faith tell you that you should investigate the course registration system used by a law school before you decide to attend it, but as my numerous registration problems should indicate, a lot can be said for a school that has figured out how to manage the needs of its students and makes it easy for them to attend the classes they enjoy.[343]

The writing course was essentially an independent study opportunity to work with a professor on a research topic of your mutual choosing. Remember my least favorite class of the second year?[344] Suffice it to say that, in raw desperation for a last-minute option, I found myself again agreeing to do a

---

[343] Conversely, you should realize in advance that you might not actually have the chance to accomplish everything you've planned for your law school career, so treasure the time you have before law school starts.

[344] See Chapter 7, Section M, on Constitutional Law and Political Theory.

paper relating to political theory – my least favorite topic in law school – and under the rules of the independent study program, I had to discuss political theory orally every week or two for around thirty minutes with the supervising professor. Though I loved the professor, I loathed the topic, and rued the course registration system that had produced the situation. In this case, it had cost me a class that I was excited about, and forced me into a situation that I would ultimately not enjoy at all.

3.   Gaining Perspective

Considered from a distance, my third-year classes were the most polar of my law school experience – the good classes were excellent and the bad ones were quite bad. Part of the problem was that in choosing 'interesting sounding classes,' I took a lot of risks on unknown professors, risks that in some cases paid off and in others made me pay for my adventurousness. Another part was that I somewhat blindly believed that the school's supposed dedication to its international program meant that its classes would be more or less safe, when in fact they were not. Past students from the classes would have made this clear to me before I took classes, and several of my friends had strong negative feelings about their international coursework, but I wrote a lot of the negativity off. In retrospect, I should have researched and trusted majority opinions a bit more while avoiding classes that just *sounded* interesting.

But all of this focus on the negative aspects of the third year drowns out a much more important story: I learned a lot about my personal areas of specialization, intellectual property law and commercial law, in the other classes I selected, and saved myself from having to do a lot of on-the-job learning when I arrived for my first day of work at the Bender law firm. I was ready to hit the ground running.

This wasn't the case with some of my classmates, but largely for reasons of luck. By the end of the third year, some people were beginning to hear that their law firms were, for economic reasons, going to reassign them to practice groups other than the ones they had been preparing to join. A number of students who had been studying corporate law were unexpectedly reassigned to become litigators or real estate attorneys as a hedge against the firms' slower transactional practices. Several especially unlucky people had their job offers delayed for six months or rescinded altogether, leaving them scrambling to re-interview at the last minute or find a way to otherwise cope with a significant lack of employment.

Preparing for such contingencies is a challenge for any student, and perhaps the best hedge against uncertainty is to have some set of backup plans – a self-created 'minor' to accompany the optional specialization or unofficial 'major' of your law school career. Coming up with a minor might just be a matter of looking to see what other practice groups your post-graduation law firm has, or what other practice groups you might want to enter if you don't get your first or even second choice when you're hired. When I entered law school, I had considered the prospect that international law might become my major, so much so that an LL.M. seemed potentially worthwhile. By my second year, I knew that intellectual property and commercial law would be my foci, and that international law at best would be a minor. By the end of my third year, and perhaps only because of bad experiences, I felt as if international law might not even be worth a second thought if it was my only remaining option.

Your own interests will likely evolve in a parallel fashion, but the important lesson is just to consider contingency plans and train yourself as broadly as possible – just in case. Through general courses such as Torts, Contracts, and Criminal Law, the first year of law school gives you as much breadth as you will most likely *need*, but you will probably *want* to have just a little bit more secondary training in an area that you feel comfortable pursuing.

E. BEYOND THE CLASSROOM

Though courses, reading assignments and papers were a substantial part of the third year, many 3Ls found ways to minimize the mental pressures of classes – rarely by pretending they either didn't exist, but more often by realizing that as third-years, they didn't have to feel dominated or overwhelmed by professors any more. Some students actually went out for rounds of golf with professors, and a number of students claimed to have spent as much or more of their third years on the golf course as they had spent in classrooms. Practicing one's golf game during the third year isn't only fun, but it's a good practical idea – it's one of those ceaselessly beloved sports that bonds lawyers to lawyers, judges, and clients, bridging otherwise apparently large gaps between generations of men and women. I've never personally had a love for golf, but I've always respected and appreciated those who have taken it up for either personal or professional reasons. Over my lifetime, its value as relaxation or a bonding tool has never decreased, and from my perspective, it's likely to continue into the distant future to be one of those subtly important skills that lawyers cultivate.

I preferred to use parts of the third year, generally vacation breaks, for travel – something I could enjoy with my girlfriend and a passion I could hopefully purge partially from my system by the time I started work at a law firm. Airfares were cheap to destinations as far away as London and Paris, Hawaii and Asia, and though I couldn't convince my girlfriend to travel to Asia, we made time and flew on student-priced fares to Europe and Honolulu, drove up to Toronto, and visited my family in Buffalo. As a 2L at the time, she wouldn't leave school without a backpack full of textbooks or things to work on. I felt as if I had to remind her that we were on vacation.

But in truth, vacation time for a 3L is very different than it is for a 2L. I could leave my worries behind and not have to worry about the consequences. She had to worry about what her grades might be like if she missed her classes, and whether she would fall irretrievably behind in her journal work if she left. All of our vacations were scheduled around deadlines. It was another reminder of what our lives would become when we officially entered the profession.

Other couples went through more considerable strains. During the interviewing and re-interviewing processes, some otherwise stable couples broke apart when they couldn't agree on a mutual city to focus on for interviews, or when one person tried but failed to get an offer of employment in the other's target city. Often, the couples went through agonizing discussions, breaking up, getting back together, and breaking up again weeks or months before their moves to separate cities. But these stories frequently had happy endings; within months after starting their new jobs, one side would be visiting the other and planning to change firms or offices in order to make things work.

Sappy though it may be, true love always prevailed in the end, despite dark days, stacks of law books and employment challenges. By the third year, students who came to law school with spouses had been more or less settled for two years, and there were no dissolutions of future engagements, only signs that new ones were imminent and old ones were soon to be consummated. This doesn't mean that relationships were always rosy, or that obviously dysfunctional relationships were fixed, but rather that good things tended to get better and those who prioritized their schedule around relationships had almost as much time as they wanted.

As had been the case in previous years, unlikely pairings continued to blossom through parties and social events at different times throughout the third year – some between 3Ls and 1Ls, some between 3Ls and 3Ls, and a couple between 3Ls and 2Ls. Many 3Ls' relationships were brief, perhaps never intended to last for more than days or weeks, and others lasted months, with their participants hoping against time in some cases that something more permanent would be forged. But to generalize, the third year was not the right time for new love within the law school's walls. These relationships fell apart more often than they stayed together, and ultimately proved to be better as temporary arrangements of convenience than anything of more lasting character. The advantage was truly on the side of those who bonded earlier.

This, of course, is bound not to be as much the case at other schools, particularly those where the school's distance from a larger city is not nearly as profound as it is in Ithaca, surrounded as it is on all sides by countryside. But then, love works in mysterious ways, and there's no reason that temporary physical separation need end something truly wonderful. It was, and shall probably always be, a matter of the willpower and interests of those involved.

F. THE SPECTER OF THE BAR

No matter how much other things may temporarily occupy one's mind during the third year, a cloud hanging over the head of every 3L is the bar exam, which by the end of the fifth semester or the beginning of the sixth has become a bit more concrete for almost every person in the class. With the exception of those who have little intention of practicing law, virtually everyone knows by this point which bar exam he or she plans to take. And this most often results in last-minute sign-ups for exams,[345] as well as bar preparation courses such as BAR/BRI, PMBR and the like. Bar prep courses may or may not have representatives personally working tables to sign people up at your law school. Signing up early – during your first year – typically gets you a better final price and early access to all of a company's preparatory materials. Price will not matter to those people whose firms cover all of their bar expenses; however, it will definitely impact those who shoulder the expenses themselves – BAR/BRI's prep courses currently cost upwards of $2200, and the far less comprehensive PMBR at least $600.[346]

In jurisdictions requiring the Multistate Professional Responsibility Exam (MPRE), well-prepared third-year students will already have received BAR/BRI preparation materials for at least the MPRE course, if not their first year classes as well. Those third-year students who have not yet taken the MPRE typically do so during the first semester of the third year, and nowhere near the time when they are supposed to be studying for the bar exam – this would be patently unwise. On a related note, many states require bar applicants to pass a separate 'moral character' certification process before they will be allowed to practice law, a process of submitting substantial documentation to the bar for a review which can take up to six months to complete. Not only should the MPRE have been finished by the start of the second semester, but moral character documentation should also be in the mail – lest you significantly delay or otherwise compromise your hasty admission to the bar.

The bar first begins to weigh on shoulders at the point during the third year when students have to complete their moral character applications and other bar-related forms. Many state bars require applicants to show up to a police station to be fingerprinted – both to verify one's identity and perhaps also to

---

[345] Some states require students to sign up for their bar exams literally within weeks of beginning the study of law, and charge significant penalty fees to those who sign up late. As law firms often shoulder the costs of bar exams, those with firm jobs will not be especially concerned by penalty fees, but others should plan ahead to the extent possible. For specific bar sign-up dates, consult your law school or visit the Law.Com bar exam information pages at http://www.law.com/students/index.html.

[346] Note that PMBR does not attempt to cover all of the subjects that BAR/BRI addresses; PMBR only prepares you for the MBE multiple-choice section of most state bar exams.

confirm one's lack of involvement in unsolved crimes – an experience which can be unsettling for especially law-abiding students. But it's just one of the formalities of the process; like other states, California requires applicants to document every residence and job they've had since age 18, provide a large collection of personal and employment references, and document any criminal history, mental health problems, or other issues in their past that may be relevant to their future practice of law.

The second stage of anxiety begins when a massive stack of BAR/BRI books – perhaps nine in all – arrives for each student by mail or requires pick-up at a nearby BAR/BRI office. Any collection of nine books, particularly ones sized like phonebooks, would worry a student who felt that he had to go through all of them, and cause considerable concern as to how anyone could handle such a burden. For now, and despite the tendency to feel otherwise, it's best not to concern oneself much with the details of bar preparation – it is factually fair to say that with the exception of those who have had a really hard time with first-year courses, the post-graduation period of bar study is more than enough time to properly prepare for a state bar exam.

Those who are disproportionately impacted by state bar administrations are foreign students – especially those hailing from civil law, rather than common law jurisdictions. While foreign LL.M. students who hoped to take the bar were at the greatest disadvantage, based not only on language skills but also not having taken many of the core subjects tested on state bars, foreign students graduating with J.D.'s also faced language-related problems, as well, with instructions and actual question content. Stories abound of LL.M. and foreign J.D. students having to repeat bar exams because of language problems.

For everyone else, it will give you no comfort when I say that you should not be concerned at this point, but hold off on worrying, at least for the moment. If you've been taking classes that coincide with those tested on your state bar, you're doing the right thing. Don't worry if you can't schedule classes that cover all of the bar subjects – many of them will be taught, and taught well, in a BAR/BRI class. So if there's any one thing you can do at this point to properly prepare for a bar exam, it's to save enough money to be sure you can take BAR/BRI immediately after you graduate. If you really, truly believe that you had problems with your first-year coursework, get BAR/BRI's Early Bird bar review audio tape series. In your final semester of law school, these will give you a head start on the review you'll need to accomplish during the summer.

G.   CLERKSHIPS

Among the most prestigious jobs one can have after law school is one that only lasts a year or two – a judicial clerkship. Clerkships come in two flavors: state and federal. A federal judicial clerkship is to law review what law review is to law school – the next step up the food chain, and one that gives its possessor even greater bragging rights and job opportunities.[347] Though some state clerkships carry a fairly high level of prestige – Delaware is perhaps the most notable one – there can be little doubt that a federal clerkship is a prize sought by many and achieved by so few as to be especially prestigious.[348]

The benefits of clerking are numerous. On a purely academic level, you can learn about courts from the inside – it's the flip side of class work in civil or criminal procedure, where you learn what happens if you fail to file a motion properly or on time; here you work for the person who makes the decision as to what will actually happen. You will probably personally write the opinions and court orders that decide cases, and thereby learn how to write like a judge.

And you will, as a consequence, go on quite a power trip.[349] Attorneys will suck up to you to curry your favor when your judge hears their cases. Depending on your clerkship, the opinions you write may be of some actual gravity in changing or enforcing existing law. Past the education and the power, you also enhance your resume in a considerable way. Law firms will likely hold employment offers open for your return to the private sector.[350] Your work will entitle you to seek professorial positions at top law schools; clerking is all but a prerequisite for employment at many schools. And your judge may well become your friend for life – so long as you get along – and an influence who could open doors unimaginable to many attorneys. If you're thinking of later work as a judge, a clerkship is an excellent place to begin.

The clerkship search is similar to, but harder than the 2L job search, perhaps even harder than the 3L and 1L job searches. Judges, like law firms during your first year, will not pay for you to fly out to interview; you pay your own way. And unlike the first year, you can't interview at a few different places

---

[347] Note that one needn't be a law review member to succeed in obtaining a clerkship; the positions are open to any applicant from a law school.

[348] Prestige is not the only factor. Though the prestige of hiring a former law clerk is considerable, law firms find that there may even be greater value in employing someone who worked for a local judge – a clerk to a local judge has better access to the way things work nearby and can deliver a lot more practical value than someone who took a prestigious federal clerkship hundreds of miles away. Clerkships localized in the state where one practices can advantageously further familiarize the clerk with local law.

[349] See Chapter 5, Section E, for the story of Professor Hale's Supreme Court Clerkship.

[350] Technically, law firms are not allowed to extend offers of employment to those who have accepted judicial clerkships – to do so risks creating the appearance of impropriety via a seeming attempt to influence individuals working for a sitting judge. As a practical matter, however, many firms make offers to summer associates before either side knows that a clerkship is imminent, and students may actually accept firm offers only later to put them on hold for a clerkship. Many, if not most firms accommodate this delay, and offer something akin to a 'wink wink' about keeping the old job offers open for the day when their clerkships come to an end.

on each trip – it's one trip per judge, and judges are even less interested in interviewing than firms are for third-years. Eligible candidates outnumber open slots by perhaps 10 times the ratio of those seeking and obtaining firm employment, even though there may be fewer total applicants. The long odds and expenses dissuade many people from seeking clerkships in the first place, as do salaries: you'll be lucky to earn 1/3 of a top private sector law firm salary during your time as a federal judicial clerk, and could earn substantially less for state clerkships. The price differential is less considerable for those who would otherwise pursue jobs with smaller law firms, or jobs with regional firms outside of major cities.

If your school holds initial clerkship informational sessions, they may well begin during the second semester of your second year or the first semester of your third. The actual clerkship search will likely begin slightly thereafter, and could conceivably continue through much of your third year. Judges typically attempt to recruit clerks one or two years in advance of their actual needs, which means that a second-year might interview for a clerkship beginning shortly after graduation, and third-years might interview for clerkships beginning either after graduation or a year into their practice with a law firm. Both the interviewing process and vacancies continue to be in a state of flux, however, as judges continue to recruit earlier and earlier, and delayed Senate confirmation of judges creates uncertainty as to when certain judges may take office and thereby require new clerks. The precise deadlines for application will thus vary somewhat from year to year and judge to judge.

Unlike the second-year job search, there are no job fairs and no on-campus interviews for clerkships. Interested candidates send out masses of cover letters and resumes to judges essentially sight unseen, based on advertised judicial openings and booklets listing judges in need of new clerks. Some candidates will look deeply at the judges whom they are applying to work for, taking their political backgrounds (if any) into account by looking to the President who appointed them, and considering the thinking behind some of their historic and recent published opinions. As many judges ask their existing clerks to screen candidates, better-prepared candidates go into interviews knowing as much as possible about all of the various people with whom they might be meeting. Their cover letters may indicate some of their personal and educational connections to the judge and perhaps the current clerks. Other candidates will be less picky and apply to any judge with an open position. In general, it helps to come from a political orientation, background, or educational institution similar to the judge you're applying to, although some judges intentionally pick candidates with different politics and many hope to pick candidates from top schools regardless of whether they themselves attended those schools. The pickiest judges tend to be those in the federal courts and at the top appellate court levels, whereas the least picky are those in trial courts and state courts.

In addition to the cover letters and resumes, candidates generally must secure two or three positive letters of recommendation from faculty at their law schools. Professors with academic or personal ties to the judges have greater sway than others, and well-known professors also tend to carry greater weight when producing letters of recommendation. But these letters can only get candidates so far. Judges are very grade- and personality-conscious, and it's hard for students in the bottom 50% of even a top law school's class to win clerkships at the federal level. Judges look for a strong feeling of personal connection or respect from the candidate, and if they feel it, they may well make an offer of employment within only hours of an in-person interview.

Unlike law firm offers of employment, judicial clerkship offers are typically very hard to turn down. Once a candidate has flown out to meet with a judge, and perhaps the judge's clerks, and is then offered a job, the candidate is generally obliged as a matter of custom to accept the offer unless something about the interview strongly suggested to the candidate that something would not be right about the employment situation. Judges frequently expect "yes" or "no" answers within a very short period of time after making the offers, and there have been rare publicized stories of judicial and student bad faith dealing such that either a judge has retracted an offer before acceptance or a student has attempted to get out of a clerkship after accepting it. Students can find their careers blemished for doing this; judges have occasionally been outed in newspapers for betraying students, as well.

Is pursuing a judicial clerkship worth your time? The answer depends on your ambitions, financial needs, and success in law school. If you attend a good school, or have solid grades or a good connection to a judge, you have a better than average chance of getting a clerkship. If you have no ambition of litigating, or becoming a judge or a law professor, going after a clerkship might not be worth the bother. It also might not be the best idea if you need a strong salary immediately after graduation and have better options, though your later starting salary at most law firms will be somewhat higher if you clerk.[351]

It's also worthwhile to mention that it's possible to squander the entire clerkship search process by aiming too high – something you might not know until you've had an extended bad run of mailings or interviews. Speaking with your law school's career office, or professors who themselves clerked, will give you an idea of where to aim on the judicial ladders – state versus federal, trial versus appellate courts, famous judges versus magistrate judges, and so on. Both resources will also be handy in suggesting courses you should plan to take

---

[351] Most law firms start former judicial clerks at one salary level higher than their normal starting salary, such that an incoming first-year associate would start out with a second-year associate's pay.

in order to make yourself a superior candidate and successful clerk; traditional recommendations include the classes Federal Courts, Conflict of Laws, Advanced Civil Procedure, perhaps Criminal Procedure, and in some cases, clinical work or seminars dealing with trials and litigation. If you're particularly interested in bankruptcy or patent courts, you should also give consideration to the special educational requirements such courts will look for in their clerks.

Unlike second- and third-year employment, which may hit 99-100% at top schools, the clerkship rates are considerably lower – 10-15% is considered quite good for a law school. That number is somewhat deceiving in that far fewer people seek clerkships than permanent legal jobs, but many more people end the clerkship hunt disappointed and without a position. If you plan to seek a clerkship, make sure you start grooming yourself for that goal early – first when you're choosing schools, then again and again when you're taking classes, meeting professors, studying for exams, choosing courses, attending social events where judges are speaking, and requesting recommendations from faculty. Every step will be critical to securing the clerkship you desire.

H. On Graduation and Options Beyond Immediate Employment

For a brief period of time surrounding the most final of final exams, the end of law school seemed anti-climactic. Most 3Ls were far from stressed out, and exams were nothing more than a formality. Some, if not most people were operating under the assumption that their third-year exams were relatively worthless – jobs secured, no more books, no more teachers' dirty looks – finishing the last semester and going on to a high-paying job of some sort or another were all but guaranteed. Some people – ones with guaranteed employment and low-risk final exams – talked about bringing flasks full of booze into at least one of their finals, and later boasted about having been entirely inebriated by the time the exam ended. I personally found myself with a celebratory bottle in hand immediately after I finished my last class, as I didn't want to wait several days for the official end of most of my classmates' exams.

A few people at my school and perhaps substantially more people outside were looking to a somewhat more stressful, but still comparatively light conclusion to law school. Uncertain job prospects meant that final grades still mattered, but by this point, grades were about as predictable as they could get. Only the tiniest fraction of law students believed that their final semester might not, for one reason or another, be their actual final semester.

There are, in fact, no big surprises in the last round of final exams – their formats don't change from the way they've been for the past five semesters, and when you're done with them, you feel only the slightest sense of accomplishment. That's because graduation, as you know well by now, is not enough in most states to make you an actual attorney. It's an event important more for families and for the law school, which finally get to see you move on beyond academia and into the next stage of your life. At least that's true for most people. Some will, of course, remain students for some period of time after law school, continuing a joint-degree program or starting a post-J.D. course of study. Some students will have already applied to LL.M. programs at other schools to fill in the gap between their J.D. and actual employment,[352] and rare others will go on to pursue degrees tangentially related to the law, perhaps in hopes of pursuing later careers in academia.[353]

Even these students will typically have spent the month or so before graduation inviting family members and friends to the official ceremonies held by their law schools. The ceremonies will range from the elaborate to the austere, and from the law school-specific to the university-wide. Owing to its independence from the larger university, my law school offered two separate graduation ceremonies – a law school Convocation attended by virtually every 3L and their families, and a University-wide Commencement held two weeks later with far less 3L attendance. Formal celebrations sounded great, but something a little less buttoned-up seemed a more appropriate way to commemorate the end of the law school experience. Eric Sprague and I organized one final party – this time, a post-exams happy hour ultimately sponsored by the Law Students Association – and titled it "Ready to Take Off?" with one final Sprague-themed poster, this one with our hero seemingly naked in front of the law school. As would be expected for any end-of-school party, especially one with an open bar tab, attendance was superb and the mood was entirely upbeat. It was a fitting near-conclusion to our time as law students.

From a staging standpoint, graduation day was also just about perfect. Letters had arrived a day or two earlier to let each of us know that we had been officially cleared for graduation; the alternative seemed all but inconceivable to most people, and there wouldn't be any last-minute worrying that someone wasn't about to actually receive a diploma. As families filed into the campus's tiny ceremonial hall, students met outside the building and adjusted the collars of the capes attached to their rented gowns. Cornell's red graduation robes looked like the costumes of medieval squires, complete with small black velvet capes and matching octagonal caps – not similar in any way to undergraduate

---

[352] Many of the post-J.D. options available to students may be found at http://www.abanet.org/legaled/postjdprograms/postjdc.html.

[353] Some of the degree options include the Doctor of Juridical Science/Doctor of the Science of Law (S.J.D.) degree, a two-year post-LL.M. or post-J.D. degree for those interested in teaching; the Master of Comparative Law (M.C.L.) degree, a one-year course in international law that many schools now fold into their LL.M. programs; the Master of Dispute Resolution (M.D.R.) degree, a one-year program; and the Master of Public Policy (M.P.P.) degree, a two-year program.

outfits. It wouldn't have been unprecedented in Ithaca if graduation day was muggy or rainy, but it was a sunny, slightly windy early afternoon in May, just cool enough in the late Ithaca spring to make comfortable the wearing of such elaborate, heavy costumes. Lines were formed and name cards were passed out to hand off to the announcer right before each of us walked up on stage. Then all of the students were led inside.

It was dark inside the small auditorium, but the cramped stage and seats were full of familiar faces – many of the school's professors arrived on stage in their own graduating caps and gowns, and families filled virtually every seat in the room. Slight celebratory music played in the background before a brief speech, which was followed by the procession of students, one by one, to shake hands with the dean and receive the applause of the assembled crowd. J.D. recipients went first, followed by J.D./LL.M. students, LL.M. students, and other international program participants. When all of the students had finished walking the stage, the crowd listened to additional, fittingly congratulatory speeches offered by one student and one faculty member who had been elected to speak by the 3L class. The student had been a sanitation worker at one point before coming to law school, had previously been elected class representative, and was widely respected for his quiet eloquence and independent thought. Our chosen faculty member was Laura Edwards, the Civil Procedure professor who had taught at least half of the class and intimidated almost as many – it was the second year in a row she had been elected speaker.

When the student spoke, he recalled the special things about our class – the camaraderie, some of the funnier and more controversial events during our time there, and the quality of the people we had been lucky enough to know. Professor Edwards implored and trusted the crowd to do great things with our lives, and to remember the motivations that had brought us that far. Both speeches were fused with passion and rippled with the sense of loss we would feel when graduation figuratively cast us to the wind. But the ceremony was far more optimistic than somber. Each speaker left the stage to strong applause, though if parents had tears in their eyes, students most definitely did not. Most would be studying for the bar exam soon thereafter and were not going to be leaving Ithaca, or each other, for at least another two months.

At the end of the ceremony, the auditorium was buzzing with excitement and pride, but when the event drew to a close, there was no tossing of caps en masse towards the sky, nor any screaming and yelling – it was unclear at that moment whether this was because the event was for graduates rather than undergraduates, or because the students were just not that sort of crowd. In retrospect, it was as much a result of the outfits as the setting and the people. We were now professionals, not carefree kids, and we marked the event not with chaos, but rather with lots of reciprocal congratulating. Friends introduced their families to one another for the first time since starting law school, and in many cases, families met students' friends for the first time, as well. Around the same time, the group walked back to the law school's courtyard together for an outdoor celebratory meal, and disbanded shortly thereafter, some attending an evening party sponsored by the law school and organized by several students. It had been dignified but passionate, orderly yet exciting. This was the end of law school that wasn't really an end at all.

CHAPTER 11

barbri
ITHACA NY
67715
JEREMY HORWITZ
113-115 VALENTINE PL. #103
ITHACA, NY 14850
SUMMER 2001
CALIFORNIA
800-995-5227
Exam results are scheduled to be mailed and available on the Internet (at 6:00 p.m.) on November 16, 2001. Please retain this badge for reference to your registration and application numbers.
http://www.calbar.org

ID CARDS, CALIFORNIA BAR EXAM AND BAR/BRI BAR REVIEW COURSE

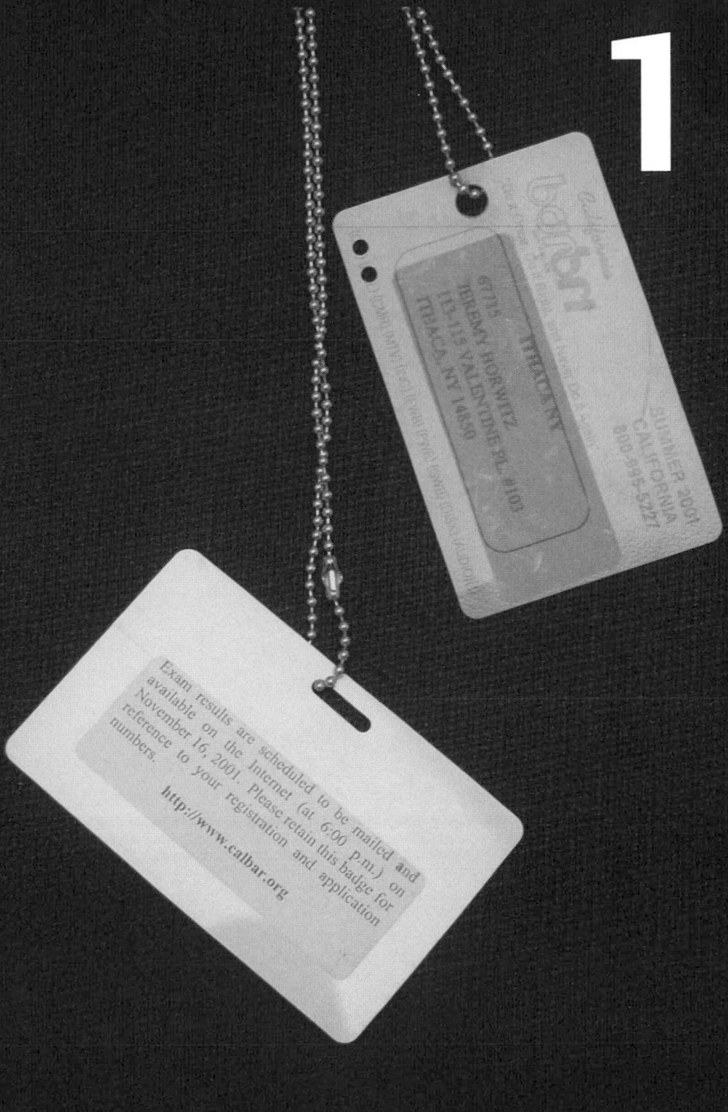

Graduation from law school is bittersweet, not only because it might be the last time you see some of your closest friends, but also because the bar exam still stands as a barrier to making full use of your law degree. In essence, graduation from law school merely means that you've finished an extended course of instruction in the law, knowledge from which must now be demonstrated to experts in the state(s) where you hope to practice.

Several introductory points should be made about bar examinations. First and foremost, bar examinations are not, by any meaning of the words, just routine tests. They are not given by law schools. They are generally not given at law schools. And even though many students feel that law school examinations are among the most challenging they've ever prepared for or taken, bar exams are in a completely different league. Like medical boards and other professional certification tests, bar exams are prepared by individuals with authority granted by the state, and they are not something you want to do more than once. Some people will fail bar exams four or five times before passing; rare people will fail the exams as many as thirty times – a feat that would require fifteen or more years to accomplish, as bar exams are offered at most twice per year. And you can't become a lawyer until you pass a bar exam. That's a long time to wait.

Secondly, the general public does not understand any of this, and people traditionally have needed to be educated one at a time. Several law students have noted that friends or relatives outside the profession expected that by scheduling their summer weddings a year in advance, but on dates very close to bar exams, the law students could just schedule their studies around the weddings. It just doesn't work that way, at least, for diligent law students taking the bar exams offered by many larger states.[354] Though the friends and relatives clearly don't understand as much when they're asking, any person who would request this is literally demanding that the law student risk the prospect of not becoming a lawyer and quite possibly losing or not finding a job.

Third and finally, though bar exams are tough, they can indeed be mastered and passed – however, your chances are often best on your first try. Over the six-year period from 1996-2001, 67% of all takers passed bar exams given in the United States, though the number has declined over those years from 70% per year to 65-66%.[355] But during the same period, almost four-fifths of first-time takers nationally passed their state bar exams. A 20% chance of failure is not good, but it's better than a 33-35% chance, for sure. And it should

---

[354] Of course, top students at schools with historically flawless passage rates for a given jurisdiction may believe themselves exceptions to the general rule; however, even the best schools often have 4-10% bar exam failure rates for their nearest major jurisdictions, and some fraction of these numbers unquestionably comes from overconfident students who are less than diligent in their studies.

[355] All bar exam statistics in this chapter are derived from annual factual statistics published by the National Committee of Bar Examiners at http://www.ncbex.org/stats.htm.

be noted that to "pass" is truly to pass. Though exams are graded, exam takers simply either score above the minimum passing number or below it. In many states, most people who pass never learn their actual scores and some people never want to know them. Some states publish the names of each exam's highest male and female scorers, but many do not. People who fail are generally given their scores solely to prepare to re-take the exams again. The information above should be sobering, not discouraging. All things being equal, your chances of passing the bar are better than your chances of failing, especially as a first-timer. This chapter will assume, however, that you want some idea of what it takes to pass the most punishing of all bar exams – California's – and that you're not going to choose to practice law in a state other than your top choice just because it has a shorter or easier bar exam.

A. WHY YOUR BAR EXPERIENCE CANNOT BE ANY WORSE THAN CALIFORNIA'S

California, like every other state, has its own bar – an official organization of practicing attorneys who, with authority of the state's highest court, set standards of admission to practice law within the state's borders. With only rare exceptions, each state's bar offers two exam administrations per year to applicants, each administration utilizing a fixed combination of essays and multiple-choice questions to determine who is and is not competent to practice law within the jurisdiction. Examination fees will likely total upwards of $1000 per exam, not including any preparatory courses you take or living expenses for the month or two you will study prior to the exam. The typical law school graduate will spend approximately $5000 in total relating to a single bar exam; most people take preparatory courses in order to avoid re-taking exams.

As suggested above, for first-time bar takers, the national average pass rate over the last six years is approximately 79%, meaning that nationally, an average of 21% of first-time exam takers were deemed unqualified to practice law by virtue of having failed the exam. But in actuality, the pass rates vary dramatically from state to state – two states often fail an average of over 35% of first-time takers, while two others fail fewer than 10%.[356]

Many states have challenging bar exams; several are reputed to be the country's worst. New York's is often claimed to be one of the hardest because it tests so many subjects – 22 or so, depending on how you count them – but there are others, including Mississippi and Virginia, with as many as 23 subjects each. New Jersey, by contrast, may seem the easiest, with only six subjects and two days of testing.[357] On paper, Mississippi's seems especially bad, because

---

[356] See Appendix B's Bar Exam Table.

[357] Some people take the New York and New Jersey bar exams simultaneously, alternating days of attendance between the two states; the theory is that even a person who bombs

you have not only all of those subjects to learn, but also three full days of examination to go through. In New York and Virginia, by comparison, the exam lasts only two days, and as a result, though you need to study many subjects, you won't actually be tested on much of what you've studied. In Virginia, however, you'll have to wear formal attire to take the exam.[358] Could it get any worse than all this?

Superficially, some state bar exams appear easy to pass. Wyoming has the country's shortest bar exam, at 1.5 days, and one state – Wisconsin – even permits those who completed three years at the state's only law school to practice law without ever sitting for a bar exam.[359] These practices are far outside the norm: two-day exams are the majority, nine states have 2.5-day exams, and seven states have three-day exams.

But length of exams and number of subjects only tell part of the story, and not even an especially important part of it. Historic passage rates give you a much better sense of just how hard an exam will be. And by that standard alone, California is just about the worst place in the country you could take a bar exam.[360] Mississippi's "especially bad" three-day exam has a typical summer passage rate of over 80%; California's three-day exam fails as many as 50% of all takers.[361] In New York, a passing score on a bar essay is a 4.5 out of

---

the tougher New York exam will wind up with the consolation prize of New Jersey passage. It works for some, but I've heard multiple tales of people failing both exams at the same time, leading one to wonder whether concentrating on just one jurisdiction might be a better idea. Notably, despite the comparatively narrow subject matter of the New Jersey Bar Exam, the state's average pass rate (72%) is slightly lower than New York's (73%).

[358] Under the Virginia Bar's rules, the "manner of dress for the examination shall conform to the standard of suitable attire for a lawyer appearing in a court of record: *i.e.*, a suit or jacket with tie for males, or a suitable dress or suit for females." You can read about this and Virginia Board of Bar Examiners policies at *Rules* Section VII (Nov. 2001), available at http://www.vbbe.state.va.us/VBBE_Rules11_2001Ver.pdf.

[359] Wisconsin doesn't require graduates of two Wisconsin law schools to take their bar exam if their schools certify them to practice law; this is truly the exception, not the norm. Note that Wisconsin does require graduates of out-of-state law schools to pass their bar exam, and the state's average first-time passage rate over six years is approximately 86%.

[360] Though Louisiana's average first-time passage rate over a six-year period (approximately 63%) is slightly lower than California's (approximately 65%), Louisiana typically has under 1,000 total test takers per year, whereas California generally has over 12,000. Thus California fails as many people in one year as Louisiana does in six. Additionally, repeat Louisiana exam-takers are substantially more likely to pass than repeat California exam-takers, such that if you fail Louisiana's exam the first time, you have a better than 50% chance of passing the second time. Not so in California, where you have about a 25% chance on your second time.

[361] The five lowest state passage rates, averaged over six years, are Louisiana (62% first-time passage), California (65%), Delaware (66%), Nevada (67%), and Maine (69%). From 1998-2001, California failed 50% of those who took its exam every year, counting both

10. In California, you might need a score of 70 out of 100 to pass, depending on the year you take the exam. It is considered grueling, despite the fact that it has around 13 testable subjects, namely because you actually have to know all of the subjects; there are true stories about people who have screamed and quit halfway through, or collapsed from heart attacks during testing. And that's honestly not even taking into account what happens when there are earthquakes or other problems that affect everyone at a test site, situations that have actually occurred and that students have actually worked through. Taken together, the length, failure rate, and high performance standards make it easy to conclude that California's bar is the country's toughest.

This isn't to say, of course, that every bar exam is a bear. Several states have passage rates above or significantly above the national average – Utah, New Mexico, and North Dakota only fail roughly 10% of the people who take their exams.[362] And several large states are above the national average, as well, including Illinois, Florida, Texas, and Ohio.[363]

Of course, aggregated bar passage rates can be somewhat misleading. Graduates of ABA-accredited schools historically have substantially outperformed graduates of unaccredited schools, and graduates of accredited in-state schools tend to outperform graduates from outside schools, enough so that one's chances of success statistically increase by simply attending an accredited school in the same state where you hope to practice.[364] Moreover, students can also take bar preparatory courses, which often raise passage rates.

Regardless of what bar exam you take, the first day will typically consist of essay writing; in California, there are three hours to complete three essays on the first morning, and three additional hours to complete a single extended "performance test" essay in the afternoon. Whereas the one-hour essays require

---

first-time and repeat takers. Prior to 1998, the state failed similar percentages, though not every year. See National Committee of Bar Examiners, *Bar Admission Statistics*, available at http://www.ncbex.org/stats.htm.

[362] The highest passage rate jurisdictions are Utah (92%), New Mexico (91%), North Dakota (90%), Montana (89%), Minnesota (88%) and South Dakota (88%).

[363] Among large states, the highest passage rates can be found in Illinois (84%), Florida (81%), Texas (81%), Ohio (80%), and Massachusetts (78%). Pennsylvania (74%), New York (73%), and California (65%) round out the large state pack.

[364] This is a good rule to follow unless you are able to attend a school ranked in the national top 10 or 15. These schools frequently have higher per-school passage percentages outside their home states than even the top schools within those states. For example, California's top-ranked Stanford (93% CA Bar passage in July 2001) was surpassed by both Yale (98%) and the University of Chicago (97%). Other top schools, such as Harvard (92%), NYU (92%), Northwestern (92%), and the University of Virginia (91%) scored high above the state average. Statistics from numerous schools, including these, are published by the State Bar of California in *General Statistics Report - July 2001 California Bar Examination*, available at http://www.calbar.ca.gov/calbar/pdfs/0701stat.pdf.

you to know specific areas of federal and state law, the performance test provides you with whatever laws you need to know, in addition to a large collection of factual documents, and requires you in a larger essay to apply the law to the facts or vice-versa. In California, each performance test counts for as many points as two essays. Notably, New York's bar exam has five essays, one performance test, and 50 state-specific multiple-choice questions on its first day. Every state has its own point calculation system, and most adjust the number of points needed to pass an exam on an exam-by-exam basis.

The second day of most bar exams consists entirely of national multiple-choice questions. Forty-eight states use the Multistate Bar Examination (MBE), a 200-question, six-hour test covering seven subjects – con law, contracts, crim law, crim pro, evidence, real property (essentially first-year property), and torts.[365] Criminal procedure is tested only lightly, and contracts typically includes questions that some state bars and law schools might separately categorize as "UCC" or "sales." The MBE is afforded different weights in each state relative to the essays; in California, the MBE is worth approximately 35% of the total points one can receive. Past takers have passed the MBE with raw scores of approximately 65%, though the numbers vary slightly from year to year. The raw score is scaled upwards to adjust for test site discrepancies.

After two days have passed, most young lawyers-to-be have finished their labors and can take a much-needed break from reality. Not so in California, which continues on the third full day with another set of three essays in the morning and a final three-hour performance test in the afternoon. No one ever said that becoming a lawyer was going to be easy.

B.   TWO LONG MONTHS OF LABOR: INSIGHTS AND AXIOMS

Unless your school schedules graduation ceremonies especially late, you should expect to have roughly two full months to study for the bar exam – a change from practices of years past, when students had as little as a month, and where the exams may in fact have been commensurately less difficult. Some schools do persist in the one-month tradition, however, a fact which would have concerned me quite a bit if I was studying for a difficult bar exam.[366]

There's good and bad news here. Let's start with the good: by the time you take the exam, no one actually expects you to remember every detail from all of your first-year classes. The bad part is that you'll essentially spend the better part of two months after graduation re-learning all of it anyway, and in some

---

[365] Only Louisiana and the State of Washington avoid the MBE.

[366] It needn't prove fatal when selecting a law school, however. In 2001, the U.S. News first-tier University of Washington School of Law proudly announced an 80% California Bar Exam pass rate for its students, despite having only a single month for preparation between graduation and the exam.

cases, gaining an accurate understanding of it for the first time.

At this point, it's worth going through a few counterintuitive, interlinking axioms of bar preparation that you'll hear during law school, and debunking them where appropriate. Getting rumors out of the way is a good first step to getting yourself prepared for what your bar experience will actually be like; these are subjects you should confirm with recent graduates from your school once you get closer to actually taking your exam.

1. *The Bar Exam is the Only Law School Experience That is Actually Worse Than People Say It Is: False.*

Bar exams are hard. They require plenty of serious advance preparation and, depending on the exam in question, may have a crushing failure rate. Third-year students often live in fear of bar exams, and those who have already passed bar exams subtly or not-so-subtly stoke that fear. In many cases, the mythology exceeds the actual experience. What will bother you more than anything is whatever level of self-induced stress you build up from beginning to end, brought on by the challenge of coping with huge amounts of material in such a short amount of time. Some people needlessly ratchet up their stress levels to the point of nausea, tremors, or physical exhaustion, but that's strictly individual psychology and by no means a necessary part of the experience. In these regards, a bar exam is no worse than the typical first year of law school, and in some ways, better because you have actually dealt with the material before, and by then should be accustomed to managing your time.[367]

A bar exam can, of course, be worse than the stories, but only if three conditions are met. First, you must be taking the exam in an objectively challenging jurisdiction. Second, you must not have really understood the testable subjects the first time you learned them. Third, you must also find it impossible to learn the subjects during the bar review process, when they are taught in a significantly easier fashion. But I doubt that you will meet all three conditions – if you sign up for BAR/BRI or a comparably comprehensive bar review course, you will unquestionably learn everything you need just by following their schedule. If you plan to prepare on your own, or think you can vacation in the break between your graduation and your exam, you will be far more likely to find both preparation and the exam itself to be awful experiences – and ones you will go through a second or third time.

Thus it follows that if you want to come closest to a guarantee of success, I

---

[367] Comparing bar exam preparation to the first year of law school may seem to some like apples and oranges, but from the standpoints of challenge, intensity, and stress, they're very similar. Some people, of course, relax during their first year of law school, just as some people relax during the bar preparation period. Most people – especially most successful people – didn't think about relaxing during either.

would recommend that you not skip even a week of bar review, and people lacking comfort with any of their bar subjects should absolutely not waste a moment of the prescribed BAR/BRI course of study. Moreover, if you have the slightest suspicion that you might not be comfortable with more than one subject, make certain that you sign up for a preparatory course. It will make your life much easier than it would be if you re-took the exam multiple times.

2.   *Your Best Law School Subjects Will Be Your Worst Bar Subjects: Partially True.*

During law school, you'll often hear it said that your best subjects on the bar exam will be your worst subjects from law school. This was at least somewhat true for me, and all of the people I've known. The causes are counterintuitive: first, the exam frequently tests subjects differently from how law professors test them. There are large areas of similarity in the subject matter, but the bar examiners are a bit more predictable than law professors in the knowledge they want you to demonstrate that you possess.

Additionally, people tend to write off areas of the exam as 'known' and therefore not meriting review based on a high grade in law school or a level of comfort with the material. It bears mentioning that every single topic, no matter how small, deserves at least a cursory re-consideration at bar time so as to be sure that your class didn't skip something the bar examiners find important.

3.   *During Bar Preparation, Cockiness Equals Failure: Typically True.*

In my experience, in difficult jurisdictions, this axiom is almost entirely accurate. Every year, a surprising number of unquestionably bright and capable people write off meaningful bar preparation for some reason or another. I've heard stories of law review editors who figured they could travel to other countries and spend most of the summer relaxing, stories of people who decided to work for part of the summer and study for only a short while, and even some stories of people who decided not to study too much at all. Though these sorts of study shortcuts work once in a rare while for a few true geniuses, and people educated at top schools can get away with a lot in gentle jurisdictions, I personally know of too many otherwise capable people who failed their first California bar exams because of this sort of thinking. Don't believe that you're Einstein unless you've done something to equal his success, and even then, at least err a little on the side of humility.

By the same token, however, once you've completed your preparation, and you feel at least somewhat ready, don't be afraid to possess confidence. Psychologically, there may be nothing better than to walk into an exam of bar exam caliber with a mild smile and a little bit less fear than you've been dragging around for the previous two months.

4. On the Bar, Lack of Preparedness Equals Failure: Totally True.

This axiom is entirely true, but the problem is ascertaining what level of preparedness is adequate. If you're taking a preparatory class such as BAR/BRI, the answer is clear: you need to learn whatever they tell you to learn, and do all of the practice essays, questions, and exams they tell you to do. If you think you can skip a preparatory class, you're increasing your risk of failure considerably, but you'll need to come to an independent conclusion about how much you need to prepare yourself for your exam.

Every state bar sets its own minimum passing level of knowledge, and while it's a good general rule to trust BAR/BRI's judgment as to what and how much you need to have studied, it's also important to be realistic about what you need to know. This does not mean that you should, at any point, say to yourself that you are just not going to read something over because you know you'll never understand it. To the contrary, you should at least give all of the materials an once-over. But you shouldn't kill yourself to understand the Rule Against Perpetuities if you didn't understand it in law school and can't quite get it after reading it a few times over. BAR/BRI will even say as much to you. There are no A's or A+'s on a bar exam.[368] Be realistic in aiming for a passing score and, unless you have something to prove to the world, don't burn yourself out trying for perfection.

5. You Can't Spend All of Your Time Studying: Totally True.

I wholeheartedly believe this axiom, even though it might appear to run counter to previous axioms on preparedness. You simply need to leave yourself small but meaningful study breaks. Preparations for bar exams have been known to drive people batty. There's a lot to study for and studying is generally an eight-to-ten-hour-per-day endeavor for first-time takers who are likely to pass. During this stretch of two months, you need to take daily breaks, at least for lunch and dinner, perhaps for as much as an hour more per day, depending on how long you spend eating. You need to have one day of the week where at least half of your day is spent continuously doing something wholly unrelated to the bar exam, and hopefully wholly unrelated to law. You also need sleep. At least six or seven hours of it every night, no matter what. And as much as you can get each night before the exam.

This axiom is coupled with a difficult reality that some people will have to accept. During this time, it may not be easy to be an active part of a family, especially in a caretaking role with significant responsibilities for children or

---

[368] Several states publish the names of the top person or people who receive the highest scores on a given exam, but this is somewhat unusual, and moreover, is practically irrelevant to anything but the fragile human ego.

other relatives. Full-time employees will also find bar preparation to tax their schedules, as well. I think it would be fair to say that the only thing worse than spending two months preparing for a bar exam is repeating it all a second time. Optimize the chances that you'll only take it once, and consider that this might mean two months of relative isolation from friends and family. Then again, others have passed while working part-time jobs or taking care of children. Your mileage will vary, but it's my gut feeling that it's important to spend a significant enough amount of time preparing that you don't throw away the time and money you've invested in any given bar administration.

On that note, two stories come to mind – the first was shared by a friend who took the California Bar Exam while sitting next to a stranger who was on his fourth try. The stranger claimed that his father had taken the California Bar 32 times before passing – if you can believe him, that equals at least sixteen years of test-taking, each time at an expense of at least several hundred dollars. The second story is of a man whom I overheard mentioning to an exam proctor that the July 2001 examination was his 10th or 11th attempt to pass and that he had been nearly bankrupted trying to become a lawyer – a move he advised others against. These two stories are clearly atypical, but illustrative of both what some people go through to become lawyers, and the amount of time it might take for someone who comes unprepared for the examination.

> 6.   *If Your State's Pass Rate is Low, Somebody From Your School, or in Your BAR/BRI Class, Has to Fail: Not True, And Misleading.*

One of the most commonly enunciated fears of first-time bar exam takers is that statistics dictate that they will fail the exam. The logic goes something like this: I'm in the bottom 50% of my class, and 50% of people fail the exam; therefore, I am probably going to fail. Wrong, statistically and practically. As a starting point, even in the incredibly difficult jurisdiction of California, 50% of all takers may fail the exam, but only 35% of first-time takers fail. Secondly, some schools have disproportionately low rates of passage, while others tend to do disproportionately well year after year, so if you're at a good school taking the exam for your first time, you're in even better shape. Third, but not last, some really smart people fail California's exam each year, and some far less brilliant people pass. In other words, there's something more to passing than being a genius and/or at the top of one's class.

In fact, the bar exam is entirely about paced preparation and following instructions. Prepare the way you're told by the experts and you will probably pass, even if you haven't had the best time, grade-wise, in law school. This holds true for every person in your class. If everyone in your class or at your school prepares properly, no one fails. But as you'll read below, not everyone will prepare properly.

7. *You Can Study for a Bar Exam While Holding a Summer Job: Depends on the Person and Exam.*

Although my initial reaction to the question of whether people should work while studying for their first bar exams is "no way," it's fair to say that my personal take is flavored heavily by my experiences with California's Bar Exam. While it's true that almost every student who tries to work while studying for California's Bar will fail the exam, a few people, of course, may pull it off, and most certainly people in other states – including New York – have passed while working at least part time for most of the summer.

People who fail tough bar exams most often do so for one of three reasons: they didn't take a bar preparation course such as BAR/BRI; they didn't follow all of BAR/BRI's instructions, either during bar preparation or during the exam itself; or they continued to have stress and time management issues even after BAR/BRI classes. This means that they will fail if they chronically disregard the standard preparatory schedule for whatever reason – especially likely if they're spending their days working instead of studying, if they're having a messy relationship breakup, or if they're in the middle of a hard-core, time-consuming relationship. This also means that they will quite possibly fail if they don't train themselves either before or during bar prep to manage their time and thereby answer questions within the timeframes recommended by BAR/BRI – 1.8 minutes per multiple choice question and one hour per essay.

If you want to be safe, treat the two months before the exam as a time for studying and training your mind, not for other distractions or activities. My philosophy is that you give up these two months now, push yourself a bit, and you'll be glad you did when you don't have to take the exam again. Many firms – assuming you're employed by one when you have to take the bar for a second time – will actually mandate that you take a two-month leave of absence to study. Better to pass the first time.

C. DAY-TO-DAY: HOW YOU MIGHT, OR MIGHT NOT PREPARE

It's hopefully now obvious from the foregoing discussion that the best way to pass your state's bar is to arrive prepared. I spent a bit of time trying to determine what it would take to prepare properly for either the New York or California bars, and the best route appeared to be the BAR/BRI prep course – owned today by The Thomson Corporation, which also owns Westlaw. There are other "competing" bar review courses, though in fact several of the other courses have been owned by the same company for a period of time. BAR/BRI is generally acknowledged to be the best of them.

1. BAR/BRI and PMBR

Upper-classmen made clear that BAR/BRI was a must-do course; it was priced at a bit above $2000, but many people believed that it almost guaranteed bar passage, if taken seriously. I came to endorse this view. Those of us with jobs at firms would have the course expense paid for; those with public sector work, or those lacking jobs, would need to pay for the course on their own. Anecdotal evidence suggests that self-teaching the bar exam subjects without professional preparatory materials yields results that are quite disappointing; so disappointing in fact that unless you're in possession of a complete set of second-hand materials, including video or audio tapes and blank outlines to complete, I would have to say that self-preparation is probably a fool's errand. If you need to get another $2000 in financial aid to sign up for BAR/BRI, do it, and if possible, sign up for the class in your first year of law school so that you can get your hands on all of BAR/BRI's law school prep materials for free. I hesitated to do this and lost out.

For bar exam purposes, BAR/BRI offers live or videotaped lectures at numerous sites in each state, and also sells at-home tapes for those who cannot attend the lectures. Mostly out of peer pressure, and based largely on a subtle pitch that plays to the fears of Type-A students, I also gave strong consideration to a "supplemental" prep course called PMBR, which offers separate three- or six-day courses focused solely on the MBE portion of the examination.[369] PMBR does not claim to be enough, on its own, to prepare you to pass an entire bar exam. Rather, it claims to help you prepare for the MBE-tested subjects, and publishes statistics -- clearly influenced by those whose primary instruction came from BAR/BRI – suggesting that high percentages of people "supplementing" with PMBR pass their bar exams.

Though I originally enrolled in both BAR/BRI and PMBR, I cancelled my PMBR enrollment after they started to change their dates and locations around at the last minute,[370] and I found it unusually difficult to contact and deal with their customer service department. I never gave strong consideration to Bar Passers or Micromash, two other courses which neither appeared to be offered

---

[369] PMBR offers a three-day course for $325-$395, a six-day course for $595-695, both courses together for $725-895, and supplementary materials such as workbooks, audio tapes, CDs, and flash cards for $50-295. The prices vary based on a student's membership in certain legal organizations.

[370] This problem is apparently not unique either to my school or to the particular year when I took the bar exam. PMBR's national promotional materials now explicitly reserve the right to change schedules and deny students the right to a refund after they've received course materials. Numerous students have found themselves in the unenviable situation of scheduling events around the PMBR dates, receiving course materials, and then being told to show up for new PMBR dates that conflict with their prior schedules.

locally or offer the same level of expertise as BAR/BRI advertised.

If you sign up for BAR/BRI, you will receive a large collection of books and a calendar they advise you to follow almost every day until the exam is administered – complete with an instruction to stop studying the night before the exam. The collection of books is almost staggering – a stack of phonebook-sized compendia of practice multiple choice and essay questions, plus three separate volumes full of extensive course outlines covering the breadth and depth of material tested on each state's bar. Every state has its own collection of BAR/BRI books, though there is overlap in materials between those 48 states using the MBE for its multiple choice questions.

If you sign up for PMBR, you will also receive additional instructions, another set of practice question books, and sets of tapes or CDs to use for practice MBE questions. PMBR will recommend that you replace significant portions of the BAR/BRI calendar with PMBR-authored lesson plans. As of this writing, PMBR appears to swap some of BAR/BRI's MBE practice questions with ones that are frighteningly hard, and administers 'practice' MBE exams of such artificially high difficulty that almost no one who takes them has a chance of passing. The tough questions and exams are supposed to motivate students to study harder, and PMBR takers often state that the program's primary advantage was the fear generated by these experiences.

Based on considerable anecdotal evidence from individuals who took PMBR and those who did not, I firmly believe that BAR/BRI's materials alone will properly prepare most students for even the difficult California Bar Exam, let alone New York's or other less challenging exams. It was not worth $325, let alone $900, to have PMBR scare me into studying hard for the exam, and after talking with people who took the class, I think that the average person would be better off adhering strictly to BAR/BRI's calendar and saving the money.

Having rendered this opinion, it's only fair to tell you that a minority of the people I know continue to recommend PMBR to others, largely because (as the logic goes) they *somehow* passed their bar exams after taking a PMBR class. The counter-argument, of course, is that these people likely would have passed even had they not taken PMBR. Most people agree that BAR/BRI's course is sufficiently rigorous, and had the PMBR-takers followed BAR/BRI's schedule precisely – something you cannot do when "supplementing" with PMBR – I get the feeling that they still would have studied more than enough to succeed.

Putting aside its classes, however, PMBR does have at least one redeeming feature. Its audio tapes and CDs of substantive lectures on the MBE subjects are only inconsistently engaging or useful, but they may be helpful on those few occasions when your eyes just get too tired to keep reading. PMBR currently sells tapes and CDs for $50 per subject, though they're also likely to be available at lower prices as second-hand items from recent law school graduates. Similarly, PMBR flash cards may be useful for those who opt not to create their own for whatever reason.

In summary, BAR/BRI is a must, and though PMBR's classes are probably unnecessary, some of their cheaper take-home materials *might* appeal to you. But don't just buy things for the sake of buying them. You will likely be tempted to spend money on anything that promises to help you pass your bar exam, and my own opinion is that you should strive to avoid that temptation. Following BAR/BRI's instructions will be enough to help most people pass their exams.

But what if you absolutely, positively can't afford BAR/BRI? Or if you can only afford the less-expensive but non-comprehensive PMBR program? First, be certain that you absolutely, positively, and certainly can't afford BAR/BRI, even if you need to finance it through loans. If there's any opportunity to take the course, take it. But if you're literally certain that BAR/BRI isn't an option, pick up a set of used BAR/BRI materials for your state's most recent previous administration, check to be sure that your state hasn't changed the scope of the examination at all, and adapt the previous year's BAR/BRI calendar for your own use. Realize up front that you will not benefit from hearing BAR/BRI lectures, and therefore, you'll need to drill the previous owner's written outlines into your head for several hours a day on your own, in addition to the other demands of the calendar. Work diligently. Here, and here alone, consider taking PMBR or purchasing the CD-based lectures. And pray. You have a much better chance of passing if you take BAR/BRI and live out the typical law student's summer bar routine, as described below.

2. The Routine

Because of BAR/BRI, the summer took on a mostly comfortable, predictable rhythm very quickly. The California BAR/BRI class at Cornell consisted of only twenty or so students, a few of whom were actually from neighboring schools; similarly, at least two California exam takers I personally knew had left Cornell to take BAR/BRI in other states, and it turned out that as many as 15 classmates were not taking the course with us. By contrast, the lecture hall for New York BAR/BRI was packed – over 100 students were jammed into that room. This was about normal for a name school in New York.

Depending on where you were studying for the exam, your BAR/BRI lectures could be either live presentations or videotapes of the live presentations. At my school, tapes started to play at approximately 9:00 each morning and ended between 12:15 and 1:30 each day. The California lecture series ran as many as six days a week; the New York series mostly for five days a week. Our task was the same in almost every lecture; we filled in short outlines – generally 30-some pages per day, occasionally longer – of subject-specific material based on straightforward information presented to us by BAR/BRI lecturers. The outlines were said to contain literally everything we needed to know for the actual bar, and this turned out to be mostly true. What minor points weren't in there would appear randomly in the practice questions we were assigned. After each class, four or five hours of additional work per day awaited us at home or in the library; I alternated between those two locations to minimize distractions and provide a change of scenery.

Each day's work consisted of brain-sapping activities such as practicing multiple-choice MBE questions, reading outlines and correct MBE answers, and/or simulating past exams' essay questions. One out of each four essays had to be mailed in to BAR/BRI's California offices, and were returned to us by mail a week later with grades. Even over separate years of BAR/BRI, people have reported the same phenomenon – nearly all of their essay grades were below passing, despite submitting answers which appeared to be very close to the sample answers BAR/BRI's books contained. The low grades continued until almost the very end, at which point they spiked up and became passing, even though people swore up and down that their work product was nearly identical throughout. Whether this is a BAR/BRI scare tactic to push students to work harder, or a means to compel students to follow very strict essay-writing guidelines is unclear at present. Given the number of people I knew who experienced the exact same phenomenon, even taking separate BAR/BRI classes, I've tended to suspect that both possibilities are somewhat accurate.

In addition to the essays, formal three-hour in-class practice examinations were administered several times throughout the course. BAR/BRI representatives received and graded these practice MBE questions, essays, and performance tests via mail. Practice MBE scores were made available via the Internet; practice essays and performance tests were returned to us in class.

I have to confess that I went through the classic bar exam 'freak out' experience at one point early in the process – perhaps two weeks into the course. In short, I was feeling emotionally overwhelmed. My social life had all but disappeared, as friends were similarly immersed in studies and it was all but impossible to get people to spend more than an hour on anything but a meal or class work. Every day seemed like the same thing: wake up, go to class, read, write, read answers to what I did wrong until it was time to go to sleep, and wake up again to do it again, six days a week. My test scores were low and I needed to keep on working.

When I freaked out, it was a sign that I needed to make a modest adjustment: I needed to allocate a little space for myself. And I needed to figure out what, if anything, was extraneous for me in BAR/BRI's schedule. The only part I cut from the calendar was the reading of outlines in advance of classes. If the classes were truly supposed to tell us all we needed to know for the bar exam, reading the huge outlines in the book would just be a waste of time for me, as I couldn't absorb all of it, anyway. This turned out to be a judicious cut, and one I never regretted. Everything I needed to learn, I learned from filling out the outlines in classes and practicing the related MBE's and essays afterwards.

3.   Taking the Practice Exams

Different people had their own 'strategies' in preparing for the practice MBE test, which was administered three or four weeks into the course. Some took the practice seriously and studied reasonably hard to see what score they could get. A few others hardly studied at all to see what they could score with only minimal effort, a strategy some had used on practice exams during the first year of law school.

One week after the grueling six-hour practice exam was over, the results came in. Two close friends who had used PMBR scored at exactly the 50th percentile on the practice MBE – I scored at the 82nd, and had been using BAR/BRI's materials exclusively. Both said that they had taken the test seriously but had been somewhat confused by the difficulty of PMBR's problems.

In each of our cases, the practice MBE grades included a breakdown of our scores on the areas that had been tested, which proved extremely useful in subsequent review of trouble areas prior to the actual exam. We could tell precisely what subjects we knew, and didn't know, in each of the MBE's key areas. I found that I was surprisingly weak on the multiple-choice questions on the First Amendment, which – true to the axiom – had been one of my best subjects in law school. Though I would only realize it later when I went to analyze what had gone wrong, my problem was that I was answering the questions as I had in my class, and I really needed to look at the questions in the way the bar examiners were asking them – with a bit less nuance.

We discovered after the practice exam that there are ways to entirely squander the BAR/BRI class, and for that matter, the bar prep period. One person who had boasted of not studying for the practice exam at all scored so low that he disappeared from the bar review course to study doubly hard on his own. Another person shamefully admitted that his score was so low that it didn't even fit into a percentile. Based on these experiences, and others like them, I think it's safe to say that it's not a wise move to waste the first three or four weeks of bar review time. Unless you're forced into it by a late law school graduation, you don't want to learn just how poorly prepared you are with only a month left before the exam.

As many people wonder at this stage how much of a correlation there is between BAR/BRI's practice MBE and the actual one, my personal feeling was that the practice exam was only modestly less difficult than the actual July 2001 MBE. The actual exam had a somewhat larger number of advanced questions, which honestly I think would have been all but impossible to prepare perfectly for, even if I'd had the combined materials from three separate bar classes. The practice essays and performance test we did for grades were very similar to the actual ones in length and content.

4.   *Going Solo*

When formal BAR/BRI classes ended two weeks before the bar exam, the balance of the calendar was essentially ours to re-design according to our own personal strengths and weaknesses. As important as the first month and a half had been to build foundational knowledge, the last two weeks were essential to address weak spots and re-consider areas that seemed easy but yet had occasioned low practice MBE scores. I determined that I would work primarily on the essays, a little bit less on the MBE's, and very little on performance tests. My graded performance tests were consistently passing and I felt comfortable with even the most difficult of the practice questions we'd been given.

The psychological pressure continued to build, despite mounting evidence that I would be at least vaguely competent when the exam took place. Admittedly, I felt okay about my practice MBE score, but I wasn't about to get complacent and lazy near the end, or let my memory slide. I also felt highly uncertain about the results of the BAR/BRI practice essays I had gotten back. Although they were in line with what friends who had previously passed bar exams had suggested, and seemed so suspiciously low as to be less than credible, they were low enough to cause me considerable concern. So I kept studying, largely in line with BAR/BRI's recommended daily schedule: mornings, afternoons and nights.

5.   *Last-Minute Preparations*

I had signed up to take my exam in Pasadena, California with two friends from law school who were also in my bar review class; it was our closest available location, though many friends were taking the exam up north in San Francisco or further south in San Diego. We were going to meet in Orange County, set up a 48-hour study group at the home of one friend's parents, then drive to Pasadena the day before the exam. They flew out to California from New York five days before the exam. Four days before the exam, I boarded the flight which begins this book, leaving behind BAR/BRI's largest volumes and carrying only a collection of bare-bones outlines and smaller practice books.[371]

There was only one major surprise in the days before the exam: my girlfriend was waiting at the airport for me when I arrived, despite the fact that we had agreed weeks earlier that we shouldn't see each other until the exam was over. We went out for dinner with my two friends and one friend's parents, a meal that was marked with laughter and general relaxation until my girlfriend and I had to part ways in the parking lot of the restaurant. There are few feelings like knowing that you can't be with someone you care about because you just

---

[371] As it turns out, I never used the practice books. The outlines were entirely adequate.

have to work too much.[372] This was far from the first or last time I had felt that way since deciding to study law.

And it was hard to appreciate in advance just how much I would work, and how important the final 72 hours prior to the exam could be. On the one hand, my two friends and I had heard the supposed axiom that failure was all but certain for the people we saw studying in the hallways outside the convention center where the exam was to be administered. On the other hand, even having followed BAR/BRI's schedule for two months, we still had plenty of information left to commit to memory in the three days before the exam.

Having practiced MBE questions rather extensively, we spent the three days before the exam preparing for the California essays – any of the subjects we had studied were fair game. As a general rule, each essay tested one topic, but "cross-over" essays were common enough, blending two subjects in a single essay. Sometimes, the examiners might only hint at a cross-over question with certain language; BAR/BRI taught us the subtle signs. We read over every outline repeatedly to cover whatever points we hadn't already memorized. We tested each other on various legal concepts and mnemonics that we believed would be helpful to know. And we handicapped the likelihood of various essay questions based on a chart of previous exam administrations.

The study sessions we went through then have been burned into my brain as indelible memories of just how serious preparation can be. We sprawled out on the couches and floors of every room of my friend's house, drew diagrams of constitutional law concepts with our fingers in the carpets, and spent pretty much every moment from morning until midnight reading, talking, or thinking about the law. We tried to relax during our meals. Conversation inevitably turned to topics on the exam. We discussed and debated every major point in our outlines. Over and over again.

Critical to the entire process, for me at least, was gentleness towards my own ego – I felt it necessary not to beat myself up for forgetting material I knew I had read over at one point or another, or for missing an issue here or there when talking with my friends. It was more important for me to absorb as much information as I possibly could while acknowledging the simple truth that I was only human. The California Bar couldn't possibly expect me to know everything; it simply wanted to know that I was at least as competent as the upper 65% of the incoming potential lawyer population, the threshold for first-time exam takers on the most recent California exam.

Though numbers such as that one had not played a major role in my day-to-day life in law school, they took on a bizarre importance in bar review, first when computing where I needed to be mathematically on the MBE and written portions in order to pass the whole exam, and second when we tried to figure

---

[372] But see the POSTSCRIPT for final reflections on this point.

out which essays were likely to show up. One of my friends taking the New York exam ran numbers through a spreadsheet to determine which subjects to study the most; we hand-computed probability charts and gave a measure of deference to BAR/BRI's 'no guarantees' predictions.

Though there was clearly tension in the nights before the exam, it was a lot better than it could have been. We kept cool heads, reassured each other, and actively sought to politely draw lines between what we could work together on, and what we had to do separately – civil procedure for example only rarely lent itself to productive group discussion, while federal securities rule 10b5 (fraud and insider trading) and section 16 (short-swing profits) quickly became the subjects of mnemonics and repeated discussion.

To some extent, we wanted to know what other people were going through, but we also didn't want to get too wrapped up in anything but the business that needed to get done – making sure we remembered as much as possible when we walked into the exam. Thus we were largely non-communicative with the outside world, though one of my friends had heard from a college buddy that some serious freaking out was taking place with the buddy's other friends – one was repeatedly vomiting from the stress, and predictably, others weren't sleeping. We took comfort primarily in the facts that we were managing to eat and sleep, remaining in control of our own abilities to keep our food down and our eyes closed.

Our common, primary stress symptom was mild paranoia – the thoughts that we might not make it to Pasadena, or could get hit by a car crossing the street somewhere. These weren't totally unfounded concerns. Someone who had graduated from our law school the year before had actually died in a car accident on his way to the Los Angeles testing center only months earlier. And the three of us had somehow, not so brilliantly, managed to turn on an hour-long MSNBC report on gruesome discoveries of the Los Angeles County Coroner's Office for our study break the night before we left for the exam. It was horrific, but we couldn't bring ourselves to turn it off. At least we could say that our minds were not totally focused on what we were about to go through.

D. JUDGMENT DAY: THE BAR EXAM COMETH

The day before the exam, we traveled to Pasadena and checked into our hotel. BAR/BRI's calendar suggested that we shouldn't study the night before the exam, but none of us followed that advice. There was always something left to think about or talk about. We couldn't help ourselves. BAR/BRI's advice was for those who were susceptible to last-minute panic attacks – you don't want to study at the last minute because you might psyche yourself out and lose your confidence. We had as much confidence as we could muster at this point; we just needed to make sure we remembered our mnemonics and looked over those things that we thought were most likely to appear.

1. The First Day

On the morning of the first day, we walked over to the Pasadena Convention Center, the only location in Pasadena where the exam was to be administered. There were a few familiar faces to be seen, but almost no one was looking to talk at this point – tension was in the air, so no one wanted to hear something off-putting and fall into a last-minute panic attack. We had heard many times that people would be sitting outside of the exam and still studying even minutes before the exam began. It was true. All three of us forced ourselves to maintain smiles as we walked into the building. We wanted to remain positive, but we also needed to keep on telling ourselves that everything was going to be OK. Each of us had knots in our stomachs.

Two main rooms were set up for the exam administration. The one we could see from the outside of the building was a typewriting room for people who had signed up in advance to type, rather than write the exam.[373] It was a relatively small room, of the size one might expect at a LSAT administration. Then we saw the hallway where we were to complete the handwritten version of the exam. This room was the sort of scene people imagine in their nightmares: a football field of empty chairs and wooden tables, manned by sentries with the power to eject people from the exam, and a large podium with a microphone in the front of the room to ensure uniformity of instructions.[374]

Our seats had been assigned based on the date and time we had registered for the exam. My friends had submitted their applications hours before I had; they were rows away from me to my front. I was in the final row of the first section of the room – as a result, there was a large gap behind me and I could move my chair wherever I desired. I squished to comfortably cross my legs under the old, low wooden table; splinters came off all over my pants and I felt hardened pieces of gum on the underside.

Every seat was marked by a white plastic identification card with a

---

[373] Those taking bar exams can typically opt to handwrite, type, or word process their essay answers, and separate testing rooms are generally designated for each form of writing. But should you use a typewriter or computer to submit your answers? Don't even think about using one of these formats to cheat – it isn't possible, and it would ultimately destroy your legal career. That aside, is mechanically-printed text superior to messy handwriting? Counter-intuitively, even with the increasing use of computers in law classrooms, the use of typewriters and computers on bar exams is dramatically less common than handwriting. A perception persists – perhaps rightfully – that graders subject typed or word processed answers to greater scrutiny, as those answers can be read word-for-word without impediment, whereas scrawled handwritten answers may receive a grader's benefit of the doubt. On balance, you probably stand a better chance of passing even a hard bar exam if you handwrite your essays rather than type them.

[374] Other states' exams are held in less intimidating surroundings, including smaller rented convention rooms at hotels.

person's name and an ID number. We had to carry the cards during the exam if we needed to use the bathrooms.

The proctors were a crowd of 40- to 70-something men and women who evinced none of the uncertainty or questionable competency of LSAT administrators. Despite their older ages, the bar proctors gave off a vaguely menacing air, just enough that people would not want to take their chances by screwing around. Once we were in this room, we were following all their rules – and to a T. We had to use one transparent bag to carry all of our belongings – wallets, pencils, pens, Bar-provided identification, and so forth. We would only start and stop writing when they told us it was okay to do so. And if someone broke the rules, there was no sense that exceptions would be made for anyone.

Every person started the first day of the exam under the same conditions, but each person's work area looked a little bit different. Mine was just a watch face and the bare collection of materials. Others had egg timers, bigger clocks, and highlighters. Hearts were racing in the moments before the examination began. We were each given thin booklets containing the first three essay questions, three regulation answer booklets numbered corresponding to the essays, and scratch paper. There would be three hours for the three essays, and then a lunch break, and then we would return for our first performance exam.

Though it would be exciting to attempt to dramatize the start of the exam, the actual moment was not truly suspenseful. Proctors had been shuffling around the room and making announcements for more than a half hour. People were tired of filling out forms, including a fingerprint verification document, and anxiety had nearly metamorphosed into listlessness when the clock started. Then people started to work in a hurry.

The big question when an exam this important begins is "what is going to be on it?" There was no way that we could have been sure until we opened it up, and thus, even opening the exam booklet can bring a crushing wave of negative thoughts upon a room full of brains that were ready to start thinking. Imagine that you know what your three worst subjects are, you skim through the three essay questions, and realize that you're not in great shape. Or that you know what your three best subjects are, and they all show up.

As it turned out, our first day of bar essays started with civil procedure, moved to what seemed like a difficult real property question, and finished with a big issue-spotting test on evidence law. These were the three subjects I absolutely did not want to be tested on, but they were also topics that were mathematically highly likely to appear on the exam. Therefore, I had prepared especially hard for each of them, despite my personal feelings. One of my friends thought that this was his favorite possible combination of essay topics. For different reasons, it wound up working out for both of us; those who were disadvantaged were only the people who hadn't prepared for their personal worst possible eventualities.

Lunch was a blur – a hurried snacking on sandwiches and chips at a nearby dive of a restaurant. We just wanted to be done with the day, and there were mixed feelings about whether or not to discuss what had just gone on – one of us didn't want to talk at all, just in case of a jinx; the other two originally were not going to talk but wound up discussing the essays. When we returned to the hall, the performance test was nothing out of the ordinary – challenging, but not fundamentally different from what BAR/BRI had showed us. It was merely a free-form three-hour extension of the marathon that had started in the morning. In all, it was not an easy day, but not a terrible one, either.

To recap, the three-day California exam tests on essays the first day, multiple choice the second day, and then essays again on the third day. When the first day had ended, we vowed to go out and have an incredibly large meal of some sort that would put us to sleep. And that we did. We ate well at a restaurant near the hotel and were almost ready to go back to bed as soon as we'd returned to our rooms. But then we had to ask ourselves, "should we study?" There wasn't much doubt that the answer was yes. We temporarily put aside our essay probability charts and spent a couple of hours just reviewing some of the bigger areas that were certain to appear on the multiple-choice MBE exam. Then it was bedtime; we were not going to stay up late worrying or pushing ourselves too much.

Right before we fell asleep, something rattled us. A friend called from New York to report that a classmate had made a potentially fatal mistake on his essays. This classmate had been stressing out about the exam for literally months, and was going berserk preparing for imaginary contingencies. But he hadn't bothered to plan in advance for his arrival at the test site, and had struggled to find parking when he arrived. Coming late to start the exam, he hurried, ignored the individually numbered essay booklets, and proceeded to write all three of his essays in the same booklet. Only at the end of the exam did he realize what he had done wrong, and pleaded for an exception to the rule. The proctors set his exam aside but could not guarantee that all three essays would be read. All three of us were taken aback, but thankfully, none of us had made the same mistake. The big question was how a person could continue working on the exam after blundering so spectacularly: would they screw up the entire second day? And would this psyche anyone else out, even though they hadn't made the same mistake?

2.   The Second Day

Our second day turned out to be memorable – administered across the country, the MBE questions were the same from state to state, so we could be sure that our friends were having similar experiences to our own. But the order of questions isn't precisely the same from place to place. The 'first' 100 of the 200 total MBE questions might be administered in a different order for different people, in different testing sites and even within the same testing room. I might have a really good time with my first 100 questions and talk at lunchtime with an equally capable friend who'd had a terrible time with his first 100, and we would have had totally different questions. Then we would reverse our experiences in the second half of the exam.

My first half was exactly like the introductory- and intermediate-level BAR/BRI questions: not so bad, but still challenging. We were amazed and amused that Horace, a hypothetical friendly old bear we recognized from a BAR/BRI sample question, appeared almost identically in an actual exam question; the randomness was enough to ease some of the tension in answering questions. The time constraints of the first half, though, created plenty of stress for everyone: three hours for 100 questions meant less than two minutes per question, and if you didn't know something, it was always difficult to quickly decide whether to think it through or just take a wild guess. My personal strategy varied depending on how tricky the question seemed to be.

Lunch was again unspectacular, and when we returned, our second half of the questions was devastatingly hard – 40 or 50 of them were as hard, if not harder, than the worst of BAR/BRI's questions, and the rest were intermediate level in difficulty. Every single person I knew felt that they might have failed the exam based on this portion alone; I couldn't imagine what it must have felt like to get those questions in the first half of the day, rather than the second. An all-day feeling of failure might have been more than I could have taken.

Regardless, answering six hours of multiple choice questions was a hell of a way to spend my birthday. When testing had ended for the day, we relaxed again. Phone calls from my girlfriend and parents were brief, and we again went out and had an excellent, large meal. That night, we went out and saw a movie: we were all looking for something relatively mindless and Scary Movie 2 fit the bill. The movie was not especially funny, and each of us probably spent at least a little bit of the movie thinking about what we'd been through – the word "little" is, in and of itself, significant, because we weren't quite as consumed with what was to come as we had previously been. It felt great to be done with two-thirds of the exam, no matter how hard it had been.

Yet there was still a slight tension in our discussions. No matter how much we had agreed in advance that we weren't going to discuss the exam, the temptation was always there, and the subject repeatedly came up in one form or another. One of my friends was not going to even speculate on his performance. The other was quietly confident that he was doing as well as he was capable of doing. I felt the same, but also began to feel that I would actually be surprised if I did not pass the exam. By contrast, some people were already freaking out and saying that they were not going to pass. If there were people out there feeling like that, and I had felt at least comfortable answering most of what had been put in front of me, I was in better shape than many people at this point. Whether the next day would spell disaster, I had no idea.

On that second night, we ran through our essay probability chart again to guess what would appear the next morning. Yet I felt strongly that we shouldn't rely upon math alone to save us; assuming that the topics for each exam were hand-selected by the Committee of Bar Examiners, there was certainly going to be at least one random topic thrown on the pile just to confound purely mathematical predictions. Looking purely at the frequency with which certain subjects were historically tested on the exam, four topics seemed equally unlikely from a strict mathematical standpoint and therefore likely to show up as a random essay. I thought that the random essay was likely to be corporations, or perhaps contracts – the latter only because I dreaded the prospect of having to write an essay on contract law. The other possibilities were wills and trusts, subjects which could be tested separately but often appeared together. We went over some of the fine points of corporations at length, discussed the major points of wills and trusts, then went over contracts to the extent that we could. But we were running out of time and needed sleep. Whatever was going to happen the next day was then more or less inevitable.

The night ended when we checked our voicemail at the hotel and discovered messages from some of our friends back in New York. Their two-day bar exam had already ended and they were already out partying – to the extent true partying was possible in the small cities where the exam was being administered. And of course, they just wanted to rub in that we still had a day of essays left to go. The New York Bar Exam takers' mood had been better from the start, though. Many of them had barely started to study until the last month before the exam, and to some extent, they could get away with that: Cornell's passage rate typically hovered from 92-96% for the New York test. It would probably take a pretty serious preparatory or exam-day problem of some sort to prevent a classmate from passing the New York Bar. They could afford to relax more during the summer, and would spend their third day recovering from hangovers instead of answering more questions.

3.   After the Third Day, They Rested

Even for those of us stuck in California, however, the mood was somewhat lighter on that third morning. Proctors almost smiled at us for the first time in three days, and the whole room's atmosphere just seemed to convey the message that the ordeal was almost over. Chatter in the room before the session began was largely upbeat. But the routine hadn't ended. Like the first day, we were given three separate essay answer booklets and, eventually, an essay question booklet. There was no doubt in my mind that all three of us were thinking at that moment about our classmate who had made a potentially near-fatal mistake at this stage – missing the instructions as to how to complete the three booklets. I took modest psychological comfort in the knowledge that I would not repeat his mistake, but simultaneously felt burdened by the reality that even something so minor could mean the difference between practicing law and re-taking the exam. Yet this day for me was neither a repeat of his first-day bar experience, nor my own. The essay question booklet was, again, an enigma until we opened it, but this time, things were definitely going in my favor. Our first two questions on the third day turned out to be my favorite topics – the first hit on constitutional law, specifically the First Amendment. The second mixed torts and professional responsibility – the aforementioned unusual cross-over we had predicted in advance. The third essay turned out to be a statistically unlikely wildcard, as we'd anticipated, and hit both wills and trusts. We had studied just what we had needed, and unlike the first day, where I was not looking forward to writing about the subjects that were ultimately tested, on this day, the words were just flowing from my pen into the essay booklets.

At lunch time, we felt pumped up about being so close to being done, and when we returned for the final three-hour performance examination, I was in my best spirits to date. The second performance exam turned out to be a relative pushover, and I was out of the room ten or fifteen minutes early – just enough time to call my parents and girlfriend to let them know I was done, and that I was feeling good. We had been told to keep our white plastic ID cards when we left the room; we would need them, we were told, to get our results when they became available online. I fidgeted with my card when I was on the phone; the exam was over, but the waiting was about to begin.

A cheer went up in the room when the proctors announced that the examination was over. People immediately streamed out of the building and into the sunshine of a typical Southern California summer day; the light and warmth, combined with the relative jubilation and feelings of first freedom, made the world seem a different place than it had been only days and hours earlier. This was to be the first night in two months without a study deadline, or any need to think about what was going to happen next. And that felt seriously weird. Half of me wanted to talk with my friends about what had just gone on. The other half just wanted to get on with my life already.

All told, we had successfully anticipated five of the six essays, including an unusual cross-over that one of my friends originally believed improbable at best. And the last day left me feeling as if I had a good shot at actually passing the exam. For all of the concern, stress and uncertainty – all of which were entirely merited as they developed – the exam had not been impossible, but just very difficult, and more like a marathon than a sprint. It was entirely possible to know the course and my abilities well enough in advance to work on my weaknesses and complete the race.

That evening, my friends went out to celebrate with the vast majority of people who had taken the California Bar, though few people were celebrating because they believed they had passed – in fact, most were celebrating solely because they were finished at least temporarily with the misery of studying. I opted to join my friends only for a quick drink or two back at the hotel, and afterwards hopped on a bus to join my girlfriend, who was waiting for me in Orange County. My friends partied the night away. I was just glad to be able to spend my first real night in months with my girlfriend.

It wasn't long before I began to feel – for the first time in a long time – that I really had no schedule to follow. It was one of those overwhelmingly important, 'checkpoint of life' feelings that started out as a whisper in my mind, growing every minute for the first couple of days after the exam. Regardless of whether I had passed or failed, I had passed a major milestone in my life. As of July 27, the rest of the summer was mine to enjoy.

E.   ONE LAST WAIT

At that point, though the pressure of the bar exam disappeared entirely for the first time in two months, and law school finally appeared entirely behind me, the biggest wait of my law student's existence was already beginning. It would be three and a half months until I would know whether or not I had passed the exam – one of the longest waits in the country, because of the sheer number of people taking the California bar. Only New York would take longer, and then, only by several days and for unusual reasons.

Our white identification cards, we were told, would enable us in November to access the California Bar's results web site. For the first few days, we would only be able to see our own names on the list; afterwards, the complete "pass list" would be made public and the whole world would know. By that time, I would already have started my new job. I didn't want to imagine what would happen if I didn't pass.

A. SUNLIGHT IN A COLLEGE TOWN

There are some days when reality outstrips your dreams.

Months of bar exam preparation had passed with heavy traffic on the small local roads and big piles of paper on my desk just waiting to be dealt with.

But when I went outside that day, that late summer day, the whole world seemed to be glowing.

The streets of Ithaca for once seemed almost empty. And I was free.

The deep golden warmth of a slow-setting sun lit the landscape perfectly, and the air was just hot enough to make me feel comfortable in my shorts and light shirt. I was able to go from my apartment to the parking lot of the law school in an unusually short four minutes. The lot was empty, so I parked alongside the building and walked in.

Everything was quiet; the building seemed abandoned. Though this would have been unusual for the law school even three weeks earlier, it was appropriate for 7:30 on a Sunday evening near the end of the summer. This was a day between years. The post-third-year law students had graduated months earlier and removed the last of their possessions from the building. Freshly-minted second- and third-year law students were finishing their work as summer associates at law firms across the country. And though most of them were already informed, a handful of wait-listed members of the brand new class of first year law students were only days away from learning that they were about to come here to study law.

As I walked through the floors of the law school's abandoned library, I thought for a moment that I might take one last look at the reading room, the beautiful, expansive wood-ceilinged room that resembled a cathedral. I could see through the locked door that warm rays of sunlight were streaming through its windows, illuminating the antique tables and chairs that weeks from now would be cloaked in darkness and full of people at this time of night. But this evening, when I left the law school to walk through Collegetown, only one other person appeared to be in the building. He was asleep, sitting up, in a study carrel. He might well have been me at another time; an earlier time.

Over the last three years, I had been in this building six or seven days a week since just about the first day I arrived here. I had never actually slept in the law school, but only because my closest bedroom had been in a dormitory only steps away. Now, having graduated, I had walked its halls for the last time as a student, and if I was to return again, it would most likely be as a short-term visitor and as a life-long alumnus. I was bidding goodbye to Collegetown, where I had eaten many hurried meals between classes and hunted innumerable times unsuccessfully for a carton of Ben & Jerry's Coffee Heath Bar Crunch in the convenience store near the law school. It was my favorite flavor, and my girlfriend's, too. Today, as I walked from the library over to that store, there were three cartons of that precise flavor just sitting in the freezer. My girlfriend wasn't in town. Without her around to help me with one of those cartons, I decided, sadly, to abstain.

Like my classmates, I had packed up most of my belongings and started them on their way to a new apartment – post-law school, post-bar exam, post-every other part of my life up until this moment. No one I knew was staying in Ithaca to practice law. I supposed that it might have been different had I attended a school in a city where there was a thriving economy and lots of demand for new lawyers, but Ithaca – like many college towns – was little more than an extended, always temporary stop in the larger plan of my life. I felt like I had greater adventures to pursue. Though my apartment had been packed, I had just enough of my clothing and possessions left to begin the next short phase of my life – one that I had been waiting to enjoy for years.

B. THE BAR TRIP

For years, it's been called the "Bar Trip" even though it's technically a post-bar trip: the vacation you take to celebrate your freedom from months of dungeon-like preparation for a bar exam. Like everything else in law school, the location and duration of the trip you plan will vary considerably from person to person and school to school. Friends often get together and plan trips abroad, or at the very least, to nearby island destinations considerably removed from libraries, books, and exam proctors. Others take extended trips around the United States. One previously well-traveled friend from California spent weeks just relaxing and surfing at nearby beaches. Whatever it is that you plan, it will most certainly be a break from the bar routine and may well be the biggest thing that you have to look forward to doing once the exam is over. My own bar trip was the thing that kept me thinking, "no matter how terrible this might be, in a few weeks, I'll be someplace much, much better."

Bar trips tend to be more spectacular than standard vacations because of three factors. First, they are extended in duration. During law school, people rarely had the chance to go away for three or four weeks at a time; for bar trips, three or four weeks is typically a minimum. The reason for this is only obvious once you've been in law school for a while and are planning to be employed shortly thereafter: the job of a young lawyer at a large law firm is typically a morning, noon, and night affair, and weekends are fair game for work hours, too. Vacation days become precious and there are few if any opportunities to use three or four contiguous weeks of time to do anything but practice law. A second factor to consider is that bar trips are frequently financed by firm stipends, which makes possible the sorts of trips one might otherwise not finance on his own.[375] This is true as much for the location of the trip as the sorts of activities one might undertake while there. The third and final factor is pragmatism on two levels: this might be your last big chance to do something you've really wanted to do, or to hang out with your law school friends, or to just do something crazy. Moreover, if you don't take a significant break after spending two hard months preparing for the bar, you're never going to be able to deal with the fast pace of law firm life thereafter.

My personal philosophy was, and is, to take full advantage of the chance to do a great bar trip. This philosophy was backed by virtually every practicing attorney I've ever spoken with, most of whom cited both their own excellent bar trips, and the pragmatic reality that they wouldn't want to work with someone who was burnt out from bar study and hadn't taken the time to rest. Even the partners who hired me for both my 2L summer and post-3L jobs told me that a long, relaxing bar trip was a must, at the very least to get your mind off of the impending results. Waiting for bar results makes you enough of a nervous wreck when you've had some time off; imagine thinking about it every day without any vacation or rest for the three months between taking the exam and finding out how you did.

My planning for the bar trip had started months before preparation for the bar exam: the hotel, airline, and other coordinating issues were just too much for me to consider doing in any serious way while preparing for the exam. But then, my trip was going to be a bit trickier than most. A couple of friends were going to drive across the country, a trip that required some planning but neither hotel nor airline reservations. Others were going to single cities or island destinations. I wanted to see Southeast Asia. Pretty much all of it. That was something I had wanted to do for as much of my life as I could remember, and especially if I could do it with my stipend, I was going to do it.

Though I won't go into all of the details, suffice it to say that my post-bar experience included three stages: the first stage was the period immediately after the exam where I spent time with my girlfriend in California going to beaches, the Del Mar race track, and several fantastic restaurants. This was my initial cooling-down period, and one that I needed in order to get in touch with

---

[375] My firm, like many at the time, was offering a significant summer bar stipend designed to cover between $10,000 and $15,000 (before taxes) of bar-related expenses, including bar study costs, food and apartment costs, and costs associated with a post-bar vacation. As economic conditions tighten in various cities, this particular perk tends to disappear or decrease on a firm-by-firm basis, though some firms and government agencies maintain their bonuses or stipends unchanged. Some firms deal with economic hardships by changing the stipend from a bonus into an advance payment on vacation days or salary, the latter of which may well mitigate one's interest in an elaborate post-bar trip.

my old self again. But no matter where I went or what I did, the preparation for the bar exam had changed me a bit. Aware that I had just taken the exam, non-law student friends and family asked me plenty of legal questions just for fun, and my brain was still sharp enough to shoot back quick answers and analysis on virtually any exam topic. After I packed up all of my possessions, I returned to spend some time with my parents, where I was still thinking pretty intensely about the exam and also trying to prepare for the trip I was about to take.

The second stage was the bar trip itself. It was scheduled to include a month and a half of travel across Southeast Asia, hitting everyplace from China to Singapore to South Korea and Vietnam, and many places in between. For a month, it was fantastic. I had daily adventures in places I had dreamed of visiting for years. I wrote, took pictures, and lived as different a life as I could imagine from that of a law student.

But in the first week of September, while I was visiting South Korea, a fax from the U.S. Department of State was slipped under the door of my hotel room, and presumably the doors of other American tourists in the hotel. The fax said that the United States had credible information that terrorists were threatening American military personnel and civilians overseas. I mentioned it to my parents that night on the telephone, but thought little more about it for several days. Arriving in Tokyo on September 11, on a totally different time zone, I accidentally turned on the television and saw that a plane had hit a tower of the World Trade Center. It seemed like an unrelated accident at the time, and I went to sleep. An hour or two later, I was awakened in my hotel by a call from my parents, letting me know that two more planes had hit the Pentagon and the other tower of the Trade Center.

Five days later, I returned to the United States, canceling my remaining plans – which would originally have had me fly to Indonesia, then Vietnam. Newspapers were reporting that Indonesian extremists were already scoping out American tourists in hotels and threatening to kill them if they had not already left the country; it seemed especially wise not to consider traveling there. If someone was going to kill me, I certainly did not want it to happen *after* I'd spent two months of my life studying feverishly for the bar.

When all was said and done, my bar trip had been a solid month of travel, interrupted only by events beyond my control. But I wasn't looking forward to flying home under such circumstances. It was a disappointing, frightening, but yet necessary end to my official period of post-bar relaxation.

The third and final stage of my post-exam experience was my return home and the days before I left to set up my new apartment in California. On the bright side, I was not thinking much about the bar exam any more; everything else I had been through, positive and negative, had dominated my thinking for many weeks at this point. I spent time with my parents and my girlfriend, who had returned for her final year at Cornell. Considering everything that had taken place – both the events of September 11 and the fact that I had been traveling in so many entirely foreign places for so long – people were glad just to have me back in one piece. There was plenty to be thankful for.

On the flip side, though, I dreaded having to fly across the country again at a time when air travel seemed so unsafe. And the economy, which was already in decline before the attacks, was now beginning to look even worse. Suddenly, all that I had planned for after law school seemed more uncertain. Who knew, for sure, what was going to happen with my job when I came out to California? And what would I do if I hadn't passed the exam?

C.   OUR WAITS END, ONE-BY-ONE

Nothing is guaranteed in life. This was as true for bar results as it was for my impending employment. When I started work at my law firm job at Bender in October, the firm's stated policy was to pay for your second crack at passing the exam if you failed the first time, and then require you to leave if you failed twice. By the time bar results were expected, the firm's policy appeared to have changed; the firm was downsizing and costs had to be cut wherever possible. You would virtually bear the costs of any second exam on your own, and there was some discussion that, under certain circumstances, people might not be allowed to stay on if they had failed the exam the first time. Needless to say, passing the bar took on a new level of importance. It might, if things were going really badly, result in instant termination.

Three 'Fall Associates' had started at the same time at Bender's office in Irvine, and especially as the days ticked down to mid-November, anticipation and anxiety for the results continued to build. Other junior attorneys good-naturedly teased us almost daily to keep us nervous; more senior associates and partners expressed quiet confidence that there was nothing to worry about. One associate suggested that the people who really had to worry were those who either hadn't prepared or had prepared yet felt they'd messed up on a couple of sections of the exam. This wasn't a lot of comfort.

I learned through the telephone that the friends I had studied with were also getting nervous, and by the week before the results, I and virtually every person I knew seemed more wound up than we had been before the exam. And unlike New York, where virtually every one of my friends was likely to pass, the California Bar's low passage rate strongly suggested that I would personally know at least a couple people who failed. One friend's comment resonated strongly with my own feelings; "if I fail the bar exam, I know that I studied as hard as I could have studied, and I don't even begin to know what I could do differently the next time." In other words, if we failed this exam, passing on a second try seemed unimaginable.

This was especially hard to handle given the small number of new associates in my office. We had bonded pretty well, and if one of us failed, it would be both emotionally and professionally challenging, given the firm's changing policy on bar failure. It was tough enough to know that the firm had already scheduled a champagne celebration for those who passed, and that one of us might not attend. We talked about making our own plans to get together right after getting the results, but no one really wanted to commit to showing up for something when they might have failed. The one Cornell grad I knew in the area was equally non-committal about making plans for that night.

Results for other states had been steadily trickling in for the past several weeks, and through the law school's informal alumni e-mail network, the news was spreading quickly. From where I was standing, it seemed as if everyone who had taken the Massachusetts, Oregon, Texas and other bars had passed – but this was only a small fraction of the people I knew. Because of the terrorist attacks, and the resultant disruptions of the lives of exam graders and administrators, New York exam takers had to wait until some uncertain date to get their results – in any case, it would be after California. Virtually everyone I knew from law school was still waiting on pins and needles.

On the day the California results were supposed to come out, we were allowed and even encouraged to leave the office early in the day to wait for our results. I had lunch with one of the other new Bender associates; you can guess what we were thinking and talking about. More than the results, we were consumed with and surprised by our own anxiety. Though neither of us would have ever done it on a normal work day, or for that matter, any normal afternoon, we both had drinks at lunch. They didn't help much.

We could have done anything that afternoon; results weren't due until 6:00pm. Yet both of us just wanted to go to our respective apartments and wait there for our results. As has become commonplace across the country, results appear first on the Internet through a web site set up by the California Bar, and then are mailed to your home address. You check the Internet first and pray first that you passed, and then that the web site was right – if it says you did – or wrong if it says you didn't.

Interestingly, the web results aren't always right. All of my friends had heard stories of people who supposedly hadn't passed but learned later that they had, the sort of emotional devastation that is hard to imagine one could ever forget, no matter how good the real news was later. Various state bars have attempted to disclaim liability for posting incorrect bar results on their web sites, and the results posted on the Internet have on more than one occasion been demonstrably wrong. The result has been that some states, including California, generate pass lists which may or may not be complete listings of those who have passed the exam. If your name doesn't appear on the list, you either failed or were unlucky enough to be left off the list. Your old-fashioned envelope will arrive in the mail to tell you your status for certain. You hope.

My personal mechanism for coping with the stress was to do what I already enjoyed doing with my free time – using the Internet, talking on the phone with friends, and so on – while occasionally checking to see if the results had been posted early. They weren't up as of 3:00pm. My phone kept on ringing and people, especially on the East Coast, wanted to know if I had passed; the results were unlikely to be posted at 6:00 their time, I had to explain. I would get on the telephone with one person and then not feel like talking. Then ten minutes later I would be in the mood to talk again. By 5:45pm, I was wondering just how nervous I would become as the last fifteen minutes counted down.

So I checked the Bar's web site one more time. This time, my computer froze for a moment. The Bar's computer was either overloaded with users or in the process of updating its files. My web browser timed out. I hit the refresh button. A screen came up asking for my name and testing ID. I could hardly believe it. I was so stunned by the fact that I was about to get my results early that I didn't have a chance to renew my anxiety. I picked up my white ID card from the exam, typed in my ID number and name, then hit the submit button. The screen cleared.

The next screen came up with a flash.

"JEREMY BRIAN HORWITZ appears on the list of persons who successfully took the July 2001 Bar Examination."

This took a moment to digest. It was almost too fast.

My first thought was: "I passed!"

But then I thought, "Did I pass?"

Is that really what this was saying? It was so convoluted. Plenty of people had taken the exam; was "successfully took" supposed to indicate that others who had completed the exam had not "successfully taken" it? No "congratulations?" There was only curt, terse language, possibly subject to later explanation that the list was inaccurate, but still, it was coupled with a fleeting sense that nothing negative had been said. That was good enough, I guessed. It could have said I didn't appear on a list. Welcome to the practice of law; ambiguity prevails even in what should be the clearest of circumstances. I took a screenshot of the result and printed it out, just in case. For all intents and purposes, I had passed. I called my parents and girlfriend to tell them the news.

Even after I spoke with them, it was only 5:50, local time. Most people didn't know their results yet, but I wanted to call everyone I knew, hear their results, and tell them mine. I wasn't worried any more, and I was pretty much certain that the people I knew would pass, too. At this point, it seemed so much more clear – just as the associate from my firm had said, I couldn't have failed unless I really knew that I had messed something up, and truly, I hadn't felt that way. As my other friend had suggested weeks earlier, I had studied my hardest, and given that I had never failed any exam in the past, how could I possibly have worked harder or done a better job? But this was all easy enough to say now that I had positive results in hand. What about everyone else?

There was plenty of excitement and continued anxiety throughout the night. I called people, people called me, and uniformly, there were congratulations all around. By the end of the night, I learned that none of my friends or co-workers had failed; hastily assembled celebrations were going on all throughout California. Some people had gotten drunk before getting their results, just to soften the blow. Other people were going to get drunk afterwards. I just wanted to go out, treat myself to a great meal, and relish the fact that I wouldn't have to go through it all again. I went with my local friend from Cornell to gorge on a seafood buffet with all-you-can-eat sushi, lobster, crab and shrimp – plus Japanese beer to wash it all down. We were both entirely relieved, happy, and by the end of the meal, quite full. It was a very good way to conclude months of apparently unnecessary concern.

We were walking out of the restaurant and discussing the evening's continued celebration options when his cellular phone rang. He became very quiet shortly after answering the phone. I could tell from what he was saying that the person on the other end of the line was confused about something. My friend was now somber and soft-spoken, attempting to be almost conciliatory. He explained that he wasn't sure what it meant, for sure, if your name wasn't on the list. He told the person on the phone just to wait for an envelope from the Bar. It was now clear that my friend had been contacted by the first non-passing person that either of us knew. When he hung up the phone, we talked about it for a little while and then tried to get back to thinking about something fun to do afterwards. Our plans wound up not working out, and we both returned to our apartments.

Over the next day or two, I learned that although all of my friends and co-workers had passed the exam, everyone I knew had only one or two degrees of separation between themselves and someone who had failed. Cornell's statistics, historically high in New York, had apparently dropped in California. Even several quality classmates had failed, dropping our California pass rate to approximately 64% -- a major fall from the prior year's 78%. But other factors might have been at play. Many of those who hadn't passed had not attended BAR/BRI classes, or had studied at least partially on their own, or had worked for a law firm for part of the summer while studying. Across the board, it seemed as if those who had failed – from my school, at least – hadn't immersed themselves quite as fully on their weekends and evenings after class as those who had passed, had skipped some significant part of BAR/BRI's instructed lesson plan, or hadn't taken classes at all.

After California released its results, New York unexpectedly announced that it, too, would be ready within several days. Suddenly the pressure went up on all of my friends awaiting New York results; would they, too, become negative statistics? When New York's results came in, though, Cornell was redeemed. Its 96% passage rate was the highest in the state, and it was almost impossible to determine who, in fact, had failed. Ironically, one Cornellian whose name did not appear on New York's pass list went through the humiliation of apparent failure, and then went so far as to enroll in another BAR/BRI class, only to learn that the Bar had erred in its initial list and left off a large number of the people who had actually passed – including him. Every telling of the story and its punchline from person to person instantly evokes the same facial grimace and subsequent anger. His experience could have been any other person's, and I feel lucky every day that I didn't have to go through that extra little hassle at the end of my educational career.

That incident aside, the final hurtles of most law students' lives had passed without incident: the vast majority of those accepted to law schools had graduated on time, and a solid majority of new graduates had passed their July bar exams on their first try.

It had taken over four years from dream to reality – it was 1997 when we started to prepare applications for law school, and 2001 when we learned that we would be licensed to practice law. In the first days after we received our results, it seemed as if anything was possible – as we had to be sworn in, we were still days from calling ourselves lawyers, but knew that we had been sculpted from stone with ancient tools and tested repeatedly by the harshest of modern standards. If we had survived law school and a bar exam, we were ready for greater challenges. Today we were junior and inexperienced, but some time soon, we would run our own firms, become partners with established firms, or go on to whatever we wanted to do in the world. At least, that was the theory.

The only thing left to do was to get sworn in. But I'm not going to describe that for you. If, after all you've read here, you aspire to practice law, that's just something you'll just have to experience on your own...

References to cycles appear several times throughout this book – educational cycles, social cycles, and romantic cycles among them. And as I write these last pages for this book, a cycle in my own life finally come to an end. Today, a year has passed since I wrote the first words of this book, and as I type these words, I'm sitting directly outside the Summer 2002 administration of the California Bar Examination. This time, thankfully, I'm only a distant observer. It's the last afternoon of the exam, my girlfriend is inside, and as of this moment she's only two hours away from completing the very last step in becoming a lawyer. I'm just here for moral support. When she finishes this exam, we'll both be done living the lives of law students, once and for all.

Though no two bar exams are precisely alike even in the same state, her experience was quite different from mine. There was no frightening set of MBE questions, though some were considered "odd" in terms of subject matter. There were two separate confusing California essays, when typically there is only one, and whereas my exam was administered in a huge convention center in Pasadena, hers was in a smaller basketball arena at the University of California at San Diego. Finally, though we decided to keep things similar by remaining apart during the summer so that she could concentrate on her studies, she invited me to keep her company during the actual exam, something we had not contemplated the year before. Though there were of course many similarities between our experiences, including the extent and style of our preparations, the stress, fatigue, and the structure of the exam days themselves, it's true that two people can have very different experiences with a single state's bar exam over only one year's time… and perhaps even the same exam.

That's equally true about the law school experience as a whole. I've focused throughout this book on what I can report as typical (and atypical but noteworthy) modern experiences, but as you're certainly aware, there are other perspectives on law school life. Some are available in print. You might hear others from lawyers, judges, or professors. Writers and practitioners seem to get a kick out of portraying law school as brutish or terrible, though in rare cases, people will state that their experiences were even less stressful or demanding than I've suggested. Even if these perspectives vary wildly, I think there's definitely something to be said for having a spectrum of opinions before you choose to undertake any serious three-year course of graduate study.

If you're still contemplating law school after reading this book, I urge you to do two things. First, make the effort to actually get some other opinions on the experience before you decide that law school's right for you. And second, once you know what you're signing up for, if you feel that it's the right choice for you, go after it. Don't be dissuaded by naysayers. If you have what it takes to survive law school, and you're willing to commit to the ups and downs of a law student's life, you should do it. Despite its challenges and predictable cycles of stress, law school is an appropriate next step in the lives of people who are truly interested in learning the law.

Ultimately, you will have to make difficult personal choices as to which schools, classes, and career options are right for you. Some will chase top grades from prestigious schools and seek high-paying jobs. Others will prefer more comfortable schools, classes, and employers. Having seen each of the extremes, I think that people will ultimately choose or fall into paths that match their own personalities and meet their individual needs. I also honestly believe that if you do the right research before you make each of your key choices, following the general principles described throughout this book, your law school experience will be happier, more exciting, and more rewarding than you can imagine.

In any case, your educational experiences, bar exam, and job search will no doubt differ somewhat from mine. But in each of these things, and in all of your other endeavors, I wish you great success in achieving your goals and safe travels towards each of them.

J. Horwitz
La Jolla, California
August 1, 2002

APPENDIX A: GLOSSARY OF LAW SCHOOL TERMS

Actus Reus: In criminal law, the Latin term for a 'guilty action,' which when combined with *mens rea* and an *injury* forms the three generally required elements for criminal culpability.

Associate: Typically, the name used for junior-level members of a legal organization, such as a *law firm*, *law review*, or other journal, as contrasted with their respective senior-level members, the *partner* and the *editor*.

Bad Law: Law which has been repealed or is otherwise no longer valid. Also, a term sometimes used too loosely by professors seeking to suggest that poorly-reasoned court decisions will, in the near future, be invalidated.

Bar: As most commonly used in law school, a self-regulating organization of all practicing lawyers in a given state governed by the highest court of that state. Even if you graduate from law school, you aren't a lawyer until you are accepted as a member of a state bar (except under limited circumstances in Wisconsin). Each state bar regulates its own admissions by using one or two annual bar exams and other requirements. See Chapter 10, Section F, and Chapter 11. There are also federal bars for individual federal courts and the U.S. Supreme Court, though with the exception of the federal Patent Bar, these bars do not require exams, only admission to the bar of the state in which the federal court is located.

Bar Exam: One of 51 difficult screening exams used by the individual U.S. states (and the District of Columbia) to limit the number of people who will be allowed to practice law within the borders of a given state. A bar exam is required in every state except Wisconsin in order to practice law; Wisconsin's exception lets you skip the bar exam only if you studied law at one of two schools in that state, otherwise, you still must pass their exam. Only some states extend *reciprocity* to people who have taken bar exams in other states, thereby eliminating the need for a lawyer to take more than one bar exam to practice in two or more states. See also *reciprocity* and *waiving in*.

Bar Review Course: A post-law school program, typically lasting for two months, designed to re-familiarize third-year law students with the subject matter of a given state's bar exam. *BAR/BRI*, listed below, currently offers the nation's most comprehensive bar review courses.

Bar Trip: An extended celebratory post-law school, post-bar exam vacation taken by many law students while waiting for bar exam results.

BAR/BRI: A business that provides preparatory services for students taking any of the United States bar exams, and also helpful pre-bar exam materials for first-year and upper-class students.

BIGlaw: Shorthand for 'big law firms' considered as a whole. Often refers to the similarities between firms with aspirations of national or international scope.

Black Letter: The clearest possible explanation of a law, a point, or collection of points about the workings of the law. Black Letter law refers to the manner in which the law may be stated succinctly by a professor or practitioner without unnecessarily drifting off into the academic or uncertain elements of that law, contrasting with *hiding the ball.*

Blackacre: The most common name for a fictional piece of land used for reference purposes by Property law professors, along with Whiteacre, Greenacre, and my personal favorite, Gatoracre.

BLUEBOOK/Bluebooking: Bluebooking is the process of correctly referencing other writers' materials when you write a legal document, a process accomplished by using a blue-covered reference book called THE BLUEBOOK: A UNIFORM GUIDE TO LEGAL CITATION. Edited and published by law students at several top law schools, the BLUEBOOK goes through slight modifications every year or two. Not all courts use BLUEBOOK citation formats, but most schools do.

Boilerplate: Widely accepted legal language included almost without a second thought in certain documents. Considered so standard or fundamental as to be almost universal, with perhaps slight tweaks for individual clients.

Brief: A formatted, broken-down set of summaries of critical elements of a decided court case. Many suggested brief formats exist, but they typically all include the following headings: name and citation, short summary of facts, procedural posture, issue(s) presented by the case, concise rule of law, holding(s), and decision.

Call-back (Interview): As described in Chapter Nine, the third stage of the interview process for law students – first, initial contact via a letter to the firm; second, a short screening interview in person or via telephone, and third, a call-back interview in person at the law firm with a number of different attorneys. If you are called back for the third stage, the firm is typically seriously interested in you, and if you do well, the firm will extend you an *offer* to work for them.

Cardozo, Benjamin N. (1870-1938): Noted New York judge whose eloquence, legal reasoning and legal writing skills propelled him to the pinnacle of prominence in the New York State courts, even earning the state international fame. Subsequently appointed by President Herbert Hoover to the U.S. Supreme Court.

Civil Procedure: A required first-year course and critically important legal subject, especially for litigators. Teaches students about the procedures used to regulate the order of events and interactions between attorneys and judges at federal civil trials. Tends to scare the hell out of first-year students. See also *procedural/substantive dichotomy*.

Clerk/Clerking/Clerkship: Typically refers to an individual's work for a judge as a 'clerk' – someone who performs tasks as requested by the judge, ranging from the menial to the ghostwriting of judicial opinions.

Code: Two meanings. First, code can mean an officially adopted set of rules, such as the United States Code, a systematic book-format integration of otherwise piecemeal laws passed by Congress. Second, code can refer to a proposed set of rules, such as the Model Code of Judicial Ethics, a compendium of widely-respected rules with which a given state's representatives might or might not replace their old rules.

Cold Offer: A mutually understood artificial offer of employment made by one law firm to a summer associate, tendered only under the implicit condition that the associate will ultimately use the competitive advantage of the apparent offer to seek employment with another law firm. Called "cold" because it is dead upon arrival. See also *offer*.

Commercial Outline: A succinct, logically-organized presentation of the biggest issues in a substantive area of law. Can range in size from a single page to over 300 pages. Contrast with *hornbook* and *treatise*.

Common Law: The body of law developed by judges (and lawyers) in courtrooms, as understood through the recorded decisions of judges and followed as binding precedents by future lawyers. Compare with *statutory law*, which is developed by legislatures.

Conclusory Thinking: To think by process of drawing conclusions first and rationalizing or explaining thereafter. The opposite of *thinking like a lawyer*.

Constitution: The primary governing document for a given jurisdiction or organization, such as the United States, an individual state, or a private group. In the event of a conflict between a constitution and any lesser rule, the constitution's provisions will generally govern. In the United States, in the event of a conflict between the federal constitution and any state constitution, the federal constitution will govern. Compare with *law, regulation,* and *statute.*

CRAC: See *IRAC.*

Δ **(Delta):** A symbol commonly used to signify the defendant in a civil or criminal case.

Demur/Demurrer: To demur in the law is to say "so what?" in court – an admission (or a 'for the sake of argument' assumption) that while an accusation against you might be correct, your conduct was neither illegal nor punishably wrongful. A demurrer is a document containing a demurring statement.

Ding Letter: Slang term for a letter of rejection from a law firm or judge to whom you applied for a job.

Disbarred: To be prohibited by a state bar from practicing law in that jurisdiction – to lose one's license to practice law in a specific place. Former President Nixon was disbarred by New York State in 1976 after resigning his presidency, and resigned from the California Bar rather than face disbarment there. This meant that Nixon could not practice law in New York or California. Former President Clinton was suspended from legal practice for five years by the Arkansas Supreme Court in January 2001 and then disbarred by the United States Supreme Court in October 2001. As a result, Clinton has to wait until January 2006 to practice in Arkansas, and could not again practice before the U.S. Supreme Court unless they reinstate him. President Clinton later requested that the Supreme Court allow him the dignity of resigning from the Supreme Court Bar rather than being forcibly removed.

Editor: Typically, the name for a senior-level member of a *law review* or other journal, used for those members of the 'board of editors' who oversee the work of associates.

Erie: One of the key civil procedure cases during the first year, *Erie Railroad Co. v. Tompkins,* 304 U.S. 64 (1938) is an introduction to the *substantive/procedural law dichotomy. Erie* stands for the proposition that when a case comes to a federal court on 'diversity jurisdiction,' namely because the two parties come from different states and want a neutral federal court to decide the case rather than a potentially biased state court, federal courts should use federal procedural law and the substantive law of the state in which they sit. In other words, since each state has its own laws and state courts typically decide cases using the laws of the states in which they sit, federal courts must follow the same laws, but may conduct day-to-day affairs in their courtrooms according to federal, rather than state standards. Like many laws, this is only noteworthy and important because of how messed up things were before the law changed.

Firm: Short for *law firm*.

Gunner: A student who is aggressive in his or her pursuit of top grades – so much so that he or she is seen as 'gunning' for (willing to shoot down) other students or aiming for the professor's attention as a top student.

Hand, Learned (1872-1961): Along with Justice Cardozo, Learned Hand was a powerhouse of the early 20th century American judiciary, similarly achieving prominence in New York – but as a federal district court judge, and then as a federal Second Circuit Court of Appeals judge. Often referred to as the finest jurist never to reach the U.S. Supreme Court.

Harm: A legally cognizable injury – typically physical damage, severe mental distress, or financial harm. Generally, in order to hold someone liable for a crime or civil wrong, there must be some actual harm. Same as *injury*.

Hearsay: Defined as "an out of court statement offered (in court) to prove the truth of the matter asserted," this classic concept in evidence law starts from the presumption that a courtroom is a sealed chamber into which only specific information can be introduced and used to prove or disprove an allegation. Statements made outside of the courtroom are presumed unreliable because the jury doesn't know or can't see the speaker in person to assume whether the statements are true.

Hiding the Ball: A process used by law teachers to obscure otherwise clear points of black letter law in order to force students to learn how to *think like lawyers* and reason out the law/answer for themselves.

Holding: In its most common law school meaning, the new or especially important legal decision(s) rendered by a specific court in a specific case. A holding is typically an explicit finding of the court on a specific critical point. The past tense of a holding is "held."

Hornbooks: High-level study guides published for every conceivable legal subject, presenting more or less up-to-date *black letter* explanations of the law as it's commonly taught in classes, though some areas of each book will go beyond or perhaps slightly omit material discussed in your school's courses. Sometimes called *treatises*.

Interview: One of the stages of a law student's job search process, which typically begins when the student initiates contact with a law firm, is put through an initial screening interview, and then, if the firm is interested, invited for a *call-back*.

Injury: See *harm*.

IRAC: One of the classic legal thinking methodologies, often suggested as the "correct" way to analyze essay questions. Begin by stating the legal <u>issue</u>, state the <u>rule</u> of law that applies to the issue, analyze how the facts in your essay get <u>applied</u> using the rule, and then state your <u>conclusion</u>. Other versions include *CRAC* – state your conclusion, then the rule, then analyze in a manner that leads eventually and logically to restatement of the conclusion.

Issue: An amorphous term that initially confuses many first-year law students. An issue in its most specific sense is a precise novel question presented by a case that's being studied. However, issues are a matter of framing; in other words, even a simple issue can be stated or examined in different ways. One professor's framing of an issue may be subtly, slightly, or significantly different from another professor's or a student's framing. Moreover, some people like to break down a large 'issue' into several smaller issues, and a given case may have several issues – either truly discrete individual questions, or interrelated questions that otherwise might be bunched together. Learning how to frame issues in a commonly acceptable way is something that law school begins to teach you, and something you'll practice for years thereafter.

Job Fairs: Gatherings of interviewing attorneys from multiple law firms, organized by law schools in order to easily expose interested students to numerous interview opportunities.

K: The symbol commonly used as shorthand for contract. The phrase O + A = K generally refers to the concept that an offer plus acceptance equals a contract.

Lateral/Lateral Attorney/Lateral Hiring: The process of transferring an attorney from one firm to another while preserving his or her relative level of seniority.

Lateral is used both as a verb and as a shorthand noun to refer to an attorney who has made a lateral move.

Law: A generic term for any rule that has been formally adopted by a given government as providing or restricting rights within the government's borders. Has lower priority than a *constitution* but greater priority than a *regulation*. Generally synonymous with *statute*.

Law Firm: A business operated by attorneys, generally divided into two classes of attorneys: *partners* – the senior owners of the firm – and associates, who have little or no ownership stake and work as the partners' employees. Law firms also hire *paralegals* and support staff (such as secretaries, file clerks, and document processing assistants) to handle many of the day-to-day tasks that their lawyers don't have time to handle.

Law French: The relatively few Norman dialect French phrases that were carried over from William the Conqueror's reign in England and are still used in the American legal system; fewer in number than Latin. Includes such words as *demurrer*, fait accompli (a presumably irreversible accomplished fact) and force majeure (force of nature).

Law Review: As part of a longstanding tradition, students publish 'legal journals,' periodicals dealing exclusively with the law, during their time in law school. A school's 'Law Review' or 'Law Journal,' specifically so titled, is typically its most prestigious legal journal, and is operated by a group of second- and third-year law students selected through competitive criteria. Legal journals, like medical journals, publish articles by scholars and practitioners, on a quarterly, bi-monthly or eight-times-annually basis. They typically resemble small books in size and shape, rather than magazines or newspapers, and their articles are densely packed with oblique legal writing and footnotes. Second-year students typically start as associates and eventually become editors. For more detail on law reviews and the concepts 'editor of a law review' and 'making law review,' see Chapter 5, Sections A and K, and Chapter 8.

Lawyer: Someone who has both graduated from law school and also been admitted to at least one state *bar* after passing a *bar exam*, without being *disbarred*. Note that one does not become a lawyer just by graduating from law school, with the single and truly unusual exception of Wisconsin, which automatically entitles graduates of two Wisconsin-based law schools to practice law within that state. Synonymous with 'attorney at law.' See also *bar*, *bar exam*, and *disbarred*.

Majority Law: A given legal standard adopted by the majority of U.S. states or jurisdictions, either through legislation or court decisions. May be used to suggest 'strong majority law' or 'bare majority law' based on levels of adoption. Courses and professors often focus upon majority law, and only focus on its opposite, *minority law*, under specific circumstances. Majority and *minority law* often replace *bad law*.

Maritime Law: The law of the seas – the laws that apply when people and property are not on the soil or within the borders of a given country.

Mens Rea: In criminal law, a guilty mind, or mental state, which is typically part of a three-part scheme for assessing culpability for a crime. A frequent maxim is that in the absence of a guilty act (actus reus), no one will be held culpable for possessing a guilty mind.

Minority Law: A given legal standard adopted by fewer than 50% of the U.S. states or jurisdictions, either through legislation or court decisions. May be used to suggest 'strong minority law' or 'very weak minority law' depending on the level of adoption. Professors only focus on minority-adopted laws in cases where (a) the law school is located in a state where a minority law standard governs, or (b) the professor believes that a new legal standard, perhaps part of a growing but still minority trend, is important enough to highlight. Contrast with *majority law*.

Model Code: Authored by law professors and interested practitioners, a model code is a comprehensive set of proposed laws taken from the best practices of courts and legislatures. See also *Restatements of the Law* and *UCC*.

MPRE: Multistate Professional Responsibility Exam. See Chapter 7, Section H.

Offer: The common, quick way of stating "offer of employment," as used in the phrases "I got an offer from…" or "I got the offer from…" a given law firm or judge. As understood in contract law, one party makes an offer and the other party must accept it in order for a valid contract or agreement to exist.

1L (One-L): The traditional shorthand name for a first-year law student.

Outlining: The process of turning one's class notes from an entire semester into a single organized document hitting on all major points covered in a single class; also the related process of assimilating and memorizing parts or the whole of that knowledge.

Partner: One of two or three classes of senior attorney with a law firm. Traditionally, a partner was a guaranteed owner of a fractional share of a law firm, such that if a law firm had 10 partners, 20 associates, and 30 people as support staff, the partners would pay the 50 employees and split the remainder – the profits – 10 roughly equal ways. In recent times, such partners have become known as "equity partners," and a new class of partners, "fixed income" partners, has been created to bestow some of the prestige of partner status upon people who do not deserve to share in the firm's profits. Fixed income partners are salaried employees, like associates, but typically oversee associate work and enjoy other perks associated with partnership. In either case, it generally takes between eight and ten years of very strong associate work to become a partner at an established large law firm, and upwards of six years at an established small firm.

π (P): The symbol commonly used to signify the plaintiff in a civil case, somewhat more rarely used to signify the prosecution in a criminal case. The letter P is sometimes written instead of the Pi symbol.

Procedural Posture: The specific history of events that brought a case to the stage at which you begin to analyze it, namely, the simple operative facts that gave rise to the trial and the various key decisions made by lower courts, and then this court. Often requested by first-year professors and contained in *briefs*.

Procedural/Substantive (Law) Dichotomy: Procedural laws or rules are the guidelines that must be followed in a courtroom or other place of official proceeding; substantive laws or rules are the general guidelines for everyday living that must be followed outside (and also inside) the courtroom, dealing with everything from criminal law to environmental law to contract law, tort law, maritime law, and everything in-between. A critical concept in first-year civil procedure.

Professional Responsibility: The legal profession's jargon for "ethics."

Rankings: A concept of critical importance to law students, both in choosing law schools and then determining one's class standing relative to others.

Rationale: The underlying explanation or reasoning behind a judicial decision or an argument. Professors and students often spend a lot of time analyzing the rationales behind decisions, and professors quite frequently challenge the supposed explanations offered by judges in reaching unusual decisions.

"Reasonable Person" Standard: A standard applied principally in tort law but increasingly in other spheres of the law, to determine what the average upstanding member of society would have done when acting appropriately in a given situation. Used as the benchmark for determining 'negligence,' or the failure to act in an appropriate/reasonable manner when the law required you to do so. Based on personal experience, relies on the jury (or finder of fact) in a trial to make a determination as to what sort of conduct in a certain situation is unreasonable, and assesses liability only if the conduct was not reasonable.

Reciprocity: State A's agreement to allow lawyers from State B to practice in State A without taking State A's bar exam, in exchange for a reciprocal privilege in State B to allow State A lawyers to practice there without taking the State B bar exam. Several states, including Alabama, California and Louisiana, have no reciprocity with other states. See also *waiving in*.

Regulation: A generic term for any low-level rule that has been formally adopted by a given government to restrict rights within the government's borders. Typically has lower priority than a *constitution* or *law/statute*.

Restatements of the Law: Model legal codes on specific substantive subjects, such as contracts, torts, and so on. Assembled by leading law professors and practitioners to reflect the best practices of courts in the nation and sometimes beyond, Restatements have been updated in second and third versions as circumstances have warranted. Examples of Restatements include the First Restatement of Contracts, the Second Restatement of Torts ('Rest.2d of Torts'), the Second Restatement of Judgments ('Rest.2d of Judgments') and the Third Restatement of Trusts ('Rest.3d of Trusts'), amongst many others. See also *UCC*.

Rule Against Perpetuities (RAP): The most universally hated single subject in all of the first year of law school, this confusing Property rule says that a future interest in property is invalid unless it must vest within the lifetime of a person in being (at the time of the interest's creation) plus a given number of years. In essence, it means that any legal attempt by Person A to control the transfer of his property to Person B will fail unless that transfer takes place within a certain number of years. It's confusing because (a) that certain number is measured in part by a third person's lifetime, (b) it assumes that person A will try to control the transfer of his property to people who might not be alive during person A's lifetime, and (c) uses unfamiliar language and tricky concepts of contingency.

Socratic Method: The interrogative 'question and answer' lecture style developed by famed Greek philosopher Socrates and practiced by many law professors today. For additional detail, see Chapter 3, Section H.

Splitting the Summer: When a student has received two or more offers, she may opt to accept two of them – with the permission of the firms involved – and split the summer in half to see which of the firms she would prefer to work for. The majority of people will not have the opportunity to split the summer between two firms, primarily because they will not have two offers to choose from and secondarily because some firms have an anti-split policy. Splits between more than two firms per summer are highly unusual. See Chapter 9, Section B.

Springgun: A classic concept from tort law – a homeowner's trap set off mechanically when a thief attempts to gain entry to a house or room with valuable property inside. Comes from the classic Iowa case of *Katko v. Briney*, 183 N.W.2d 657 (1971), where thieves repeatedly pillaged a dwelling to steal bottles and jars; owner Briney responded by setting up a gun that would blast automatically when a thief attempted entry. For reasons explained in tort law through the *Katko* case, the use of deadly force to defend uninhabited property is generally illegal.

Statute: Another term for 'law' that also can mean a formal document that contains a law within its pages. Statutes typically do not contain regulations, which are often considered to be lower-level.

Stevedore: A dock worker, namely one who unloads and loads ships – an outdated term often brought up for a day or two in contracts classes for no apparent purpose but to see if students bothered to look up what it means.

Syllogism: A classic concept relating to deductive reasoning, a skill required of law students. A syllogism is a collection of three phrases: a major premise, a minor premise, and a conclusion that follows from the combination of those two premises. An example is: All dogs have hair; you have a dog; therefore, your dog must have hair. Students tend to try to find holes in the syllogisms, and professors generally tell them to ignore the holes.

Thinking Like a Lawyer: An amorphous concept referring to the skills learned during law school – namely how to examine concepts in many different ways, including ways that contradict, agree with, run parallel to, or improve upon other concepts that have been or will be discussed. Also refers to a lawyer's ability to 'think in the alternative,' 'think on one's feet,' analyze problems according to a specific methodology (such as *IRAC*), and go beyond conclusory or illogical thinking.

3L (Three-L): The traditional shorthand name for a third-year law student.

Tort Law: The law governing injuries/harm caused to people, and in some cases their property.

Tort-feasor: One who committed a tort.

Treatise: A comprehensive and logically organized explanation of an entire substantive area of law, such as civil procedure, torts, or constitutional law, complete with specific references to case precedents and/or statutes that comprise the law. The comprehensiveness contrasts with a *commercial outline*, which serves the same general function but in a far more cursory way. Some treatises are specific to individual states' laws. See also *hornbook*.

2L (Two-L): The traditional shorthand name for a second-year law student.

UCC: The Uniform Commercial Code, a model system for handling contracts and sales between people and business entities, paralleling the Restatement of Contracts but surpassing it in actual use – parts of the UCC have been adopted by almost every one of the United States and also by some foreign countries.

UCCC: The Uniform Consumer Credit Code, passed by seven states to govern the credit industry and protect consumers who seek credit. Of only minor interest unless you hope to practice in a state that tests it on bar exams.

Waiving In: Gaining permission to practice law before a specific court or within a specific jurisdiction without taking that jurisdiction's bar exam; a privilege frequently limited to lawyers who have actually practiced law for a number of years in their home state.

As of 2002, there are over 51 bar examinations administered simultaneously in the United States, including one for each state and one for the District of Columbia.[376] These exams have plenty in common, though each also has something to set itself apart. This table is a comparative guide to the length, subjects tested, and other key characteristics of these 51 bar exams. For additional information on any given exam, you should consult the individual bars of each state – perhaps through their web sites, links to which can be found through the "Law Students" and "Bar Exam" pages of Law.com.[377]

The first table begins with six-year weighted average pass percentages, placing somewhat more weight on summer exams than winter ones, as far fewer people take winter exams.[378] Next the table lists the length of each exam in days, then today's current MPRE score requirements, if any, for each jurisdiction. An MPRE is typically taken before the bar exam, and your score must be at least the number listed for the state(s) you hope to practice in at the time you're admitted to the bar. States change these numbers on occasion, and typically publicize changes at least a year in advance.

Every exam consists of at least two parts. Today, 49 of the 51 exams use the MBE (Multistate Bar Examination), a seven-subject, 200-question multiple choice exam that takes one full day (with two three-hour, 100-question sessions) to administer. The MBE mostly covers typical first-year subjects – Constitutional Law, Contracts & Sales, Criminal Law, Real Property and Torts – but also tests a modest amount of Criminal Procedure and a considerable amount of Evidence, subjects that are often optional at law schools. Some states, including New York, may also use state-specific multiple-choice questions.

Each state has essays, and most states write their own essay questions. Fifteen states do or may use questions from the MEE (Multistate Essay Examination), a six-question, three-hour essay test,[379] often in addition to questions of their own. Some states are deliberately ambiguous as to whether they use MEE questions, and though the MEE is written for examinees across the country, each state grades its own MEE tests, and some states require that students address both majority law and state distinctions. The table distinguishes between states that have specifically warned that state distinctions might be tested on their MEEs, and those that have not. Consult your state's bar for recent updates.

Over half of the jurisdictions also have one or two "performance tests," essays that simulate real-life demands of actual law firm practice. Twenty-six of the 51 jurisdictions currently use one or two essays taken from the MPT (Multistate Performance Test);[380] the table indicates one or two. Some states, including California, write their own performance tests that are similar to the MPT, but perhaps longer or focused on other subjects.

Note that testing of the UCC varies from state to state. A special UCC column appears for those states identifying the UCC as a separate testable subject.

---

[376] Though additional bar exams are administered in U.S. affiliates and territories such as Guam, the N. Mariana Islands, Puerto Rico, the Republic of Palau, and the U.S. Virgin Islands, they are excluded from this book's scope of coverage.

[377] See http://www.law.com/students/index.html.

[378] Separate six-year summer and winter pass rate breakdowns appear after this table.

[379] For more information on the MEE, see http://www.ncbex.org/tests/mee/mee.htm. Note that Hawaii apparently uses a seventh essay question on its bar examinations.

[380] For more information on the MPT, see http://www.ncbex.org/tests/mpt/mpt.htm. Note that Alabama will also use the MPT as of July 2003.

TABLE B-1	STATE BAR EXAM SUBJECT MATTER COVERAGE AND MPRE REQUIREMENTS								
State	Pass %; 6. Yr. W. Avg.	# Days	Min. Req'd MPRE Score	MPT Used & # of MPTs	Con Law (State, Federal, and MBE Used)	Contracts & Sales	Crim Law & Proc.	Evidence	Real Prop.	Torts
Alabama	74	3	75	N	FED/MBE	Y/MBE	Y/MBE	Y/MBE	Y/MBE	Y/MBE
Alaska	74	2.5	80	Y-2	AK/FED/MBE	Y/MBE	Y/MBE	Y/MBE	Y/MBE	Y/MBE
Arizona	80	2	85	N	AZ/FED/MBE	Y/MBE	Y/MBE	Y/MBE	Y/MBE	Y/MBE
Arkansas	74	3	85	Y-2	FED/MBE	Y/MBE	Y/MBE	Y/MBE	Y/MBE	Y/MBE
California	65	3	79	N	FED/MBE	Y/MBE	Y/MBE	Y/MBE	Y/MBE	Y/MBE
Colorado	81	2	85	Y-2	FED/MBE	Y/MBE	Y/MBE	Y/MBE	Y/MBE	Y/MBE
Connecticut	81	2	80 or C/PR class	N	CT/FED/MBE	Y/MBE	Y/MBE	CT/FED/MBE	Y/MBE	Y/MBE
Delaware	66	2.5	85	Y-2	FED/MBE	Y/MBE/MEE	DE/FED/MBE	Y/MBE	Y/MBE	Y/MBE
D.C.	74	2	75	Y-2	FED/MBE	Y/MBE	Y/MBE	Y/MBE	Y/MBE	Y/MBE
Florida	81	2	80	N	FL/FED/MBE	Y/MBE	Y/MBE	Y/MBE	Y/MBE	Y/MBE
Georgia	83	2	75	Y-2	FED/MBE	Y/MBE	Y/MBE	Y/MBE	Y/MBE	Y/MBE
Hawaii	74	2	85	Y-2	FED/MBE	Y/MBE/MEE	Y/MBE	Y/MBE	Y/MBE	Y/MBE
Idaho	75	2.5	85	Y-2	FED/MBE	Y/MBE/MEE	Y/MBE	Y/MBE	Y/MBE	Y/MBE
Illinois	84	2	80	Y-1	FED/MBE	Y/MBE/MEE	Y/MBE	Y/MBE	IL/FED/MBE	Y/MBE
Indiana	84	2	80	Y-2	IN/FED/MBE	Y/MBE	Y/MBE	Y/MBE	Y/MBE	Y/MBE
Iowa	84	2.5	80	Y-2	FED/MBE	Y/MBE	IA/FED/MBE	Y/MBE	Y/MBE	Y/MBE
Kansas	85	2	76	N	FED/MBE	Y/MBE/MEE	Y/MBE	Y/MBE	Y/MBE	Y/MBE
Kentucky	81	2	75	N	FED/MBE	Y/MBE/MEE?	Y/MBE	Y/MBE	Y/MBE	Y/MBE
Louisiana	62	3	80	N	FED		Y	Y		Y
Maine	69	2	75	Y-1	FED/MBE	Y/MBE	ME/FED/MBE	ME/FED/MBE	Y/MBE	Y/MBE
Maryland	75	2	0	N	FED/MBE	Y/MBE	Y/MBE	Y/MBE	Y/MBE	Y/MBE
Mass.	78	2	85	N	FED/MBE	Y/MBE	Y/MBE	Y/MBE	Y/MBE	Y/MBE
Michigan	80	2	75	N	FED/MBE	Y/MBE	Y/MBE	Y/MBE	Y/MBE	Y/MBE
Minnesota	88	2	85	Y-1	FED/MBE	Y/MBE	Y/MBE	Y/MBE	Y/MBE	Y/MBE
Mississippi	87	3	75	Y-2	MS/FED/MBE	Y/MBE/MEE	Y/MBE	Y/MBE	Y/MBE	Y/MBE

State	Pass % 6 Yr. W. Avg.	# Days	Min. Req'd MPRE Score	MPT Used/ # of MPTs	Con Law (State, Fed.,& MBE Used)	Contracts & Sales	Crim Law & Proc.	Evidence	Real Prop.	Torts
Missouri	81	2	80	Y-1	FED/ MBE	Y/MBE/ MEE	Y/MBE	Y/MBE	Y/MBE	Y/MBE
Montana	89	2.5	80	N	MT/FED/ MBE	Y/MBE	Y/MBE	Y/MBE	Y/MBE	Y/MBE
Nebraska	86	2	85	N	FED/ MBE	Y/MBE/MEE	Y/MBE	Y/MBE	Y/MBE	Y/MBE
Nevada	67	2.5	85	Y-1	FED/ MBE	Y/MBE	Y/MBE	Y/MBE	Y/MBE	Y/MBE
N.Hampshire	75	2	79	N	NH/FED/ MBE	Y/MBE	Y/MBE	Y/MBE	Y/MBE	Y/MBE
New Jersey	72	2	75 or C	Y-1	FED/ MBE	Y/MBE	Y/MBE	Y/MBE	Y/MBE	Y/MBE
New Mexico	91	2.5	75	Y-2	FED/ MBE	Y/MBE	Y/MBE	Y/MBE	Y/MBE	Y/MBE
New York	73	2	85	Y-1	NY/FED/ MBE	NY/FED/ MBE	NY/ FED/ MBE	NY/FED/ MBE	NY/FED/ MBE	NY/FED/ MBE
N. Carolina	80	2	80	N	FED/MBE	Y/MBE	Y/MBE	Y/MBE	Y/MBE	Y/MBE
North Dakota	90	2	80	Y-2	FED/MBE	Y/MBE/MEE	Y/MBE	Y/MBE	Y/MBE	Y/MBE
Ohio	80	2.5	85	Y-2	FED/MBE	Y/MBE	Y/MBE	Y/MBE	Y/MBE	Y/MBE
Oklahoma	83	2	75	N	FED/MBE	Y/MBE	Y/MBE	Y/MBE	Y/MBE	Y/MBE
Oregon	74	2	85	Y-1	FED/MBE	Y/MBE	Y/MBE	OK/FED/ MBE	Y/MBE	Y/MBE
Pennsylvania	74	2	75	Y-1	PA/FED/ MBE	Y/MBE	Y/MBE	PA/FED/ MBE	Y/MBE	Y/MBE
Rhode Island	72	2	80	N	FED/MBE	Y/MBE	Y/MBE	Y/MBE	Y/MBE	Y/MBE
S. Carolina	83	3	77	N	FED/MBE	Y/MBE	Y/MBE	Y/MBE	Y/MBE	Y/MBE
S. Dakota	88	2	75	Y-2	FED/MBE	Y/MBE/MEE	Y/MBE	Y/MBE	Y/MBE	Y/MBE
Tennessee	79	2	75	N	TN/FED/ MBE	Y/MBE	Y/MBE	Y/MBE	Y/MBE	Y/MBE
Texas	81	3	85	Y-1	FED/MBE	Y/MBE	Y/MBE	Y/MBE	TX/FED/ MBE	Y/MBE
Utah	92	2	80	N	UT/FED/ MBE	Y/MBE/ MEE?	Y/MBE	Y/MBE	Y/MBE	Y/MBE
Vermont	77	2	80	N	FED/MBE	Y/MBE	Y/MBE	Y/MBE	Y/MBE	Y/MBE
Virginia	73	2	85	N	FED/MBE	Y/MBE	Y/MBE	Y/MBE	Y/MBE	Y/MBE
Washington	76	2.5	0	N	WA/FED	Y	Y	Y	Y	Y
W. Virginia	76	2	75	Y-2	FED/MBE	Y/MBE/MEE	Y/MBE	Y/MBE	Y/MBE	Y/MBE
Wisconsin	86	2	0	N	FED/MBE	Y/MBE	Y/MBE	Y/MBE	Y/MBE	Y/MBE
Wyoming	72	1.5	75	N	FED/MBE	Y/MBE	Y/MBE	Y/MBE	Y/MBE	Y/MBE

State	Admin Law	Agency	Bankrup. & Creds' Rights	Civ Pro / Pleading & Practice	Commerc. Paper / Negotiable Instrum'ts	Conflict of Laws	Corps / Business Org's	Equity	Family Law / Domestic Relations	Partn'ships
Alabama		Y		Y			Y	Y		Y
Alaska				Y			Y		Y	
Arizona				Y			Y			Y
Arkansas		Y/MEE		FED/MEE	Y/MEE	Y	Y/MEE	Y	Y	Y/MEE
California				Y			Y			
Colorado	Y	Y		CO/FED	Y		Y		Y	Y
Connecticut	Y	Y		Y	Y	Y	Y	Y		Y
Delaware		Y		DE/FED			Y	Y		Y
D.C.		Y/MEE		FED/MEE	Y/MEE	Y/MEE	Y/MEE		Y/MEE	Y/MEE
Florida				FL			Y	Y	Y	Y
Georgia		Y		GA/FED	Y	Y	Y		Y	Y
Hawaii		Y/MEE		FED/MEE	Y/MEE	Y/MEE	Y/MEE		Y/MEE	Y/MEE
Idaho		Y/MEE		FED/MEE	Y/MEE	Y/MEE	Y/MEE		Y/MEE	Y/MEE
Illinois		Y/MEE		IL/FED/MEE	Y/MEE	Y/MEE	Y/MEE	Y	Y/MEE	Y/MEE
Indiana	Y	Y		Y	Y		Y		Y	Y
Iowa				IA/FED			Y		Y	
Kansas		Y/MEE		KS/FED/MEE	Y/MEE	Y/MEE	Y/MEE		Y/MEE	Y/MEE
Kentucky	Y	Y/MEE		KN/FED/MEE	MEE?	Y/MEE	Y/MEE		Y/MEE	Y/MEE
Louisiana				LA/FED	Y					
Maine		Y	Y	ME/FED	Y	Y	Y	Y	Y	Y
Maryland		Y		MD	Y		Y		Y	Y
Mass.		Y		MA/FED	Y		Y		Y	Y
Michigan		Y	Y	MI/FED	Y	Y	Y	Y	Y	Y
Minnesota	Y		Y	Y					Y	Y
Mississippi	Y	Y/MEE	Y	MS/FED/MEE	Y/MEE	Y/MEE	Y/MEE		Y/MEE	Y/MEE

State	Admin Law	Agency	Bankrup. & Creds' Rights	Civ Pro / Pleading & Practice	Commerc. Paper / Negotiable Instrumt's	Conflict of Laws	Corps / Business Org's	Equity	Family Law / Domestic Relations	Partn'ships
Missouri	Y	Y/MEE		MO/FED/MEE	Y/MEE	Y/MEE	Y/MEE	Y	Y/MEE	Y/MEE
Montana		Y		Y			Y		Y	Y
Nebraska		Y/MEE		FED/MEE	Y/MEE	Y/MEE	Y/MEE		Y/MEE	Y/MEE
Nevada		Y		NV/FED	Y	Y	Y		Y	Y
N.Hampshire		Y	Y			Y	Y	Y	Y	Y
New Jersey										
New Mexico	Y	Y		NM/FED	Y	Y	Y	Y	Y	Y
New York		Y		NY/FED	Y	Y	Y	Y	Y	Y
N. Carolina		Y		Y	Y		Y	Y	Y	Y
North Dakota		Y/MEE		FED/MEE	Y/MEE	Y/MEE	Y/MEE		Y/MEE	Y/MEE
Ohio		Y		Y	Y		Y			Y
Oklahoma	Y	Y	Y	OK/FED	Y	Y	Y		Y	Y
Oregon	OR/FED	Y		OR/FED	Y		Y		Y	Y
Pennsylvania				PA/FED	Y	Y	Y		Y	
Rhode Island		Y	Y	RI	Y	Y	Y	Y	Y	Y
S. Carolina				Y	Y		Y	Y	Y	
S. Dakota		Y/MEE		FED/MEE	Y/MEE	Y/MEE	Y/MEE		Y/MEE	Y/MEE
Tennessee		Y		TN/FED	Y	Y	Y		Y	Y
Texas		Y	Y	TX/FED			Y		Y	Y
Utah	Y		Y	FED/MEE	Y/MEE	Y/MEE	Y/MEE		Y/MEE	Y/MEE
Vermont	Y	Y	Y	VT	Y		Y	Y	Y	Y
Virginia		Y	Y	VA	Y	Y	Y	Y	Y	Y
Washington	Y			Y	Y		Y		Y	Y
W. Virginia		Y/MEE		FED/MEE	Y/MEE	Y/MEE	Y/MEE		Y/MEE	Y/MEE
Wisconsin				Y			Y		Y	Y
Wyoming	Y	Y		Y	Y		Y		Y	Y

State	Profess. Respons. (Ethics)	Secured Transacts.	Tax	Trusts & Estates	UCC	Wills	Also Tested/Other Notes
Alabama			Y	Y	Y	Y	Will start MEE testing in July 2003
Alaska							Products Liability, Remedies
Arizona	Y			Y	Y	Y	Community Property
Arkansas		Y/MEE		Y		Y	
California	Y			Y		Y	Community Property, Remedies
Colorado		Y		Y		Y	
Connecticut	Y	Y		Y		Y	Personal Property, Suretyship
Delaware				Y	Y	Y	
D.C.		Y/MEE		Y/MEE		Y/MEE	
Florida	Y			Y		Y	
Georgia	Y	Y	Y	Y		Y	Damages, Remedies
Hawaii		Y/MEE		Y/MEE			
Idaho		Y/MEE		Y/MEE		Y/MEE	
Illinois		Y/MEE		Y/MEE		Y/MEE	Suretyship
Indiana			Y	Y		Y	Personal Property
Iowa				Y		Y	
Kansas	Y	Y/MEE		Y/MEE		Y/MEE	Employment, Personal Property
Kentucky		MEE?	Y	Y/MEE	Y	Y/MEE	Personal Property
Louisiana							LA Civil Code I, II, III
Maine	Y	Y	Y	Y		Y	Recently changed from 2 MPTs to 1 MPT (July 2002)
Maryland	Y						
Mass.	Y	Y		Y		Y	Consumer Protection, Mortgages
Michigan	Y	Y		Y		Y	Insurance & Workers' Comp, Personal Property
Minnesota	Y		Y	Y		Y	
Mississippi	Y	Y/MEE	Y	Y/MEE	Y	Y/MEE	Workers' Comp

State	Profess. Respons. (Ethics)	Secured Transacts.	Tax	Trusts & Estates	UCC	Wills	Also Tested/Other Notes
Missouri		Y/MEE		Y/MEE		Y/MEE	
Montana	Y		Y	Y	Y	Y	Water Law, Workers' Comp
Nebraska		Y/MEE		Y/MEE		Y/MEE	
Nevada	Y	Y		Y		Y	Community Property, Remedies
N.Hampshire			Y	Y	Y	Y	
New Jersey							
New Mexico	Y	Y		Y		Y	Amer. Indian Law (2/2003), Community Property, Personal Property
New York	Y	Y	Y	Y		Y	Insurance & Workers' Comp, Personal Property, Mortgages
N.Carolina	Y	Y	Y	Y		Y	Mortgages, Suretyship & Liens
North Dakota		Y/MEE		Y/MEE		Y/MEE	
Ohio	Y	Y				Y	Personal Property
Oklahoma	Y	Y	Y	Y	Y	Y	Consumer Protection, Remedies
Oregon	Y	Y	Y	Y		Y	Remedies
Pennsylvania	Y	Y	Y	Y			Mandates one-day Bridge the Gap class
Rhode Island		Y		Y		Y	
S. Carolina				Y		Y	Insurance, Legal Writing & Research, Trial Advocacy
S. Dakota		Y/MEE		Y/MEE		Y/MEE	
Tennessee	Y	Y				Y	Personal Property, Remedies
Texas			Y	Y	Y	Y	Consumer Protection, Oil & Gas
Utah	Y	Y/MEE	Y	Y/MEE	Y & UCCC	Y/ MEE	
Vermont	Y	Y	Y	Y		Y	Personal Property
Virginia	Y	Y	Y	Y		Y	Local Gov't Law, Personal Property, Suretyship
Washington	Y			Y	?	Y	Community Property, Consumer Protection, Zoning
W. Virginia		Y/MEE		Y/MEE		Y/MEE	Water Law
Wisconsin	Y	Y	Y	Y			Associations, Sole Proprietorships
Wyoming		Y		Y			Mortgages, Oil & Gas

The following table lists the weighted average first-time passage rates for all 50 state bar exams and the District of Columbia, ranked from highest to lowest passage rate.

TABLE B-2	*State Bar Exam First-Time Passage Rates, Ranked Highest to Lowest*		
State or District (Ranking)	*Percent Passing Bar Exam on First Try - 6-Year Weighted Average*	*State or District (Ranking)*	*Percent Passing Bar Exam on First Try - 6-Year Weighted Average*
Utah (1)	92	Tennessee (27)	79
New Mexico (2)	91	Massachusetts (28)	78
N. Dakota (3)	90	Vermont (29)	77
Montana (4)	89	Washington (30)	76
Minnesota (5)	88	West Virginia (30)	76
South Dakota (5)	88	Idaho (32)	75
Mississippi (7)	87	Maryland (32)	75
Nebraska (8)	86	New Hampshire (32)	75
Wisconsin (8)	86	Arkansas (35)	74
Kansas (10)	85	Alabama (35)	74
Indiana (11)	84	Hawaii (35)	74
Iowa (11)	84	Oregon (35)	74
Illinois (11)	84	Pennsylvania (35)	74
Oklahoma (14)	83	D.C. (35)	74
S. Carolina (14)	83	Alaska (35)	74
Georgia (14)	83	New York (42)	73
Connecticut (17)	81	Virginia (42)	73
Missouri (17)	81	Wyoming (44)	72
Florida (17)	81	Rhode Island (44)	72
Colorado (17)	81	New Jersey (44)	72
Kentucky (17)	81	Maine (47)	69
Texas (17)	81	Nevada (48)	67
Michigan (23)	80	Delaware (49)	66
Arizona (23)	80	California (50)	65
Ohio (23)	80	Louisiana (51)	62
N. Carolina (23)	80	*Average*	*79*

TABLE B-3	STATE BAR EXAM WINTER FIRST-TIME PASSAGE RATES, 1996-2001						
State/District	1996	1997	1998	1999	2000	2001	6yr/avg.
Alabama	70	66	68	66	56	66	65.3
Alaska	81	67	70	65	66	85	72.3
Arizona	75	81	72	80	80	72	76.7
Arkansas	86	77	77	61	63	73	72.8
California	60	62	57	52	50	53	55.7
Colorado	82	82	77	75	73	77	77.7
Connecticut	87	84	81	82	76	76	81.0
Delaware	No winter exam in this state						
D.C.	53	83	61	65	71	53	64.3
Florida	82	85	82	79	71	79	79.7
Georgia	88	76	74	70	72	74	75.7
Hawaii	63	60	75	56	63	68	64.2
Idaho	77	68	76	67	64	79	71.8
Illinois	86	84	80	81	78	79	81.3
Indiana	74	88	92	87	86	73	83.3
Iowa	86	80	83	85	82	85	83.5
Kansas	87	93	87	90	87	85	88.2
Kentucky	80	81	86	86	84	76	82.2
Louisiana	51	54	54	48	51	59	52.8
Maine	77	84	83	61	67	64	72.7
Maryland	77	79	83	77	78	69	77.2
Massachusetts	75	76	72	70	71	68	72.0
Michigan	81	86	79	67	69	72	75.7
Minnesota	83	84	77	81	91	86	83.7
Mississippi	81	84	82	75	85	90	82.8
Missouri	86	81	81	80	67	75	78.3
Montana	No winter exam at this time			89	81	83	84.3
Nebraska	77	87	89	88	71	72	80.7
Nevada	No winter exam in this state						
N.Hampshire	69	77	73	69	62	76	71.0
New Jersey	70	68	60	63	55	58	62.3
New Mexico	95	94	92	93	95	88	92.8
New York	69	67	65	64	60	58	63.8
North Carolina	67	76	73	68	71	87	73.7
North Dakota	No winter exam at this time			86	100	n/a	93.0
Ohio	92	89	75	76	70	74	79.3
Oklahoma	87	88	87	78	78	82	83.3
Oregon	79	74	68	63	73	83	73.3
Pennsylvania	70	76	73	65	67	63	69.0
Rhode Island	79	88	71	74	60	58	71.7
S. Carolina	88	83	75	79	74	85	80.7
South Dakota	83	88	82	84	75	94	84.3
Tennessee	74	72	76	82	76	81	76.8
Texas	76	81	73	78	77	70	75.8
Utah	92	93	86	79	97	87	89.0
Vermont	71	68	86	78	80	77	76.7
Virginia	76	66	68	71	64	69	69.0
Washington	73	78	83	80	79	83	79.3
West Virginia	59	64	67	80	100	27	66.2
Wisconsin	86	90	86	94	92	78	87.7
Wyoming	36	82	68	69	67	80	67.0

TABLE B-4	STATE BAR EXAM SUMMER FIRST-TIME PASSAGE RATES, 1996-2001						
State/District	1996	1997	1998	1999	2000	2001	6 yr avg.
Alabama	78	80	83	78	78	73	78.3
Alaska	83	76	75	70	71	71	74.3
Arizona	83	84	81	79	79	82	81.3
Arkansas	84	74	72	78	58	85	75.2
California	69	75	65	64	71	70	69.0
Colorado	89	83	79	83	82	79	82.5
Connecticut	84	85	83	79	76	82	81.5
Delaware	n/a	62	70	57	69	73	66.2
D.C.	78	75	78	85	78	74	78.0
Florida	84	84	82	80	79	81	81.7
Georgia	88	86	83	85	84	88	85.7
Hawaii	76	81	83	73	79	80	78.7
Idaho	81	75	83	77	65	78	76.5
Illinois	86	87	82	83	84	85	84.5
Indiana	78	91	90	81	84	84	84.7
Iowa	78	86	84	82	87	87	84.0
Kansas	83	87	87	87	81	79	84.0
Kentucky	84	65	82	82	83	83	79.8
Louisiana	69	62	63	66	67	74	66.8
Maine	81	63	72	70	48	70	67.3
Maryland	76	69	74	71	76	75	73.5
Mass.	83	84	79	80	79	83	81.3
Michigan	84	89	82	81	83	73	82.0
Minnesota	92	93	88	90	88	93	90.7
Mississippi	94	93	85	84	86	91	88.8
Missouri	83	86	85	78	81	81	82.3
Montana	94	91	89	86	91	92	90.5
Nebraska	97	88	86	90	87	86	89.0
Nevada	69	67	66	69	62	70	67.2
N. Hampshire	77	77	78	85	77	63	76.2
New Jersey	78	77	72	76	75	77	75.8
New Mexico	89	94	91	90	87	94	90.8
New York	78	78	78	75	79	79	77.8
N. Carolina	80	85	79	78	76	96	82.3
N. Dakota	90	85	86	89	86	94	88.3
Ohio	90	79	76	75	76	83	79.8
Oklahoma	84	81	85	85	80	82	82.8
Oregon	77	74	71	72	72	81	74.5
Pennsylvania	75	81	76	75	74	77	76.3
Rhode Island	67	61	69	80	65	89	71.8
S. Carolina	90	86	82	73	84	88	83.8
S. Dakota	86	90	87	84	92	95	89.0
Tennessee	81	81	77	77	83	81	80.0
Texas	84	83	82	83	80	84	82.7
Utah	92	93	94	91	91	97	93.0
Vermont	88	80	76	81	67	75	77.8
Virginia	80	76	72	75	74	75	75.3
Washington	73	73	68	80	80	75	74.8
W. Virginia	80	85	83	81	78	72	79.8
Wisconsin	92	86	88	87	77	79	84.8
Wyoming	76	78	69	66	73	82	74.0

APPENDIX C: SAMPLE WRITING COMPETITION SUBMISSION

The following is provided as an imperfect but actual reference sample of one type of legal writing capable of winning a law review/journal Case Note writing competition, as authored over a three-week period and only modestly cleaned up for publication. Footnotes herein largely conform to BLUEBOOK standards of citation and formatting endeavors to match common contemporary law review and journal standards. Can you spot the mistakes (not including the start of footnotes at #381)?

WHEN A LIE BECOMES A FELONY:
THE HISTORY AND DANGERS OF FEDERAL FALSE STATEMENT PROSECUTIONS

INTRODUCTION

Following the Supreme Court's decision in *Brogan v. United States*,[381] there is little doubt that 18 U.S.C. § 1001[382] enables prosecution of any person who knowingly and willfully makes materially false statements to certain federal investigators.[383] Most notably, the 1998 *Brogan* decision expressly rejected a 45-year old judicially crafted exception[384] to section 1001 that had permitted criminal suspects to utter simple[385] false denials of guilt with impunity.[386] Commonly known as the "exculpatory no" doctrine, this exception was originally thought necessary to reconcile the text of section 1001 with Congressional intent,[387] as well as to guard against perceived encroachments on a criminal suspect's Fifth

---

[381] 118 S. Ct. 805 (1998).

[382] Defendant Brogan was charged under the version of 18 U.S.C. § 1001 in effect at the time of his arrest. *See* 18 U.S.C. § 1001 (1994).

[383] *See Brogan*, 118 S. Ct. at 808, 812 (noting then-existing statutory language limiting prosecutions to "any matter within the jurisdiction of any department or agency of the United States"). *Compare* 18 U.S.C. § 1001 (1994) *with* 18 U.S.C.A. § 1001 (West Supp. 1999) (reflecting present scope of the statute and explicit applicability to all three branches of government in various forms).

[384] *See* Brief for Petitioner at 7, Brogan v. United States, 522 U.S. 398 (1998) (No. 96-1579) (describing the beginning of the exculpatory no doctrine in United States v. Levin, 133 F. Supp. 88 (D.Colo. 1953)).

[385] *See Brogan*, 118 S. Ct. at 808 (noting "considerable variation" among circuits as to what constitutes 'simple').

[386] *Id.* at 811, 812 (rejecting the doctrine).

[387] *See* United States v. Tabor, 788 F.2d 714, 717 (11th Cir. 1986); *see also* Paternostro v. United States, 311 F.2d 298 (5th Cir. 1962) (discussing relationship of the false statements statute to an existing perjury statute). *But see* United States v. Cogdell, 844 F.2d 179, 186 (4th Cir. 1988) (Wilkins, J., concurring in part and dissenting in part).

Amendment[388] right against self-incrimination.[389] Supporters of the exception later claimed that it stood as a bulwark against the manufacturing of new false statement crimes by otherwise impeded federal investigators,[390] and prevented prosecution of witnesses who unwittingly provided inaccurate information.[391]

This Note will argue that although the *Brogan* decision brought needed clarity to section 1001 jurisprudence, it simultaneously removed a check on dangerous misuse of prosecutorial authority. The Note will begin by discussing cogent statutory and judicial history leading to the *Brogan* decision, and will then move on to an examination of the decision, its concurring opinions, and its joint dissent. Having touched upon several notable false statement prosecutions, including *Brogan*, the Note will ultimately analyze the potential for dangerously aggressive application of the law in light of the simplified *Brogan* standard.

I. ORIGINS AND INTERPRETATION OF 18 U.S.C. § 1001

A.   The Statute and its Exception

One hundred and thirty five years of legislative history separated enactment of the earliest precursor to 18 U.S.C. § 1001 and the Supreme Court's decision in *Brogan v. United States.*[392] Originally enacted in March of 1863, the first statute specifically proscribed false statements made with the purpose of creating or supporting fraudulent claims against the government.[393] Until 1934, Congress made only slight alterations to the statute,[394] and courts applied the statements language only where the government had suffered pecuniary or property loss.[395]

---

[388] U.S. CONST. amend. V. The Fifth Amendment provides, in pertinent part: "No person . . . shall be compelled in any criminal case to be a witness against himself . . . ."

[389] *See, e.g., Paternostro*, 311 F.2d at 303; *Tabor*, 788 F.2d at 718-19.

[390] *See* Brief for Petitioner at 19-20, Brogan v. United States, 522 U.S. 398 (1998) (No. 96-1579); Brief of National Association of Criminal Defense Lawyers as Amicus Curiae in Support of Petitioners at 21-22, Brogan v. United States, 522 U.S. 398 (1998) (No. 96-1579).

[391] *See* Amicus Brief at 19-20, *Brogan* (No. 96-1579); Stephen Michael Everhart, *Can You Lie to the Government and Get Away With It? The Exculpatory No Defense under 18 U.S.C. § 1001*, 99 W. VA. L. REV. 687, 692 (1997).

[392] *See* Hubbard v. United States, 514 U.S. 695, 704-07 (1995) (describing origins of statute).

[393] Although the original statute had more than one purpose, the false statements portion is the sole focus of this Note. For discussion of the statute's origins, see *id.* at 703-08.

[394] These changes included adjustment of penalties, addition of a second purpose requirement, and making the statute applicable to frauds against corporations in which the government held stock. *See id.* at 705-06.

[395] *See generally* United States v. Rodriguez-Rios, 14 F.3d 1040, 1047 & n.15 (5th Cir. 1994) (en banc) (suggesting language might also cover cases where the United States was only intended to suffer such a loss).

In 1934, Secretary of the Interior Harold Ickes requested that Congress expand the scope of the statute specifically to aid in enforcement of the National Industrial Recovery Act of 1933 (NIRA),[396] namely cases where the United States would have been misled without suffering any measurable loss.[397] Congress responded by removing the statute's purpose requirements,[398] broadly rewriting the statute to authorize prosecution of whomever "knowingly and willingly... make[s] or cause[s] to be made false statements or representations... in any matter within the jurisdiction of any department or agency" of the United States.[399] With several minor changes,[400] this amended 1934 language became the basis for 18 U.S.C. § 1001, the modern federal false statements statute codified in 1948.[401]

While the language of the statute remained largely the same for nearly half a century after its codification, judicial interpretation of that language changed substantially. At the heart of the change was an ongoing debate over a paradox of statutory construction nestled in the 1941 case *United States v. Gilliland*.[402] Where the language of a statute is unambiguous, the plain language canon of statutory construction precludes judicial interpretation of the statute to conform with apparent legislative intent.[403] In apparent contravention of that rule, the *Gilliland* Court had held that the plain language of the statute unambiguously enabled prosecutions for false statements unaccompanied by a governmental loss,[404] yet

---

[396] *See* United States v. Gilliland, 312 U.S. 86, 94 & n.7 (1941) (discussing the National Industrial Recovery Act of 1933, 48 Stat. 195, 200, specifically Section 9(c)); *Rodriguez-Rios*, 14 F.3d at 1045-47.

[397] *See Gilliland*, 312 U.S. at 94.

[398] *Rodriguez-Rios*, 14 F. 3d at 1046-47 (noting that the purpose 'requirement' was removed, having discussed both "the purpose of obtaining" and "a purpose to cheat" separately above).

[399] Although the "knowingly and willingly" language has long appeared in the statute, its applicability as a scienter check on broader application of the false statements clause of the sentence may be more recent. *See* 18 U.S.C. § 1001 & note (1994) (Historical and Revision Notes) (discussing then-current section 1001 and its predecessor, 18 U.S.C. § 80). *See also* Staples v. United States, 511 U.S. 600 (1994) (explaining modern application of "knowingly and willingly" language to each element of offenses not deemed regulatory or strict liability in nature); *Rodriguez-Rios*, 14 F. 3d at 1048 & n.21.

[400] *See* Hubbard v. United States, 514 U.S. 695, 706 (1995) (discussing removal and addition of language); *Rodriguez-Rios*, 14 F. 3d at n.16 (discussing division of old § 35 into separate parts and later separate statutes).

[401] *See* 18 U.S.C. § 1001 (1994).

[402] 312 U.S. 86 (1941).

[403] Though established for generations, this canon has been given new life in recent years. *See* United States v. Gonzales, 520 U.S. 1, 8 (1997) (quoting Marshall, C.J.: "Where there is no ambiguity in the words, there is no room for construction. . . ."); 2A NORMAN J. SINGER, SUTHERLAND ON STATUTORY CONSTRUCTION § 46.01, at 73-74 (4th ed. 1984); 1 WAYNE B. LAFAVE & AUSTIN W. SCOTT, JR., SUBSTANTIVE CRIMINAL LAW § 2.2, at 105-06 (1986 & Supp. 1999). *See also* Brogan v. United States, 118 S. Ct. 805 *passim* (1998).

[404] *Gilliland*, 312 U.S. at 90-91, 93-94; *Rodriguez-Rios*, 14 F. 3d at 1047 & n.17.

seemingly indicated elsewhere in the decision that the language was ambiguous and had been interpreted with reference to Congressional intent.[405] Thus after the *Gilliland* Court noted that Congress intended "to protect the authorized functions of governmental departments and agencies from... perversion" in the statute,[406] a majority of the federal circuits eventually came to interpret this "authorized functions" language as a test for applicability of section 1001 to a given prosecution.[407] Where the defendant had not perverted the authorized functions of a government agency, the statute would not apply; perversion of function was most unlikely where the defendant falsely provided "mere negative answers" to an agent conducting a federal investigation.[408] This was the foundation of the "exculpatory no" doctrine, embraced initially at the appellate level by the Fifth Circuit in *Paternostro v. United States*.[409]

Both the exculpatory no doctrine and the authorized function test proved controversial within the federal circuits,[410] leading courts to debate section 1001's semantics[411] and interactions with other federal false statement laws.[412] As the debates led to new uncertainties as to Congressional intent, some courts searched for additional independent justifications for the doctrine. The Fifth Circuit embraced the authorized function test in *Paternostro*, but later occasionally applied the doctrine with reference to the Fifth Amendment, suggesting that the right against self-incrimination permitted false exculpatory denials where silence

---

[405] *Gilliland*, 312 U.S. at 93 (noting "congressional intent to protect the authorized functions of governmental departments and agencies . . .").

[406] *Id.*

[407] *See, e.g.*, United States v. Cogdell, 844 F.2d 179 (4th Cir. 1988); United States v. Tabor, 788 F.2d 714 (11th Cir. 1986); Paternostro v. United States, 311 F.2d 298 (5th Cir. 1962); United States v. Ehrlichman, 379 F. Supp. 291 (D.D.C. 1974).

[408] *Paternostro*, 311 F.2d at 304 (discussing patterns exhibited in lower court rulings).

[409] *Id.* at 298.

[410] The "authorized function" quickly became a source of confusion. *See Id.* at 303 (quoting the earlier case of United States v. Davey (D.S.D.N.Y. 1957): "Is the authorized function of the Bureau to extract from the suspect only the truth, or, in view of the Fifth Amendment proscribing compulsory self-incrimination, to hear and record only such statement as the accused desires freely and voluntarily to make?"). The circuits also sparred over whether the doctrine itself was applicable at all, and if it was, what sorts of statements should be protected, and why. For a retrospective, see Everhart, *Supra* note 11, at 690-705.

[411] *See, e.g.*, *Paternostro*, 311 F.2d at 298, 300-301 (holding that "mere negative answers to certain questions propounded by Federal agents" did not "constitute 'statements' within the meaning of that word as it appears in § 1001" and therefore were not covered by the statute).

[412] Courts opted not only to interpret the modern false statements statute in the context of its pre-*Gilliland* history, but also attempted to reconcile its provisions with those of an existing perjury statute. *See id.* at 302-03. The courts reasoned that Congress could not have intended to subject minor matters to possible punishments exceeding those for perjury and therefore that Congress must have intended to constrain application of the statute to deliberate perversions of 'authorized functions' of government. *See id.* at 302-05.

would be unnatural and potentially incriminating.[413] Following the Fifth Circuit's lead, the Eleventh Circuit in *United States v. Tabor*[414] allowed both the authorized function test and Fifth Amendment to serve as independent justifications for the doctrine. By contrast, the Ninth Circuit created its own five-step test for application of the doctrine, a test which simultaneously implicated the abandoned history of section 1001, the authorized function test, and the Fifth Amendment.[415] The Fourth Circuit adopted the Ninth Circuit's test over a single dissent[416] in *United States v. Cogdell*,[417] and the Eighth Circuit's variation on exculpatory no considered both the authorized function test and Fifth Amendment concerns[418] despite a recognition that the doctrine had no textual basis in the statute.[419] By the mid-1990s, the First and Seventh Circuits had flirted with the doctrine but had not developed lasting tests,[420] while the Third, Sixth, Tenth and D.C. Circuits all stood on uncertain ground.[421]

B. Initial Dismantling of the Exception

As the circuits debated the scope and merits of the exculpatory no doctrine, several important Supreme Court decisions were changing the criteria by which the doctrine's validity would ultimately be judged. An ambiguity in Fifth Amendment jurisprudence received a particularly noteworthy clarification.

---

[413] Giles A. Birch, Comment, *False Statements to Federal Agents: Induced Lies and the Exculpatory No*, 57 U. CHI. L. REV. 1273, 1281-82 (1990).

[414] 788 F.2d 714 (11th Cir. 1986) (reversing conviction of defendant who lied to a federal agent about a violation of state law which the federal agent could not himself have prosecuted). *See also* Birch, *supra* note 33, at 1282 & n.45.

[415] *See* Birch, *supra* note 33, at 1283-84.

[416] United States v. Cogdell, 844 F.2d 179, 185-187 (4th Cir. 1988) (Wilkins, J., concurring in part and dissenting in part) (presaging the reasoning of Justice Scalia's majority opinion in *Brogan*).

[417] *Id.* at 179.

[418] *See* Birch, *supra* note 33, at 1283-84 & n.48.

[419] *See* Brief for United States at 12 & n.5, Brogan v. United States, 522 U.S. 398 (1998) (No. 96-1579).

[420] *See* Brief for United States at 17 & n.8, *Brogan* (No. 96-1579) (claiming First and Seventh Circuits did not support exculpatory no). *Compare* Birch, *supra* note 33, at 1284-85 (suggesting First Circuit abandoned doctrine but Seventh adopted it) *with* Everhart, *supra* note 11, at 701 (stating First and Seventh Circuits accepted doctrine). *See also* Brief for Petitioner at 7-8 & n.2, Brogan v. United States, 522 U.S. 398 (1998) (No. 96-1579); Brief of National Association of Criminal Defense Lawyers as Amicus Curiae in Support of Petitioners at 12, Brogan v. United States, 522 U.S. 398 (1998) (No. 96-1579) (claiming that Fifth and Seventh Circuits accepted doctrine).

[421] *Compare* Brief for United States at 19, *Brogan* (No. 96-1579) (stating that all had neither accepted or rejected the doctrine) *with* Everhart, *supra* note 11, at 701 (claiming that the 10th did adopt it).

Though their 1964 ruling in *Murphy v. Waterfront Commission of New York Harbor*[422] acknowledged the legitimacy of the Fifth Amendment as a tool to protect a suspect against "the cruel trilemma of self-accusation, perjury or contempt,"[423] the Court's 1980 decision in *United States v. Apfelbaum*[424] concluded that the Fifth Amendment's right to remain silent under interrogation did not include a right to make false statements.[425] Disappointing as *Apfelbaum* may have been for guilty suspects whose resorts to silence could be used against them,[426] the implications for section 1001 were equally apparent; the exculpatory no doctrine had lost the Fifth Amendment as a crutch.[427]

Resolution of the Fifth Amendment debate was only one of the reasons[428] behind the Fifth Circuit's abrupt decision in *United States v. Rodriguez-Rios*[429] to entirely overrule the exculpatory no doctrine it had initiated in *Paternostro*. Significantly, the Fifth Circuit cited canons of statutory construction, including the plain meaning rule[430] and post-*Paternostro* statutory construction precedents[431] which provided adequate protections for defendants under even a plain language reading of section 1001. Shortly after the *Rodriguez-Rios* decision, the Supreme Court signaled its own return[432] to similar rules of statutory construction, holding in *Staples v. United States*[433] that the knowledge requirement of a statute prohibiting otherwise legal conduct applies to each element of the described offense.[434] If *Staples'* statutory interpretation was applied to section 1001, the new emphasis on its existing plain language would insure that the "false, fictitious or

---

[422] 378 U.S. 52 (1964).

[423] *Id.* at 1596 (per Goldberg, J.). The trilemma was later discussed by Birch and Everhart and expressly rejected as unfounded by Judge Smith in *Rodriguez-Rios* and then Justice Scalia in *Brogan. See* Brogan v. United States, 118 S. Ct. 805, 809-10 (1998); United States v. Rodriguez-Rios, 14 F.3d 1040, 1050 (5th Cir. 1994) (en banc); Everhart, *supra* note 11, at 693-700; Birch, *supra* note 33, at 1276.

[424] 445 U.S. 115 (1980).

[425] *Id.* at 117. *See also Rodriguez-Rios*, 14 F.3d at 1049-50 (citing previous Supreme Court precedent for the same proposition); United States v. Cogdell, 844 F.2d 179, 187 (4th Cir. 1988) (Wilkins, J., concurring in part and dissenting in part) (citing another Supreme Court precedent for the same proposition).

[426] *See, e.g., Rodriguez-Rios*, 14 F.3d at n.26.

[427] *See supra* note 43.

[428] *Rodriguez-Rios*, 14 F.3d at 1049-1050.

[429] *Id.* at 1040.

[430] *See supra* note 23.

[431] *See Rodriguez-Rios*, 14 F.3d at 1044, 1048.

[432] *See* United States v. Gonzales, 520 U.S. 1 (1997); *supra* note 23.

[433] 511 U.S. 600 (1994).

[434] *Id.* at 606-09. *See also* United States v. X-Citement Video, Inc., 513 U.S. 64 (1994) (extending *Staples'* scienter principle to apply even in the face of statutory language suggesting otherwise).

fraudulent statements or representations" would have to be "knowingly and willingly" made by the defendant. Even without an exculpatory no exception, therefore, unintentional falsehoods would not be punishable.[435] Moreover, the Court's 1997 decision in *United States v. Gonzales*[436] suggested that it would indeed emphasize a statute's existing plain language,[437] even in the face of legislative history supporting an alternative interpretation.[438] Like *Apfelbaum*, the *Staples* and *Gonzales* decisions revealed important shifts in the Court's perspectives on issues tangential to the false statements statute.

Crucially, the judicial debate over Congressional intent regarding section 1001 finally came to an end as a result of the Supreme Court's 1995 decision in *Hubbard v. United States*.[439] Confronted by a defendant who had been convicted under section 1001 for making false statements in a federal bankruptcy court, the *Hubbard* majority held that a court was not a "department or agency" of the United States as defined in the section.[440] By implication, neither was any subdivision of the Legislative branch.[441] Only executive agencies or departments were certainly covered. Fearing the loss of "integrity of legislative and judicial functions and proceedings," Congress was inspired by *Hubbard* to restructure and clarify section 1001,[442] primarily to make certain that the section applied in at least a limited fashion to all three branches of government[443] but also explicitly restricting false statement prosecutions to "materially" false, fictitious or fraudulent statements and representations.[444] Where *Staples* had made possible a section

---

[435] This would be the case both because of the difficulty of proving an innocuous falsehood to have been made knowingly and willingly, as well as the Eighth Amendment's protection against severe punishment. *See* United States v. Wiener, 96 F.3d 35, 40 (2d Cir. 1996), *rev'd sub nom.* Brogan v. United States, 118 S. Ct. 805, 815 (1998); Everhart, *supra* note 11, at 712-13. Note also the subsequent 1996 Amendment to 1001, discussed *infra*, making prosecutable only "materially false, fictitious, or fraudulent statements," thereby excluding trivial falsehoods as well. *See* 18 U.S.C.A. § 1001 (West Supp. 1999).

[436] 520 U.S. 1 (1997).

[437] *See supra* note 23.

[438] *See Gonzales*, 520 U.S. at 5 (presenting the alternative interpretation suggested by the dissent of Justice Stevens).

[439] 514 U.S. 695 (1995).

[440] *Id.* at 715. *See also* H.R. REP. NO. 104-680, at 2 (1996), *reprinted in* 1996 U.S.C.C.A.N. 3935, 3936.

[441] Hubbard, 514 U.S. at 717 (Scalia, J., concurring) (indicating that *Bramblett*'s dictum and holdings were rejected).

[442] *See* H.R. REP. NO. 104-680, at 3939 (stating explicitly that the legislature wanted to clarify the law and that it would like to see more extensive use of the statute, especially including communications made to Congress).

[443] *See* H.R. REP. NO. 104-680, at 3936.

[444] *See* False Statements Accountability Act of 1996, Pub. L. No. 104-292, 110 Stat. 3459 (1997); 18 U.S.C.A. § 1001 (West Supp. 1999).

1001 interpretation excluding unintentional falsehoods from prosecution,[445] the 1996 Congressional Amendment explicitly foreclosed prosecution of trivial false statements, as well. In forcing Congressional action on the section, *Hubbard* ultimately eliminated any residual need to consider Civil War- or FDR-era legislative history when applying the false statements statute.

II. *BROGAN V. UNITED STATES* AND THE ENDING OF "EXCULPATORY NO"

While Congress was drafting its 1996 revisions to 18 U.S.C. § 1001, the Second Circuit was contemplating the false statements statute's exculpatory no exception.[446] Following much of the logic from the Fifth Circuit's renunciation of exculpatory no in *Rodriguez-Rios*, the Second Circuit explicitly rejected the exception in *United States v. Wiener*.[447] The *Wiener* case was an appeal by two of twelve original defendants to their convictions for making false statements to federal investigators.[448] While serving as Union delegates, James Brogan and Reinaldo Roman had illegally accepted money from an employer of Union members.[449] Interviewed separately at their homes by federal agents, Brogan and Roman falsely denied accepting cash from the employer. Both were informed that lying to federal agents was a crime, but neither chose to modify his answers before the conclusion of his interview; both were convicted under the false statement clause of section 1001.[450] Brogan's case differed from Roman's only in that Brogan's "no" denial was simpler than Roman's,[451] and that the federal agents knew before asking Brogan that he had in fact accepted the money from the employer.[452] Brogan's denial, simple in nature and apparently harming no one, was therefore an ideal test case in that it was as close to a 'true' or 'pure'

---

[445] *See supra* notes 19 & 54.

[446] The Second Circuit heard arguments in United States v. Wiener on April 4, 1996, and decided the case on September 16, 1996. *See* United States v. Wiener, 96 F.3d 35 (2d Cir. 1996), *rev'd sub nom.* Brogan v. United States, 522 U.S. 398 (1998). Congress started work on the False Statements Accountability Act in May, 1995 following the May 15, 1995 decision in *Hubbard*, and passed the Act in September, 1996. *See* H.R. REP. NO. 104-680, at 3935, 3937.

[447] *Wiener*, 96 F.3d at 35.

[448] The original appeal included three defendant-appellants and convictions under two separate statutes. Robert Wiener, the named defendant, was not a party to the appeal. *See Id.* The Second Circuit opted to resolve by summary order the appellants' convictions for unlawfully receiving money from an employer, leaving for separate decision applicability of the exculpatory no defense to the false statements charge against only Brogan and co-defendant Reinaldo Roman. *See Id.* at 36.

[449] *Id.* at 36 (reciting facts).

[450] *Id.*

[451] *Id.* (describing Roman's responses as "nothing" or "none," Brogan's as "no").

[452] *Id.*

---

exculpatory "no" as possible;[453] rejection of the exception in such a case would render it inapplicable to all similarly situated defendants. After the Second Circuit affirmed both of Brogan's convictions and rejected the exculpatory no exception, the Supreme Court granted certiorari solely on the issue of the exception.[454]

Decided almost fifty-seven years after *Gilliland*, *Brogan v. United States*[455] definitively resolved the statutory construction paradox that had undermined *Gilliland's* holding and spawned the exculpatory no doctrine. After acknowledging the diversity of decisions that had come in the wake of *Gilliland*,[456] the Supreme Court rejected first the 'perversion of governmental functions' test, suggesting that the circuits had created the test from what was intended to be "a comment" in *Gilliland*.[457] Moreover, Justice Scalia, writing for the majority, described as unimaginable a false denial of guilt that would not pervert a governmental function in an investigation.[458] Next the Court disclaimed any Fifth Amendment support for exculpatory no,[459] dismissing the "cruel trilemma" suggested in *Murphy*[460] and citing *Apfelbaum* to note the limits of the Amendment's protections.[461] Justice Scalia therein deemed "implausible" the premise that a section 1001 defendant could "be unaware of his right to remain silent" based on "the modern age of frequently dramatized '*Miranda*' warnings."[462] Penultimately the Court belittled the argument that prosecutors would abuse section 1001 if the doctrine disappeared,[463] stating that the petitioner had provided no historic evidence to that effect, and concluded the decision by rejecting the doctrine itself, citing the plain language of the statute that had been in dispute since *Gilliland*.[464] In sum, the *Brogan* majority adopted without question much of the reasoning that had fueled the Fifth and Second Circuits' renunciations of exculpatory no, closing the door on a long-standing doctrinal debate by resort to a deceptively simple principle of statutory construction.

---

[453] *See* Brief for Petitioner at 3-4, Brogan v. United States, 522 U.S. 398 (1998) (No. 96-1579).

[454] *See Wiener*, 96 F.3d 35 (2d Cir. 1996), *cert. granted*, 117 S. Ct. 2430, 138 L.Ed.2d 192 (1997); Transcript of Oral Argument at 3, Brogan v. United States, 522 U.S. 398 (1998) (No. 96-1579);

[455] 118 S. Ct. 805 (1998).

[456] *Brogan*, 118 S. Ct. at 808. *But see infra* text surrounding note 86 (naming Brogan as a suspect whose denial misled no one).

[457] *Id.* at 808-09.

[458] *See Id.*

[459] *Id.* at 809-10.

[460] *See supra* note 43.

[461] *Brogan*, 118 S. Ct. at 810.

[462] *Id.*

[463] *Id.*

[464] *Id.* at 812.

Having concurred only with the judgment of the majority, Justice Ginsburg's separate opinion[465] gave additional thought to two interrelated issues Justice Scalia had brushed aside: she pinpointed Brogan's denial as an example of a false denial of guilt that had not misled anyone,[466] and noted that the Brogan case itself was an example of the potential for abuse of section 1001.[467] Expressing strong concern that the Government would use the statute to manufacture new crimes for suspects whose initial offenses had become 'nonpunishable,' Justice Ginsburg urged Congressional action to address "the sweeping generality of § 1001's language."[468] In dissenting from the majority's opinion, Justices Stevens and Breyer established their agreement with Justice Ginsburg's concerns, but concluded that they could not agree with even the judgment of the court because its statutory construction was neither the only one available nor the best option in light of the apparently stronger lower court support for the alternative conclusion.[469]

III. ANALYSIS

Following *Brogan*, the standard for false statement prosecutions is unquestionably clearer: investigators have the power to charge suspects with violations of section 1001 after almost any material falsehood, constrained only by their discretion and the prospect that the trier of fact might not find the statute's requisite culpability.[470] Though this clarity is arguably preferable from both policy and practitioner's standpoints, in as much as it creates a simple test allowing prosecution of any falsehood shown material to an investigation, the simplicity belies the danger of usage that can defeat statutes of limitation. For example, an investigator may obtain a felony conviction[471] after simply getting a suspect to lie

---

[465] *See id.* (Ginsburg, J., concurring in judgment). Note that Justice Souter wrote a brief opinion concurring in the Court's opinion in all but its treatment of the potential for misuse of the statute, an issue on which he joined Justice Ginsburg. *See id.*

[466] *Id.*

[467] *See Brogan*, 118 S. Ct. at 812 & n.1 (stating that the statute "arms Government agents with authority not simply to apprehend lawbreakers, but to generate felonies . . . "); *id.* at 814 (citing Sherman v. United States: "The function of law enforcement is the prevention of crime and the apprehension of criminals. Manifestly, that function does not include the manufacturing of crime").

[468] *See id.* at 813, 816-17.

[469] *See id.* at 817-18. (Stevens and Breyer, JJ., dissenting).

[470] *See* Brogan, 118 S. Ct. at 815 (Ginsburg, J., concurring); United States v. Wiener, 96 F.3d 35 (2d Cir. 1996), *rev'd sub nom.* Brogan v. United States, 522 U.S. 398 (1998) (apparently leaving open this question and the improbable issue of whether ignorance of this law could be a defense).

[471] The conviction, notably, carries a maximum five-year jail term and substantial fine. *See* 18 U.S.C.A. § 1001 (West Supp. 1999). For an examination of situations in which substantial penalties will be assessed, see U.S. SENTENCING GUIDELINES MANUAL § 3C1.1 cmt. 4 (1998).

about a material fact relating to a crime the investigator could not prosecute, as was the case in *Tabor*.[472] The investigator could add a section 1001 felony charge to any original substantive charge simply by eliciting a false denial of a material fact prior to arrest, as occurred in *Brogan*.[473] Perhaps the investigator could elicit a lie about a crime that has not yet occurred, as was the case in *Rodriguez-Rios*, failing to convict on that crime but succeeding on the section 1001 charge.[474] All of these denials would be independent federal felonies today. Contrary to Justice Scalia's aforementioned suggestion,[475] the petitioner did demonstrate what many people would agree to be prosecutorial excesses in section 1001's history;[476] the real issue is whether "exculpatory no" was the appropriate remedy.

Furthermore, Justice Scalia's analysis of the right to remain silent gave only shallow attention to another legitimate concern. Whether or not one believes that "frequently dramatized" *Miranda* warnings suffice as notice to section 1001 defendants for due process purposes, the Fifth Amendment only protects a person "in any criminal case" from being a witness against himself.[477] *Miranda* warnings are issued when a suspect is taken into custody, not prior to informal discussions or formal interviews with federal agents, a false statement in either of which might become the basis of a section 1001 prosecution. *Miranda* may not provide a person with a clue as to what her rights are before arrest. Moreover, section 1001 applies beyond criminal cases to "any matter within the jurisdiction" of the three branches of government, including testimony before Congressional committees. Since evoking the Fifth Amendment before a Congressional committee or subcommittee has not been "frequently dramatized" in recent years, perhaps Justice Scalia would make an exception for those section 1001 prosecutions.

Events transpiring during the *Wiener* and *Brogan* cases offer additional cause for concern. Justice Ginsburg cited subtle changes made in the United States Attorneys' Manual from 1988 to 1996 and 1997 to evince "dubious propriety [in] bringing felony prosecutions for bare exculpatory denials."[478] The changes could be interpreted less charitably. Acting Solicitor General Seth Waxman noted that the Manual's policy reflects concern over use of limited prosecutorial resources.[479] One might argue that the initial policy was inspired

---

[472] *See supra* note 34.

[473] *Brogan*, 118 S. Ct. at 807-08 (stating facts of the case).

[474] Rodriguez-Rios was charged for his initial statement that he was carrying no more than $1,000. *See* United States v. Rodriguez-Rios, 14 F.3d 1040, 1042 (5th Cir. 1994) (en banc). At the time of his arrest, he had not yet left the country without filing the 4790 report. *Id.*

[475] *See supra* text accompanying note 83.

[476] Brief of National Association of Criminal Defense Lawyers as Amicus Curiae in Support of Petitioners at 21-22, Brogan v. United States, 522 U.S. 398 (1998) (No. 96-1579) (discussing *Tabor* and *Rodriguez-Rios*).

[477] U.S. CONST. amend. V.

[478] *See* Brogan v. United States, 118 S. Ct. 805, 815 (1998); U.S. DEPT. OF JUSTICE, 3A U.S. ATTORNEYS' MANUAL, § 9-42.160 (1988 & Supp. 1996).

[479] Transcript of Oral Argument at 29, 32, Brogan v. United States, 522 U.S. 398 (1998) (No. 96-1579).

by then-unquestioned judicial construction of the law and that the changes revealed a perceived potential for rejection of the doctrine. If the threat to wasting resources came chiefly from existence of the exculpatory no defense, the Court's rejection of the defense ensures that prosecutorial resources used in section 1001 cases will be well spent. Given that some federal prosecutors were willing to manufacture section 1001 crimes from mere false denials of guilt prior to *Brogan* and in the face of a manual instructing otherwise, there is little reason to believe that they will exercise increased restraint in its wake.

CONCLUSION

Having demonstrated that the exculpatory no doctrine is neither permitted by the text of 18 U.S.C. § 1001 nor supported by present legislative intent, the Supreme Court in *Brogan* distilled a simple standard for federal false statement prosecutions from a pool of divergent lower court opinions. Those opinions, however, diverged for good reason: lacking an exception, section 1001 enables investigators to incarcerate suspects for words rather than actions. Allowing suspects to lie to the government might be an inappropriate check on that broad grant of power, but the history of section 1001 jurisprudence strongly suggests that a check of some sort will be necessary.

The following class outline excerpts are intended to serve as several examples of how personal outlines may be created; however, it should be stressed that none of these outlines is intended to be complete. They just provide a sense of how several traditional law school subjects may be understood or condensed into quick reference tools.

Property

Law of Gifts

Three requirements for a valid gift of <u>present ownership</u> and possession:
(1) Donative intent : Donor must intend to presently part with ownership of the asset.
(2) Delivery of asset: Manual delivery mandatory when possible; when manual delivery is impossible, either constructive delivery (delivery of means of access to the thing) or symbolic delivery (a writing stating the gift). If actual delivery is feasible, no other means suffices.
- Customarily, it suffices where owner voluntarily, volitionally parts with dominion and control over the item.
- Delivery of a check does not suffice as delivery of the asset until check is cashed. Donor can always cancel check until cashed.
- You only keep that from a shared security box which was actually delivered to you, even if the box is deemed 'joint tenancy;' that term is only for the bank's protection.
(3) Acceptance by the Donee – Donee can always refuse the gift.

Gift Causa Mortis – made in contemplation of imminent death. To be valid:
- Death must be imminent; if no death, gift is revoked.
- Can be revoked before death; is not an absolute gift.
- Symbolic delivery not allowed in Newman v. Bost – only manual or constructive.

Where owner intends to make a gift of something other than present possession, physical transfer of the item is not necessary. Under Gruen v. Gruen, a transfer of a remainder in a famed painting does not require physical transfer of the painting; a document specifying the non-possession rights suffices. BUT you must intend to transfer the other rights NOW, not at death.

Criminal Law

Law of Murder: Unlawful taking (killing) of human life with malice aforethought.
- Definitions:
  - Human Life (when does it begin? During pregnancy? When does it end? Brain death is the current endpoint.).
  - Malice Aforethought - Not just evil ideas in advance of the killing, but rather:
    (1) intention to inflict death or grievous bodily harm
      Starts out as Second Degree murder.
      Becomes First Degree murder if premeditated.
      Becomes only manslaughter if in heat of passion.
    (2) knowledge that you'll probably cause death under circumstances evincing a depraved indifference to human life, If only reckless or negligent, then only manslaughter.
    (3) murder in commission of any felony; some states define felony-linked murder as 1st Deg.
    (4) interference with an officer conducting a lawful arrest.
- Sample classification systems: Pennsylvania – Willful & Premeditated Murder is first degree; all felony murder is 2nd degree; all others are third degree. NY Statute defines 1st degree in terms of who the victim or accused is – if victim is a cop or the accused is a life-termer in prison, then it's 1st degree and punishable by death.
- Premeditation: Two views – the Carrol view and the Anderson view. At a minimum, killer need only think "what about the consequences" and answer, "consequences be damned."
  - Carrol: Not enough time not a defense – "no time is too short for a wicked man to frame in his mind the scheme of murder;" premeditation may be inferred from conduct and circumstances, such as using a deadly weapon (Commonwealth v. Carrol; shooting wife abruptly in head with pistol).
  - In People v. Anderson, Calif. court for premeditation (killing of a young girl by drunk houseguest) looks to [1] evidence of D's planning acts prior to the killing; [2] motive, [3] deliberate manner of killing for premeditation. It needs to find at least #1, but minus strong #1, it needs some #2 + some #1 or some #3. Multiple stab wounds indicate lack of premeditation, this court says. But many courts say that there needn't be prolonged reflection – consideration of any dimension, including punishment or consequence or methodology, suffices. Common law says that Caroll's crime is worse than Anderson's, but MPC doesn't try to get into the mind of the criminal and doesn't deal with premeditation. Apply MPC for 210.2; it treats Caroll and Anderson the same.
- No such thing as consent to murder
- Can be excused by self-defense or necessity; self-def can lead to imperfect justification manslaughter, where you think you have a right to use self-

defense but don't; rather than as a complete defense to murder you mitigate down to manslaughter

- Mitigation: Heat of Passion. An actor must have been both objectively and subjectively provoked, and there must NOT have been a subjective or objective cooling off – reasonable in that enough time passed that a reasonable person would have cooled off. Some jurisdictions are dispensing with the objective period b/c a reasonable person would always have cooled off. Provocation minus cooling off period can equal heat of passion mitigation from a Murder 1 charge down to voluntary manslaughter (State v. Thornton, weak law student who walks in on his wife with a bigger man, who is shot and killed somewhat accidentally). Victim's act must have been calculated to arouse ungovernable passion, something that would unquestionably slight the D. Note that in Texas, Thornton could have gotten off entirely – not just mitigation but complete defense. Examples of legit. Provocation:
  - o extreme assault/battery upon D
    - ▪ Classic assault: Fear of the blow, not the blow itself. V shoots at you, then runs out of ammo, and you shoot them.
    - ▪ Classic battery: If small D is punched in face by big V and D shoots back.
  - o mutual combat: Barroom brawl out of hand, guy pulls knife.
  - o D's illegal arrest (mall security guard not a real officer)
  - o injury or serious abuse of D's close relative, hearing about it generally not enough, but that's changing.
  - o sudden discovery of spouse's adultery (is walking in on people getting dressed enough?)
  - o POSSIBLY (but never shown in textbook), a special level of verbal provocation more serious than illegitimate provocation B below. (State v. Shane; no example given)
  - o Broadly, anything that could provoke someone could be submitted for jury consideration (Maher v. People; man shoots V he saw going into woods with wife; believed adultery and had other reasons to believe adultery). At least let the jury hear.
  - o Extreme Emotional Disturbance: Must be created from outside of oneself, must be both subjective and objective, not peculiar to D. Just about anything could be EED causative, though, not just one of the 6 categories of Heat of Passion. Is this in the right spot? (It's provocation?)
  - o Objectivity of provocation: Must be judged from the position of a reasonable person in the shoes of the D, considering the age or other relevant characteristics of D (Camplin case where young boy is raped by older man, whom he kills in response).
  - o Examples of illegitimate provocation: [a] Verbal attack (Girouard v. State; wife attacking husband's sex prowess). [b] Verbal information as to spouse's adultery (State v. Shane; wife tells husband she's been cheating; he kills her).

Torts

Law of Negligence (carelessness, as opposed to intentional harm caused to another)
Failure to meet an implicitly or explicitly recognized standard of prudent
behavior with resulting damages to another. Four elements must be shown:
Duty, Breach, Causation (Actual and Proximate), and Damages.

- DUTY: Foreseeability first (via eye of vigilance test, and any obvious
precautions already taken, statute maybe)
  - Remember: No duty to rescue. Be careful in defining rescue – no duty will
  exist for something that looks like a rescue (taking a ride home in winter
  after leaving a bar), but is not (the bar is still open).
    - Consent defense can lower duty. Also consider NPS re: duty.
  - Then special relationship. Seems obvious between doctor-patient,
    - BUT informed consent to procedure may modify duty of care, via
    primary assumption of risk, to use of reasonable means. Consent
    given by third-party proxy only valuable when reliably representing
    P.
    - AND similarly, signing of a waiver may modify scope of the duty for
    same AoR reason, though if waiver is not accompanied by informed
    consent, ct. will not honor it.
    - Note: A facility (golf course) can be liable for foreseeable actions
    taken by its users.
  - Additional duties owed to users of land (see 335, 337, 339 (for kids)).

- BREACH: D's behavior was not reasonable. Start with look at BPL, see whether
all available Bs have been used.
  - AND note that addt'l B is only necessary where cheaper than expected
  accident costs it would avoid.
  - Moreover, a B that prohibits any use of the good/service is too major
  unless PLs have historically been frequent and/or frequently extremely
  damaging. (Golf balls will always escape from golf course, but do they
  frequently harm people? Also; if ball bounces off protective device and
  hits someone, at least there was a protective device there.)
  - Be sure a given B precaution was necessary and not just a voluntary action
  on D's part.
  - Any insufficient D behavior should be cited.
    - Be careful: Was D entitled to do what he was doing? Would what he
    did likely cause a breach?
  - BREACH APPROACH 2: Look at Custom. In the case of a hospital, if they
  followed custom, this ends the inquiry altogether. In other cases, if
  industry standard has otherwise been followed (a valid defense), TJ
  Hooper's approach (cheap and easy must be done) must be proved by P if
  he wants to win. A key to TJ Hooper is showing that this is an odd industry
  where normal mkt. forces wouldn't create appropriate custom. Cheap and
  easy solution isn't necessarily OK where it creates other problems.

- BREACH APPROACH 3: Negligence Per Se. Includes statute-like regulations pertaining to safety; must be state-sponsored, not from a club or organization.
  - Defeats any defense of reasonable care based on custom, BPL, anything else. Not necessarily conclusive evidence of neg.
  - If safety, must be –specific- in nature. If it just says to use reasonable care, that's same as pure negligence.
  - BUT a Licensing Statute may not provide evidence of negligence.
  - UNLESS the licensing statute deals with specific kinds of negligent conduct, or otherwise deals only with the sort of people who cause harm. (Is the illicit behavior in statute likely to be the cause of harm here?)
- BREACH APPROACH 4: Res Ipsa Loquitur. Has evidence of negligence been destroyed? (Prong A) Harm doesn't happen w/o negligence. Facts should support this. If rate of error is shown, doesn't work; you really need % chance that given error stems from negligence. (B) Exclusive control. See below.

- CAUSATION (ACTUAL): As close to a pure link as possible should be shown. If there are other reasons the injury might have occurred, actual becomes tricky. Look at the injured party and show that they were unlikely to have been hurt another way. Must be established by P.
- CAUSATION (PROXIMATE): Could the initial sort of harm have been reasonably foreseen for this particular P? If so, liability for the actual extent of harm. Only if nothing bad could have been foreseen would Palsgraf apply. Use ZONE OF FORESEEABILITY test here (common sense).
  - On tricky Proximate questions, make arguments for and against.
  - Passage of time tends to make connection more remote. 2 weeks is stretching it.

- DAMAGES: Was the plaintiff certainly hurt? In a medical context, for example, even a patient receiving an emergency transfusion containing a fatal disease has problems proving damage. He would have died immediately if not for the transfusion, now gets to live longer.
  - Be sure to explain why damages would be recoverable, if asked.
  - No liability for mental/consortium/purely consequential economic loss. Property harm is NOT PCEL. But revenue loss is. A jury question.
  - Purely consequential economic loss can be recovered for where there is also physical touching of some kind. (Read 'touching' liberally.)
  - Recovery for emotional harm OK where there is also harmful or offensive physical contact, sometimes even where there is no physical contact (California only).

Corporations

The **Fiduciary Duties of the BOD** (Loyalty, Disclosure, Care and Fair Dealing)

- **Loyalty**: Board members owe duties of loyalty to the corp. They must put corp's interests ahead of any personal interest. Any breach renders K of director unenforceable.
    - o Corporate Opportunity Doctrine: They must present an opportunity squarely (fully) to the BOD and offer BOD right of first refusal. If not, this is a violation of loyalty to the corporation (and not S/H directly, so they can't sue). Test for violation of corp. opp:
        - Most courts ask if a reasonable investor in the corporation would have allowed corp to pass up the opportunity when they made their initial investment in the corp.
        - NY court: Problem only if a director takes opp. in which the corporation has an *interest* (financial interest) or a tangible expectancy (such as a contractual option to invest).
        - Majority Test: Director is absolved if he (1) made full disclosure and (2) gave the corporation the chance to take the opportunity. Director is liable if he chose not to fully disclose, even if the opportunity was ostensibly outside of the corporate charter (e.g. bank starting insurance business) or beyond the corp's ability to pay (a $30-million investment opportunity for a $6-million company).
    - o BOD may not limit liability of directors for breach of this duty, only the breach of the duty of care.

- **Disclosure**: Director must disclose any financial/material involvements with another corporation with which director's corp is contemplating business. Officers must fully and honestly disclose any information relevant to the transaction.

- **Care**:
    - o **The Director's Personal Duty** of Care:
        - A director must act with ordinary care in the discharge of his duties.
        - Similar to the previous duties, but applies only when allegedly careless director was not personally benefiting at the expense of the corporation.
        - Court will only interfere if P can specifically allege that director:
            - Did not act in good faith, OR
            - Did not act in corporation's best interest, OR
            - Did not act with ordinary care.

- o The **Board of Directors' Aggregate Duty** of Care:
  - ▪ The test to assess breach of this duty is light, however: the Rational Business Purpose Rule. So long as the directors used proper procedures in reaching their decision, courts will leave them alone so long as any rational business purpose might be imagined for that decision.
  - ▪ Courts have found liability where directors did not appear to use proper procedures and deliberate (formally meet) enough. (Litwin and Smith v. Van Gorkom cases.)
  - ▪ BODs will not be held liable for doing one of the following:
    - • Turning down bids at substantial premiums, so long as they considered the options.
    - • Making bad decision, after receiving fairness opinion from bank expert.
    - • Reaching bad decision, so long as there was a formal deliberation process.
  - ▪ How a BOD should defend bad decisions in court: (Prof's test)
    - • Avoid duty of loyalty problem by showing no self-dealing or conflict of interest. This makes it a duty of care issue.
    - • Show that BOD knew/addressed the issue
    - • Show BOD properly informed itself, at least minimally.
    - • Show BOD's action was anything but completely irrational.
  - o **Corps may limit, in their articles of incorporation, the personal liability of directors who breach their duties of care, but not breaches of loyalty.**

- • **Fair Dealing:**
  - o You will not violate this duty if you: (State ex. rel. Hayes)
  - o Have full disclosure of director's relationship to companies involved in a deal/transaction, AND disclose all particular facts regarding the transaction that other directors ought to know about, AND only disinterested directors approve deal.
  - o OR if full disclosure is impossible, disclose director's relationship to, and win approval of *disinterested* s/hs (those who do not own shares of both corporations).
  - o OR hope that the court finds the transaction to have been fair.
  - o NOTE: Hayes court essentially eliminated C prong and replaced it with an A&B test; disclosure, despite the rule announced

above by most legislatures, continue to be of primary interest to courts.

- **Parent-Subsidary Duties**: A parent owes subsidiary, and sub's minority shareholders, fiduciary duties. Therefore the parent's BOD owes duties to two different companies and four different shareholder groups.
  - o Test: Did parent's obtain an advantage to the disadvantage of the subsidiary?
    - If the parent and subsidiary both benefited (i.e. minority was not disadvantaged), the light **business-judgment rule** applies and courts will be loathe to interfere unless the plaintiff meets burden of proving that parent's conduct could not have any rational business purpose. D almost always wins.
    - If the parent receives a benefit to the exclusion/expense of the subsidiary, courts will apply the harsh **intrinsic fairness** test instead, forcing the parent to prove the transaction was unfair to the minority shareholders. Plaintiffs almost always win on this test.

- **Executive Duty to Supervise**: Directors will be liable for failure to supervise employees if:
  - o Directors had direct knowledge of criminal/illegal acts of their managers, even if managers acted only recklessly.
  - o OR directors should reasonably, in conduct of their business, have had cause to investigate "red flags"
  - o OR where BOD has failed to attempt, in good faith, to create an information/reporting system for employees. This is a controversial point and the level of reporting needed is uncertain, but Prof suggests at a minimum:
    - Hold a meeting
    - Discuss nature of business and the risk of exposure to claims for failure to supervise.
    - Consider what sort of info system would be necessary given the nature and risk, with special attention to legally mandated conduct and reporting requirements. (Caremark)
  - o Prof says: Duty to Supervise is now an extension of the Duty of Care, both are measured by essentially a negligence standard. BODs will be OK so long as they take reasonable measures to investigate and plan.

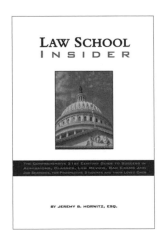